RESCRIPTING SHAKE

Building on almost 300 productions from the
Alan Dessen focuses on the playtexts used
Shakespeare's plays: the actual words spoken, the scenes or segments omitted or transposed, and the many other adjustments
that must be made – as with references to swords in a production
that features handguns and grenades. Directors *rescript* to streamline the playscript and save running time by cutting speeches or entire scenes, as well as to eliminate obscurity, conserve on personnel,
and occasionally cancel out a passage that might not fit with a particular "concept." They *rewright* when they make more extensive
changes, moving closer to the role of the playwright, as when the
three parts of *Henry VI* are compressed into two plays. Rescripting can yield practical, narrative, and conceptual gains but can
also involve losses or diminutions, so that Dessen calls attention to
price tags and *trade-offs*, both the pluses and minuses of a director's
rescripting or rewrighting. He analyzes what such choices might
exclude or preclude and explains the exigencies faced by actors
and directors in placing before today's audiences words targeted at
players, playgoers, and playhouses that no longer exist. The results
are of interest and importance as much to theatrical professionals
as to theatre historians and students.

ALAN C. DESSEN is Peter G. Phialas Professor of English at the
University of North Carolina, Chapel Hill. He is a member of
the Editorial Boards of *Shakespeare Quarterly, Studies in Philology*,
and *Renaissance Drama*, and editor of the *Shakespeare Performed* section of *Shakespeare Quarterly*. His previous books include *Elizabethan
Stage Conventions and Modern Interpreters* (Cambridge, 1984), *Recovering
Shakespeare's Theatrical Vocabulary* (Cambridge, 1995), and *A Dictionary
of Stage Directions in English Drama, 1580–1642*, co-authored with
Leslie Thomson (Cambridge, 1999).

RESCRIPTING SHAKESPEARE

The Text, the Director, and Modern Productions

ALAN C. DESSEN

University of North Carolina, Chapel Hill

CAMBRIDGE
UNIVERSITY PRESS

CAMBRIDGE UNIVERSITY PRESS
Cambridge, New York, Melbourne, Madrid, Cape Town,
Singapore, São Paulo, Delhi, Mexico City

Cambridge University Press
The Edinburgh Building, Cambridge CB2 8RU, UK

Published in the United States of America by Cambridge University Press, New York

www.cambridge.org
Information on this title: www.cambridge.org/9780521007986

First published 2002

A catalogue record for this publication is available from the British Library

ISBN 978-0-521-81029-6 Hardback
ISBN 978-0-521-00798-6 Paperback

Cambridge University Press has no responsibility for the persistence or
accuracy of URLs for external or third-party internet websites referred to in
this publication, and does not guarantee that any content on such websites is,
or will remain, accurate or appropriate. Information regarding prices, travel
timetables, and other factual information given in this work is correct at
the time of first printing but Cambridge University Press does not guarantee
the accuracy of such information thereafter.

To Cynthia, Murph, and ACTER

Contents

Acknowledgments

The writing of this book was made possible by a National Endowment for the Humanities fellowship at the National Humanities Center in Research Triangle Park, North Carolina. The supportive staff at the Center made possible a fruitful nine months, and for a third time NEH funding helped me generate a book-length project.

Earlier versions of chapters 7 and 8 have appeared in *Yearbook of English Studies* 23 (1993): 65–79 and *Shakespeare's Sweet Thunder: Essays on the Early Comedies*, edited by Michael Collins (Newark, Delaware, 1996), and the section on massed entries in *The Winter's Tale* in chapter 9 draws on my essay in *Medieval and Renaissance Drama in England* 8 (1996): 119–27. I am grateful to the University of Delaware Press and the Editors of *YES* and *MaRDiE* for permission to incorporate those items. Since the mid 1970s I have written many reviews and theatre essays from which I have drawn paragraphs and sections, so I am grateful to the Editors of *Shakespeare Quarterly* and *Shakespeare Bulletin* for permission to use that material.

As a scholar and inveterate playgoer with no backstage or rehearsal room experience, I have benefited greatly from my contact with theatrical professionals who have been generous with their time so as to give me what limited grounding I have in matters theatrical and save me from many missteps. I would therefore like to single out at least some of the many individuals who have put up with my questions and were generous in sharing their insights and expertise. From the Oregon Shakespeare Festival where starting in 1974 I got my baptism as a frenetic playgoer: Jim Edmondson, Audrey Stanley, Pat Patton, Mimi Carr, Megan Cole, Barry Kraft, Hilary Tate, Elizabeth Huddle, Denis Arndt, Rex Rabold, Larry Paulsen, Henry Woronicz. From the ACTER program: Bruce Alexander, Gareth Armstrong, Jane Arden, Vivien Heilbron, David Rintoul, Michael Thomas, Patrick Stewart, Bernard Lloyd, Tony Church, Sam Dale, Annie Firbank, Eunice Roberts, Patrick Godfrey, Jennie Stoller, Clifford Rose. From the RSC, RNT, and other United

Kingdom venues: Tim Piggott-Smith, Philip Voss, Richard Cordery, Deborah Warner, Juliet Stevenson, Fiona Shaw, David Bradley, John Woodvine, Barry Kyle, Brian Cox, Estelle Kohler, Basil Henson, Sonia Ritter, Paul Shelley, Alan David, Jasper Britton, Christopher Saul. From Stratford Festival Canada: Martha Henry, Peter Moss, David William. From Shakespeare Santa Cruz: Michael Edwards, Paul Whitworth, Molly Mayock, Bruce A. Young, J. Kenneth Campbell.

On the academic side, my greatest debt is to Homer Swander, but I have gained much from interchanges with (and often objections from) John Styan, Cary Mazer, Michael Friedman, Michael Warren, Steven Urkowitz, Phyllis Gorfain, Leslie Thomson, Lena Orlin, Catherine Belsey, Russell Jackson, Andrew Gurr, James Lusardi, June Schlueter, James Bulman, Miranda Johnson-Haddad, and Paul Nelsen. I have also learned much from a series of performance-oriented seminars at the Shakespeare Association of America and, in particular, from the sixteen participants in the 1995–96 NEH Institute at the Folger Shakespeare Library devoted to "Shakespeare Examined Through Performance."

My special thanks go to the RSC, RNT, and Globe press officers who often helped me get access to productions and to my editor at Cambridge University Press, Sarah Stanton, for almost two decades of support and good counsel. For Cynthia (whom I have dragged to too many Shakespeare plays) here is a production that is not classical, young adult, or improvised.

Note on documentation

The chapters that follow draw upon roughly 280 of the productions I have seen over the last twenty-five years. Unless otherwise noted, references to the RSC are to productions in the two large theatres (the Royal Shakespeare Theatre in Stratford, the Barbican in London) as opposed to the Swan, The Other Place, and the Pit. I do not distinguish between OSF productions at the Elizabethan Stagehouse and the Bowmer, RNT productions at the Olivier and Lyttleton, and SFC productions at the Festival Theatre and the Avon. When I supply two consecutive years for a RSC production (*Richard III*, 1995–96), the later date refers to a remounting at the Barbican in London or on tour which was the version I saw. With very few exceptions I sidestep cinema and television productions (a different genre and different set of problems) and only introduce stage productions I have actually seen. See the appendix for a list of productions cited.

Abbreviations

DC	The Shakespeare Theatre, Washington, DC
ESC	The English Shakespeare Company marathon of history plays in Chicago 1988
Globe	The Globe Theatre, London
OSF	The Oregon Shakespeare Festival, Ashland, Oregon
PRC	The Playmakers Repertory Company, Chapel Hill, North Carolina
RNT	The Royal National Theatre, London
RSC	The Royal Shakespeare Company
SFC	Stratford Festival Canada, Stratford, Ontario
SSC	Shakespeare Santa Cruz, Santa Cruz, California
TOP	The Other Place

"Let it be hid": price tags, trade-offs, and economies

"a short tale to make"
Polonius, 2.2.146

In the final speech of *Othello* Lodovico issues the command: "The object poisons sight,/Let it be hid" (5.2.364–65).[1] According to scholars who gloss the line, "the object" and "it" refer to the bodies of Othello and Desdemona ("the tragic loading of this bed" – 363). Jacobean beds had curtains whereas our beds do not, so that in those first performances at the Globe the poisoned sight could be hidden after Lodovico's line by closing a bed curtain, an option usually not available today. Recent directors, moreover, resist such closing off of the two or three dead figures on the bed because they prefer to have that tragic loading the final image as the lights go down (such diminution of onstage illumination was not possible at the Globe), often accompanied by an onlooking Iago. The preferred choice today is therefore to treat Iago rather than the figures on the bed as the object that poisons sight and direct him to be "hid" or taken offstage. Furthermore, directors such as Brian Bedford (SFC 1991) and Michael Attenborough (RSC 1999)[2] have chosen to keep Iago as an onstage observer of an Othello and Desdemona still visible on the bed. Their solution is worthy of Alexander the Great with the Gordian knot: cut "Let it be hid."

In singling out such a problematic moment (and a large cluster of such moments are found in final scenes), my goal is to explore the theatrical rationale behind a director's choice and point to both the gains and losses – in this instance the possible diminution of a major motif or image, the refusal of those Venetians onstage to face fully the horrors or poisoned sight generated by tragic error. The asset of offering the playgoer a powerful final image crafted by the director should be played off against the blurring or loss of another potentially powerful climactic image, here a refusal to "see."

As evident in this example, my focus is on choices made by today's theatrical professionals, more specifically the choices made about the playtexts to be used – the actual words to be spoken, the scenes or segments to be omitted or transposed, the many other adjustments that must be made – for example, the treatment of references to *swords* in a production that features handguns and grenades. From many conversations over the last twenty-five years I have gained a healthy respect for the commitment and expertise of actors and directors, so I will not mount an attack against the director-as-vandal or sing hymns to uncut playscripts. Indeed, as my years increase and my staying power in a theatre seat diminishes, I am less sanguine about four-hour renditions of *Hamlet* and *King Lear* (that is no country for old people). Rather, I will spell out (I hope accurately and sympathetically) the exigencies faced by actors and directors in placing before today's audiences words and effects targeted at players, playgoers, and playhouses that no longer exist.

In taking on such a task I am building on my previous work in two related but discrete areas. Since 1977 as a theatre historian I have published four books in an attempt to recover features of the first performances of the plays of Shakespeare and his contemporaries. During that same period as a performance historian I have written a book on the onstage history of *Titus Andronicus* and close to thirty theatre essays devoted to recent productions of Shakespeare's plays, usually with a focus on the shows I managed to see in a given year. In these twin pursuits I have wrestled repeatedly with the evidence about the first performances of English Renaissance plays and since the mid 1970s have also seen an enormous number of Shakespeare productions in North America and England (often fifteen or more per year).

My goal in this book is to fuse these two bodies of material so as to draw upon my expertise in the dramaturgy and staging practices of the 1590s and early 1600s in order to shed some light on problems and choices found in the 1990s and early 2000s. Readers familiar with the wealth of studies linked to what has become known as "Shakespeare in Performance" may rightly wonder about the need for yet another such investigation.[3] My own approach to such issues has changed considerably since the mid 1970s when I began a series of annual reviews of the Oregon Shakespeare Festival season. In particular, evaluative comments about the work of actors, directors, and designers (what I now think of as the hits-runs-and-errors method) have been superseded by a focus upon choices, especially those that strike me as "new" or provocative or worthy of putting "on the record" (I rarely write with prospective ticket-buyers in mind). In collecting such material while simultaneously puzzling over the limited evidence about the first performances of the same plays, I have made various connections that I hope will be illuminating to others and not merely a rehashing of the plentiful scholarship of the last decade and more. Again, my goal is not to attack directors or editors for failing to understand the original playscripts but to play off then versus now in a fashion that I hope will be useful to the theatre historian, the theatrical professional, the student of these plays, and the playgoer.

The starting point for today's director is the received text, almost always a modern edition of the play in question. Subsequent choices and adjustments then range from the tiny (a single word) to the massive (as when a two or three-part play is compressed into one). To describe this process of turning an English Renaissance printed text into a playscript for today's actors and playgoers I use two terms. For me, *rescripting* denotes the changes made by a director in the received text in response to a perceived problem or to achieve some agenda. For more extensive changes I use the term *rewrighting* to characterize situations where a director or adapter moves closer to the role of the playwright so as to fashion a script with substantial differences from the original.

The forms of rescripting vary widely. To cite a few categories, directors make adjustments in order to (1) streamline the playscript and save running time by cutting speeches or entire scenes, (2) eliminate obscurity (in mythological allusions, difficult syntax, and archaic words), (3) conserve on personnel by eliminating figures completely (Lovell in *Richard III*) or telescoping together various lesser characters (Antenor-Margarelon in Trevor Nunn's 1999 RNT *Troilus and Cressida*), (4) sidestep stage practices appropriate to the Globe that might mystify today's playgoer or actor, and occasionally (5) cancel out a passage that might not fit comfortably with a particular agenda or "concept." Examples of rewrighting include presenting the three parts of *Henry VI* as two plays (or more radically one) or the two parts of *Tamburlaine*, *The Honest Whore*, or *The Fair Maid of the West* as one (see chapter 7) and factoring in material from the 1594 *The Taming of a Shrew* to "complete" the Christopher Sly story apparently left incomplete in the First Folio's *The Taming of the Shrew* (see chapter 8).

To discuss these choices is to enter a murky area, one where the vested interests of the scholar or theatre historian can easily be at odds with the "real world" reflexes of the theatrical professional. Rescripting decisions can yield practical, narrative, and conceptual gains but can also involve some losses or diminutions. Throughout my presentation the emphasis will therefore be upon what I term *price tags* and *trade-offs*, both the pluses and minuses of a director's rescripting or rewrighting. Any movement of a Shakespeare play from page to stage involves hundreds of interpretative decisions. In many instances (as with Lodovico's "Let it be hid") to opt for X means to diminish or even eliminate Y – a trade-off situation true of all interpretative choices but particularly those that take place in the theatre. For example, to seek broad, farcical effects in a scene from a Shakespeare comedy is often to achieve a short-term gain at the expense of some long-term effect or "build" that is diminished or denied. To play Morocco and Arragon in *The Merchant of Venice* as buffoons is to entertain the audience during those three scenes at the risk of changing, even subverting the way an audience eventually sees and evaluates Bassanio's choice of the leaden casket in 3.2. The implications found by various critics in the golden and silver choices can evanesce if the speeches that enunciate the rationale behind those choices are eclipsed by laughter at a scimitar-waving Morocco and a lisping, affected Arragon.

Such interpretative decisions are further complicated when the production in question is geared to a "concept," a new historical period, or an elaborate set (hence the term "Designer's Theatre"). For many theatrical professionals and playgoers, such design choices or transpositions into other eras introduce new excitement and liberate the imagination. For less sanguine observers, such choices diminish Shakespeare by prizing ingenuity over substance. The spectrum of opinion can be summed up by two remarks overheard in Stratford-upon-Avon in the summer of 1985. First, a member of the Royal Shakespeare Company noted that only the bold director dared to do a "traditional" production of Shakespeare. In contrast was a remark heard in the foyer of the theatre: "I've saved for five years and come 5,000 miles to see three shows in Stratford, and not one of them was in Elizabethan dress" (the three were set in 1850, 1959, and 1985).

This debate over "pure" Shakespeare versus transposed or "Designer's Theatre" Shakespeare will not be soon resolved. The purist's stock response (play the Quarto or Folio version with as few trappings as possible) will not necessarily lead to a show that will play in Peoria (although it might do well in Urbana). Remember, some of the most memorable productions this century have realized significant meanings and effects (sometimes in long-neglected scripts) through such transpositions (as in Tyrone Guthrie's 1956 *Troilus and Cressida*). In tackling elaborate designs, transpositions into new periods, and other "strong" directorial decisions, I will therefore forgo any absolute "purist" stance, for such choices would not be made were there not effects or meanings to be gained.

Rather, my recurring questions will be: what is the cost or price exacted for these gains? What do such choices exclude or preclude? Wherein lie the trade-offs? If some massaging of elements in the received scripts is to be expected, how much rescripting is "legitimate" to gain a more sympathetic Shylock or an anti-colonialist Ariel? Where is the line between interpretation and translation? In posing such questions, I admit, my own purist gene is never fully recessive, but my goal is to present as judiciously as possible the rationale of both the director and the theatre historian.

In some instances that rationale includes a sense of financial and theatrical exigency. Many of the productions I will be discussing are linked to large theatrical companies with significant resources in terms of budget and personnel: the Royal Shakespeare Company; Stratford Festival Canada; the Oregon Shakespeare Festival. But what if you are a director of a regional repertory company in Virginia with less than four weeks to set up *The Tempest*, your first Shakespeare production ever, and, moreover, you are working with actors with little experience in doing such plays (so that both your Prospero and Ariel have never before done a professional Shakespeare production)? Wherein lies the incentive to dig deeply into the script and wrestle with apparent oddities or difficulties? Rather, if Prospero's masque in 4.1 (notoriously difficult to bring off) is giving you trouble, why not cut it and reshape the end of 3.1 (Prospero's observation of Miranda and Ferdinand) to take the omission into account? Similarly, in a 1974 interview Michael Kahn observed that he was "cutting less and less," with such editing "very often to do with our inadequacies rather than Shakespeare's." For example, his first choice would be, despite the obscure jokes, to include the musicians in *Romeo and Juliet* (4.5.96–146), but to cut this sequence means "a great deal of money less on salaries, three fewer costumes, and also four minutes that the audience isn't going to understand anyway because they don't have any clues about Simon Catling and 'heart's ease' and all that."[4] To do such rescripting or rewrighting is therefore to "solve" the problem within your time limit and resources. In such situations wherein lies the inducement to dig deeply for solutions (and maybe come up with nothing) when you can simply cut the Gordian knot and save precious rehearsal time by using the blue pencil? Why privilege Shakespeare and his "intentions" anyway?

Nonetheless, the alternative approach – to play a full text and wrestle with the subsequent problems – is not a stance limited solely to professors far removed from the practicalities of the theatre but is found in the work of such directors as Deborah Warner and Sir Peter Hall and has led to some remarkable productions. In this context Hall's diary entries on his 1975 RNT *Hamlet* are revealing. Given enormous pressure to cut this very long script owing to mounting costs, he laments "So what am I to do?" Although initially reluctant to direct this show, Hall notes: "But I now have a line, an excitement, something to get the adrenalin going" and then adds tellingly: "I don't want to *interpret* the play by cutting it." In the next day's entry he observes: "It seems to me that we have come some distance in the last twenty-five years in understanding the rhythm of a Shakespeare play, how it operates, how one segment reacts on another. We have also come some way in understanding how to speak the verse. But we still cut the text like barbarians. Do we know *what* we cut? And don't we normally cut either to fit some preconceived theory for the production, or because we simply can't make the passage work? I think my future direction in Shakespeare must be to reveal the total object as well as possible. I feel in my blood now that I know how. The cost implications of full length will have to be got over somehow."[5]

WORDS, WORDS, WORDS

Directors such as Hall and Deborah Warner (in her uncut or nearly uncut productions of *Titus Andronicus*, *King John*, *King Lear*, and *Richard II*) represent one end of a broad spectrum of approaches to rescripting. In the chapters that follow I provide a road map of such choices by means of a wide array of examples placed in a series of sometimes overlapping categories. The most provocative situations arise from a director's decision to update or improve the received text, but in this introductory chapter I will focus primarily on choices linked to practical considerations, most often the desire to cut down on running time and to eliminate elements perceived as obscure, excrescent, awkward, or beyond the resources of a given company.

The logic behind such pragmatic cuts is spelled out by Tom Markus in his description of how he prepared *2 Henry IV* for the Colorado Shakespeare Festival. In his view, "play doctoring is necessary as a result of the differences in the knowledge and beliefs of a contemporary audience from those of one in Shakespeare's era." Included therefore among his guide-lines for such "play doctoring" or rescripting are: "shorten each scene as much as possible . . . eliminate everything that might confuse an audience . . . cut all characters who are unnecessary to the scene . . . cut all scenes which do not advance the story . . . cut or change all words that are archaic or obscure."[6] Here in extreme form is the rationale for directorial intervention to bring Shakespeare's plays more in line with today's idiom and expectations.

To start at the most fundamental level (in keeping with Markus's injunction to "cut or change all words that are archaic or obscure"), students of Shakespeare regularly encounter situations wherein a specific word may vary from text to text. Most famous are the many variations in Second Quarto/Folio *Hamlet* such as *solid* versus *sallied/sullied* flesh (1.2.129), *despised* versus *disprized* love (3.1.71), and *scullion* versus *stallion* versus *scallion* (Q1's delectable version – 2.2.587), but also well known in editorial circles are items such as Othello's base *Indian/Judean* (5.2.347) and Juliet's *name/word* (2.2.44). Here is where editors make choices in behalf of their readers. Directors, who may or may not be aware of these interventions, face comparable problems when presenting speeches and interactions to their auditors. An editor may present to the reader a difficult passage and then gloss it by means of an explanatory note, but directors, fearful of losing their auditors and not getting them back, regularly cut or simplify syntactically complex passages or otherwise streamline long speeches, with mythological allusions particularly vulnerable. In the eyes (or ears) of a director, the need for a steady flow of communication without jolts (in the spirit of Markus's "eliminate everything that might confuse an audience") takes precedence over textual purism – assuming there is anything "pure" in these muddy waters.

Many of these directorial alterations are tiny and go unnoticed even by veteran playgoers – as when at the outset of *The Taming of the Shrew* (OSF 1991) the hostess's reference to the *thirdborough* (Induction.1.12 – *headborough* in the Folio) was changed to *third-constable*. In two rival 1999 productions of *Antony and Cleopatra* the Globe director retained Enobarbus's comment that Antony at Philippi "was troubled with a rheum" (3.2.57), but the RSC director changed *rheum* to *cold*. In the 1994 RSC *Twelfth Night*, Sir Toby described Cesario to Sir Andrew not as "fencer to the *Sophy*" (3.4.279) but rather to "the *Shah of Persia*." Beatrice grieves that a woman must "make an account of her life to a clod of wayward marl" (2.1.62–63), but the director of the 1989 OSF production changed *marl* to *sod*. In Steven Pimlott's *Hamlet* (RSC 2001) the poisoned sword wielded by Laertes in the fencing match was not *unbated* but *unblunted* (see 4.7.138, 5.2.317). In Brian Bedford's 1991 SFC *Othello* Iago called Roderigo a *pimple*, not a *quat* (5.1.11); Desdemona was described as a *treasure craft*, not a *land carract* (1.2.50); and Othello referred to a *reed*, not a *rush* and *judgment day*, not *compt* (5.2.270, 273). Nicholas Hytner's *Twelfth Night* (Lincoln Center 1998), widely seen on television in the

United States, provided an unusually large number of such changes: for example, *sink-a-pace* became *hornpipe* (1.3.130–31), *con* became *learn* (1.5.174), *revolve* became *consider* (2.5.143), *chev'ril* became *kid* (3.1.12), *pilchers* became *sardines* (3.1.34), and *barricadoes* became *stone walls* (4.2.37).[7] In the same director's *The Winter's Tale* (RNT 2001), to avoid an unwanted laugh during the final moments at what initially might seem an incongruous image Paulina said not "I, an old *turtle,* / Will wing me to some wither'd bough" (5.3.132–33) but *turtledove.*

Often changes are occasioned by a combination of difficult phrasing and tangled syntax. In his *Coriolanus* (RSC Swan 1994) David Thacker sidestepped a notable puzzle (to which the Arden 2 editor devotes a long note) by cutting "make you a sword of me?" (1.6.76). A pet passage of mine in piecing out an interpretation of *King Lear* (Kent's disquisition on the "holy cords" [2.2.73–80]) is regularly omitted or pared back onstage (as in Adrian Noble's 1993 RSC production) owing to syntactical difficulty and the presence of phrases such as "halcyon beaks." I should note, however, that when in a lecture at the Oregon Shakespeare Festival I lamented the absence of these lines from the 1976 production, director Pat Patton shrewdly noted that in discussing it for my auditors I instinctively paraphrased the passage, rearranging the word order and explaining the hard words, an option not available to the actor playing Kent. Comparable passages also disappear, as when Brian Bedford (SFC 1991) eliminated Othello's "Exchange me for a goat" phrasing (3.3.180–83), presumably because of "exsufflicate and blown surmises," and several other hard passages (e.g., Brabantio's lines on "the bruis'd heart" being "pierced through the ear" – 1.3.219). Perhaps most subject to such changes is *Love's Labor's Lost* with its many puns and learned quibbles. Even a lightly cut production such as OSF 1980 omitted both the fox-ape-humblebee passage involving Armado, Moth, and Costard (3.1.83–103) and the final forty lines of 4.1, a witty and bawdy exchange among Boyet, Rosaline, Maria, and Costard. Also often pared back are a variety of obscure or syntactically difficult passages in *All's Well That Ends Well* (OSF 1975, DC 1988, PRC 2001), especially the speeches of Lavatch – and Jon Jory (OSF 1975) omitted this figure entirely and substituted three *commedia* jesters who provided acrobatics, mimicry, and dumb shows and, after his exposure in 4.3, received Parolles as one of their own.

Sometimes in-the-theatre changes occur when words or phrases are deemed offensive or politically incorrect. Prominent among the casualties are Portia's comment on the departed Morocco "Let all of his complexion choose me so" (*The Merchant of Venice*, 2.7.79), the third witch's "Liver of blaspheming Jew" (*Macbeth*, 4.1.26), and Benedick's "if I do not love her, I am a Jew" (*Much Ado About Nothing*, 2.3.263). The first two items are often omitted, whereas Benedick's *Jew* has been changed to *knave* (OSF 1989), *fool* (RSC 1990) or, as reported to me from another recent production, *jerk*. Moreover, some directorial ears are more sensitive than others. The director of the 1995 DC *Macbeth* changed Macduff's "Be not a *niggard* of your speech" (4.3.180) to *miser*, and the director of the 1995 PRC *Othello* omitted such lines as "Your son-in-law is far more fair than black" (1.3.290) and "Haply, for I am black" (3.3.263).[8] The latter cut may also have been influenced by Othello's subsequent comment that "I am declin'd / Into the vale of years" (3.3.265–66), for in this production a youngish actor was cast in the role ("the vale of years" also disappeared in RSC 1999 where a thirty-year-old Ray Fearon played Othello). In a virtually uncut *Othello* (SFC 1979) Othello's famous speech building to his suicide was not interrupted by the brief lines from Lodovico and Gratiano, a standard adjustment. In this instance, however, the two interjections were not omitted to enhance the dramatic rhythm but because, in a production that was to end its run with a series of matinees for high school students, the director and her actors were fearful of losing this climactic moment when Lodovico, in front of 2,000 teenagers, exclaimed: "O bloody period!" (5.2.357).

Changes or elisions are not linked solely to obscurity or political correctness. Iago tells Othello that Cassio used the handkerchief to "wipe his *beard*" (3.3.439), but if the actor is clean-shaven, *beard* becomes *mouth* or *face*. Similarly, Malcolm's "ne'er pull your hat upon your brows" (4.3.208) will often disappear (as in OSF 1987) if directed at a Macduff not wearing a hat. In *The Tempest* Antonio mockingly describes Adrian as a *cockerel* (2.1.31), but, given a small cast for a touring show, David Thacker (RSC Swan 1995) opted for an Adriana played by an actress and therefore changed the term to *hen*; similarly, if Alonzo is played by an actress as Alonza (PRC 1998), Ariel's "three men of sin" (3.3.53) directed at Alonso, Sebastian, and Antonio becomes inappropriate, so *men* became *creatures*. In a production of *Hamlet* (RSC 2001) in which the same older actor doubled as the ghost and Osric, the director cut references to "young Osric" (5.2.196, 259). Productions of *Much Ado* often omit Borachio's line to Conrade "Stand thee close then under this penthouse, for it drizzles rain" (3.3.103–4) as in RSC 1990 where the garden set had no such overhang. Also often adjusted is Tybalt's angry comment on Romeo's presence, "This, by his voice, should be a Montague"

(1.5.54), as when Jim Edmondson (OSF 1975) inserted a dance between Romeo's speech (44–53) and Tybalt's reaction and therefore changed *voice* to *face*.

As evident in such examples the rationale behind pragmatic cuts can vary widely. Whether for practical or conceptual reasons, directors of *The Winter's Tale* (e.g., RSC 1981, RSC 1992) omit Leontes's first reaction to Hermione's "statue" ("Hermione was not so much wrinkled, nothing / So aged as this seems") and Paulina's response ("So much the more our carver's excellence, / Which lets go by some sixteen years" – 5.3.28–31). An award-winning Falstaff (John Woodvine) explained to me that Sir John's camomile passage at the outset of his rendition of Henry IV (that starts "for though the camomile, the more it is trodden on, the faster it grows" – 2.4.399–401) disappears because if it is included the beat is too long for an actor to sustain. Adrian Noble cut the opening lines of 1.2 from his *Henry V* (RSC 1984) because in his production the dialogue between the two clergymen that constitutes 1.1 was presented with Henry V and various lords in view elsewhere onstage; since the Archbishop never exited, Henry's call for his presence ("Where is my gracious Lord of Canterbury?" – 1.2.1) became superfluous. A small pragmatic adjustment was made by director Mark Rucker in his production of *Titus Andronicus* (SSC 1988). In the script, Marcus's first line after the four murders in 5.3 is: "You sad-fac'd men, people and sons of Rome," but at some performances the rapidity of these murders elicited titters from the Santa Cruz audience. Since in this rendition Marcus was addressing his lines to the playgoers rather than to actors playing onstage Romans, the actor had the option to omit the first three words so as not to label a gaggle of giggling onlookers as "you sad-fac'd men."

Adjustments also occur when shows are updated to later periods. The 1998 Cheek by Jowl *Much Ado About Nothing* was set in turn-of-the-century England, so that Dogberry and Verges became bobbies, the watch carried *truncheons* rather than *bills* (3.3.41), swords were eliminated (the various challenges in 5.1 were realized by means of gloves), and various lines inappropriate to 1900 were gone (e.g., "What a pretty thing man is when he goes in his doublet and hose and leaves off his wit!" – 5.1.199–200). In her *The Taming of the Shrew* (RSC 1995) Gale Edwards omitted Biondello's elaborate description of the approaching Petruchio and Grumio (3.2.43–71) which was out of phase with the actual costuming or mode of transportation: this Petruchio arrived in a red Fiat and sported multi-colored, parrot-like feathers, a toucan-beaked hat, a boxing glove on his left hand, green boots, and a huge codpiece; Grumio was a bridesmaid in a pink tutu, pink tights, and a pink veil. Elsewhere Edwards crafted some new dialogue to accommodate Tranio's Elvis outfit for his "Lucentio" (United Kingdom reviewers saw him as Gary Glitter). The Folio's true Vincentio is dismayed at Tranio's "silken doublet," "velvet hose," "scarlet cloak," and "copotain hat," but this Vincentio cited "diamond fingers," "a silver shirt," and "winkle-pickers"; Tranio responded: "Why, sir, what 'cerns it you if I wear Armani?" – as opposed to "pearl and gold" (5.1.66–67, 75–76).

Always of potential interest when the action is placed in a later period is what happens to references to the original weaponry. Most common is the adjustment of individual words, as in Jude Kelly's *Othello* (DC 1997) where Patrick Stewart said "Keep up your bright *arms*" (1.2.59) in lieu of *swords* (the weapons of choice here were revolvers). In a comparable production (RNT Cottlesloe 1997) Sam Mendes had his Othello threaten Iago with a revolver in 3.3 which the latter appropriated and used to shoot Emilia in 5.3 while Othello tried unsuccessfully to use a sword against his nemesis. Most elaborate was Matthew Warchus's modern dress *Hamlet* (RSC 1997) which had plentiful handguns and even a shotgun for Laertes in 4.5 but no blades until the climactic fencing match, so that in the cellarage scene the injunction was to swear "Upon my *life*" not "Upon on my *sword*" (1.5.147). As Hamlet, Alex Jennings threatened suicide in "To be, or not to be" with a pistol pulled out of a paper bag; this same weapon was produced in 3.3 to threaten the praying Claudius (Jennings dropped the bullets, so was forced to fumble and reload, so that "Up, sword" [88] was cut) and was used in 3.4 to threaten Gertrude and kill Polonius with a single shot. In the final moments this Hamlet did use the poisoned sword and wine but additionally shot Claudius's body three times (the body jerked at the first shot), a choice that generated a somewhat different flavor for "the rest is silence."

At the other extreme are those theatrical purists who resist *any* changes even if "obvious" errors. To cite two examples, as Corin in the 1992 OSF *As You Like It*, actor Barry Kraft took on the challenge of actually playing the First Folio's "*pood* pasture" (TLN 1226, 3.2.27 – "that pood pasture makes fat sheep") rather than accepting the universal editorial emendation to *good*. Kraft wafted his hand under his nose and grimaced so as to convey clearly the sense of *manured* (and Ashland playgoers who chuckled were not aware of anything unusual in this line reading). Similarly, actor Bill Christy in Homer Swander's 1991 Santa Barbara production of *The Taming of the Shrew* refused to accept as a misprint Petruchio's line "Borne in *Verona*, old *Butonios* sonne" (TLN 756, 1.2.190) where all other

editors and readers have emended *Butonios* to *Antonio's* (clearly established
elsewhere as the name of Petruchio's father). In what may be the ultimate
in textual purism, Christy played the line as a joke at Gremio's expense,
with *Butonio* an equivalent to *Buttinsky*, a meddler (again, the moment
was amusing and *did* made sense in context). Admittedly, such extreme
instances "prove" nothing, for, despite such actorly ingenuity, a director
faced with a textual oddity or obscure pun may well ask: why should
I include in 2000 a 400-year-old joke that needs a footnote?

DISPOSABLE PARTS

Some of Shakespeare's plays are relatively short (several of the comedies,
Macbeth, *The Tempest*) even by today's standards and therefore *could* be presented uncut or at least without major omissions, but other well-known
scripts (e.g., *Richard III*, *Hamlet*, *King Lear*) are almost always streamlined
so as to avoid four hours in the theatre. To play all or even most of the text
of *Hamlet* found in today's editions (as in the Kenneth Branagh film) is
to strain the resources of a theatre company and sometimes the patience
of an audience. Veteran *Hamlet*-watchers are therefore not surprised to
find Reynaldo or Fortinbras absent from a given production or to see in
3.2 the dumb show or the play-within-the-play but not both.

Playgoers familiar with both the received texts and today's productions
can readily make their own lists of rarely included scenes or sequences:
the Chorus to Act 2 and Peter and the musicians (4.5.102–46) in *Romeo
and Juliet*; the carriers, Gadshill, and the chamberlain in *1 Henry IV* (2.1);
Ventidius with the body of Pacorus in *Antony and Cleopatra* (3.1); large
chunks of the first courtier scene in *The Tempest*, especially the "widow
Dido" exchange (2.1.77–102). Both the RSC 2000 and Almeida 2000
directors omitted Berkeley's brief appearance to confront Bolingbroke
in *Richard II*, 2.3; several directors of *2 Henry IV* (ESC 1988, OSF 1989,
RSC 1991) have cut Warwick's account of Hal crying in the next room
(4.5.82–87). Libby Appel's *The Merchant of Venice* (OSF 1991) was typical in telescoping together the two Morocco scenes (2.1, 2.7), eliminating entirely Old Gobbo from 2.2 (a choice that resulted in an awkward
Launcelot–Bassanio encounter), and cutting Launcelot Gobbo's appearance to deliver a message in 5.1 and his exchange with Lorenzo in which
the latter accuses him of getting the Moor with child (3.5.37–42). Indeed,
veteran playgoers are sometimes surprised to see a particular scene
or sequence that is almost always cut. For example, although Michael
Attenborough in his 1999 RSC *Othello* streamlined his script, he did include Othello's brief appearance in 5.1 to cheer on a murder in the

dark, a moment rarely seen onstage.[9] I have seen several productions of *Richard II* without the Duke–Duchess–Aumerle scenes (5.2–5.3) and often encountered major omissions in Act 2 of *Richard III*. Similarly, I have yet to see a stage production of *Henry VIII* that includes in 4.2 Queen Katherine's vision (the term that precedes the long stage direction in the Folio) or in 5.2 the curious inside/outside sequence involving Cranmer standing at the door awaiting his call to the council.

Some short scenes strike directors as cuttable but turn out to serve a practical function. Pat Patton told me that he initially cut the scrivener's scene (3.6) from his 1978 OSF *Richard III* but quickly reinserted it when he discovered the need for a time lapse between 3.5 and 3.7. Readers will also note that this scrivener's observation – "Who is so gross / That cannot see this palpable device? / Yet who's so bold but says he sees it not?" (3.6.10–12) – places him in the series of moral compromisers that includes Brackenbury in 1.4, the Cardinal in 3.1, and the Mayor in 3.5. Patton did cut 4.5 at the cost of not having his playgoers hear from Stanley that Richard's strenuous wooing in the previous scene had failed to win the hand of Princess Elizabeth. Similarly, some directors seeking to trim back another long script, *The Winter's Tale*, choose to omit 3.1 (Cleomines and Dion's account of their experience at the oracle) although again the brief scene serves as a bridge between the Leontes–Antigonus confrontation that ends 2.3 and the trial of 3.2 (the 1997 Globe director provided a wordless procession over the stage).

Directors of *As You Like It* must confront the problem: what to do with the curious 4.2 that starts with Jaques's "Which is he that kill'd the deer?" Again, this scene serves a practical function – to allow for the passage of two hours during which Orlando saves Oliver and the latter reports back – but does so in a puzzling way, at least given the lines that survive in the Folio. One solution is to provide some form of ritual blooding with a large number of actors and even the carcass of a deer, but I have seen several productions where the Folio's lines were gone to be replaced by some form of mimed action. For example, at the end of 4.1 in the 1990 SFC production a forester chased a woman across the stage with 4.3 following immediately; in the 1985 RSC production Celia fell asleep at the end of 4.1, Jaques trailed a bloody white silk sheet across the stage, and hunters fired at her as she writhed and became enveloped in the silk – all to present her nightmare (of sexual awakening?). Also relevant here is one of the standard cuts in this script, Touchstone's speech on horns and cuckoldry (3.3.51–63), for both this rarely heard passage and 4.2 are linked by the Elizabethan obsession with horns, a source of considerable humor then but of less interest today.

Some solutions to perceived problems are so familiar that playgoers may no longer have a good fix on the original script. For example, those playgoers familiar with *Macbeth* onstage are taken aback when Hecate appears in 3.5 to chastise the witches or when the English doctor is included in 4.3. The omission of Hecate is supported by a scholarly narrative about interpolations from Middleton's *The Witch*. In contrast, the paring back of 4.3 is linked to a widely shared conviction among theatrical professionals that this England scene is too long. During a spate of productions over a recent two-year span I saw and heard Hecate three times and the English doctor twice, so that I can attest that both episodes when included can contribute to a sense of the whole – as with Malcolm's comment about the English king's "heavenly gift of prophecy" (4.3.157) that can resonate with the riddling comments from the witches.

What is bedrock to one director may be disposable to another. When I saw the touring version of Peter Brook's RSC *A Midsummer Night's Dream* (Chicago 1971) only two passages from the play were included in the printed program, one of them the Theseus–Hippolyta exchange that includes "The best in this kind are but shadows; and the worst are no worse, if imagination amend them" (5.1.211–12), but this speech was omitted by Dennis Bigelow (OSF 1979). In her *King Lear* (Young Vic 1997) Helena Kaut-Howson included moments that are usually cut such as the Edmund–Curran beginning to 2.1, the Quarto-only Kent scene (4.3), and the Kent-gentleman coda to 4.7, but omitted such meaty and potentially telling passages as Cordelia's two asides in 1.1, Edgar's asides in 3.6 and 4.6, and, from the final scene, Edgar's "The gods are just" and Goneril's "the laws are mine, not thine;/ Who can arraign me for't" (5.3.171, 159–60). In his *King Lear* (DC 1991) Michael Kahn made many of the usual cuts in the final scene including Edgar's account of meeting Kent (a Quarto-only passage) and the bringing in of the bodies of Goneril and Regan (5.3.205–22, 238), but other omissions were atypical. Goneril did not say "Who can arraign me for't?" (160), no gentlemen appeared with a bloody knife (222), and, in perhaps the unkindest cut of all, Edmund said "The one the other poison'd for my sake" but not "Yet Edmund was belov'd!" (5.3.240–41). For both actor and playgoer today, those four omitted words can provide a major clue about what has been driving Edmund (going back to Gloucester's dismissive lines at the beginning of 1.1). In this latter instance, to economize can affect a significant through-line.

Also revealing are the varied approaches to *Coriolanus*, 5.5 in which Volumnia, Virgilia, and Valeria are seen *"passing over the stage"* (5.5.0) while a spokesman for Rome praises them as "the life of Rome" and others respond "Welcome, ladies, / Welcome!" (1, 6–7). This scene is sometimes omitted as disposable (OSF 1980) or reduced to a procession over the stage without the accompanying speech (SFC 1981). However, to include 5.5 can yield some meaningful effects, whether to provide a fleeting sense of Volumnia's pride in saving Rome or show her dismay at the danger to her son who had stated that his decision to capitulate to her pleas, though "a happy victory to Rome," may prove "most mortal to him" (5.3.186, 189). David Thacker (RSC Swan 1994) had Virgilia and Valeria smile as they circled the stage but Volumnia (who knew what was in store for her son) look grim. Even more tellingly, Terry Hands (RSC 1989–90) used 5.5 to set up one of the major images in his production. The speech in praise of the women's efforts (delivered by Valeria) was followed by a ceremony in which the son of Coriolanus, dressed in a black cloak, was presented with a sword. This boy had been brought onstage in 1.2 where Volumnia clearly had appropriated him from Virgilia. Now in 5.5, after receiving the symbolic ceremonial sword, the boy shed his cloak to reveal beneath it a white military uniform identical to that worn earlier in Rome by his father. A grim but proud Volumnia led the boy around the stage so as to show off the new martial hero being groomed to replace the son she had helped to destroy in 5.3, a climactic image of grandmother and grandson that was stunning – and, in its implications for the future, highly disturbing.

Within a week in August, 1979 I saw two very different productions of *1 Henry IV*, both heavily cut. Both directors omitted 2.1 and 4.4 (standard cuts); the director at the North Carolina Shakespeare Festival also cut Francis the drawer and some other sizeable chunks; the SFC director omitted Vernon's description of Prince Hal (4.1.97–110), Hal's disposition of the day's honors in the final scene (5.5.25–31), and most of Hotspur's pre-battle speeches, including all of the "time of life is short" passage (5.2.81–88). Of particular interest is a moment pared down in both productions, Hal's rescue of his father from Douglas at Shrewsbury. The Quarto speech reads:

> Hold up thy head, vile Scot, or thou art like
> Never to hold it up again! The spirits
> Of valiant Shirley, Stafford, Blunt are in my arms.
> It is the Prince of Wales that threatens thee,
> Who never promiseth but he means to pay.
>
> (5.4.39–43)

In North Carolina, all these lines were gone; Hal entered, saw his father fighting with Douglas (the Quarto stage direction reads: "*They fight; the*

King being in danger, enter Prince of Wales"), and attacked. In Ontario, Hal spoke the first line and a half and then rescued his father. Even an academic purist can appreciate how all or most of these lines might drop out in rehearsal as impediments to the flow of the action or as violations of plausibility. In "the real world," would a son, seeing his father "*being in danger,*" go through five blank verse lines before coming to the rescue? In addition, the SFC director told me that the line starting "It is the Prince of Wales" was, in his terms, a "white gloves" passage with a formal or prissy ring to it that he found inappropriate to the scene and to Hal's character. In both productions the lines therefore disappeared, and few playgoers were aware of their absence.

What then can be said in behalf of these five lines? Throughout the play a wide range of figures, including Falstaff, Henry IV, and the rebels, are associated with not paying their debts and not keeping their promises. In contrast, Prince Hal does honor his debts and promises, whether those made in his early soliloquy (where he vows to "pay the debt I never promised" – 1.2.209), in his reply to Falstaff in the major tavern scene ("I do, I will" – 2.4.481), or in his interview with his father (where he vows, among other things, to force Hotspur to "exchange / His glorious deeds for my indignities" – 3.2.145–46). Here, just before his climactic fight with Hotspur, the Prince appears as a vengeful warrior, visibly bloodied (5.4.2), who embodies in his arms "the spirits" of those who have already fallen (Shirley, Stafford, Blunt). But in this speech he describes himself not as Hal, Prince Henry, or the Prince but as "the Prince of Wales," the Crown Prince, the heir to Henry IV, the role that epitomizes the debt he never promised; and he further characterizes that Prince of Wales as one who, unlike almost everyone else in the play, "never promiseth but he means to pay." Both in action (this rescue of his father) and in metaphor, Hal here fulfills a role, a debt, a promise that is central to the final movement of Part I (and of Part II as well). To cut these lines is then to achieve a modest gain in the flow of the battle and to avoid what might or might not be a "white gloves" passage but at the cost of losing a major signpost that can point towards some distinctive meanings embodied in Hal's emergence as the Prince of Wales and eventually Henry V.

The pros and cons of streamlining were highly visible in Matthew Warchus's widely seen *Hamlet* (RSC 1997). With a running time of just over three hours the script was heavily cut and adapted (according to the program the acting text "has been specially cut and partially restructured by the director with reference to the First and Second Quartos and the Folio"). Gone were Fortinbras, the ambassadors, Marcellus, Reynaldo,

and all of 1.1; "To be, or not to be" was moved from 3.1 into 2.2; a version
of the Horatio–Gertrude scene unique to the First Quarto was included.
In lieu of 1.1 appeared a film sequence of a youthful Hamlet with family
and dog romping in the snow. The subsequent emphasis was upon the
family and upon the boardroom rather than the kingdom (this show did
not highlight political or cosmic issues), so that Polonius was described
in the program's plot summary as "an old family friend." Cutting the
first scene drastically changed the nature of the ghost who appeared in
a tuxedo in the midst of the 1.2 festivities (most of what remained of
Shakespeare's Act 1 took place at the same raucous wedding party) and,
as I discovered, undermined the figure of Horatio who lost his defining
scene. This ghost offered Hamlet a polite request not a command and
when he departed in the equivalent to 1.5 was compared by one reviewer
to a party guest drifting away in search of some breakfast. The production
ended with Horatio's epitaph, followed by another view of the initial film
sequence of Hamlet's childhood with a voice-over narrative drawn from
Horatio's speech to Fortinbras.

The choice made by Warchus and others to omit the Polonius–
Reynaldo section of 2.1 is targeted by David Bell ("Many directors too
easily give up trying to find the point") in a brief section on "Trusting
the Playwright" in his manual for directors. Bell starts with the imperative: "If you trust the play enough to stage it, trust its author" and adds:
"If you alter or cut whenever you have difficulty you may miss something
important." As Bell notes, with this section omitted "Polonius is merely
a doddering, harmless old fool" whereas "those seventy-five lines reveal
him to be an expert, ruthless spy" and "a force to be reckoned with and
used." When Hamlet kills Polonius, "Does he kill a harmless old fool, or
a machinating intelligence agent?" He concludes: "So think twice before
you cut those seventy-five lines. Chances are they have more to do with
the play than you do."[10]

A comparable choice is the elimination of onstage plebeians in *Julius
Caesar*. Some directors get considerable mileage out of the three crowd
scenes (1.1, 3.2, 3.3), but others make these figures disappear. Most extreme was John Wood's production (SFC 1978) where the souvenir program listed actors to play citizens and Cinna the poet, but both the
opening scene (1.1) and the killing of Cinna (3.3) were omitted, the onstage crowd was gone from the Forum scene (3.2), and even the offstage
shouts in 1.2 were replaced by symbolic chords. Not only did Brutus and
Antony direct their 3.2 orations at the theatre audience, but Calpurnia
was included in the scene (she brought the will to Antony and remained

onstage until the end). In lieu of the scripted 1.1 Edward Hall (RSC 2001) started with a black-shirted ensemble singing a Fascist hymn ("We bring forth the new world from the ashes of the old . . . The republic makes us strong") and a tickertape welcome for Caesar, but, although the Forum scene started with actors scattered throughout the auditorium, their responses to Brutus were audible and meaningful, and during Antony's oration a large number of black shirts assembled onstage to provide a powerful scene.

Omitting 1.1 and 3.3 may be unusual, but leaving the plebeians out of one or more scenes is not. To avoid what he termed yet another static "pressed toga" rendition Michael Kevin (OSF 1991) used a streamlined script that had no onstage plebeians in 1.1 and especially in 3.2 where Brutus and Antony targeted their orations at the playgoers; he also omitted many lines and phrases, the second account of Portia's death (4.3.181–93), and large chunks of the battle sequence that follows 5.1. In this 1.1 an angry Flavius vigorously presented his speeches but, without the cobbler and without a visible crowd, a playgoer had difficulty determining what the tribune was angry at – and no actors were available to slink away "tongue-tied in their guiltiness" (1.1.62). The onstage plebeians in the Forum scene were also eliminated by Terry Hands (RSC 1987) and Mark Rylance (Globe 1999). At the Globe, actors mingled with the standees and heckled the onstage orators during 1.1 and 3.2, and at the end of the latter scene a few actors climbed onto the stage, but no onstage crowd was visible for either scene – though Antony still spoke his line: "Nay, press not so upon me, stand far off" (3.2.167).

For this choice the price tag is high. The Globe director seized an opportunity to generate in-the-theatre excitement by stationing actors in the midst of the groundlings, but I am not the only *Caesar*-watcher who finds this approach counter-productive. In general terms, figures in this play repeatedly invoke idealized images of Romans or "noble Romans," most notably in Brutus's argument against swearing an oath (2.1.114–40), but such formulations must be tested against the onstage behavior of "real" Romans in these three scenes. More specifically, in these streamlined productions (as opposed to Edward Hall's approach in RSC 2001) the third plebeian's response to Brutus, "Let him be Caesar" (3.2.51), was either omitted or blurred (usually all that was heard from the crowd was a recorded chant of "the will" in response to Antony), whereas that particular moment can emerge as one of the most telling in this tragedy. Does Brutus hear this line? If so, how does he react to a response that contradicts the stated rationale for what he has been saying and doing? Also eliminated with no visible crowd for a playgoer is the stage business when Antony says to the departing plebeians "You have forgot the will I told you of" (3.2.238) and draws them back – what I think of as the yo-yo effect. For this choice Bell's warning ("you may miss something important") seems appropriate.[11]

ACTOR EXIGENCIES

Disposable lines or segments can sometimes be linked to the limitations of the available personnel. I have no wish to single out productions where elements may have been omitted or diminished because a director deemed a particular actor incapable of sustaining a given speech or scene. Rather, I would like to introduce three instances of exigencies occasioned by particular situations.

First, problems can arise when, owing to a shortage of personnel, actors with distinctive faces or voices must reappear to fill out crowd scenes. Directors who choose to downplay or conceal such recycling can resort to masks, as in the Globe 1998 *The Honest Whore*, or lighting, as in the final scene of the Almeida 2000 *Coriolanus* where the Volscian citizens appeared above in the dark. Often affected is *Richard III*, 3.7 where Richard and Buckingham seek and win the support of the Mayor and a group of citizens. Pat Patton (OSF 1978) opted for an elaborate coronation in 4.2, but, in this show without an intermission, lacked time for costume changes and therefore faced a shortage of personnel for the 3.7 citizens. The four actors available had recently been seen as Rivers, Grey, and Vaughan (3.3) or as Clarence (an actor well known to Ashland playgoers), so Patton kept the four figures muffled and stationary while Richard performed above with his two priests and Buckingham cavorted below. This static presentation of the citizens left underdeveloped the play's presentation of "England" and "the people" and, along with the director's omission of 2.3 with its three citizens and his downplaying of the Mayor in 3.5, left one dimension of the script unexplored.

Without doubt the most severe economies I have witnessed on-stage have been found in the ACTER productions in which five British actors, working with minimal costumes and properties, bring a complete Shakespeare play, often uncut, to United States colleges and universities. Decisions about how to realize the script vary widely in these directorless shows. Some groups have chosen to leave everything to the playgoer's imagination, as in the Spring 1985 *As You Like It* that provided no visible bloody napkin, verses, or weapons, whereas other ensembles have opted for some costumes or properties, often as "signatures" to help the playgoer discriminate among various characters and locales. For example, when actors are playing multiple roles, the reappearance of a figure after a considerable absence can puzzle a spectator not familiar with the script (e.g., Oliver in *As You Like It*, 4.3; Antonio in *Much Ado About Nothing*, 5.1), as can the appearance of a new figure late in a play (Mariana in *Measure for Measure*, 4.1).

To sustain their multiple roles, the actors must overcome many hurdles, particularly for the playgoer who would rather look than listen (as one colleague pointed out to me: "This is definitely *not* entry-level Shakespeare"). Surprisingly, some moments that would appear the most daunting have proved to be high points of a production – as when the actor playing Orlando must also play Charles and therefore wrestle himself in 1.2. A theatrically exciting moment was occasioned by such an exigency in the Spring 1985 *As You Like It* when Patrick Godfrey's Jaques finished his account of the seven ages of man ("second childishness, and mere oblivion, / Sans teeth, sans eyes, sans taste, sans every thing" – 2.7.165–66) with an expansive gesture that extended his hands horizontally – at which point he collapsed backwards into the arms of an entering Orlando so as suddenly to "become" old Adam. The ironic counterpointing already present in the script (where Jaques's cynicism is played off against Orlando's care for Adam) was here heightened in a manner that was meaningful, moving, and, in its own way, "magical." A different kind of effect was generated in three different productions of *The Winter's Tale* (Fall 1989, Spring 1990, Spring 2001) by the appearance of Florizel and Perdita in 5.1, for, given the ACTER allocation of parts, the two young figures were played by the same actors who had played Polixenes and Hermione. Given such casting, when Leontes welcomed Florizel and Perdita "As is the spring to th' earth" (5.1.152), he was in fact visibly welcoming a version of the two figures he had rejected and plotted against in the "winter" part of this romance. Some of his lines therefore acquired a special resonance: for example, his assertion to Florizel that "Your father's image is so hit in you / (His very air) that I should call you brother" (127–28).

Shakespeare's plays, however, were not scripted for five actors, so inevitably some features are lost or blurred in these productions, especially in ensemble scenes where a playgoer must imagine the reaction of a figure not visible – as when the Prospero actor is also playing his brother Antonio in *The Tempest*, 5.1. In the ACTER *King Lear* (Spring 1989) the group decided that the Lear actor (Bernard Lloyd) could not maintain his role in 2.4 and also play Cornwall who, albeit with relatively few lines, confronts his father-in-law. In this rendition Cornwall was therefore not a visible presence until after Lear's exit near the end of the scene, a choice that led to the omission of one telling line, Cornwall's affirmation that he was the one who put Kent in the stocks ("I set him there, sir" – 2.4.199). This cut in turn eliminated one of the series of hammer-blows against Lear that generates the exit into the storm, so that a small but essential part of the build was gone, an omission that led to a diminution of the dynamics and potency of Lear's situation. For this and related reasons, this scene was, for me, the least satisfying in this show, so that the "stripping" of Lear and the genesis of "O, reason not the need!" (264) were not fully realized.

Personnel problems may be linked not only to the size but also to the composition of a given company. In particular, the role in Shakespeare's time of the child or boy actor must be taken into account when assessing the challenges of translating the original theatrical vocabulary into our idiom. As opposed to a comparable group today, an Elizabethan or Jacobean theatre company could count on the availability of three to five skilled boy actors to play a range of roles. What difference does the absence of such a resource make today?

When such a question is posed, the usual response is to contrast the presentation of female roles by their "playboys"[12] with that provided by today's actresses and to focus upon gender issues, metatheatre, and the much cited "Some squeaking Cleopatra boy my greatness / I' th' posture of a whore" (*Antony and Cleopatra*, 5.2.220–21) with a particular emphasis upon the possible erotic or homo-erotic reactions from the original playgoers. Lost in such analyses, however, is the simple fact that the Lord Chamberlain's or King's Men had boys to play boys, pages, youths, or young men and therefore had more theatrical options than a comparable group today, especially if a young age was important for a given effect. The pursuit of gender-related agendas can obscure an awareness of how often in Shakespeare and other comparable plays (*Edward II*, *The Duchess of Malfi*, *The White Devil*) the age of a boy can be important to a scene or a larger effect, and, moreover, changes in his age could affect significantly the dynamics or potential meanings.

If indeed a range of qualified boy actors is available to a theatre company then or now, a variety of possibilities emerge that can best be summed up by a series of questions. How old are or should be Arthur and Prince Henry in *King John*? Henry VI in *1 Henry VI*? Rutland, Richmond, and especially Prince Edward in *3 Henry VI*? The two princes in

Richard III? Moth in *Love's Labor's Lost*? Sebastian in *Twelfth Night*? Lucius in *Julius Caesar*? Fleance, Donalbain, young Macduff, young Siward, and two of the three apparitions in *Macbeth*? The son of Coriolanus? Mamillius in *The Winter's Tale*? Admittedly, some small parts *are* often played today by young actors (young Macduff, Mamillius, the children in *The Merry Wives of Windsor*, the son of Coriolanus), but what if the option were readily available to cast X as a ten or twelve-year-old so that an Arthur or Fleance would strike the playgoer as particularly vulnerable?

The practical consequences of a dearth of talented boy actors is evident in *As You Like It*, 5.3, the presentation of "It was a lover and his lass," which is scripted for Touchstone, Audrey, and two singing pages. Of the many productions I have seen only a tiny fraction have followed the Folio here. For example, Lucy Bailey's one major change in the Folio script (Globe 1998) was the rescripting of this scene for musicians, Touchstone, and Audrey but no singing pages and no dialogue. An exception was John Hirsch's production (SFC 1983) in which the song was indeed sung by two pages. Moreover, this production started with the cruel society of the bad duke as depicted by soldiers, gratuitous violence, onstage gloom, and a beggar boy singing a doleful version of this same melody. The happy sunlit delivery of the song in 5.3 was therefore a positive (*in bono*) rendition that helped to set up the mood of the denouement. John Caird (RSC 1989–90) also brought on two boys for 5.3 (and introduced other child actors elsewhere), but Audrey did most of the actual singing, thereby making some of Touchstone's lines after the song irrelevant. Richard Monette (SFC 1990) provided only one verse of the song but then moved into an extensive dance that involved Audrey and a host of male foresters (but no pages), a lively moment that was comparable to Anne-Denise Ford's 1986 OSF production that introduced an elaborate rustic clogging at this point. Equally distinctive was David Landon's college production (University of the South, 1990) that brought on not two pages but five female singers who clustered around Touchstone and, while singing the verses, stroked and fondled him, with Audrey intermittently aware of such activity and Touchstone responding in kind. Radical surgery was performed by director Scott Wentworth (New Jersey Shakespeare Festival 1999) who omitted 5.3 entirely and rather used an ensemble singing of the song to replace 4.2 (also omitted).

As a sampling of choices makes clear, few directors are willing to omit completely "It was a lover and his lass," but if the song is to be included it most likely will be sung either by Touchstone or Audrey (depending upon the talents of the two performers in the roles) or by other adult members of the company – and sometimes as an ensemble number by the entire company. Once the singers have ceased to be boys or pages, however, Touchstone's response to "young gentlemen" and perhaps his wish that "God mend your voices" (5.3.34, 40–41) become irrelevant and his tone inappropriate. Whatever function the scene originally served other than the presentation of a delightful song is keyed to the ages and status of the young singers, but today's playgoers rarely get the opportunity to see the possibilities explored onstage.

Ironically, the Fall 2000 ACTER *As You Like It* provided the most fully realized version that I have seen. Here, in this five-actor genre with its obvious limitations, the group's two actresses played the pages, with one of them reverting to the role of Audrey as needed (at which point the remaining actress held her colleague's signature baseball cap in lieu of the missing page). Throughout the four verses of the song Touchstone was on the stage floor, so that he kept trying to get up and talk after each of the first three verses, but the singers silenced him by persisting with their song. For the first time I got the full force of the closing dialogue, especially Touchstone's "I count it but time lost to hear such a foolish song" (5.3.39–40), and was encouraged to see a connection between this scene and the time motif so prevalent in this script.

Another provocative moment was showcased by Matthew Warchus's *Volpone* (RNT 1995). In Act 4 of the script Lady Would-be accosts Peregrine whom she mistakenly believes is a cunning courtesan in disguise as a man, so that in the orginal production by Shakespeare's company a boy actor playing a woman was accusing a male actor playing a man of being a woman disguised as a man (as if in *Twelfth Night* Olivia had accused Sebastian of being a woman disguised as a man). However, in this production a woman (indeed, a well-known actress, Cheryl Campbell) was playing Lady Would-be and a tall male adult actor was playing Peregrine. Moreover, to generate a large comic effect the actress straddled Peregrine who was on the stage floor and felt for his/her breasts.

But what about the original Jacobean production? As I am suggesting, one key is: how old was the "man" playing Peregrine? Was he clearly an adult actor (one of the share-holders) so that Lady Would-be is badly mistaken as was true at the RNT? Or was he a youth, one who would clearly be able in other circumstances to play a female role or woman's part so that such a possibility would be part of the joke? Indeed, what would be the effect if the Peregrine actor at the original Globe production was one who had recently played a heroine or even a courtesan (e.g., Cressida or Mrs. Overdone)?[13] Such casting today, however, would be impractical, to say the least, and would lack the resonance that might have been conveyed in the 1600s.

WHO SPEAKS THE SPEECH?

A less visible form of streamlining, particularly in the history and Roman plays, is to reassign speeches to new speakers, whether to create some special effect, to enhance a role that is deemed underdone, or most often to economize on personnel. As already noted, the most efficient way to achieve the latter goal is to eliminate figures entirely, as when a production of *Richard III* omits Vaughan, Lovell, and the children of Clarence (2.2), or telescope them together, as when the scrivener's speech (3.6) is delivered by the Mayor (ESC 1988), Stanley (RSC TOP 1992), or Brackenbury talking to the keeper (OSF 1993). Indeed, I was told by the artistic director of a regional United States repertory company that saving one actor's salary by such a move (in this instance in a production of *The Tempest*) can pay for the set. Admittedly, in some situations economy is not a virtue – as in those amateur or school productions where the goal is to involve as many participants as possible (though casting calls at United States universities often produce a disproportionate number of women, with one result a production of *The Tempest* on my campus that featured Alonsa, Trincula, and Gonzala). Nonetheless, the reassignment of speeches is a standard practice that can produce some interesting effects, especially when a newly manufactured through-line or character emerges.

One technique not linked to economy is to turn a single speaker's lines into a group effort, usually to add clarity and theatrical punch to an expository passage. Typical are 1.1 of Bill Alexander's *Cymbeline* (RSC 1989) and the Rumor prologue to *2 Henry IV* (RSC 1982, OSF 1989, RSC Swan 2000) which were broken down for presentation by a larger group of actors or voices. In his *Henry V* (DC 1995) Michael Kahn did a great deal of rearranging for more voices, most notably in the choric passages which were presented by the entire cast along with pantomimed action. In Steven Pimlott's *Richard III* (RSC 1995–96) the three citizens' lines at the end of 2.3 were reallocated for choric presentation, and the scrivener's lines in 3.6 were orchestrated for three voices. In Tim Albery's *Macbeth* (RSC 1996) all three murderers rather than the scripted first murderer spoke with Macbeth at the outset of the banquet scene.

Far more common is a reassignment of speeches occasioned by theatrical exigency, most often limitations in the personnel available. If you
are a touring company presenting *The Tempest* and Edward Bond's *Bingo*,
you may find yourself short on actors if, as with David Thacker's production (RSC Swan 1995), you choose to have Ariel and three other
island spirits onstage for the entire show. In this version, the Adrian in
Alonso's retinue became Adriana and took over Francisco's speech in 2.1
(the latter disappeared); in 1.1 Ariel spoke the master's line and a spirit
played the boatswain; in 5.1 the appearance of master and boatswain
was gone. Such changes can be nearly invisible, as in Ian Judge's *Troilus
and Cressida* (RSC 1996) where Diomede's lines in 2.3 were distributed
among the other Greek generals so that he was gone from the scene. In
his *Volpone* (RNT 1995) Matthew Warchus trimmed Jonson's four avoca-
tori down to three with no significant loss, but Michael Kahn's rendition
(DC 1996) not only collapsed the four judges into two but also endowed
one of them with both the moral-authoritative lines of the first avocatore
and the venal lines of the fourth.

Such compressions are most likely to be found in the less familiar
scripts that also contain a large number of named figures. Typical are
two productions of parts of *Henry VI*. In his Part I (OSF 1975) Will
Huddleston had his actors do extensive doubling and tripling of smaller
roles, as would have been true in the 1590s, but he also eliminated
some figures and telescoped others together. Gone from this production were Alençon, whose lines were either omitted or divided among
Reignier and the Bastard of Orleans; Exeter, whose speeches were given
to Warwick (1.1), the Mayor of London (3.1), or Bedford; and Falstaff
whose two appearances (3.2, 4.1) disappeared along with the description
of his cowardice (1.1.130–34). The Governor of Paris was combined with
the spokesman for Bordeaux, so that the same figure who swore fealty to
Henry VI in 4.1 also lectured Talbot in 4.2. Bedford did not die in 3.2 but
lived on to serve as a choric figure (with Exeter's speeches) and replace
Sir William Lucy as the frustrated messenger to York and Somerset in
Act 4.

Clearly, something was lost with these changes. Without Falstaff the
audience misses a major example of the perversion of English chivalry,
a preparation for the attitudes that eventually destroy Talbot. Bedford's
death in a chair while watching the battle in 3.2 parallels Mortimer's
death in 2.5, while the demises in sequence of Salisbury, Bedford, and
Talbot demonstrate the withering of the heroic code after the initial
death of Henry V. However, given the complexity of the events onstage,

especially for a United States audience not versed in such history, even the dedicated purist can sympathize with the director's dilemma.

Such exigencies were also evident in Katie Mitchell's *3 Henry VI* (RSC TOP 1994). Since this production was designed to go on tour, what happens when you stage this complex script with a group of fifteen actors that includes only two women and no children? In this rendition, Lady Bona disappeared from 3.3; Rivers in 4.4 was played by the Queen Margaret actress; Richmond disappeared from 4.6; Rutland and Prince Edward were young men rather than boys; Northumberland and Exeter became through parts that absorbed other roles (e.g., Oxford, Somerset). Admittedly, Mitchell might have made some of the same choices had she had twenty-five actors, but the presence in this company of a talented twelve-year-old or a third actress would have opened up various options.

For example, to introduce a very young and vulnerable Rutland in 1.3 (to be brutalized by Clifford) can enhance the horrors perpetrated by the Lancastrians at the outset, just as a very young Richmond can make a strong statement in 4.6 – and the onstage age of Prince Edward can have a decided effect upon some key moments. In contrast, like most directors dealing with this script Mitchell included Clarence from the top even though the received text has him first appear in 2.2 (the role was probably designed to be played by the same actor who played his father, York). Mitchell's York actor reappeared as the French king and the Mayor of York rather than as his own son, so that a 1990s concern for a fuller through-line for Clarence overrode any possible signals in the early printed texts. Since there is no discernible reason why Edward and Richard but not Clarence should be present in 1.1, 1.2, and 2.1, here is a suggestive example of our logic or set of priorities being played off against Shakespeare's exigencies or strategy.

Another often modified history play is *2 Henry IV*. Granted, this script contains some famous moments (the dying Henry IV's final interview with his son, Henry V's rejection of Falstaff), but those moments come in the final third of the show by which point both Henry IV and Prince Hal have had little onstage time – as opposed to Falstaff, who is far less attractive than the figure with the same name in Part I, and the rebels, who lack a charismatic leader comparable to Hotspur. As a result, especially when dealing with United States audiences, directors often feel compelled to make various adjustments. A common choice is to pare down considerably the rebel scenes (1.1, 1.3, 2.3, 4.1/4.2) and focus instead upon Falstaff, the tavern world, Justice Shallow, and the recruits so as, if coherence is deemed out of reach, at least to offer entertainment.

Director Henry Woronicz (OSF 1989) felt that to shortchange the rebels, including the weighty speeches in 4.1/4.2, is to eviscerate the play and alter radically the experience of the playgoer. He did pare down a few speeches and, for practical reasons, omitted the toasts in 4.2, but these rebels kept most of their lines in what emerged as a lightly cut script. Rather, to gain added clarity he chose to telescope various lords together so as to reduce the number of actors needed and to avoid confusing his audience unfamiliar with the events and major players. Lord Bardolph disappeared from this show (so as to avoid being confused with Falstaff's Bardolph); Mowbray replaced Morton in 1.1 and therefore appeared in the whole sequence of key rebel scenes; Coleville also appeared earlier (in 1.3) as did "Russell," a figure invented for the purpose. Elsewhere, in a move I have come to expect when watching this play, the Lord Chief Justice, who in Shakespeare's script is offstage between 2.1 and 5.2 (possibly because the same actor was playing Henry IV), took over lines from Westmoreland and Warwick, including some meaty speeches in 3.1 and 4.4/4.5.

A shortage of personnel can affect the comedies as well. With a relatively small cast for his *Twelfth Night* (Young Vic 1998) Tim Supple had only one actor available to arrest Antonio in 3.4, so that officer had a gun rather than a sword to restrain his prisoner. Such a shortage of personnel was evident again in 5.1 when that same officer brought Antonio to Orsino and then had to exit (leaving his prisoner unguarded) in order to reappear as the priest. Supple's solution was elegant in its simplicity: the officer chained Antonio to an upstage post – no guard was needed. In Declan Donnelan's *Much Ado About Nothing* (Cheek by Jowl 1998) Antonio, Leonato's brother, disappeared with his lines taken over by Ursula who became Leonato's sister. A Cheek by Jowl signature device is to use the ensemble of actors (those not involved in a given scene) as an onstage chorus or entity. To open the show the entire cast presented a song and then reappeared just before the interval at Don John's "every man's Hero" (3.2.107) to cluster around the three men and sing "Men were deceivers ever." After the interval the group appeared briefly in response to Dogberry's "Are you good men and true?" (3.3.1), then re-entered at the end of 4.2 to remain onstage for the rest of the show (e.g., the whole group moved forward to look over Benedick's shoulder as he read aloud his sonnet in 5.2). By adroit use of this ensemble the director turned his relatively small cast into an observing public that paid close attention to the action and added theatrical life to the narrative.

Economies in casting can result from the number of actors available or a director's concept or some combination of the two. Jerry Turner and Dennis Bigelow's *Pericles* (OSF 1989) used only eleven actors (and one musician), with those actors costumed initially as sailors on a set that started and ended as a ship. As one of these sailors the Gower actor was not only the story-teller but also a participant who played Simonides and Lysimachus. In his South African *Titus Andronicus* (RNT Cottlesloe 1995) Gregory Doran made various script changes linked to economy and personnel. Gone from this production was Mutius (so that this Titus arrived in 1.1 with three sons, not four) and with him a large chunk of intra-family conflict at the outset. Also gone was young Lucius, Titus's grandson (who was replaced when necessary by a loosely defined black "boy"), so again a significant part of the family emphasis was pared back along with the boy's lines in 3.2, 4.1, 4.2, and 5.3. Sir Peter Hall's *King Lear* (Old Vic 1997) was based on the First Folio text "with a few verbal corrections" (according to the program) so that the second half, with the briefer versions of 3.6 and 4.2 and no 4.3, was streamlined. As part of a repertory season, the casting was linked to the actors available (e.g., three of the four actors from a very successful *Waiting for Godot* played Lear, Gloucester, and Edgar). The necessary economies led to choices that would have made sense to the King's Men: the quick reappearance of the France and Burgundy actors as knights in 1.4; the same actor as the servant killed in 3.7, the old man of 4.1, the doctor in 4.7, and various other gentleman or messenger roles in 1.4, 4.6, and 5.3.

Inevitably, some economies carry price tags. *Julius Caesar* poses major casting problems, for of the play's many speaking parts only five recur after the assassination (Brutus, Cassius, Antony, Lucius, and Caesar's ghost). The requisite doublings and triplings can therefore create anomalies. To cite one example, Mark Rylance's 1999 Globe production retained Cassius's warning to Publius that the latter should depart lest Caesar's supporters "do your age some mischief" (3.1.93) though Publius was being played by the youngish actor who also played Lucius. Edward Hall (RSC 2001) chose to replace Publius with Cicero who was played by the only older actor in the cast. Yet another choice was made by Terry Hands (RSC 1987) whose Publius actor doubled as Artemidorus (and later Lepidus). The reassurance given to this older establishment figure by both Brutus and Cassius was therefore given to the actor who moments earlier (2.3.1–16, 3.1.3–9) had been an outsider trying to warn Caesar about the conspiracy.

In two 1993 productions of *Antony and Cleopatra* (RSC 1992–93, OSF) the directors (John Caird, Charles Towers) made a host of adjustments to the smaller parts, especially the many followers of Antony and Caesar. Agrippa and Maecenas, figures prominent before Act 5, have no scripted lines in 5.2 (as opposed to Dolabella, Proculeius, Gallus, and one or more Roman guards), but few playgoers will fuss if in a quest for theatrical economy Agrippa is the one to capture Cleopatra. To use the same group of actors who attend Caesar in 5.1 to storm Cleopatra's monument in 5.2, however, is, as I discovered, to strip Caesar of his retinue at the end of 5.1 so as to have him justify his course of action towards Antony to the only figure still available, Decretas, the bringer of Antony's sword and news of his death. To have Caesar defend his policy to such a non-entity seemed to me totally illogical but apparently did not trouble either director.

This choice was especially weak for me, moreover, because of my memory of Sir Peter Hall's 1987 RNT production. Here, at the news of Antony's death in 5.1, Tim Piggott-Smith's Caesar was hit hard (and was not play-acting for public consumption). His subsequent exit was particularly telling (one of my favorite moments in this show), for in departing to offer justification for his war against Antony ("Go with me, and see / What I can show in this" – 5.1.76–77), he was directing his appeal for understanding and approval not at his retinue in general and certainly not at Decretas but at an older, statesman-like Agrippa (played with great force and intelligence by the late Basil Henson) who, as far back as 2.2, had been stressing duty to Rome over personal considerations. This same Agrippa had tried to soften Caesar's reaction to Octavia's plight in 3.6 but had been overruled by his master's anger at the slight and by the reported Roman reaction to Antony's behavior in Egypt. Now, at the end of 5.1, Caesar crossed the stage and exited with his train, but Agrippa responded with a nod of the head and headed off in another direction, distancing himself (as a Roman loyal to something larger than any one individual) from Octavius's vengeful choices that, as played by Piggott-Smith, had led to this ending. For the first time a production made clear to me why Dolabella, Proculeius, and others, but not Agrippa, are central to the final sequence with Cleopatra, for the director here set up a clear parting of the ways between a well-defined Agrippa and this Octavius.

Other adjustments by Towers and Caird are worth noting. Towers chose to replace the eunuch with an anonymous servant, so that various lines given to Mardian in the Folio were included but their point or impact was drastically changed. Having an impressive male figure deliver to Antony the news of Cleopatra's supposed death does not elicit the same response as when the words are delivered by a eunuch, especially when Antony responds "O, thy vild lady!/She has robb'd me of my sword" (4.14.22–23). Caird greatly enhanced the role of the soothsayer who became a prominent figure in this show, not only in his two scripted scenes (1.2 with Charmian and Iras, 2.3 with Antony) where he was an eerie presence, but also at various points thereafter (e.g., just before the interval) where apparently he was to suggest larger forces at work. This same distinctive figure then appeared as the fig-man who brought the asps to Cleopatra (though here the scripted lines jarred with the director's concept). Little was done, however, with the suggestive noise under the stage in 4.3 (less distinctive than other sound effects in the show) or the puzzling deaths of first Enobarbus, then Iras, so that a directorial image (an eerie, mysterious soothsayer) superseded the mysteries actually supported by the language or actions in the script.

ECONOMIES AND CONCEPTS

Of particular interest are those situations in which such reassignments or rearrangements are used not only to economize or to allow for the absence of child actors but also to enhance a through-line or further a particular interpretation. In his *Richard III* (RSC 1995–96) Steven Pimlott had a well-known actor (Victor Spinetti) playing a relatively minor role (the Bishop of Ely) so, regardless of any historical anomalies, the actor took on as well the Cardinal who violates sanctuary in 3.1 and the Archbishop in 2.4 (the program listed the "character" played by Spinetti as "Archbishop"). One result was that this pared-down production included a scene (2.4, the queen seeking sanctuary with her younger son) that is usually omitted by directors seeking to streamline this long script. In his *Coriolanus* (RSC Swan 1994) David Thacker made various adjustments but did include the often cut meeting between Adrian and Nicanor (4.3). These two figures then reappeared as Aufidius's aides in 4.7 and 5.3 and as the conspirators in 5.6 so as to emerge as figures of substance who corresponded to the two tribunes in Rome.

A good example is Jim Edmondson's *Henry VIII* (OSF 1984). On a practical level, to simplify or streamline Shakespeare's complex historical scene this director eliminated or telescoped together various lesser figures (e.g., Doctor Butts, Lord Abergavenny, the Lord Chancellor) and sought to establish more through-lines for his actors. For example, in the Folio Surrey does not appear until 3.2 where he functions as one of the lords who confront and bring down Wolsey (historically, Wolsey had arranged for Surrey to be in Ireland so as to be unavailable as a source of support for his father-in-law, Buckingham), but in this production Surrey appeared at Buckingham's side in the opening scene (taking on the role given Lord Abergavenny in the Folio) and was a continuing presence thereafter. In an even more striking adjustment, the key figure in the undoing of Buckingham in this rendition was not his "surveyor" but his "secretary," a figure then identified as Stephen Gardiner, who soon emerged (after being preferred to the king by Wolsey) as a major figure in his own right. The director not only gave this Gardiner some lines that the Folio assigns to other lords but also added stage business at several key points so that, both with Buckingham and Wolsey, his choice of self-interest over loyalty became highly visible and could be compared to the quite different choices made by Cromwell – a clear theatrical contrast that heightened a major motif developed elsewhere in the play. With this composite Gardiner figure, the director succeeded in developing a through-line that aided playgoers trying to find their way in what can seem a fragmented action.

A comparable but less successful adjustment was made in 5.5. The Folio stage direction that begins this final scene introduces a host of figures drawn from Holinshed but omits Cromwell and Gardiner. Most directors would wish to economize here so as not to introduce any new personages but still provide as resplendent a scene as possible. Edmondson therefore substituted Gardiner for the figure named "Garter" in the Folio who delivers the opening speech in praise of Elizabeth (the only speakers for the remainder of the scene are Cranmer and Henry). Like his other adjustments in the spirit of economy and through-lines, this telescoping made sense in practical terms and, in addition, brought onstage a second figure in an impressive bishop's costume to add to the visual display. But, unlike the other adjustments, this telescoping together of Gardiner and Garter had interpretative implications that I found troubling. Should a Gardiner who had just received his comeuppance from a newly enlightened Henry be rewarded by being given the opportunity to pronounce this benediction? Perhaps here the director was emphasizing forgiveness in the spirit of the romances, but this choice seemed strong on economy but weak on narrative logic.

A particularly provocative rescripting of a single figure was the enhancement of Seyton (pronounced *Satan* by Macbeth) in Jim Edmondson's *Macbeth* (OSF 1987). According to Edmondson, the genesis of the idea came from Macbeth's comment: "There's not a one of them but in his house / I keep a servant fee'd" (3.4.130–31) and the follow-up question: what if "a servant fee'd" (or perhaps "the perfect spy o' th' time" – 3.1.129) were in Macbeth's house too, though provided not by him but by someone or something above Macbeth (somehow to him as he is to the thanes)? This Seyton was therefore a mysterious, ominous presence lurking around the Macbeth's household. First, in 1.5 he started the message to Lady Macbeth about her husband's imminent arrival, then gave way to two exuberant youths; he was then seen above at the end of 1.6 after the arrival of Duncan, was waved off by Macbeth to begin 1.7, and was seen again in the doorway above (in the light) during the Macbeth–Banquo interchange in 2.1, at one point making eye contact with Fleance who was seated, below. After the departure of the two Macbeths with their bloody hands at the end of 2.2, Seyton came down the staircase with a lantern to do the porter's lines – played, for the most part, grimly, rather than for laughs, so that his "What are you?" (2.3.16) became a challenge to the playgoers. Seeing some drops of blood left behind by Macbeth, Seyton wiped them off with his glove, so clearly this figure was aware of what had just happened. Although he then played his lines to Macduff to get the usual laughs, the effect nonetheless was insidious, for we realized this banter was a smokescreen to "cover" for the Macbeths so that they will have time to change clothes and wash off the blood. In Act 3, this Seyton was increasingly surly and hence slow to react to orders from Macbeth. Although told to leave when Macbeth starts his interview with the two murderers, he went to the door, then sneaked back to the stage pillar to eavesdrop. In 3.3 as is often the case he appeared as the third murderer. During the banquet scene Seyton interestingly did *not* see the ghost (he was as puzzled by Macbeth's actions as were Lady Macbeth and the guests), so he stayed next to the stage pillar, watching, and then observed the last part of the scene from the shadows above.

Up through the intermission (as usual, after the banquet scene), the director had provided a suggestive presence in the background, with the added innovation of having his Seyton also play an insidious porter. Immediately after the intermission, however, came the radical innovation in this concept, for Edmondson chose to include much of the Hecate material of 3.5 *and* to give the lines to Seyton. So, in this rendition, "Hecat" of line 1 became "Seyton"; "mistress" of line 6 became "partner"; and lines 14–16 ("Get you gone" through "morning"), 20–27, and 34–36 were cut. After Seyton/Hecate appeared and exited above, the witches played the caldron scene (4.1), minus the appearance of Hecate and the other three witches, with 3.6 then following (an often used inversion). As a result, this Seyton emerged as someone or something not a "man" but, in various senses, "above" the witches (who soon after talked about their "masters" when setting up the apparitions). Seyton/Hecate, according to the dialogue that begins 3.5, is or looks "angerly"; the witches, moreover, during Edmondson's caldron scene, were fearful of the power they (or Macbeth) have invoked. These three figures then disappeared from the play, but Seyton remained very much in sight (and in this production had a stage life that extended beyond his last lines in the Folio). Including most of Hecate's speech, moreover, introduces at least one very suggestive passage otherwise lost ("And you all know, security / Is mortals' chiefest enemy" – 3.5.32–33) and gives us a third figure who "sees" the witches (even though he did not see Banquo's ghost).

In Act 5 the director then got a further pay-off from both the lines in the Folio and one significant addition. As in Acts 2 and 3, a lurking Seyton observed the sleep-walking from above; just as he hovered around the murder of Act 2, so now he was a witness to the consequences. Normally, Seyton (or the doctor) arms Macbeth in 5.3, but, in this production, despite Macbeth's repeated calls for the armor, Seyton resisted the request (" 'Tis not needed yet" – 33), so, although Macbeth does enter with the armor on in 5.5, he was left vulnerable for as long as possible, with the suggestion that this Seyton has become something no longer under his control. Although never a docile servant in this production, this climactic refusal to arm as requested made a strong statement to the audience. Then Seyton, standing in the same spot above from which he had witnessed Lady Macbeth's sleep-walking, observed Macbeth deliver the "tomorrow" speech.

At this point, Seyton drops out of the play as scripted in the Folio, but in this production he did appear again. At the end of 5.7 (just before the Macbeth–Macduff confrontation of 5.8), Malcolm and Siward appear briefly to note how "The tyrant's people on both sides do fight" and how their supposed foes "strike beside us"; they then ascended the stairs and entered the castle (5.7.24–29). But here the director gave Siward's first phrase ("This way, my lord") and his last ("Enter, sir, the castle") to Seyton who led the two victors up the stairs and into what was the domain of his former "master," Macbeth. Although not part of Edmondson's rationale, it should be noted that the Folio here prints the same speech prefix ("*Sey.*") for Siward or Seyward that had consistently been used for Seyton, though in the script clearly two not three figures are involved in the scene.

In making this change, the director has left us with a provocative final view of Seyton and his possible new relationship with Malcolm. Is the cycle to start all over again, as in the Roman Polanski film which ends with Donalbain seeking out the witches? The impression I received was rather that some forces are always there, waiting (just as the witches confronted both Macbeth *and* Banquo). Seyton was then visible, again above, at the final entrance of Macduff with Macbeth's head, but the ending, with no *exeunt*, just a fade-out of the lights, was diminuendo, with an overall sense of weariness rather than eeriness. The director placed no special emphasis upon Seyton above in the final moments, but he *was* there, so that some issues had not been resolved. Rather, a figure linked to the witches was still lurking, hovering (with *hover* an appropriate verb going back to "Fair is foul, and foul is fair, / Hover through the fog and filthy air" – 1.1.11–12), so that one figure linked to the moral–political pollution remained in sight. Giving two half-lines in 5.8 to Seyton does involve some rewrighting (even allowing for the ambiguous speech prefixes in the Folio), but that change was a small price to pay for a potent pay-off. What, after all, is (or should be) the role of the witches or the forces of darkness in this tragedy?

Edmondson's choices in his *Henry VIII* and *Macbeth* demonstrate how rescripting with economy in mind can readily turn into a reconception of key elements. The price tags and trade-offs linked to such reconceptions will be a major topic in the chapters that follow, but let me conclude this introduction with a telling example of rescripting in the service of a particular interpretation, David Thacker's 1993 RSC production of *The Merchant of Venice*. Lines perceived as obscure or superfluous were cut (e.g., some of Launcelot's part in 2.2, Portia on the Scottish lord in 1.2) as were references to "valor's excrement" (3.2.87), Scylla and Charybdis (3.5.16–17), *Alcides* (which was changed to *Hercules* at 2.1.35), and a pent-house not appropriate to this staging (2.6.1–2). Also omitted were passages deemed potentially offensive: Portia on Morocco's "complexion" (2.7.79); Lorenzo on Launcelot's getting the moor with child (3.5.37–42); and even Portia on Bassanio as her lord, governor, and king (3.2.165). Whether to save a set change or otherwise assist the flow of the action (so as to make 1.3 and 2.2 a continuous unit), the first Morocco scene (2.1) was streamlined and moved later so as to be joined with the second (2.7), a widely practiced rescripting that can significantly affect the rhythm and potential meanings of Act 2.

Also of interest were the various alterations occasioned by the shift of the play's setting from the 1590s to the 1990s. To bring the action

into a world of computers, cellular phones, and CDs Thacker made
a series of small changes that include the omission of references to
sixteenth-century coins and liveries (2.7.55–59; 2.2.109, 116) and the
adjustment of Morocco's *"this* scimitar" to *"the* scimitar" (2.1.24) so as to
eliminate the property entirely. Also gone were other items apparently
deemed anomalous in a 1990s setting, including Shylock's punning invocation of rats/pirates (1.3.23–24) and the jailer of 3.3 whose function was
taken over by Solanio (so that at 3.3.9 Shylock's "Thou naughty jailer" became "Signor Solanio"). Especially revealing was a tiny change in the trial
scene, the substitution twice of *man/men* for *slave/slaves*, so that Shylock
indicted the assembled Venetians by noting that "You have among you
many a purchas'd *man*" and later noted: "You will answer, / 'The *men*
are ours'" (4.1.90, 97–98). Presumably, slaves and slavery were deemed
anomalous in 1993 Venice, but here in particular the difference in weight,
resonance, and even mere sound struck me as significant with a decided
loss in the trade-off.

Most tellingly, Thacker made a series of related changes, especially in
3.1, to help create a more sympathetic Shylock. Playgoers familiar with
The Merchant of Venice on the stage are aware of various directorial moves
that can soften Shylock's image – most commonly cutting or adjusting his
"fawning publican" aside in 1.3 (often omitted is "If I can catch him once
upon the hip, / I will feed fat the ancient grudge I bear him" – 46–47)
and Jessica's speech on her father's hatred of Antonio (3.2.284–90). As
Ralph Berry notes, to pare down, alter, or eliminate such passages "is
to reduce sharply the element of predetermined hatred in Shylock's
attitudes and throw the weight of his later conduct on to the disaster of
his daughter's flight with a Christian," so that such cuts can "prepare the
way for a more sympathetic treatment of Shylock allied to an ironic and
sceptical view of the Venetians."[14] To include these two passages does not
ensure a sense of Shylock's premeditation, but omitting them makes the
sequence (merry bond, elopement, then revenge on Christians through
Antonio) more readily accessible.

Thacker not only cut these two passages but also took the refashioning
of Shylock farther than any other production I have seen. For example, this Shylock (David Calder) started 2.5 in an elegant room (with a
prominent photo of either Jessica or Leah) wearing a smoking jacket and
putting classical music on his CD player (as opposed to Launcelot with his
walkman), a cultivated, mellow image further enhanced by many pauses.
Similarly, 3.3 was played not in the street but around a desk, with Antonio
not under arrest. The major rescripting took place in 3.1. Most obviously,

the two halves of the scene were reversed, with the Shylock–Tubal section coming first (although without the "fee me an officer" punch line – 3.1.126) to be followed (rather than preceded as in the received text) by the taunts from Salerio and Solanio. The famous "Hath not a Jew eyes?" speech (53–73) was therefore generated or "motivated" not only by the venom of the Venetian Christians (as scripted by Shakespeare) but also by the news of Jessica's escapades (news which in the Quarto follows the speech). In the first beat as rescripted by Thacker, moreover, most of the lines dealing with Jessica's spending spree in Genoa were gone as was the relevant part of Shylock's reaction (e.g., "Fourscore ducats at a sitting, fourscore ducats!" – 3.1.111–12). As a result of such cuts, Shylock's reaction to the loss of his money (as opposed to his reaction to Jessica's elopement) was significantly muted, indeed just about gone, to the extent that Salerio and Solanio's mocking account of ducats and daughter in 2.8 (presented as yuppy gossip in a wine-bar) now seemed extreme, unfair. Rather, this version of 3.1 not only did not reinforce the account of Shylock's reaction presented in 2.8 but contradicted it.

In sifting through hundreds of possible examples accumulated from my playgoing (and, with very few exceptions, I will be drawing only upon productions I have actually seen) I will pursue in the chapters that follow various issues raised in this chapter and set up appropriate categories and sub-divisions so as to pose a series of questions. What is the effect upon a playgoer when a play designed for uninterrupted performance is broken by an interval/intermission? What happens when a director omits or severely pares back a long or seemingly redundant speech (e.g., Friar Lawrence's summary at the end of *Romeo and Juliet* of what the playgoer already knows)? What is blurred or lost when the three parts of *Henry VI* are presented today as two plays (or, more radically, one) – as is the usual practice? What are the results when the Christopher Sly material found in the First Folio version of *The Taming of the Shrew* is either omitted from a production or augmented by material from the 1594 *The Taming of a Shrew*? Chapter 2 will be devoted to comparable script choices in recent productions of plays by Shakespeare's contemporaries (Kyd, Marlowe, Jonson, Webster, Ford – directors feel less compunction about rescripting this material), but overall the emphasis will be upon choices linked to the Shakespeare canon where a wealth of interesting and potentially revealing examples is available. Also to be factored in are a variety of vexed editorial–bibliographical questions about how to interpret or improve the early printed texts (various Quarto editions, the 1623 First Folio) that provide our only evidence about the original playscripts, so that my final chapter will be devoted to the editor as rescripter.

Given limitations in budget, personnel, rehearsal time, and audience attention spans, directors will continue to rescript Shakespeare's plays. To return to my first example, Bedford and Attenborough's choice to cut "Let it be hid" epitomizes a decisive Alexander-like approach to a Gordian knot problem (with few playgoers choosing to complain). Nonetheless, I confess a preference for the alternative approach detailed by the Archbishop of Canterbury who, after praising Henry V's expertise in divinity, commonwealth affairs, and discourse of war, continues: "Turn him to any cause of policy, / The Gordian knot of it he will unloose, / Familiar as his garter" (*Henry V*, 1.1.45–47). According to Canterbury, the hero–king is to be singled out because he can "unloose" the intricate knot rather than cut it. For me, the richest images and effects continue to be linked closely to the original signals and strategies. In this formulation, moreover, Lodovico's "Let it be hid" is designed to set up an indictment of just that mentality that would sidestep the unpleasant, the difficult, or the challenging in favor of easier, more palatable solutions. In our age or in any other age, rescripting of what survives in Shakespeare's quartos and First Folio is a fact of theatrical life, but my question remains: at what price?

2

Rescripting Shakespeare's contemporaries

"Comparisons are odorous"
Dogberry, 3.5.16

Given the lip service (Macbeth terms it "mouth honor") paid to Shakespeare's artistry, some theatrical professionals are hesitant about rescripting, at least in its most visible forms. Such restraints can disappear, however, when the script in question is linked to Kyd, Marlowe, Jonson, Dekker, Marston, Webster, Middleton, Ford, or Beaumont and Fletcher. When confronting such less prestigious playwrights, directors can more readily imagine themselves as an Elia Kazan reshaping and giving fuller meaning to raw material provided by a Tennessee Williams. To investigate the rescripting process in this group of plays (labeled "primitive" by one director I talked with) is then to see the same kinds of omissions and alterations found in productions of Shakespeare but on less contested ground.

To deal with such material is to run various risks. First, readers in tune with the major plays of Shakespeare are less likely to be familiar with *Every Man In His Humour*, *The Fawn*, *The Maid's Tragedy*, or *The Broken Heart* so may find some of the accounts that follow mystifying. Moreover, the rationale behind the adjustments to these non-Shakespeare plays is often comparable to that outlined in chapters 1 and 3, so that there is a danger of redundancy. Nonetheless, to focus on the rescripting of such plays is to see with added clarity issues and problems basic to this study, a consummation devoutly to be wished.

STREAMLINING THE SCRIPT

As might be expected, productions of Elizabethan and Jacobean plays, particularly those with significant amounts of topical material, are routinely streamlined or otherwise adjusted. In his production of Jonson's *The Alchemist* (RSC 1991–92) Sam Mendes cut or changed words and lines to eliminate obscurity and add to his maniacal pace; gone, for example, was Lovewit's dismissal of Surly as a "an old *harquebuzier*" (*musketeer*) who was unable to "prime his powder, and give fire, and hit, /All in a twinkling" (5.5.56–58), while in the play's final speech Face's invocation of his *country* ("yet I put myself /On you, that are my country" – 5.5.162–63) was changed to *jury*.[1] Just as different Shakespeare directors often make the same cuts in a given script, directors of Jonson's *Volpone* (e.g., Matthew Warchus RNT 1995; Lindsay Posner RSC Swan 1999) also regularly pare back or eliminate certain elements, such as the Act 1 entertainment put on for Volpone by his dwarf, eunuch, and hermaphrodite; the Scoto of Mantua speeches of Act 2; and material from Sir Pol, Peregrine, and Lady Would-be scenes, especially the latter's speech on obsession (3.4.101–12). In his RSC *Volpone* (TOP 1983) Bill Alexander used a very full script, but when moving to the Pit in 1984 he shortened the playing time by over thirty minutes, so that gone or reduced in London were some of these items as well as all of Volpone's Act 5 taunting of the legacy hunters in the street.

More extensive cuts or changes are not unusual. In his production of Jonson's *The Devil is an Ass* (RSC Swan 1995) Matthew Warchus surprised no one by omitting passages of topical satire highly relevant to 1616 but murky today. Indeed, one actor complained to me about the difficulty of playing key scenes in a show where the central joke about the English legal system was almost impossible to get across to today's playgoer. Gone therefore were large chunks of inaccessible material linked to Jacobean projects and monopolies and gone too was Jonson's underdeveloped Manly–Everill link. This trimming back seemed justified by the results (e.g., a maniacally intense Fitzdottrel, a comically hapless Pug, and an energetic, highly inventive Merecraft), so that another unwieldy (and, to our ears, mystifying) play was made not only accessible but both funny and meaningful. More extreme was the DC 1996 *Volpone* in which Michael Kahn cut most of Sir Pol's material, including all of his Act 5 tortoise shell scene, inserted a TV-style commercial in place of Scoto's rhetoric, and provided song-and-dance numbers by dwarf, eunuch, and hermaphrodite as the Act 1 entertainment, as Volpone's song to Celia, and as a feel-good curtain call. Much streamlining was also visible in Dekker's *The Shoemakers' Holiday* (OSF 1987) where Jerry Turner pared down Hammon's part, gave the "inner linings" speech often cited by critics (11.40–51) to Margery rather than Simon Eyre, and made many adjustments to the final scene (e.g., gone were references to London features such as Leadenhall as too obscure for a west coast

United States audience). Also heavily cut was Jonson's *Bartholomew Fair* (Regents Park 1987) as directed and adapted by Peter Barnes.

A small but suggestive omission was made by director Laurence Boswell in his 1998 RSC production of *Bartholomew Fair* at the Swan. Here the acting script was surprisingly full so that the show including the interval lasted three and a half hours. A few segments were gone (e.g., all of 3.1) as were some Latin quotations; the vapors scene (4.4) was pared back and simplified (Val Cutting was omitted), as were the puppet play and Adam Overdo's "overdone" speeches. What struck me as especially interesting, however, was the omission of a chunk of a long speech from the the the opportunistic Quarlous.

In Jonson's formulation Winwife, Quarlous, and Grace are smarter and more observant than the various fools, so that it is Winwife who spots the Edgworth–Nightingale activity during the theft of Cokes's second purse and Quarlous who uses that knowledge to his advantage, just as he uses Dame Purecraft's offer of marriage, Trouble-All's identity, and Overdo's warrant. Actor Rob Edwards did a fine job with Quarlous's key speeches and moments in the final movement of the play, particularly his climactic speeches to Overdo with the often-cited line ("remember you are but Adam, flesh and blood" – 5.6.99–100) and his reaction to Dame Purecraft's offer ("It is money that I want; why should I not marry the money, when 'tis offer'd me? . . . I were truly mad, an' I would not!" – 5.2.80–85). But one potentially revealing passage was missing. When, after the successful theft of the license, Edgworth offers access to a whore, Quarlous reacts with indignation ("If I had not already forgiven you a greater trespass, or thought you yet worth my beating, I would instruct your manners, to whom you made your offers"), and, after the cutpurse's exit, he adds: "I am sorry I employ'd this fellow; for he thinks me such: *Facinus quos inquinat, aequat* ["Crime makes equal those whom it stains"]. But, it was for sport" (4.6.22–24, 27–29). Whether because of the Latin phrase or for reasons of economy, these lines were cut.

With so much of this long and complex script included, to fuss over the absence of this passage may seem churlish. Although insulted by the cutpurse's violation of social distance or decorum, Quarlous nonetheless admits to having been brought down to Edgworth's level and made his equal, but he then dismisses his own complicity by labeling it *sport* – a provocative term as used here and elsewhere by Jonson. For example, in their seduction of Win Littlewit, Whit and Knockem tell her that she may lie with as many men as she pleases, and she responds: "What, and be honest still? That were fine sport" (4.5.43). The omitted passage therefore provokes some shrewd questions. Are the various actions carried out in the Fair such as prostitution and theft merely *sport*? Or are we to see not *sport* but *crime* that is either unrecognized or, when recognized, unpunished or uncontrolled because those smart enough to realize what is going on decide to employ the criminals rather than stop them? To omit these lines is to save running time and eliminate a possible source of confusion in a Latin quote but also to diminish Jonson's treatment of crime and complicity.

Running time rather than obscurity was the issue underlying the heavy cutting in the 1998 Globe production of *The Honest Whore*, for director Jack Shepherd and adapter Mark Rylance chose to compress this two part play into one unit. Inevitably, some losses or diminutions resulted from this streamlining. For example, Candido's speech on patience that climaxes Part I was included in this production, but I found its positioning just before the interval at the end of an abbreviated version of Part I to be less telling than if it had served its original function as the climax of the show. Rather, I was given less encouragement at this moment to think in retrospect about all that had preceded this summary speech, for in a variety of ways preparatory material or "build" was omitted that would have enhanced various effects.

One cut struck me as particularly significant. In the production as in the script the duke (Infelice's father) gets a doctor to give Infelice a potion ("a sleepy charm" – 1.3.13) so that, like Juliet, she is presumed to be dead (the opening scene is her supposed funeral interrupted by a distraught Hippolito), and the duke then banishes the doctor. Omitted from the production, however, was the duke's subsequent attempt to get the doctor to poison Hippolito and the complications that ensue. This omission streamlined the story at the cost of decidedly changing our evaluation of the duke.

Streamlining, of course, need not be limited to comedy, as was evident in Philip Franks's 1995 Greenwich Theatre production of *The Duchess of Malfi* which was crafted to tour with eight men, four women, and one boy. The relatively small number of actors available combined with the difficulties posed by Webster's script yielded a series of choices that generated significant problems, so that the director's adjustments added up to more than a simple recycling of personnel as courtiers, armed men, executioners, and madmen.

A major hurdle in staging Webster's tragedy today is what to do with Act 5. Given the intensity of 4.1 and 4.2, especially evident in this production thanks to the stature achieved by Juliet Stevenson's Duchess when facing death, an inevitable letdown follows, a letdown that directors seek to remedy by liberal cutting. I am not one to defend every iamb in

Webster, who can be both sloppy and prolix (though once in my playgoing life I hope to see Pescara in 5.1), but this director went much further than usual in his cuts and adjustments so as to elicit audience laughter at several points. Although the echo scene worked well, little else made full sense. With a shortage of personnel, Ferdinand had no doctor, so that he struck out at Delio who, along with Castruchio, served as "the Court"; similarly, no servant was available to carry off Antonio's body (which therefore stayed onstage) and then be killed by Bosola, a casual act of violence that can affect a playgoer's evaluation of his supposed repentance. Losing Pescara not merely from 5.1 but from the play as a whole meant the loss of a distinctive voice; similarly, the absence of Antonio's son onstage as a final image significantly changed the larger equation, with only Castruchio (as usual, played as a fool) and Delio (here usually portrayed as a klutz) alive at the end (with a new line manufactured for the former). The Cardinal's poisoning of Julia was included but not her preceding meeting with Bosola, so that the logic behind the behavior that leads to her death was radically altered, with no possible link to the Duchess's wooing of Antonio in Act 1 (here in particular knowing Webster's script turned out to be a huge disadvantage). Whatever the intent behind such changes, the result was a major falling off from the heights of Act 4, so that the playgoer was left with a series of staccato murders, a piling up of bodies, and a Bosola who would not die but kept popping up and nattering on.

Such an extreme form of streamlining that verges on rewrighting can be instructive. As noted earlier, a director will not stay a director very long if he or she does not find and sustain a shared vocabulary with the nonspecialist playgoer unfamiliar with the script in question. But a large gap exists between cutting topical references in a satiric comedy that would mystify such a playgoer (as in *The Devil is an Ass*) and omitting figures and speeches many would deem necessary to an understanding of key moments or relationships. Such large-scale changes are less common in Shakespeare scripts (at least in English language stage productions, as opposed to movies or productions in translation), but the same problems persist.

IMPROVEMENTS

As with streamlining, directors dealing with non-Shakespeare Elizabethan, Jacobean, and Caroline scripts feel less compunction about "improving" the efforts of the original playwright. One device is the transposition of elements, often to enhance the telling of the story. The one significant change in Gayle Edwards' production of *The White Devil* (RSC Swan 1996) came when one of the two dumb shows in 2.2 (the murder of Isabella) was repositioned after the trial of Vittoria (3.1). This transposition did set up an intelligible narrative (the trial is linked to the murder of Camillo, not Isabella, whose death is made known to Francesco and others afterwards) but nonetheless does have implications for a playgoer. The story told in the rescripted version may be the same, but, given Vittoria's suggestive yew tree speech to Bracciano in 1.2 (Flamineo notes: "She hath taught him in a dream / To make away his duchess and her husband" – 257–58), a spectator's awareness of Isabella's murder before rather than after the trial can make a significant difference to his or her evaluation of Vittoria's spirited defense of herself at her arraignment. Moving the dumb show of Isabella's murder later makes Vittoria's response to the Cardinal less problematic and changes the situation set up by Webster.

Another source of such transpositions is a director's decision where to place an interval (UK) or intermission (US) in plays not designed for such a fifteen to twenty-minute break in the flow of action. In his production of Ford's *'Tis Pity She's a Whore* (OSF 1981) Jerry Turner opted to climax his first act with the death of Hippolyta (4.1), a big scene with a full stage that then could be cleared of properties during the intermission (a choice familiar to playgoers from productions of *Macbeth* which often are broken after the banquet scene). But such a decision must take into account not only where to stop (some kind of climactic moment) but also where to start up again. In this instance, the interchange between Richardetto and Philotis (4.2) that follows in Ford's sequence provides a flat and most unpromising beginning for a final movement.

So, having made the decision to end his first act with 4.1, Turner transposed the next two scenes and started his second act with Soranzo's jealous tirade against the pregnant Annabella (the beginning of 4.3), a moment that *does* pull an audience back into the world of the play. Such a transposition (not uncommon in Shakespeare productions – see chapter 4) does solve the problem – but at a price. For a playgoer, the choices acted out by Richardetto and Philotis in 4.2 mean something very different if, as in Ford's script, they closely follow Hippolyta's death and immediately precede Annabella's exposure rather than if they follow 4.3. Richardetto sends Philotis to a nunnery not because of Annabella's disgrace in 4.3 (a chain of thought implied by Turner's transposition) but because of what he has glimpsed of the power of that "One above" who "begins to work" (4.2.8–9) and what he has learned from Hippolyta's fate wherein the revenger seeking to poison an enemy only succeeds in poisoning herself. To the reader or playgoer solely interested in the incestuous love of Giovanni and Annabella, 4.2 may seem only a final dose of subplot to be endured before the main event, but the scene does orchestrate a set of attitudes towards human actions in the context of a larger framework of importance to the dramatist. To change the placement of this scene is then to change that context, and, in effect, to change radically the meaning and function of the sequence as a whole.

These two directorial transpositions of sequences set up by Webster and Ford certainly are not of the earth-shaking variety and would likely go unnoticed, especially in a successful production (as was the case in both of these shows). Nonetheless, the sequence of elements can be an integral part of theatrical effect and meanings, often in unanticipated ways.

Some in-the-theatre improvements are a response to on-the-page problems noted by editors and scholars. In his OSF 1979 *Doctor Faustus* Jerry Turner created his own blend of the two early printed versions of this script, so that gone were the horse-courser, the Vanholts (the sequence devoted to getting out-of-season grapes was added to the Emperor scene), the throne and hellmouth, and the final scene with the scholars. He and his actors were still confronted with the absence of a transition between scenes 5 and 6 (2.1 and 2.2 in modern editions), a gap that has puzzled many readers and has led to the postulation of a lost scene. How are we to imagine Faustus moving from his delight in the books presented to him by Mephistophiles after the signing of the pact (the end of scene 5) to his repentance (the beginning of scene 6)? The problem was solved adroitly with no break in the action by rearranging the series of books in the 1604 A-text (only one book is presented in B) so that the third book became not the one devoted to herbs and trees but the one devoted to the characters and planets of the heavens. Faustus's reading of this last book caused him to look up and, as a result, be reminded suddenly of what he had just signed away, a recognition that in turn generated the lines that begin the next scene in both A and B: "When I behold the heavens, then I repent" (A 628, B 570).

Often a director's improvements are linked to imagery, particularly when the scripted effect is deemed obscure or out of phase with the period in which the production is set. In his RSC 1998 *Bartholomew Fair* Laurence Boswell made a host of such changes to update a 1614 script to the 1990s. For example, in the script to get access to Cokes's purse Edgworth the cutpurse "*tickles him in the ear with a straw twice to draw his hand out of his pocket*" (3.5.150), but this Edgworth handed Cokes a beer and a joint so as to occupy both his hands. Similarly, in the final sequence of Jonson's text both Mrs. Overdo and Win Littlewit are transformed into "green women" or whores; Jonson's language was retained, but the two figures appeared not in green but in sexy low-cut gowns wearing platinum blonde wigs. Other directors insert distinctive images of their own in lieu of those suggested in the script. In Marlowe's *Edward II* a figure designated only as a "Mower" (presumably someone carrying a scythe) points out the king to his pursuers who then arrest him; the Mower's only lines are "Upon my life, those be the men ye seek" and "Your worship, I trust, will remember me?" (4.7.46, 117–18). In his RSC 1990 production at the Swan, Gerard Murphy presented not a mower but a bloodied Gaveston who stayed high above for this segment of the scene pointing at the king. In his 1996 Cheek by Jowl *Duchess of Malfi* Declan Donnelan included the madmen who are brought in to torment the Duchess in 4.2 but without Webster's dialogue. Instead, the mad figures presented a dumb show in which one of them was crowned and then was transformed into a pregnant woman who gave birth to a baby doll, an obvious indictment of the Duchess.

Two productions of *The Revenger's Tragedy* show a director making improvements. Di Travis (RSC Swan/Pit 1987–88) made few cuts in Stratford but, as with Bill Alexander's *Volpone* cited earlier, streamlined her script for the move to London where she omitted all of 1.4, the beginning of 2.1 with Dondolo, and several other passages. Trevis also provided several insertions. First, she invented a new character, described in the program as a "Scavenger," who starting in 1.1 was present in various scenes and, in the final image of the show, confronted Antonio, the only other figure left on stage, as the latter wandered around (and tripped over) the many onstage bodies. In addition, she expanded the role of the Duchess, a figure who has few lines in the second half of the script. Trevis fashioned roughly twenty-five new lines for the brief exchange between the Duchess and Spurio that begins 4.3 to heighten both their adultery and their ambition and then inserted another twenty-five lines of her making into 5.1 to set up an onstage confrontation between the Duchess and the new duke, Lussurioso, that resulted in her banishment as well as her sons' denial of her. A story line left underdeveloped in the script was thereby extended so that the ranking female figure of the play was given a much bigger rejection or send-off.

Jerry Turner (OSF 1984) made more extensive changes, small and large, in the original script. Presumably for added clarity, Act 1 was reshuffled, so that this production started with an abbreviated 1.4 (with Antonio mourning over the coffin of his wife), then moved to the trial of 1.2, then 1.1, then 1.3. Gone therefore was the keynote position granted Vindice and the skull in the script's first scene; gained, at least for spectators unfamiliar with the play (presumably most of the audience), was an increased emphasis upon the fate of Antonio's wife (acted out in a dumb show) as a pivotal event. Also to aid the playgoer, in a move common in Shakespeare productions, Turner introduced Vindice's name (not cited in the dialogue until 3.5) earlier (e.g., Castiza apostrophized him in 2.1). To reinforce one strand of the story line he inserted a scene at the end of Act 3 in which Antonio, who had been observing events from above, told a lord that justice now had been done after the deaths of the old duke and his youngest son.

Turner then made a series of changes in Act 5. The two sets of masquers in 5.3 did not appear in identical costumes; Vindice shared his last speech with Hippolito; the fourth lord in 5.3 was not sent off for execution but was killed on the spot by Vindice (so an eighth body accumulated onstage) – a choice that gave additional support to Antonio's verdict on Vindice moments later. After all, would you want a figure with such a quick trigger finger lurking around *your* dukedom? A final macabre effect was provided by the curtain call in which the women on stage were shocked as various fallen figures, one by one, rose like zombies from the dead. In neither of the two productions did the audience see a blazing star as a supernatural manifestation in the final scene (Trevis had her actors look out over the heads of the audience). In Turner's show, moreover, the first audible thunder (keyed to Vindice's "There it goes!" – 4.2.199) was preceded by a flickering of lights in the theatre so as to suggest a "real" storm (my first reaction, shared by others, was that the theatre was undergoing a "real" power failure).

A highly visible creator of distinctive onstage images is director and designer Philip Prowse, as witnessed by his two RNT productions of Webster's tragedies: *The Duchess of Malfi* (1985–86) and *The White Devil* (1991). Both shows included substantial cuts, striking design choices, and a variety of innovations. In *The White Devil* two dumb shows displayed the murders of Camillo and Isabella but without Webster's scripted effect (no vaulting horse for the former, a mirror rather than a poisoned portrait of her husband for the latter); the lawyer and the ambassadors were gone from the trial of Vittoria; Isabella's ghost made an extra appearance to her husband. In the script Zanche in Act 5 tells Francesco the truth about the earlier deaths of Camillo and Isabella ironically *after* the successful revenge has been completed against Bracciano, the causer of those deaths; with this interchange cut, a major irony was eliminated – and Francesco's "Tush for justice" (5.3.267) lost most of its punch. In *The Duchess* the director made many of the standard cuts in this long script (e.g., Antonio's description at the outset of the French court, large chunks of Act 5 including Pescara–Julia-Delio in 5.1) but factored in a monkish Death who remained onstage throughout and at key points was a visible part of the action (e.g., at the Duchess's wooing of Antonio in Act 1, at Antonio's dropping of the horoscope in Act 2, at Ferdinand's appearance in 3.2 to menace his sister and her subsequent telling Bosola the truth about her marriage to Antonio). In Act 5 the Duchess entered with Death, walked around the stage, did her echo speeches from up-stage, then stayed in view (as did several other figures including the mad Ferdinand), eventually being paired with Death. The goal was to counter the usual Act 5 letdown by having the Duchess be a significant presence throughout the final sequence (as opposed to her role in the script only as an echo), but at times the accumulation of the onstage figures inserted by the director overwhelmed the action.

As with the transposition of scenes, such improvements can have un-foreseen results. Of particular interest is one seemingly small change that turned out to have larger implications. Readers of *The Duchess of Malfi* have long been troubled by an apparent anomaly at the beginning of Act 3. The key sequence in Act 2 combines the birth of the Duchess's first child, Bosola's finding out of this secret, and the reactions of the two brothers to this news in 2.5, where the cool but deadly Cardinal restrains a frantic Ferdinand who vows horrible revenge upon the child and the unknown father. But moments later in dramatic time at the beginning of the next scene (3.1) we discover that not only has Ferdinand's rage not been translated into immediate action (as strongly suggested in 2.5), but, even more surprising, that the Duchess and Antonio have had time to produce two more children.

Clearly, the illogic of this time sequence and the begetting of more children troubled Prowse and his cast, so Antonio's lines to Delio about the additional children (3.1.5–7) were cut, and the remainder of the action (streamlined in many other ways as well) proceeded with only one child for the Duchess (as is usually the case, the reference to a son by the original Duke of Malfi [3.3.69–71] was cut). This production there-fore accomplished what many readers and teachers have wished for: it "improved" Webster by eliminating some of the clumsiness occasionally found in his plays – here his casual approach to time or narrative.

Like all such choices, however, this improvement carried with it a price tag, one I would not have recognized without having seen this show. In particular, if the play provides only one (rather than three) offspring from the Duchess and Antonio, that child (in this production, an infant rather than a boy) must accompany Antonio when he flees at the end of Act 3 and then be presented as dead (along with his father) to deceive the Duchess in 4.1. That disposition, in turn, means that no children are left behind with the Duchess during her ordeal in Act 4. For example, her final words to Cariola before the latter is forced offstage are: "I pray thee, look thou giv'st my little boy / Some syrup for his cold, and let the girl / Say her prayers, ere she sleep" (4.2.203–5). These lines reveal another dimension of the woman about to be destroyed by the Arragonian brethren (e.g., the nurturing mother), but, with no such children available, they were omitted from this production. Also gone for the same reason were Bosola's order that "some other strangle the children" (239), his display of the bodies to Ferdinand, his anguished question ("Alas, how have these offended?"), and Ferdinand's response ("The death / Of young wolves is never to be pitied" – 257–59) with its preview of his forthcoming lycanthropy.

After assessing both the initial cut and the chain reaction that followed, I am left with a series of questions. Do the gains in credibility or narrative economy that result from this intended improvement outweigh the loss in pathos and imagery? What effect can or should the presence of these two children have upon our reaction in Act 4 to three major figures (the Duchess, Bosola, and Ferdinand)? How can we best describe the rationale or strategy that underlies Webster's making such a choice that initially strains our sense of time and continuity but, in the long run, yields as pay-off some rich meanings and effects? This production, moreover, placed great emphasis upon sickness, madness, and violence in Act 4 (e.g., by keeping the mad folk onstage throughout the Duchess's ordeal), but the absence of the reference to her children and to medicine in her final moments subtly changed the alternatives Webster provides to such widespread disease. Admittedly, this tragedy does have its anomalies (Webster, like Homer, may nod), but does such an improvement undermine a logic or rationale behind Webster's choices? What price consistency?

I had the same reaction to several choices in Michael Boyd's production of Ford's *The Broken Heart* (RSC Swan 1994). Overall the director provided a powerful and often moving in-the-theatre experience wherein various effects, including the fully realized use of dance, controlled movement, and music, conveyed successfully the disciplined, even repressed emotions that underlie the action. Moreover, several of the difficult moments were handled very well (e.g., Orgilus bleeding to death onstage). Nonetheless, two distinctive directorial choices warrant scrutiny.

First, Orgilus's murder of Ithocles by means of a trick chair is a note-worthy bit of stage business that calls attention to itself, however staged, but Boyd's streamlining of the script gave a very different spin to this highly distinctive moment. The previous scene (4.3) starts with King Amyclas in his chair of state and builds to a duologue between Orgilus and Ithocles. In Ford's script these two figures then *exeunt*, so that 4.4 begins with their re-entry to join the women lamenting Penthea's death along with one line from a servant who, pointing to the death-trap chair, says to Orgilus: " 'Tis done; that on her right hand" (4.4.1). The director, however, omitted the first fifteen lines of 4.4, including the servant's line, so that no women appeared and Orgilus and Ithocles did not leave the stage. Rather, the playgoer saw Orgilus make an adjustment to what had previously been the king's throne, a property which then became the chair that trapped Ithocles.

This change struck me as highly significant. What in Ford's script is a potential *analogy* (the throne of a dying king may be somehow linked to a chair that traps a murder victim) has in this production become an *equation* wherein the identical chair serves both king and murderer. One taunt that Orgilus directs at Ithocles supports such a link ("Caught, you are caught, / Young master. 'Tis thy throne of coronation, / Thou fool of greatness" – 4.4.21–23), but for me this rescripting raised a series of intrusive and potentially counterproductive questions. Was this device always there on the throne? If so, how did Orgilus (not a part of any inner circle) know about it? How am I to understand a Sparta where such a device is readily available to be used on the ruler, whether father or daughter? Indeed, why should I be thinking about such questions?

Equally distinctive was Boyd's reshaping of the play's most famous moment, Calantha's death from a broken heart after she had earlier con-tinued her dance outwardly unaffected by the news in rapid succession of the deaths of her father, her lover, and Penthea. To enhance this climactic sequence, the director made a series of cuts in Act 5, the most signifi-cant being to have Calantha, after delivering her explanatory speech that refers to "the silent griefs which cut the heart-strings" (5.3.75), move downstage away from the coffin of Ithocles to deliver very powerfully her "Crack, crack" (77) and at that point die of her broken heart. In contrast,

Ford's Calantha not only has several more lines after the "Crack, crack" but also attends to "the song /I fitted for my end" (79–80), so that only at the end of that song ("Love only reigns in death; though art /Can find no comfort for a broken heart") does she die or allow herself to die.

Today's actress or playgoer may find good reasons to omit the song and instead have Calantha die on a highly theatrical "Crack, crack," but that choice changes significantly her degree of control over her "heart" so as to transform the central image of the play. I recognize the potential difficulties of staging this sequence as scripted by Ford, but I also wonder about the wisdom of tinkering with such an important moment which might have proved to be powerful in its own distinctive terms, especially in a production which elsewhere made such telling use of music and song. As with the rescripting of the trick chair, the adjustments here did yield a potent theatrical effect but an effect somewhat removed from Ford's own strategy. Should we be seeing a parallel to Penthea who, in starving herself, also fashions her own death according to a self-devised script? Should Calantha's death be juxtaposed with her verbalized "Crack, crack" or with the final insight in the song she has arranged for the purpose – that "no comfort for a broken heart" can be found in "art"?

THE DIRECTOR AS EDITOR

Streamlining a Shakespeare or other script from this period is usually linked to economy, obscurity, or some exigency (e.g., limitations in personnel, budget, or resources). To "improve" Webster or Ford is rather to react to a perceived problem in the narrative or staging so that the director, in effect, moves into the realm of the editor. In recent years the presence of more than one early printed text for several Shakespeare plays (for example, *Hamlet, King Lear, Othello*) has attracted considerable attention from scholars and critics not part of the editorial community with the subsequent controversies generating problems that in turn affect what happens in a production. How directors deal with various non-Shakespeare plays that also exist in multiple versions can therefore be instructive.

Jonson's early comedy, *Every Man In His Humour*, has survived in the original 1598 Quarto (set in Italy) and also in a later version (set in England) revised by the playwright for publication in his 1616 Folio. Director John Caird (RSC Swan 1986) chose to work with the later Folio script which most readers agree to be superior, but he also opted to include in the final scene some Quarto material, most notably a major speech, young Knowell's long defense of poetry, which for whatever reason Jonson did not retain in his revision. One member of the cast defended this insertion on the grounds that (1) Jonson omitted this speech from the revised Folio version because in the interim he had written *Poetaster*, a play devoted to poets and poetry; (2) the moment is needed to set up a reconciliation of son and father which otherwise will not take place; and perhaps most important (3) here is a fine speech not to be lost – that climaxes with a distinction between the "slubber'd lines" of "brainless gulls" or "empty spirits, /And a true poet; than which reverend name /Nothing can more adorn humanity" (5.3.318–25). In the Folio revision in lieu of this thirty-line impassioned speech, however, Jonson provides a eight-line prose defense of the worthy poet by the witty Justice Clement followed by young Knowell's ironic rejoinder: "Sir, you have sav'd me the labor of a defense" (5.1.239).

At issue here is a potential gap between Jonson's sense of narrative or thematic climax and ours. The Italian version of *Every Man In* is the work of a playwright in his mid twenties who had yet to write such plays as *Every Man Out of His Humour* and *Poetaster* that treat in depth the role of the poet or satirist. The date of composition of the revised version of *Every Man In* is uncertain (probably at least a decade later than the original) but is clearly the effort of a playwright fully in command of his medium who has written *Volpone* and perhaps *Epicoene*. The Italian ending that includes the defense of poesy reads to me more like the ending of a Shakespeare comedy or the efforts of a young poet–dramatist with an emphasis upon reconciliation (particularly of father and son) and high ideals, as opposed to the less idealized "English" ending. Both endings deal with good versus bad poets, but the Folio version, centered more on Justice Clement and Brainworm than the Quarto's father and son, also develops issues dealing with marriage and soldiership. As with comparable situations in Shakespeare's plays where multiple versions are available (including the additional Christopher Sly material found in *The Taming of a Shrew*), the presence of such elements or choices amounts to a do-it-yourself kit that can be irresistible to an editor or director, but to make such adjustments or improvements is to create a third entity that corresponds to neither A nor B. In such instances whose sense of an ending should prevail?

Outside of the Shakespeare canon, the textual muddle that has generated the most controversy among editors and scholars is Marlowe's *Doctor Faustus*. This play has survived in two early printed versions, the shorter A-text of 1604 and the longer B-text of 1616, both of which

found their way into print well after the playwright's death in 1593.
Until recently, most editions of this play have been conflations that,
as with many comparable editions of *Hamlet* and *King Lear*, provide an
editor's combination of elements or readings from both of the early
versions, with the longer B-text usually (but not always) the control or
copy text. Directors, in turn (like Jerry Turner cited earlier), tend to
take considerable liberties with the editorial text, particularly with the
various comic scenes that do not involve Faustus himself, moments that
have been prized by few readers.

In his 1989 RSC production in the Swan Barry Kyle chose to build on
the shorter A-text and, in addition, work with thirteen actors, all of them
men. The temptation was strong, I was told, to factor in elements from
the B-text (e.g., several Mephistophiles speeches near the end – B 1983–
85, 1988–94), but during the rehearsal process resistance to such editing
grew (as opposed to the situation in *Every Man In*), so that a "purist"
stance emerged. This production had many strengths: the Good and
Evil Angels came across effectively as inner voices; Marlowe's Wagner
was transformed into another Faustus in the making, by the end nearly
a Charles Manson figure. Still, to no one's surprise some elements in
the A-text were gone or transposed, with several of the alterations of
potential interest. In particular, for this director and group of actors the
psychological took precedence over the supernatural in the telling of the
story, a weighting familiar to Shakespeareans in productions of *Hamlet*
and especially *Macbeth*.

For example, the role of the various devils as scripted was diminished,
in part for logistical reasons. The B-text calls for a much greater diabolic
presence than the A-text (for me, the major distinction between the two
versions), but the devils who enter to drag Faustus off to Hell in both
texts (A 1505, B 2088) were not seen in this production. The presentation
of the Old Man is another feature that distinguishes the two early texts,[2]
with for once the A-text having more material, a speech by the Old
Man after Faustus exits with Helen of Troy (A 1377–86). That speech
was included, but the devils who are directed to enter to torment this
figure (A 1380) were cut. Also omitted was an earlier exchange in this
scene in which Faustus asks Mephistophiles to torment the Old Man,
and the latter responds: "His faith is great, I cannot touch his soul, / But
what I may afflict his body with, / I will attempt, which is but little worth"
(A 1345–47). Without this exchange and without the appearance of devils,
the Old Man's final lines, that include "My faith, vile hell, shall triumph
over thee" and "Hence hell, for hence I fly unto my God" (A 1383, 1386)

lose much of their force and, more important, do not provide a yardstick to measure Faustus on such issues as faith, bodily pain, and leaping or flying to God.

The other change I found revealing came a bit earlier. Few readers of this tragedy will leap to the defense of its "middle" (Acts 3 and 4 in modernized editions), the scenes that depict Faustus's activities during his twenty-four years of profit and delight after signing his pact with Lucifer. The last such episode in both A and B-texts is the protagonist's encounter with the Vanholts where he supplies out-of-season grapes for the pregnant Duchess, a scene that follows the practical joke Faustus plays on the horse-courser. Kyle transposed these two scenes so that the interaction with the Vanholts preceded that with the horse-courser; moreover, he omitted the speech that closes the horse-courser sequence (the punch line for the episode in both early texts) in which the protagonist gloats that "Faustus has his leg again, and the Horsecourser, I take it, a bottle of hay for his labor" (A 1217–19).

Behind this change lay a desire by director and actor to improve Marlowe's presentation of Faustus's growing torment or apprehension, a progression that started with his evident discomfort in his scene with the Emperor and was followed by the show for the Vanholts (the duchess was presented in blue, very pregnant, a Virgin Mary figure) and finally by a reconception of the horse-courser encounter which was played as a nightmare vision (the horse-courser was portrayed as a diabolic figure with talons). What in both early printed texts is a successful practical joke at the expense of the horse-courser became something decidedly different at the Swan.

As with the insertion of the Quarto speech in *Every Man In*, two incompatible senses of theatre or structure collide here. Although such reflexes may be deplored in many academic circles, many readers, actors, and directors are most comfortable with some form of psychological realism and therefore seek to establish a progression of states of mind that makes best sense in such terms. This Faustus, who lost his leg while writhing on the floor in pain, was clearly not a practical joker duping a bargain hunter. Readers may disagree about the function of this episode (at least those readers who assume it does have a function), but for me the point lies in a fairly obvious analogy: both the horse-courser and Faustus have made a bargain (for a horse at a low price, for twenty-four years of indulgence) that seemed like a good idea at the time but has a catch (don't ride the horse into the water, you must sign away your immortal soul) that leads to an unfortunate conclusion. The tragic fate of Faustus is here previewed in comic terms by the discomfiture of the bargain hunter whose horse turns into a bundle of hay. Such use of analogy or analogical reasoning, however, is unlikely to work for playgoers at the Swan, so that the director's choice here is an excellent example of rescripting to make a 1590s play conform to 1980s play logic.

The changes in *Doctor Faustus* point to some larger issues important for this study as a whole – in particular, the question: what constitutes "obscurity" for today's playgoers (and actors)? As noted in chapter 1 and in my discussion of satiric comedy, directors may omit or change passages owing to hard words, difficult syntax, or mythological allusions, but more fundamental (and often harder to perceive) are differences between then and now in theatrical procedures or ways of thinking – which I think of in terms of *conventions* (the terms upon which players and playgoers agree to meet) or *theatrical vocabulary*. The inclusion of an episode owing to its analogical relationship to the main plot would not have surprised a reader or playgoer in the 1590s but can be highly esoteric, even mystifying today.

Comparable examples are not hard to find, as in a revealing change made by Jerry Turner in the final scene of *The Revenger's Tragedy* (OSF 1984). According to the script (5.3.40), with Lussurioso and three nobles seated at the banquet table: "*Enter the masque of revengers*" (Vindice, Hippolito, and two other lords). These masked figures in distinctive costumes dance, pull out swords, and kill the four seated figures (in this production, with strangling cords). Then, with the departure of these four and with four bodies left onstage, "*Enter the other masque of intended murderers*" (Ambitioso, Supervacuo, Spurio, and a fourth lord) who "*coming in dancing*" discover the bodies of Lussurioso and his group (48). Frustrated by their inability to carry out their intended violence, these new arrivals turn on each other, so that within moments only one (the anonymous fourth lord) is still alive and seven bodies are left onstage.

In his rendition of this sequence, Turner made a significant change in the script. In the previous scene as scripted, aware of the revels and masque to be performed, Vindice had set up his murderous plot with the observation that his group will "take pattern / Of all those suits, the colour, trimming, fashion, / E'en to an undistinguish'd hair almost" (5.2.15–17). According to his plan, these revengers will gain access to their victims by wearing costumes identical to the other set of masquers. These lines, however, were cut in the Oregon production; the two sets of masquers then wore different costumes, presumably to avoid confusing an audience already puzzled by the plot complications of this unfamiliar play.

Turner's choice to differentiate clearly between the two groups of masquers provokes the question: what point or strategy lies behind this confusing conflation in the script? The key moment for an answer is the arrival of the second set of revengers. What is or should be the effect upon a spectator, then or now, when a second group of four, wearing costumes identical to the first group, appears with murderous intent? These are "the bad guys" (two of them inept villains verging on caricature, a third the cynical bastard, Spurio), as opposed to Vindice and his cohorts who supposedly are on the side of justice and morality. To an audience watching a production dictated by the Quarto, however, this second group is indistinguishable from the supposed "good guys" who have just committed four murders and left the bodies onstage. Critics may argue at length about the size of the gap between Hamlet and Laertes as revengers, but here the dramatist has narrowed that gap to just about nothing, to the point that, in both costume and action, the two sets of murderers are indistinguishable. The director's desire for added clarity (or for a second set of visually exciting costumes) can therefore blur an equation for the viewer's eye that, if confusing, is confusing in a provocative way. For me, these paired entrances and actions act out something distinctive not only about this play but about revenge tragedy in general, a genre in which the "taint" of revenge (as suggested by the ghost in *Hamlet*, 1.5.85) often narrows the initial gap between the protagonist and those he opposes. Here a sense of patterning that makes a modern interpreter uncomfortable can lead to revealing insights into the strategy implicit in the original script.

Similarly, other elements in the original theatrical vocabulary can pose problems today. As noted earlier, to take on a Jacobean satiric comedy is often to confront elements now deemed obscure or unplayable, a situation that regularly leads to some kind of streamlining. In Giles Block's production of Marston's *The Fawn* (RNT Cottlesloe 1983) the director and his actors had to contend with many features in the script alien to a modern audience, for Marston had designed this dramatic satire for child actors (and their distinctive assets and conventions) and for the coterie audience of the private theatres. In particular, major problems, whether for reader or director, arise in the final movement when an interpreter tries to account for how the dramatist sought to tie together diverse strands by means of Cupid, various allegorical figures, and the

Ship of Fools, all of which appear to be Marston's way of broadening and deepening a spectator's sense of what the play has been about.

But, as in *The Tempest*, masques and allegorical personae do not translate well into the modern idiom, whether for actors or spectators, so here in this final movement was where the director made his major changes in the original script (otherwise only slightly cut or adapted). First, Marston sets up his climax with the signal: "*Drunkenness, Sloth, Pride and Plenty lead Cupid to his state, who is followed by Folly, War, Beggary, and Laughter*" (5.1.139). In his role as presenter, Hercules-Fawnus explains this pageant to the puzzled Duke Gonzalo (and to the spectator), noting that "Triumphant Cupid," who is "Led in by Sloth, Pride, Plenty, Drunkenness, / Followed by Folly, War, Laughter, Beggary," now "Takes his fair throne" (143–51). Cupid (with the aid of Hercules-Fawnus) then cites his statutes, brings various offenders "to the bar" (243, 262, 378), and sentences most of them to the Ship of Fools, at which point they exit. The play then builds to the exposure of the climactic foolishness, that of Gonzalo himself, and the revelation of first the marriage between Tiberio and Dulcimel and then the identity of Fawnus. Many of the effects Marston calls for here are typical of early Jacobean comedy (e.g., the arraignments) and some are linked to the particular skills of the child actors (e.g., the major role allotted Cupid, the allegorical pageantry, the large number of actors available).

But the director at the Cottlesloe had a company of limited size and an audience not in tune with allegory or Parliament of Love conventions. Moreover, the script, as it survives, has many silences about how to stage this dramatic sequence, especially the Ship of Fools. So the director, in effect, worked with what he had, making several judicious cuts and changes. First, the most visible part of his set was a large tree, needed, according to the script, for Tiberio to gain access to Dulcimel's chamber (5.1.0), so that, at his entrance, Cupid was placed not in a throne (as signaled in line 151) but in the tree, from which position he delivered his judgments. Second, the director and designer ignored the dialogue references to a "bar," a standard property for Elizabethan and Jacobean trial scenes (cited in several playhouse manuscripts); rather, the indicted figures stood alone in a neutral stage area while Fawnus read the law and the charges against them. Third, no attempt was made to provide any elaborate representation of the Ship of Fools; rather, the spectator saw during the sequence a small, flat model or picture visible over the back wall of the set and later revealed to be mounted on the handle of Puttotta's broom. The figures under sentence then exited through the same door, leaving the spectator with no real sense of a "place" or entity for the ship despite the heavy emphasis in the dialogue. Finally (and undoubtedly for practical reasons), Marston's masque involving Cupid and eight allegorical attendants was reduced to Cupid and five ladies wearing small masks, four of them also wearing small sashes with lettering (hard to read from any distance) that identified them as the first four of the allegorical entities (Sloth, Pride, Plenty, Drunkenness – Hercules's reference to the other four figures was cut).

I do not wish to overrate Marston's ending or the scope of this play, but he did choose to climax his action with a series of arraignments (after a play full of poses and partial exposures) and then went to some lengths to provide a context for those arraignments with Cupid led in by and in some way defined by eight allegorical figures, including, surprisingly, War and Beggary. Somehow, if the play *is* coherent, the masque, the role of Cupid, the arraignment at the bar, and the Ship of Fools are designed to provide a context that pulls together the romance story and the series of exposures into a whole that follows from what Hercules and Marston originally set in motion. Perhaps the original logic is linked to something literary or mythological alien to the modern actor or spectator (e.g., Marston could be building upon the labors of Hercules or the motif of Hercules at the crossroads, both familiar in the Renaissance). This production, I should note, *did* realize many facets of the play up until this point, but with Cupid in the tree (rather than on a throne), with no bar and no distinctive ship, and with no real point to the allegorical presence (e.g., perhaps an appropriate allegorical persona could have led off each of the ejected men), whatever logic may have been basic to Marston's sense of his ending has been blurred or lost. Such a diminution or translation may be inevitable; moreover, this climax may not have been fully realized in the first place. But to see the difficulties faced by the modern director confronting Marston's script and the choices he feels he must make is to see a particularly revealing example of the gap between our expectations and the evidence provided by an early Jacobean comedy comparable to *Measure for Measure*.

Another play that poses significant problems for a modern production is Beaumont and Fletcher's *The Maid's Tragedy*, so that some interesting choices were on display in both the 1981 RSC version (TOP) directed by Barry Kyle and the 1997 Globe version directed by Lucy Bailey. Beaumont and Fletcher are very much of an age and not for all time, so that many of their effects do not translate well into our idiom and, in fact, often defy our expectations. Kyle in particular did some heavy cutting, not only of the masque in 1.2 but also of various highly rhetorical passages of patterned language that provide variations upon a given theme or emotion (the Beaumont and Fletcher aria or recitative). Aspatia in particular lost many lines, but so did almost every figure in the "big" talky scenes.

Such elisions (to be expected) were less revealing than two outright cuts made by the director at points where the effects provided by the original dramatists place particular strain upon our notions of realism or credibility. Both of these moments, moreover, represent for me Beaumont and Fletcher signature passages – choices characteristic of their distinctive sense of theatre and, as a result, alien to us today. The first moment is in 3.2, a typical Beaumont and Fletcher "big scene" (and one at the heart of this play) where Melantius persuades his best friend Amintor to reveal what is troubling him (that Evadne, Amintor's new wife and Melantius's sister, was and still is the king's mistress and has married Amintor only for show). What makes this scene so odd for the modern sensibility is the patterned, highly artificial movement that builds, *twice*, to the same series of actions wherein one friend draws his sword in anger, the second is forced to draw also, the first relents, and both end up sheathing their weapons. That the same process happens twice is what makes the scene so distinctive. The first sequence (in which Melantius, angered by the apparent insult to his family honor, challenges his friend) does appear psychologically plausible in our terms; in contrast, the second (in which Amintor decides he has been wronged, draws his sword, and forces Melantius to do likewise) may seem forced or artificial by our standards of psychological realism or dramatic progression.

This second drawing and sheathing of swords (what I think of as "the re-run effect") also struck Kyle as odd or anomalous, so he cut it from his production. In a letter in response to my queries, he noted that this series of cuts had been made before rehearsals began. In his terms: "Some archaic features of classical texts, I do believe, are beyond redemption for a modern audience – not all, but some – and I'm afraid that the stop–start effect of the duel in this scene reminded me of Monty Python's Flying Circus." As Kyle describes the situation, "the more genuinely and strongly the actors played those deeply serious emotions the *funnier* it would get" (i.e., for an audience at The Other Place). He also pointed out that one of the major barriers to his setting the action "in an Aga Khan-ish world on a Greek island" was "extended swordplay," so for this and other reasons he "was therefore trying to avoid sword-fights." So here is an obvious example of a *very* distinctive Jacobean theatrical strategy – again, a Beaumont and Fletcher "signature" – that a modern director has deemed unworkable or unpalatable for his actors and audience. As a playgoer, I enjoyed the scene I saw, but I also sense the presence here of a distinctive Jacobean theatrical effect that may shed light upon Shakespeare's plays, especially in the choice of patterned action over psychological realism.[3]

The other revealing change came at the climax of the play when Aspatia, disguised as her own brother seeking revenge for her supposed death, provokes Amintor into a fight in order to get herself killed – in effect, using the man who has jilted her as a means of committing suicide. The dramatists have her–him strike and then kick Amintor who finally draws his sword ("a man can bear /No more and keep his flesh") and mortally wounds her. During the confrontation, he comments that his opponent "canst not fight" and that her blows "are quite besides"; rather, she only spreads her arms and takes his blows, defenseless, upon her breast (5.3.95–103).

Both the fight and most of Amintor's lines written to accompany that fight were gone from this production and from the Globe production as well. Again, Kyle writes "that in this case I made the cuts after trying very hard to direct the scene with all the lines intact," but, he adds, "the naturalistic question immediately arose of how would Aspatia know how to handle a sword." More important, in his wish to heighten the clear sexual imagery of the scene (with its emphasis upon desires, dying, and penetration) he decided "that it was less silly but also *truer* to the very specific psychological line being developed by Beaumont and Fletcher to replace swordplay with her violent provocation of Amintor followed by a rush of blood to his head and a single fatal stabbing." As in the re-run effect of 3.2, a striking image involving extended swordplay was deemed inappropriate or chancy (in the sense of being liable to produce unwanted laughter) and at odds with the yardstick of psychological truth. Conversely, the reader of Beaumont and Fletcher might conclude that, especially in such big moments, our sense of psychological realism may be superseded by something else – and defining that something else would then be a major task for students of this tragedy or Jacobean tragicomedy, including the late plays of Shakespeare.

RESCRIPTING FOR A "CONCEPT"

The most highly visible examples of rescripting are linked to a director's "concept" and often involve added material or special effects, most commonly at the beginning and end of a production so as to serve as a framing device. Barry Kyle's modern-dress production of Marlowe's *The Jew of*

Malta (RSC Swan 1987) opened with Machiavel (spelled in the Quarto Machevil and pronounced that way here) rising from below on a trapeze and speaking his Prologue slowly and deliberately in a strong Italian accent with his presence further reinforced by smoke and distinctive music. In the play proper the same actor (John Carlisle) reappeared as Ferneze, the Governor of Malta, the epitome of Christian hypocrisy and Barabas's primary antagonist. For the play's last speech after the death of Barabas the actor took off the Ferneze wig and, supported by the smoke and music of the Prologue, delivered the final line and a half ("let due praise be given / Neither to fate nor fortune, but to heaven" – 5.5.122–23) in the Machevil voice. The device was especially effective for that play-goer who remembered Machevil's original lines – most notably the assertion that those who "read me," attain power, and then "cast me off" are in turn "poisoned by my climbing followers" (Prologue.11–13). By this choice the play's final word, *heaven*, was totally undermined (in keeping with Machevil's assertion that religion is "but a childish toy" – Prologue.14), and a frame was established that suggested a larger cynical force underlying the power politics in Malta.

Middleton and Rowley's *The Changeling* is one of the most often pro-duced non-Shakespeare scripts of the period. However, those readers, playgoers, and theatrical professionals who are fascinated by the Beatrice–DeFlores–Alsemero story are often less interested in the second plot that involves Isabella, her two suitors, Lollio, and Alibius. The re-cent ninety-minute television production (BBC 1993, directed by Simon Curtis, adapted by Michael Hastings) with Elizabeth McGovern, Bob Hoskins, and Hugh Grant omitted this second plot completely. Directors in the theatre may not do such radical surgery but still regularly pare back the madhouse material.

A notable exception was Richard Eyre's 1988 RNT production which, according to his program note, was set in "a Spanish slave colony of the nineteenth century" to make apparent the "interdependence of rank and money." Here the madhouse was an essential part of the director's concept: "Madness runs through the play like a vein charged with infection.... People are either robbed of their reason by nature or accident, or are insane in a metaphorical sense: robbed of their reason by sexual passion." The second plot was therefore showcased rather than pared back. This production started and ended in a dim light with the same image: a large number of ragged figures in a pile and a central grate in the stage floor so as to suggest a madhouse or prison. From its midst the group pushed up two figures not in rags (Alsemero, Beatrice) and pushed them together (initially they were automata with no animation). Alsemero then moved into the lines that begin 1.1 gradually taking on energy or "character," but the playgoer was left with a sense of a story generated in a madhouse. The set reinforced this concept by displaying throughout the show two visible sides with three levels of metal steps that could represent either the castle or the madhouse (with the fools on one side, the madmen on the other) so that even during the castle scenes a sense of madhouse as place was present (in this show the set became a major character in its own right). The production ended with Alsemero (the show's initial "actor") standing alone over the bodies of Beatrice and DeFlores and then being surrounded by madfolk who pulled him into the pile where he had started in 1.1. The show therefore ended where it had begun so that madness and the madhouse emerged as the dominant image or symbol.

A particularly good example of the freedom in rescripting a director may feel possible in a play not part of the Shakespeare canon is provided by Michael Boyd's *The Spanish Tragedy* (RSC Swan 1997). Boyd did much eliding of Kyd's long rhetorical passages but did not take out any major elements, so that he presented more of this ungainly script than I had anticipated. Included were the two Portugal scenes (1.3, 3.1), the Andrea-Revenge frame (central to the director's concept), an amalgamation of the 1592 Don Bazulto scene (3.13) with the 1602 Bazardo or painter scene, and a delightful (and very funny) rendition of Hieronimo's entertainment for the king in 1.4. Overall, the show was well paced and was well received by audiences unfamiliar with the story.

This production started with a line from Hieronimo's lament in Act 4 ("Here lay my hope" – 4.4.90) projected onto the rear curtain (after the interval three more lines from this same passage were included), but the key to Boyd's interpretation lay not in Hieronimo's lines but in the final two words of the script, "endless tragedy." The show started with a jumble of unintelligible voices, a repeated sound effect (which eventually I understood to be everyone telling their story endlessly), and Don Andrea seated, unmoving, with a cloaked and hooded Revenge at his side and behind them the entire cast seated at a table. This inert Andrea, who at the outset repeatedly faltered in his delivery of his lines, had to be animated, prodded, even jump-started by Revenge, so that the playgoer witnessed not a willing but an enforced telling of this tale. Andrea and Revenge were then not a constant onstage presence (as suggested in the script). The former came onstage to offer his complaints in the subsequent choric scenes (1.5, 2.6) and was present during some of the action involving Bel-Imperia, Horatio, Balthazar, and Lorenzo, but Revenge was not in sight (though late in Kyd's Act 3 Revenge did appear in a procession across the stage that also involved Andrea and Hieronimo).

Boyd then made some major adjustments starting in 3.15. Gone was Kyd's dumb show to be replaced by a Revenge who, in response to Andrea's continuing complaints, called forth Balthazar in armor who repeatedly stabbed Andrea who then stayed on the floor for much of Act 4. The effect was to display the power of Revenge and the subservience of Andrea (or humanity); he/we are not in control but must repeat the experience as dictated by this force. As the "Soliman and Perseda" play-within-the-play developed, Andrea was placed in the midst of the action (e.g., exulting over the deaths of his enemies, embracing the dead Bel-Imperia). In the final coda (4.5) Andrea was overjoyed at the outcome of events (and here the director pared back the end of his first speech so as to eliminate the references to the good fates expected for Andrea's friends). Then, after Revenge had the final words in Kyd's script ("For here though death hath end their misery, / I'll there begin their endless tragedy" – 4.5.47–48), he removed his hood to reveal himself to be Hieronimo (the program had listed no actor as playing Revenge). At this point the stage went dark, the lights came up again, and the same process started again with Horatio rather than Andrea being animated and prompted by Revenge to deliver the play's opening lines (up through "My name was . . . " – 1.1.5) until his voice was drowned out by the other voices. The effect was summed up by one reviewer as an "endless brutal recycling" in which "the characters think they are acting on their own behalf" but "we can see that they are being used by the gods to fulfill a design of which they are unconscious."[4]

The foregoing account of directorial choices is selective, not comprehensive, and, like the chapters to follow, is based upon material from productions I have actually seen. In starting with plays that may be unfamiliar to many readers my goal has been to bring into focus a series of questions. Our notions about drama or character or going to the theatre work (or appear to work) for Shakespeare's plays and, we assume, for the plays of his contemporaries. But do they? Why indeed are the masques or other allegorical presentations that recur in these playscripts so problematic in modern productions? What prevents us from appreciating or valuing such moments as the re-run effect in *The Maid's Tragedy* or the identical masquers in *The Revenger's Tragedy*? One answer is that Elizabethan and Jacobean dramatists, including Shakespeare, had access to a language of the theatre that included signifiers or ways of signifying that have been screened out by later notions and assumptions linked to psychological realism and narrative credibility – hence our impulse to improve Webster and streamline Marston's denouement.

Given such a gap between then and now, some degree of rescripting may be inevitable, but once the process begins, where does one draw the line? Inevitably, some changes reflect laziness or a desire to cut the Gordian knot rather than wrestle with a problem. As noted in chapter 1, when in doubt, why not simply cut the offending line or scene, especially when the original playscript is unfamiliar to just about everyone in the audience? Here different directors take decidedly different stances, so the practices of a Deborah Warner or Katie Mitchell (whose RSC 1991–92 *A Woman Killed With Kindness* was very faithful to the received text) are very different from Jerry Turner's approach to *Shoemaker's Holiday* or Philip Franks's approach to *The Duchess of Malfi*. A high degree of rewrighting, as in Stephen Jeffreys's adaptation of Brome's *The Jovial Crew* (RSC Swan 1992), leads to the question: why stage these plays at all today? Do they reveal something distinctive about their world or is the goal to adapt them so that they reveal (or appear to reveal) something pointed about ours?

3

Adjustments and improvements

> "But in this changing, what is your intent?"
> *Love's Labor's Lost*, 5.2.137

A variety of motives – practical, commercial, and conceptual – lie behind the various forms of rescripting. Streamlining is often a pragmatic choice linked to a lack of resources (a shortage of personnel, a limited theatrical space), a judgment that the targeted playgoers will not stomach the full length of a given script, or merely a director's impatience with the original language and theatrical practice (so "cut to the chase" thinking). Of greater interest are the varied conceptual concerns that lead to rescripting. Like *The Fawn, The Revenger's Tragedy*, and *The Duchess of Malfi*, Shakespeare's plays are replete with problematic moments, many of them linked to the material conditions or cultural practices of the 1590s and early 1600s, that have troubled editors, critics, and students. Directors, with their own resources in mind (variable lighting, sets, actresses rather than boy actors to play female roles), therefore regularly adjust or improve the situation in their effort to find a common language with playgoers who lack scholarly glosses. This chapter will deal with several directorial strategies designed to deal with perceived difficulties and anomalies and at times advance specific agendas.

SOLVING PROBLEMS

Over the years scholars have expressed dissatisfaction with some of Shakespeare's narratives as set forth in the Quartos and the Folio and as a result have postulated supposed missing scenes. Directors in turn have factored in additional material to bridge such apparent gaps. For example, Act 2 of *The Merchant of Venice* is often streamlined by combining the two Morocco scenes (2.1, 2.7) so that, depending upon the positioning of the recombination, either the sequence 1.3 through 2.6 or 2.2 through 2.8 can take place in Venice without a shift back to Belmont. Gregory

Doran (RSC 1998) went a step farther by adding a new scene after 2.6 where Shylock, returning home from his dinner with Antonio and Bassanio, fought his way through a group of revellers (and was bloodied in the process), had a glimpse of the eloping Jessica, called out to her to no avail, and finally was seen bouncing off the walls of his house. Similarly, just before the interval (taken after 3.2) of his *Much Ado About Nothing* (Cheek by Jowl 1998) Declan Donnelan used the upper right balcony to provide a brief view of Hero at her "window," then a glimpse of Margaret's impersonation, so that the playgoers saw a version of the missing scene postulated by some scholars. A different insertion was provided by Bill Alexander (RSC 1990) who had Beatrice walk across the stage by herself at night in Act 3 so as to justify her having caught a cold (3.4.53, 64) and therefore not having shared a bed with Hero at the crucial time (4.1.147–49). All three directors sought to close perceived gaps in the story as told in the Quartos.

Although many readers are not troubled by the narratives in the received texts of *Merchant* and *Much Ado*, other problems or anomalies do cry out for some kind of resolution. A good example is provided by the sub-plot involving the Host, horses, and supposed Germans in *The Merry Wives of Windsor*. Peter Moss (SFC 1978) decided that the original script was keyed to information available to a Windsor insider but lost to us today. He therefore chose to omit completely this abortive Host–Germans plot and any Garter-related material (e.g., 5.5.56–73), pare back other sub-plots (so that 4.1 with its language lesson was gone), and highlight the comedy provided by Ford and Falstaff. Similarly, Michael Kahn (DC 1990) cut 4.1, 4.3, and chunks of 4.5 so that the Host received no comeuppance; rather, the Sir Hugh/Dr. Caius lines at the end of 3.1 ("let us knog our prains together to be revenge on this same scall, scurvy, cogging companion, the host of the Garter" – 118–21) were the last a playgoer heard of any retaliation by parson and doctor against their tormentor. Kahn, however, did insert additional onstage business for Fenton and Anne, especially at the beginning and end of 1.1 (kisses, noises to befuddle Slender) in order to provide more substance to that part of the narrative, so that these two lovers were more of a presence than in any other production I have seen.

In contrast, two other directors chose to improve rather than omit the plot against the Host. Jon Cranney (OSF 1980) provided an additional brief scene between 4.4 and 4.5 in which Pistol, Dr. Caius, and John Rugby hurriedly donned disguises and conned the Host in broken German. Rather than creating a new scene Terry Hands (RNT 1995)

attached the Host–Bardolph lines that constitute the brief 4.3 to the beginning of 4.5 so as to have all of the Germans–horses plot in one long
tavern sequence (4.5, 4.6, 5.1) and in the process make as much sense
out of this material as it ever does. The cuts or adaptations in these four
productions reflect the directors' responses to a perceived weakness or
gap in the received text, a perception shared by many readers.

Another problem for scholars and readers that has led to adjustments
in the theatre is linked to two related passages in *Measure for Measure*: the
duke's soliloquy in tetrameter couplets (3.2.261–82) and his subsequent
soliloquy during the brief conference between Mariana and Isabella
(4.1.59–64). A long note in the New Variorum edition[1] records dissatisfaction going back to the eighteenth century with the latter passage, a
meditation on how "place and greatness" are vulnerable to "millions of
false eyes" (4.1.59). Why does the duke express these sentiments at this
point? Moreover, in practical terms is this speech long enough to allow
for the Isabella–Mariana conference that takes place offstage? Similarly,
does the tetrameter couplet speech, which starts "He who the sword of
heaven will bear / Should be as holy as severe" and moves to a plan of
action in "Craft against vice I must apply" (3.2.261–62, 277), make sense
in its Folio position? In defense of the later speech in the received text
Katherine Lever notes: "The time has obviously been foreshortened,
but this was permitted by the theatrical convention that time could be
presumed to elapse during a soliloquy," but many directors agree with
A. P. Rossiter about the 4.1 soliloquy that the earlier speech in couplets
"could equally well go in here – providing a necessary explanation and
at a point where the Duke must be alone."

To deal with this perceived problem directors have resorted to a variety
of solutions. The Fall 1997 ACTER actors borrowed some script choices
from an earlier Peter Brook production, so that they placed their intermission mid way in the duke's couplet speech after "O, what may man
within him hide, / Though angel on the outward side!" (3.2.271–72) and
moved the remainder of this speech (273–82) to replace the duke's 4.1
soliloquy and cover the Isabella–Mariana conference. Steven Pimlott
(RSC 1994–95) chose to omit the duke's 4.1 Folio soliloquy but not to
replace it with a section of the 3.2 speech; rather, his choice was elegant
in its simplicity – the duke stood silent onstage and looked impatiently
at his watch. Jim Edmondson's solution (OSF 1986) was more elaborate
than most: he repositioned the 4.1 speech as the Prologue and broke up
the 3.2 speech so that one part was placed at the end of 3.1 just before
his intermission and the remainder replaced the original soliloquy in

4.1 – and no lines were left at the speech's original placement at the end of 3.2.

Exactly what constitutes a problem or anomaly may vary. Readers are sometimes surprised at the appearance of Fabian rather than Feste as one of the comic conspirators in *Twelfth Night*, 2.5, but directors usually do not make adjustments. Exceptions are Martin Platt (PRC 1992) who factored Fabian into the earlier revelry scene (2.3) and Bill Cain (OSF 1988) who eliminated the figure entirely giving most of his lines to Feste (see chapter 5). The letter or box-tree scene in *Twelfth Night* is often streamlined somewhat so that a few of the cryptic comments from the eavesdroppers disappear (e.g., Sir Toby's "And with what wing the staniel checks at it!" and Fabian's "Sowter will cry upon't for all this, though it be as rank as a fox" – 2.5.113–14, 123–24), but usually Malvolio's lines remain intact. However, Nicholas Hytner (Lincoln Center 1998) omitted a passage so that Malvolio, after reading the letter supposedly from Olivia, did not say: "She did commend my yellow stockings of late, she did praise my leg being cross-garter'd" (166–67). The director or actor's rationale for this adjustment is clear, for later in this scene Maria tells the other conspirators that "He will come to her in yellow stockings, and 'tis a color she abhors, and cross-garter'd, a fashion she detests" (198–200).

To omit Malvolio's supposed "memory" is therefore to eliminate an anomaly, a possible source of confusion. When would Malvolio have worn such an outlandish outfit? Given Maria's comment, how could Olivia have commended or praised it? An alternative view, however, is that this anomaly should not only be included but stressed. With or without reference to recent controversies about recovered (and perhaps bogus) memories, a more sanguine interpreter of the scene can argue that Maria's explanation is given such a climactic placement to cause a reader or playgoer to reassess just how far Malvolio has gone or will go to hold on to his pipe dream or delusional vision that he is Olivia's beloved. Indeed, noting this particular omission in the classroom has generated some fruitful discussions of Malvolio's mind set and the scene as a whole.

TRANSPOSITIONS

One way to solve an apparent problem in the theatre is therefore to omit the anomalous item: the celebration of the killing of the deer in *As You Like It* (4.2); the Duchess of Malfi's children other than her eldest son; all references to horses and Germans in *Merry Wives*; Malvolio's memory of Olivia's praise; the second account of Portia's death in *Julius Caesar* (4.3.181–93).[2] To adjust or improve the received text a director may also reposition significant items, whether to enhance the narrative, eliminate a perceived anomaly, or advance a particular interpretation – as with Gayle Edwards's handling of a dumb show in *The White Devil* and Jerry Turner's handling of two post-intermission scenes in *'Tis Pity* noted in chapter 2 and David Thacker's transposition of the two sections of *The Merchant of Venice*, 3.1 noted in chapter 1. A good example is provided by a much discussed moment, Henry V's response at Agincourt to a "new alarum": "The French have reinforc'd their scatter'd men./Then every soldier kill his prisoners" (*Henry V*, 4.6.35–37). Readers have disagreed about what Henry's decision reveals about his strategy and values, but playgoers often do not get to experience the effect as scripted in the Quarto and Folio. Rather, directors either omit this command entirely or move it (RSC 1977–78, DC 1995) so that it comes after the Fluellen–Gower speeches that immediately follow (4.7.1–54). This solution turns the English killing of their French prisoners into a reaction to the French slaughter of the English boys (" 'Tis certain there's not a boy that's left alive" – 4.7.5) and therefore makes a problematic moment less troubling, though many readers feel that the king's command *should* be troubling or problematic.

Will Huddleston made two less controversial changes in his *1 Henry VI* (OSF 1975). First, he streamlined a major sequence by placing earlier the initial meeting of Vernon and Basset, the contentious supporters of York and Somerset, that is placed in the Folio after Talbot's first appearance before Henry VI (3.4.28–45), so that rather than being interrupted by this private quarrel 3.4–4.1 became one continuous action in front of the king that climaxed with Vernon and Basset's public confrontation (4.1.78–122). Later in the script Joan de Pucelle's final scene (5.4) falls into two parts, with the English taunting of Joan followed by York's parley with the Dauphin, but Huddleston reversed the two sections so that Joan's accusations about the father of her child, wherein she names the Dauphin, the Bastard, and Reignier (5.4.72–78), were directed at those figures who remained above after the parley.

Often a transposition is keyed to a director's sense of narrative climax or efficiency. In his *All's Well That Ends Well* (RSC 1989–90) Barry Kyle found the progression of questions directed at the blindfolded Parolles in 4.3 to be anticlimactic and therefore rearranged the three beats or segments so that the revelations about the numbers in the French army (129–69) came last as the climactic treason and the comments about the

Dumaines and Bertram (171–302) preceded them. In the final scene of his *As You Like It* (SFC 1990) Richard Monette cut the duke's speech after Hymen's hymn (5.4.147–48) and moved Phebe's "I will not eat my word" response (149–50) to an earlier position after Hymen's line to her ("You to his love must accord,/Or have a woman to your lord" – 133–34). The change was welcomed by the actress who found a better psychological through-line but altered the potential value of that hymn, here sung by the ensemble, as a factor in moving or changing Phebe. In his *King Lear* (DC 1991) Michael Kahn moved the fool's prophecy (3.2.80–96) to the end of 3.6 so that the actor had a tour de force moment as he delivered most of these lines while being brutalized by Cornwall's men looking for Lear.

The rationale for transpositions can vary widely. Thanks to Peter Brook's landmark production (RSC 1970–71), to double Theseus/Oberon and Hippolyta/Titania has become a familiar move, but some directors balk at Brook's metatheatrical choice to have his actors playing the fairy king and queen proceed to an upstage door and then turn triumphantly to "become" Theseus and Hippolyta. The Quarto, however, leaves no space at this point, for the entrance of Theseus and his train at 4.1.103 follows immediately upon the *exeunt* of the fairies, with only a sound effect ("*Wind horn*" – 102) intervening. To allow for the desired doubling while also taking into account costume changes and verisimilitude some directors (OSF 1979, RSC 1999) have moved Bottom's soliloquy that ends 4.1 to the space between the departure of the fairies and the arrival of the court figures. This transposition therefore solves one problem but at a price, for Bottom, the only human to interact knowingly with the fairy world, then delivers his prose account of his dream before rather than after the lovers' account of their experiences, a decided change in theatrical rhythm that alters the sequence of three awakenings and denies Bottom's "most rare vision" (4.1.204–5) its climax position.

Another familiar move is to reposition the choric speeches in *Henry V* that precede Acts 2 and 4. Adrian Noble (RSC 1984) enhanced the role of Ian McDiarmid's Chorus by keeping him onstage throughout the show as a mediator between the audience and the action and by parceling out some of his speeches to heighten their impact. The chorus before Act 4 was broken up into three parts: lines 1–22 preceded 3.7, the first scene after the interval; lines 22–47 preceded 4.1; and the remainder preceded 4.2; and the chorus to Act 2 was split in two: lines 1–11 preceded 2.1; the remainder, with some adjustments, preceded 2.2. These

divisions not only expanded a spectator's sense of this figure's role in
the play but also opened up various new possibilities for gestures or
links. For example, when the Chorus revealed that "the French, advis'd
by good intelligence / Of this most dreadful preparation, / Shake in their
fear" (2.Chorus.12–14), he got a striking ironic effect by means of a gesture that linked "this dreadful preparation" to the exiting Pistol, Nym,
and Bardolph. Overall, this rendition of the Chorus strengthened the
continuity of the events and the meaning of some individual moments,
especially for the spectator unfamiliar with the script.

Henry Woronicz's *2 Henry IV* (OSF 1989) provided two distinctive
transpositions. First, he yoked together 5.1 and 5.3 to create one long
Falstaff–Shallow sequence that preceded 5.2 (our first view of Hal as
Henry V). The price tag for this splicing was a considerable change in
the rhythms of the two individual scenes, so that Falstaff's speech that
ends 5.1 lost its climax position, and Silence's changed behavior was less
striking. Moreover, Falstaff's lines that end 5.3, especially "the laws of
England are at my commandement. . . . woe to my Lord Chief Justice"
(136–38), mean something very different when positioned before rather
than after Henry V's choice of that Justice as "father to my youth"
(5.2.118).

More successful was the director's rescripting of the material in
Shakespeare's 3.1, the first scripted appearance of Henry IV. The well-
known speech that begins this scene that climaxes with "Uneasy lies the
head that wears a crown" (31) stayed in its customary position and was
the last utterance heard before the intermission. But the second half
of Shakespeare's 3.1 (Henry's interaction with various lords) was moved
earlier between 1.3 and 2.1. In the latter part of 1.3 the Archbishop moved
from below to above to deliver the lines describing Richard II – in effect,
evoking the image of the previous king. During this speech, with the
rebel leader in a commanding position above, Henry IV moved slowly
downstage below in a half-light so that this troubled figure was in view
during the Archbishop's evocation of the kingdom's present ills ("What
trust is in these times?" – 1.3.100) and then began the repositioned 3.1
sequence from that downstage spot. At the close of this reconstituted 1.4,
the king moved above to take a seat on the throne that remained in view
throughout the show, staying motionless in regal silence until the middle
of 2.3 when he slowly took off his robe, gloves, and other accoutrements
to become one of the drawers at the beginning of 2.4. Near the end of
that tavern scene he again donned his regal robes to deliver the speech
that begins 3.1. The director's splitting of 3.1 introduced Henry into the

action much earlier, giving him two appearances rather than one in the first half of the show, and used his brooding presence to underscore the diseases of the kingdom.

In my playgoing experience transpositions of scenes most commonly are linked to an effort to minimize set changes. Here Shakespeare's presentation of distinctive locales, generated, with few exceptions, by means of a combination of dialogue, costumes, and portable properties, sometimes does not mesh comfortably with a director or designer's reflexes on how best to display a forest, throne room, or other distinctive place. One of my few memories of Jack Landau's *Antony and Cleopatra* (Stratford, Connecticut 1960) is the rearrangement of scenes in Acts 2 and 3 to avoid Shakespeare's movement back and forth between Egypt and Rome; rather, the director presented consecutive sequences in one or the other locale and therefore (at some cost) managed to keep in place for a long stretch the elaborate Egyptian throne room set. Similarly, a rendition of *The Two Gentlemen of Verona* (Regents Park 1987) strung together all the Verona scenes at the outset so as to make possible a continuous presence for the rest of the show of an elaborate "Milan set" (the forest scenes of Acts 4 and 5 were done in the green areas to the left and right of the audience).

Such instances call attention to a revealing gap between then and now. The onstage storytelling of Shakespeare and his contemporaries is often keyed to the rapid alternation of scenes and locales as befits their flexible open stage, but that flexibility or openness can collide with today's sense of "design" or "set" that precludes such alternations. The collision is most visible in productions of *As You Like It* where, to avoid elaborate set or costume changes, the court scenes, including 3.1, are sometimes strung together as one unit before the action moves to 2.1 and the "Forest of Arden set," so that a playgoer sees 1.2, 1.3, 2.2, 3.1 – then either 2.1 or 2.3, then 2.1. Here a pragmatic approach to "place" supersedes the original sequence, with any loss of scenic counterpoint or any confusion in the plot deemed an acceptable trade-off. However, such transpositions do make a difference. For example, the rationale for Oliver's murderous plot against Orlando revealed by Adam in 2.3 may be understood very differently if (as in PRC 1983) the playgoer has already witnessed 3.1, the interview between Oliver and Duke Frederick.

Perhaps the best-known transposition is the movement of "To be, or not to be" from its familiar Second Quarto/Folio placement in 3.1 before the nunnery scene to the previous scene, often after Hamlet's "except my life, except my life, except my life" (2.2.216–17). Directors who make this adjustment (e.g., Ron Daniels RSC 1989, Richard Monette SFC 1994, Matthew Warchus RSC 1997) seek to provide a better context for Hamlet's thoughts of suicide and to remove what some interpreters see as an anomaly when the soliloquy appears in 3.1 – the pause or indecision exhibited in Hamlet's first appearance after his decision at the end of the previous scene to use *The Murder of Gonzago* to "catch the conscience of the King" (2.2.605). In a program note, moreover, Daniels, like some readers, found justification for the change in "the structure of the First Quarto" where this soliloquy *is* placed earlier – though no mention was made of other unique or distinctive features of that anomalous text (Polonius being named Corambis, a unique Gertrude–Horatio scene). Members of Daniels's cast I talked with strongly approved of this repositioning, for theatrical professionals wedded to psychological realism are puzzled by a speech on suicide that follows hard upon a decision to take action ("the play's the thing" – 2.2.604).

Many things, however, are changed, even put out of balance, by this adjustment. One result in Daniels's production was a stripped down version of 3.1 that lacked not only the famous soliloquy but also the subsequent nunnery scene with Ophelia (also moved to Act 2) and Claudius's "harlot's cheek" aside on his conscience (49–53), a useful, even highly significant building block to his prayer speech in 3.3. In this rescripting, moreover, the playgoer's first view of the "antic" Hamlet was no longer the fishmonger exchange with Polonius followed by the meeting with Rosencrantz and Guildenstern, then the arrival of the players, but now became "To be, or not to be," followed by the intensity of the nunnery scene which no longer immediately preceded the advice to the players, the exchange with Horatio, and the play-within. The meditative soliloquy comes across very differently as an initial element in a long progression, especially as delivered by Mark Rylance's Hamlet dressed in soiled striped pajamas, as opposed to a much later part of that progression. The nunnery scene did gain some force from being closer to Ophelia's report to her father in 2.1, but, in turn, lost a great deal without having as context Hamlet's interactions with Polonius both in the fishmonger exchange and at the appearance of the players (in this production, Hamlet and Polonius intensely disliked each other). As noted in chapter 2, placement of such major elements *is* a significant part of theatrical meaning, so that this choice had both obvious and subtle effects upon a playgoer's sense of the whole.

Such transposing was much in evidence in Trevor Nunn's production of *Troilus and Cressida* (RNT 1999). Confronted with this long and difficult script Nunn made various cuts, but more extensive rescripting was signaled by a program note that announced that "for this production, both the Quarto and folio texts have been used in a version wherein the play has been edited and in part re-arranged." That rearrangement significantly affected the action before the interval, so that a playgoer witnessed the following sequence: Prologue; the middle of 1.2 (the return of the Trojan warriors); the beginning of 1.3 (up to the arrival of Aeneas); 1.1; the rest of 1.2; 2.2; the end of 1.3; 2.1; 3.1; 2.3; 3.2.

For the playgoer unfamiliar with this daunting script the director's reshaping helped to create a clearer narrative. With the two opposing forces onstage during the Prologue, pantomimed actions singled out Helen, Paris, and Menelaus (and, as usual, the latter became a running joke). A subsequent skirmish then set up the next element, a return from battle (1.2) during which Pandarus identified for Cressida and the audience a series of Trojans including Hector and Troilus. By the end of this sequence the playgoer had witnessed the equivalent of an extended program note or introduction. In addition, having the Trojan council scene (2.2) where Hector initially argues in favor of sending back Helen precede Hector's challenge to the Greeks (end of 1.3) simplified matters and eliminated what some have perceived as an anomaly.

Such gains by means of reordering, however, should be weighed in terms of potential losses or diminutions. A distinctive feature of this unusual script is the way scenes comment on each other or work in counterpoint, as when the tawdry view of love in 3.1 (the Helen–Paris–Pandarus scene) precedes 3.2 (the first meeting of Troilus and Cressida) or when 2.1/2.3 (the two anti-heroic Thersites–Ajax scenes) bracket 2.2 (the Trojan council with its emphasis upon Honor and chivalric idealism). Nunn's rescripting was strong on clarity and narrative continuity but reduced the ironic or deflationary effects built into the script, not to mention the impact of various verbal–poetic links (e.g., *deed* in 3.1–3.2) so as to raise some provocative questions about the links between narrative sequence and potential meanings.

INSERTIONS

Since a major goal of much rescripting is to streamline playscripts that directors (and some playgoers) deem too long, the insertion of additional material would not appear to be a necessary or even desirable practice. However, directors regularly use a variety of techniques to clarify or enhance their story lines (as with the Cranney and Hands productions of

Merry Wives) or occasionally to enforce a particular effect or interpretation by means of material not in the received text.

Many such insertions or substitutions are not of the earth-shaking variety. Hamlet lectures the players that "those that play your clowns speak no more than is set down for them" (3.2.38–40), but then or now opportunities to gain some short-term effect are hard to resist. In the CSC (New York City) 1986 *The Merchant of Venice*, Launcelot Gobbo in 2.2 factored in a line that named his mother Gretta – so Gretta Gobbo; in the SSC 1984 modern dress *1 Henry IV* at the end of 4.2 Bardolph walked offstage with a walkie-talkie calling "Come in, Camp Peto." Such insertions can be musical. In the RSC 1997 *Hamlet* the gravedigger sang not the scripted "In youth when I did love" (5.1.61–64, 71–74) but "September Song"; in the RSC 2000 *Richard II* Richard appeared in the deposition scene whistling "God Save the King" whereas in the RSC 1987 *Titus Andronicus* the figures setting the banquet table in the final scene entered whistling "Heigh ho, it's off to work we go." In his *As You Like It* (PRC 1983) Greg Boyd began his second act after the intermission with a rock version of sonnet 147 and to heighten (or send up) the love-at-first-sight of Oliver and Celia in 4.3 played Placido Domingo singing "Be My Love." Following theatrical tradition some productions of *Richard III* (e.g., OSF 1978) include in 4.4 Colley Cibber's "Off with his head. So much for Buckingham." Two of the three August 2000 RSC Stratford productions in the Royal Shakespeare Theatre were preceded by a request over the public address system for playgoers to turn off their pagers, watches, and mobile phones, but the third, Lynne Parker's *The Comedy of Errors*, started with a Prologue that, in the spirit of the play's opening scene, delivered a comic threat of execution for any such offender in the audience during the performance.

More substantive is the insertion of figures into scenes where they are not specified in the script, as in the Donmar 1982 *Hamlet* where an ominous Osric was a significant presence starting in 1.2. In one category, a director may bring X onto the stage in a situation where one would expect him or her to be present but no such signal is provided – perhaps owing to casting problems in Shakespeare's company (most commonly in history and Roman plays with a large number of named figures). As noted in chapter 1, in *3 Henry VI*, 1.2 Richard of York's sons persuade him to forgo his pact with the Lancastrians, but the arguments are presented by Edward and Richard with Clarence absent from the scene. Clarence is also absent from 2.1, so that he does not actually appear in the early printed editions until 2.2, probably because in the first performances the role was played by the same actor who had played his father (who last appears in 1.4). Directors regularly introduce Clarence into 1.2 and 2.1 and sometimes make other small adjustments in order to signal who he is.

Comparable is the problem for an editor or director: should Cassius appear in 2.2 as part of the group that escorts Caesar to the Capitol (he is not cited in the stage directions or dialogue of the Folio)? Again, the scholarly explanation for this silence is that the actor in the original productions who played Cassius was needed to play Caius Ligarius and therefore was not available for 2.2 (Ligarius's presence *is* scripted here). But should such a scholarly–historical explanation linked to a theatrical exigency that no longer exists pertain to a production today? Sir Peter Hall (RSC 1995) chose to include both Ligarius *and* Cassius in 2.2 and solved the obvious problem (why would Cassius be present but not mentioned?) by having Caesar greet all the senators named in his welcoming speech but snub Cassius by walking right by him. This choice made sense out of Caesar's failure to include Cassius in his greetings and fit neatly with both Caesar's comments about Cassius and Cassius's resentment of Caesar in 1.2.

Similarly, given sufficient personnel, directors will bring figures on-stage who are mentioned in the dialogue but not included in the surviving stage directions. The best-known instance is the Indian boy who sometimes appears as part of Titania's train in *A Midsummer Night's Dream*, 2.1 and then may be seen being spirited away by Oberon in 4.1. In the Folio the son of Coriolanus appears only in 5.3 as part of the attempt to save Rome where he has his single speech (127–28), but, as in Almeida 2000, playgoers often see him playing silently during the first Volumnia–Virgilia scene (1.3) and as part of the three ladies' triumphant return to Rome (5.5). Many theatre companies find staging the history plays a strain upon their resources (so that Lovell, Vaughan, and the ghosts of Henry VI and Prince Edward regularly disappear from *Richard III*), but I have seen several productions where Jane Shore appeared in one or more scenes, most commonly with Hastings in 3.2, and George Stanley as well. Indeed, Steven Pimlott (RSC 1995–96) listed Jane Shore in his program – she was portrayed as a black prostitute who, while in bed with Hastings, stroked the messenger although she was subsequently ignored by a Catesby who was strictly business. Less common is John Caird's choice in his *Antony and Cleopatra* (RSC 1992–93) to bring onstage Cleopatra's son, Caesarion, at her capture in 5.2 so that, like George Stanley, he could be taken away as a hostage. To our sensibility a Lovell or Vaughan may seem redundant whereas an Indian boy or a Jane

Shore may spark interest – and here Shakespeare's propensity for threes, whether in sub-villains (Ratcliffe, Catesby, and Lovell) or victims (Rivers, Gray, and Vaughan) has been superseded by a desire for economy.

Another figure cited in the script but not brought onstage in the Folio is Isbel, the woman Lavatch wants to marry in *All's That Ends Well*, 1.3. However, Michael Kahn (DC 1988) made Isbel an active part of Lavatch's appeal to the Countess for permission to marry in 1.3; later at court in 2.4 Lavatch made a pass at a court lady so as to explain his change in 3.2 ("I have no mind to Isbel since I was at court" – 12). The various reconciliations in the final scene then included a reuniting of Lavatch and Isbel so that this particular strand was fleshed out or completed. Similarly, directors of *Measure for Measure* sometimes include an onstage Kate Keepdown who, according to Mrs. Overdone (3.2.199–201), bore Lucio's child. In Nagle Jackson's 1972 Milwaukee Repertory Company production after the duke's sentence on Lucio ("thou shalt marry her" – 5.1.518) and the latter's response a huge hooded figure (the largest actor in the company) came racing onto the stage, picked up Lucio, and carried him off.

If a large number of actors is available, as is often the case in SFC productions, a director is under considerably less pressure to economize and indeed may craft additional roles – as in the 1987 OSF *Macbeth* where the presence of additional children added to the effect of the violence against the Macduff family in 4.2 or the 1977 SFC *Richard III* where the Mayor's wife was a highly visible presence in 3.7 when Richard sought support from a large onstage crowd. More actors available means more options. A good example is provided by the death of Macbeth (SFC 1990) where the puzzling Folio signal directs a fight with Macduff, an *exeunt* for the two, an immediate re-entry, and then the killing of Macbeth. To avoid a possible letdown in intensity, director David William chose not to provide elaborate swordplay for both young Siward versus Macbeth and Macduff versus Macbeth, but kept the first encounter very brief and in lieu of the second presented a sudden appearance of the witches below and a group of figures above that included Lady Macbeth, Lady Macduff, her son, Banquo, and one of Banquo's kingly descendants. The final moments of Brian Bedford's Macbeth therefore yielded him a vision of what he had destroyed (his equivalent to his wife's sleepwalking images) so as to heighten forcefully the emphasis upon conscience and guilt. Given the large number of actors involved in the final sequence, however, only the size of the company made such a reprise (and subsequent strong image) possible.

Similarly, in crafting *As You Like It*, Shakespeare, probably thinking in terms of the casting resources available to the Lord Chamberlain's Men, did not bring back Le Beau after his exit in 1.2, despite his suggestive final lines to Orlando ("Hereafter, in a better world than this,/I shall desire more love and knowledge of you" – 284–85), nor did he offer any indication of what happens to old Adam after 2.7. Presumably, the actors playing those parts reappeared in other guises (e.g., as Jaques, Martext, William, Jaques de Boys, or Hymen). With no such casting limitations, Richard Monette (SFC 1990) did bring Le Beau back at the end of 2.7 (and also in 5.4) for a visible reunion with Orlando and, in similar fashion, staged an onstage reunion of Adam with Oliver and Orlando in 5.2 and with all three brothers in 5.4. John Caird (RSC 1989–90) provided comparable moments with his Adam but not with Le Beau, a part taken by the actor who later played Jaques. The high point of Jim Edmondson's OSF 1992 production was the end of 2.7 where not only Orlando but also Le Beau, Charles, Dennis, and others from outside the forest joined the banished duke in an elaborate ceremony reminiscent of Thanksgiving that climaxed with a larger group below bearing lanterns and circling around a log pile and a smaller group circling above, all played off against a solitary seated Jaques.

Another device is to insert a significant event or image not included in the script (as with the additional scenes in *The Merchant of Venice* and *Much Ado About Nothing* cited earlier), a choice common in cinema productions not limited by the practicalities of the stage but less common in the theatre. In *Troilus and Cressida*, 2.2 Cassandra bursts onto the stage to interrupt the Trojan council, but Ian Judge (RSC 1996) kept his Cassandra onstage throughout the scene, initially at the downstage end of the council table with her back to the audience, then standing and mostly ignored by the bored men, and finally, comforted only by Helenus, on the floor upstage huddled against the wall. In his *Measure for Measure* (OSF 1986) Jim Edmondson factored in various figures not scripted in the Folio: the two gentlemen who interact with Lucio in 1.2 accompanied him to seek out Isabella in the convent (1.4) and were present at Pompey's arrest (3.2); Friar Thomas not only consulted with the duke in 1.3 but also was onstage for the duke's dialogues with Juliet (2.3) and Isabella (3.1); and Mrs. Elbow was included in the Elbow–Pompey–Froth confusion of 2.1 and appeared with a baby in the final scene (the sight of a woman holding a baby, whether Mrs. Elbow, Juliet, or Kate Keepdown, is by no means unusual at the end of this play).

Insertions to aid a playgoer confronting an unfamiliar script can take many forms. Early in the run of his *Henry VIII* (OSF 1984) director Jim Edmondson discovered some confusion among his spectators as to exactly who was on trial in 1.2. To clarify the situation he chose to introduce a kneeling and somewhat humbled Buckingham for part of this scene. This director, moreover, cut 5.4, the penultimate scene that involves the Porter, his man, the Lord Chamberlain, and the offstage crowd, a sequence that includes obscure language and difficult jokes. Something is needed at this point, however, to provide time for costume changes for the climactic christening, so Edmondson chose here to recapitulate a sizable portion of the Prologue. At the outset of this production two figures later to be the two choric gentlemen appeared above to share these lines, while below in dumb show the audience watched Buckingham, Wolsey, Katherine, and Anne move about the stage. In the reconstituted 5.4, these four appeared again as "shades" and remained as silent observers of the final scene (Anne's presence, although appropriate to the desired pattern, struck some observers as questionable in that she was still alive). The reintroduction of these four figures as witnesses to the climax of the play added some measure of continuity to an unfamiliar and sometimes puzzling narrative.

Another category of insertions is the placement onstage of acts of violence only implied or reported in the received text, sometimes to emphasize the brutality of a regime. Such moments are already there in various scripts, most notably the blinding of Gloucester in *King Lear* (3.7), but additional actions are regularly factored in. The battle sequence in David Thacker's promenade *Julius Caesar* (RSC TOP 1993) included one woman being pursued and threatened with rape and another wheeling a soldier in a pram. In his *Richard II* (RSC TOP 2000) Steven Pimlott did not interpret Bolingbroke's command to Northumberland "see them dispatch'd" (3.1.35) to mean that Bushy and Green should be taken off the stage and executed. Rather, Bushy got out part of his two-line speech (31–32) before being summarily shot by a pistol-wielding Hotspur, and then Bolingbroke himself shot Green. Similarly, in his *Richard III* (RNT 1990) Richard Eyre did not have Rivers and Grey *exeunt* at the end of 3.3 but had them executed onstage, and Tom Haas (PRC 1979) had the playgoer see Macbeth kill Duncan's two grooms.

A good example is the death of Bardolph in *Henry V*, a telling moment in Kenneth Branagh's film version which shows the hanged body. The script, however, provides only Fluellen's narration, that climaxes with "his nose is executed, and his fire's out," and the king's response:

"We would have all such offenders so cut off" (3.6.105–08). As staged by Terry Hands (RSC 1977–78) the execution took place just offstage and was controlled by Alan Howard's Henry V who gave a clear signal and then reacted in full view of the audience to his decision. Adrian Noble (RSC 1984) took this effect one step further by bringing Bardolph onto the stage, so that, with the audience looking on, Kenneth Branagh's Henry gave the order, Exeter garrotted the kneeling figure, and for the remainder of the scene Bardolph remained fixed in this position in the center of the stage, his hands tied behind his back, occasionally dripping blood from his mouth. The implications of the king's choice (or the suppression of Prince Hal by Henry V) could not have been presented more starkly.

Director Laird Williamson made use of two very different types of inserted material in his *All's Well That Ends Well* (DC 1996). First, a lengthy pre-show sequence started with a seated Lavatch and two children (younger versions of Bertram and Helena) who disappeared to be replaced by their adult counterparts. The end of this sequence in which an amorous Bertram made a move to seduce Helena and she pulled away then set up his displeasure with her in 1.1 and her virginity speech. Moreover, some by-play between Parolles and Lavatch was designed to explain the latter's hostility towards the former. The goal of this wordless prologue or induction was to help playgoers get a better fix on this unfamiliar narrative (my unscientific exit poll suggested that the results were at best mixed).

More controversial was Williamson's treatment of Bertram's final words – in the received text only "Both, both. O, pardon!" – in response to Helena's comment that she is "but the shadow of a wife you see, / The name and not the thing" (5.3.307–08). The director moved the Lafew–Parolles beat that follows this exchange earlier so that Bertram's final statement gained a climactic position before the king's closing speech and then, given the inadequacy or ambiguity many readers have found in Bertram's four words, had the actor deliver sonnet 109 (which starts with "O, never say that I was false of heart" and ends with "For nothing this wide universe I call, / Save thou, my rose, in it thou art my all"). The choice eliminated much ambiguity, greatly diminished the potential hurt of the ending, and in effect transformed the final moments. What many interpreters find to be the most provocative problem in the play – how to deal with the comic resolution – was here solved by an infusion of new material from elsewhere. The result was a decidedly more upbeat interpretation than I have found in other recent productions (this Bertram was clearly repentant) but one that for me lacked theatrical punch.

This kind of bold directorial move, especially in such a climactic moment, may be unusual, but other insertions *are* commonplace. In her production of *3 Henry VI* (RSC TOP 1994) Katie Mitchell added various speeches, most notably at the end of 1.1 where Exeter was given a coda derived from the Bishop of Carlisle's dire prophecy in *Richard II* (4.1.137–44). In his presentation of the two tetralogies of history plays (ESC 1988) Michael Bogdanov cut Henry IV's soliloquy on his "unthrifty son" (*Richard II*, 5.3.1–12) from its Quarto placement and re-inserted it at the end of *Henry IV*, 1.1. Most familiar is the situation in *Richard III*, 1.1. As already noted, this script (the second longest in the canon next to *Hamlet*) is usually pared back, with material not involving the title figure especially vulnerable. Nonetheless, to enhance Richard's role a long line of actors and directors have factored into his famous opening soliloquy material from his comparable soliloquy in *3 Henry VI* (3.2.124–95) and even from his "I am myself alone" speech after the murder of Henry VI (5.6.68–93). Here many facets of the "world" of the play (Clarence's children in 2.2, the three citizens in 2.3, the figures seeking sanctuary in 2.4, the scrivener in 3.6, Stanley/Urswick in 4.5) and some of the rhetoric (e.g., with the three queens in 4.4 or Richmond in Act 5) is deemed dispensable, whereas the prospect of additional rich material for the title figure is highly attractive.

Comparable to such appropriation of material from a previous play in a sequence is the recycling of some distinctive element in the play in question so that X appears both in its "normal" place and elsewhere as well. My one vivid memory of Edward Amor's 1968 University of Wisconsin *Julius Caesar* is that the assassination of Caesar was shown three times: as a prologue before 1.1; in its scripted position in 3.1; and as the final element after the battle, deaths, and reactions. Similarly, Jerry Turner's *Richard II* (OSF 1987) started with some material from Act 5 (Exton's speech in 5.4, some of Richard's prison soliloquy and the beginning of the groom's speech from 5.5), then presented the play in normal order although minus various elements (1.2, 4.1.1–100, 5.2–5.3). What emerged was a revealing collision between a modern director's sense of narrative or patterning (as in our sense of "flashback") and a different (and perhaps inaccessible) sense of patterning in the original wherein events under the second king (Henry IV) echo or recapitulate with differing results events under Richard II – as with the throwing down of gauntlets in 1.1 and 4.1.[3] In particular, the role of York facing a potential rebellion against the reigning king by Bolingbroke, Northumberland, and others in 2.3 as opposed to his comparable situation when confronting Aumerle in

5.2–5.3 can reveal much about the loyalties engendered by the two very different monarchs. This director's distinctive rewrighting set up a highly visible marker in our theatrical vocabulary as an alternative to what is already there implicitly in the original, albeit not seen or not valued if seen.

PRE-SHOWS AND FRAMES

By far the most common type of insertion is typified by Williamson's prologue to *All's Well*, for directors sometimes feel the need to provide additional context for their playgoers in the form of such an induction or dumb show that precedes the first scripted lines of a play. Drawing upon a series of RSC productions, Robert Smallwood calls attention to a recurring phenomenon, "the little directorial dumb-show (and some-times not altogether dumb) that so often begins the evening" wherein a director is "creating a free space for himself before the authorial text comes along to restrict that freedom and to cramp his style."[4] Some of the examples cited "greet one when one enters the theatre, however early one gets there" whereas others "do not begin until the official starting time printed on the theatre ticket, usually after some sort of music cue and short black-out" (80). An example of the former is John Caird's *As You Like It* (RSC 1989–90) where when the doors opened at 7:00 pm to admit playgoers for a 7:30 show "most of the cast were on stage dancing to music of the 1930s" and subsequent actions and interactions ensued so that "the boundaries between playing area and auditorium were being examined and challenged." Smallwood notes that "The whole approach of the production, its basic concept, depended upon the ideas set up in that elaborate silent induction preceding the first line of the text and invit-ing us to wonder, to feel uncertain and confused, about the boundary between auditorium and stage, real world and play world; to consider, in short, the question of where the play begins" (76–77).

As Smallwood goes on to note, the most elaborate pre-show inser-tions that take place after the official starting time are variations on the Christopher Sly material in *The Taming of the Shrew* (see chapter 8). Such additions can be found even when Sly has disappeared completely – as in OSF 1978 where Judd Parkin started with a raucous Punch and Judy show, an accompanying song about a husband and his shrewish wife, and a meeting between Kate and Petruchio punctuated by a blow. Owing to what many perceive as an abrupt beginning, productions of *Measure for Measure* also regularly provide pre-show material. Jerry Turner (OSF

1977) not only set his production in Freud's Vienna but also sought to establish an intense psychological emphasis by means of two-and-a-half minutes of stage business before the first spoken line. After the brief appearance of a nun, the duke descended a staircase, seated himself, and pondered his book of state with Viennese waltzes in the background; when the music turned discordant, he rapped his leg with a riding crop in obvious anguish, at which point the playgoers saw behind him the shadowy figure of a naked woman, hanging by her wrists, being whipped. Ultimately, the duke broke off this vision and, in a shaken voice, called out for Escalus (1.1.1).

Comparable examples are not hard to find. Michael Bogdanov's *1 Henry IV* (ESC 1988) started with the entire cast doing a lively rendition of "The Ballad of Harry Leroy." Michael Kahn's *Henry V* (DC 1995) not only rescripted the opening Chorus to have it spoken by a series of actors but inserted other material as well, most notably Henry V's rejection of Falstaff that concludes *2 Henry IV*. Bill Cain's *The Two Gentlemen of Verona* (OSF 1989) started with a four-minute induction that included singing, dancing, sight gags, and athleticism in which an older and repentant Proteus retold his story in the manner of the Ancient Mariner. Given his choice to set his *All's Well That Ends Well* (OSF 1992) in 1910 Europe, Henry Woronicz changed Lavatch from a fool to a poet who read a Prologue (sonnet 87), spoke the Epilogue in lieu of the king, and served as a silent onstage presence during several key Helena scenes (2.5, 3.2, 5.3). The director also began his show with a formal ball at Rossillion so that almost five minutes elapsed before the first line was spoken; playgoers therefore had ample opportunity to observe Helena's lesser status and her obvious affection for Bertram. Michael Kevin's Etruscan *Julius Caesar* (OSF 1991) started with a soothsayer, his acolytes, and an elaborate ritual sacrifice; the soothsayer subsequently kept appearing at key moments (e.g., during Brutus's soliloquy in 2.1) to supply weapons, wine, even a line of dialogue so as to underscore a supernatural dimension – to the point that individual responsibility or autonomy was undercut. An extended ritual beginning was also provided for Deborah Warner's *Richard II* (RNT Cottlesloe 1995) where, with a kyrie as background music, playgoers saw a priestly figure silently move objects from seven stands and, behind a scrim, the investiture as king of Fiona Shaw's Richard. Helena Kaut-Howson's *King Lear* (Young Vic 1997) began with the Lear actor (Kathryn Hunter) as a patient in a wheelchair pushed in by an attendant in a distinctive cap and green jacket (this figure became the fool), followed by the entire cast split into groups and acting out visions or dreams that involved three women (the daughters) and figures around a tub. Hunter's Lear then re-entered dressed in black for 1.1. The show's final image was the same attendant from the opening moments pushing in an empty wheelchair.

Such pre-show activities have been regular features of productions at the new Globe. Lucy Bailey's 1998 *As You Like It* began with a singer and musicians in the yard presenting a ballad recounting the story of old Rowland de Boys and his sons while mimed action on the stage showed among other things Jaques the scholar happily receiving his books and Oliver lurking malevolently on the side. In his extensive review of the 1998 season, Richard Proudfoot observes: "This invented prologue was symptomatic of general directorial unease about how to get the play started." He adds: "Lengthy horseplay and music preceded the first scene of *The Merchant*; the opening funeral in *The Honest Whore* made up for its lack of ceremony by proceeding under the gaze of characters who are not on in the first scene"; and "In *A Mad World* general turmoil by most of the cast turned into a mimed fight which culminated in Follywit being knocked down by the large actor who would return as the Constable in the final scene." For Proudfoot: "Except in the Dekker play, these inventions took up time that might have been better spent in launching straight into the opening scenes. It was apparently assumed that audiences would take five or ten minutes to stop moving and talking, or to get used to looking at the stage, and that only then could the real show begin."[5]

As suggested in several of these examples, the most elaborate effects result when a director provides both Prologue and Epilogue so as to frame the received text. Such a situation is most often seen in productions of *The Taming of the Shrew*, where the two Christopher Sly scenes found in the Folio are combined with material found in the 1594 Quarto of *The Taming of a Shrew* or with other "new" scenes (as in Bill Alexander's 1992 RSC production). Not only *The Taming of a Shrew* but also several other comedies of the period (*Mucedorus, James IV, Every Man Out of His Humour*) provide such framing, so that a historical precedent of sorts does exist.

To cite two distinctive examples of such framing, in his *Richard II* (RSC TOP 2000) Steven Pimlott had his Richard (Sam West) begin 1.1 just as Bolingbroke later began 4.1 by donning a jacket taken from the back of a chair and a crown from its seat, then locking the doors, at which point the lights came up and he addressed Gaunt with the script's opening lines. These actions were preceded, however, by the unjacketed and uncrowned Richard in semi-darkness delivering the opening section of his prison soliloquy, starting with "I have been studying how I may compare / This prison where I live unto the world" (5.5.1–10), and, from later in the same speech, "But whate'er I be ... With being nothing" (5.5.38–41). More such insertions followed. After the interval (taken after 3.2), the show resumed with Richard and Bolingbroke, again in plain dress without crowns, meeting in mid stage, with the latter delivering some of Richard's lines that build to "Tell thou the lamentable tale of me, / And send the hearers weeping to their beds" (5.1.40–45); to begin the garden scene (3.4) the queen reprised some of the lines from Richard's 5.5 prison speech ("I have been studying ... hammer it out" (5.5.1–5).

The most telling changes and insertions came in the final scene. The king received the series of messages from Northumberland, Willoughby and Ross in unison, Hotspur, and finally Exton with Richard's body; each departed after his speech leaving the king alone onstage except for the Common Man figure seated upstage (his placement for Richard's comparable opening beat before 1.1). The king's speech to Exton extended through lines 43–44 ("With Cain go wander thorough shades of night, / And never show thy head by day nor light") at which point Exton spoke Bolingbroke's lines from 1.3 ("Where e'er I wander, boast of this I can, / Though banish'd, yet a true-born Englishman" – 1.3.308–9) and exited. At this point Henry IV locked the door, took off his jacket placing it on the back of the chair, and took off his crown placing it on the chair so as to cycle back to the show's opening image presented by the previous king (or actor) – and again the Common Man figure was upstage. Henry then sat on the box that contained Richard's body and, as actor, had the option of playing various endings: on Press Night he delivered the first line from the next play ("So shaken as we are, so wan with care"); when I saw the show later in the run he presented again the shorter version of the 5.5 prison soliloquy lines.

The rationale behind such changes and insertions, I was told, was to go beyond the basic story to something bigger, even mythic, involving the larger problems linked to Power (not limited only to the two situations of these two kings). Certainly the insertions heightened a sense of a recurring cycle, so that the body under Henry IV at the close echoed the fate of Woodstock at the outset as reinforced by the onstage grave visible in the early scenes. Moreover, as opposed to Jerry Turner's OSF 1987 production cited earlier that also recycled some of Richard's prison lines, Pimlott did not make substantial cuts in the script. Nonetheless, gone from Henry IV's final speech as scripted in the Quarto (5.6.45–52) was the promise, whether heartfelt or hypocritical, of "a voyage to the Holy Land" so as "To wash this blood off from my guilty hand" (49–50) and "Lords, I protest my soul is full of woe/That blood should sprinkle me to make me grow" (45–46). This latter couplet in particular telescopes together the play's richly developed images of blood, garden, and even manure (as in Carlisle's "The blood of English shall manure the ground" – 4.1.137) so as to provide a climax or pay-off however interpreted. Pimlott got a different pay-off keyed to some highly visible markers of his own devising, so that readers and playgoers must judge the results of the trade-offs for themselves.

A second notable example of framing is supplied by Henry Woronicz's *2 Henry IV* (OSF 1989). At the outset the Ashland audience was confronted with a group of strolling players who arrived with their costumes and properties to join in the final song presented by the pre-show musicians and eased into the first scene. Actors not involved in a given scene then observed their colleagues from the sides of the stage; Henry IV remained on his throne above as a visible presence throughout much of the first half; occasionally, an actor had to be cued by his fellows (e.g., Pistol, onstage to observe Doll's arrest, had to be reminded to leave). The most striking effect in the production then came in the play's final beat after the rejection of Falstaff. The conversation between the Lord Chief Justice and Prince John was moved earlier before Falstaff's final dialogue with Shallow and the others (who were not arrested). Meanwhile Henry V had ascended to the throne above and, dressed in formal robes, was seated, stony-faced and regal, on the throne upon which his father had sat earlier. The last line in the show was from Falstaff: "I shall be sent for soon at night" (5.5.89–90), but a dubious Shallow, Pistol, Bardolph, and the boy trailed off the stage. Falstaff remained, waiting, even though no change was to be seen in Henry V above.

At this point the strolling players concept re-emerged, for the other "actors" (for whom "the play" had ended) slowly gathered up their properties and costumes and departed (with some glances behind at "Falstaff" who remained downstage in the light, waiting). Finally (with music in the background all this time), the actor started to take off his ruff, turned upstage, looked above at the unmoving figure, and began to depart into the darkness (the "wait" was over, Henry V had not sent for him) so that the playgoer was left with the vision of Hal-Henry V stonily seated on his throne above. The show then ended with an enormous burst of sound (as if a huge door had slammed) and darkness – with no visible movement from the king. As played here, Falstaff tried but failed to resist closure, but Henry V ended up out of the world of the play, removed into history or some other realm. The climactic moment in this show was therefore not Henry V's rejection speech but rather this moment of waiting, denial, and continuity. As a playgoer, I missed the sense of "arrest" that seems to me a dominant image in Shakespeare's ending but was much impressed by the many strands that came together here to form a highly potent climax to a difficult script.

RECONCEPTIONS

As seen especially in Pimlott's *Richard II* and Woronicz's *2 Henry IV* some adjustments or insertions, both tiny and highly visible, are designed to advance a directorial agenda or "concept." Sometimes a particular passage if included would jar with what the playgoer is seeing. In his production of *A Midsummer Night's Dream* (OSF 1979) Dennis Bigelow provided a very distinctive Oberon who was malevolent, even diabolic, so that I was not surprised that this figure did *not* say "But we are spirits of another sort" so as to distinguish himself and his followers from Puck's "Damned spirits all" (3.2.388, 382). Similarly, as part of a strategy to make Bertram less objectionable in his production of *All's Well That Ends Well* (OSF 1975) Jon Jory cut his line to Parolles at Helena's entrance: "Here comes my clog" (2.5.53). In an exchange in *As You Like It* Jaques is or appears to be bested by Orlando ("I was seeking for a fool when I met you"; "He is drown'd in the brook; look but in, and you shall see him" – 3.2.285–87), but in SFC 1978 Jaques was played as far shrewder and more knowledgeable than Orlando so that these lines were cut. In Jerry Turner's *2 Henry VI* (OSF 1976) Alexander Iden was portrayed as a buffoon rather than a champion, so that his major speech describing his size and prowess (4.10.45–54) was omitted. Matthew Warchus's 1993 West End *Much Ado About Nothing* provided a Don Pedro who was highly troubled by the falling out with Benedick in 5.1, a weighty interpretation that did not mesh with all the elements in the script, particularly some of the banter. The director therefore darkened the tone of the Claudio–Don Pedro gibes at Benedick in Act 5 and then omitted completely Don Pedro's witty response to Dogberry ("First, . . . thirdly, . . . sixt and lastly, . . . and to conclude . . ." – 5.1.220–23) that obviously did not fit with the prevailing tone as chosen.

As noted in chapter 1, directors such as David Thacker (RSC 1993) regularly make such adjustments to create a more sympathetic Shylock. Comparable rescripting is standard practice to eliminate troubling images and thereby enhance the stature of other key figures. Romeo regularly loses not only some of his "savage-wild" lines (5.3.33–39) but also his scripted mattock and crow of iron, and similar adjustments are often made in the final scene of *Coriolanus* (see chapter 5 for discussions of both situations). As noted earlier, Othello's appearance in 5.1 to cheer on a murder in the dark is almost always cut. With few exceptions (e.g., RNT 1980) directors of *Othello* also omit completely (SFC 1994) or significantly pare down the protagonist's eavesdropping lines as he watches Iago and Cassio supposedly discuss the latter's affair with Desdemona (e.g., "O, I see that nose of yours, but not that dog I shall throw it to" – 4.1.142–43). Both the eavesdropping and the cheering on of a murder ("O brave Iago, honest and just" – 5.1.31) underscore an ugly, shameful, degraded side of Othello, a side that some theatrical professionals would prefer to suppress (Salvini, for one, found the eavesdropping scene "not in accord with Othello's character").[6] How then should a playgoer react to a reading of Oberon, Bertram, Jaques, Shylock, Romeo, Coriolanus, or Othello that requires rescripting to sustain it?

An omission or transposition can set up an interesting effect. In his *Richard III* (OSF 1978) Pat Patton cut six lines (2.1.41–46), starting with Edward IV's "A pleasing cordial," so that Buckingham's oath, in which he asks God to punish him "With hate in those where I expect most love!" (35), was juxtaposed neatly with the entrance of Richard at line 46. For the near violence in *The Tempest*, 2.1 Sam Mendes (RSC 1993) chose to freeze Sebastian and Antonio with their swords poised over Gonzalo and Alonso (this show had many such figures frozen in place) so that Ariel could warn Gonzalo, but to achieve this stage image Sebastian's line ("O, but one word!" – 2.1.296) had to be omitted. More substantive were director Henry Woronicz's adjustments in his 1989 OSF *2 Henry IV* so that Henry IV could die onstage at the end of 4.5. Woronicz cut the king's order after his swoon to "bear me hence / Into some other chamber" (4.4.131–32) and changed the final speech of Act 4 from "But bear me to that chamber, there I'll lie, / In that Jerusalem shall Harry die" (4.5.239–40) to "But leave me in this chamber; here I'll lie; / In this Jerusalem shall Harry die." In this rescripting a strong onstage moment was gained at the cost of an equally strong irony, for in Shakespeare's script at the point when he swooned Henry had been "in Jerusalem" without knowing it and now may or may not reach that place again before he dies.

In his *Richard III* (RSC 1995–96) Steven Pimlott, as is usually the case, made substantial cuts in 4.4 (e.g., chunks of Richard's wooing of Elizabeth, all the messengers before Catesby). More distinctively, in this version Stanley did not exit but stayed on at the end of 4.4 and, in an abbreviated eight-line version of 4.5, said just enough to explain his dilemma and announce Elizabeth's decision to betroth her daughter to Richmond.[7] In his program note Pimlott stated that at Richard's wooing of Elizabeth "she has already promised her daughter to Richmond," a decision confirmed by the continuity of Stanley's presence here and by the queen's exit in which she visibly wiped off Richard's kiss. That her choice had already been made before Richard's wooing, however, is far less clear if 4.5 is a separate scene as scripted and therefore to be understood as taking place at some later time. This bit of rescripting was therefore needed to underscore the director's interpretation.

Rescripting can also aid in developing a psychological through-line. For some years directors have gone to considerable lengths to present a Cressida who is somehow sympathetic rather than treacherous or sluttish (as in many older readings). The most successful rendition in this vein I have seen was Juliet Stevenson's Cressida as directed by Howard Davies (RSC 1985). One of several hurdles in any defense or justification comes in 3.2, the first meeting of the two lovers, particularly the latter part of the scene which can easily be interpreted cynically if Cressida's speech that climaxes with "Stop my mouth" (3.2.117–33) is seen as a calculated ploy to elicit a kiss from a bashful, hesitant lover. To forestall such a reaction Davies did some rescripting earlier in the scene. In the script Pandarus has a prose speech ("She's making her ready" – 30–34), then exits; after five verse lines from Troilus, Pandarus brings in Cressida ("Come, come, what need you blush?" – 40) who is wearing a veil ("Come, draw this curtain, and let's see your picture" – 46–47). The director, however, cut Troilus's five lines; Pandarus started to exit up the onstage staircase only to have Cressida minus the veil come racing down the stairs past him to stand motionless facing Troilus. Here and later Stevenson's playing of impetuosity effectively conveyed a love and commitment that belied any sense of calculation. This particular entrance, a major component of that interpretation, would not have been possible, however, if a seemingly reluctant veiled Cressida had been led in by her uncle.

A special case is provided by the ESC 1988 series of history plays where at least some playgoers saw the seven productions in sequence rather than as discrete items. To enhance the continuity between plays Michael Bogdanov therefore made various adjustments. Some of these changes were very small, as in the Epilogue to *Henry V* where the speaker's reference to events during the reign of Henry VI "which oft our stage hath shown" (13) became "soon our stage will show" accompanied by a look at his watch. More substantive was the rescripting of the final moments in *1 Henry IV* where, after wounding Hotspur in the thigh, Falstaff exited with the body (5.4.129), at which point the action shifted to the fate of Worcester and the ransom of Douglas in 5.5. With Henry IV still onstage, Falstaff re-entered with his claim that he, not Hal, had killed Hotspur, so that the king, overhearing most of this exchange (5.4.138–153), departed no longer believing in his son. A stunned Hal, again estranged from his father, threw down his sword, and Falstaff had the final lines in the production (5.4.162–65), so that the playgoer was prepared for Hal's backsliding in 2.2 of the next play from his apparent triumph at Shrewsbury.

Frequently adjusted or improved is *Timon of Athens*. In his program note (OSF 1978) Jerry Turner described this script as a "work in progress" or "a dramatic incompleted fable," so that it should be viewed "not as something perfect, but as something flawed, experimental, and in process." To economize on characters and add to the narrative flow he therefore inserted 2.1 and the beginning of 2.2 (where the senator decides to dun Timon) before the first banquet (1.2), cut the fool's appearance in 2.2, gave the lines of the strangers of 3.2 to the poet, transposed 4.1 (Timon's first tirade against Athens) and 4.2 (Flavius and the servants), ran together the two Flavius scenes in 4.3 and 5.1, and cut the soldier looking for Timon (5.3).

More significant than such cuts and transpositions was the design, for this was a production keyed to a distinctive set. The first half was placed in an opulent "modern" living room of couches and pillows, beiges and whites, classical statuary and columns, banners, an enormous stone head, and, suspended from the ceiling, a seven-foot ocean liner in an eight-foot case; Timon's guests were costumed so as to associate them with oil and shipping with the "room" reeking of money, power, and superficiality. The high point (and major image) of this show then came in 3.6 (Turner cut 106–21, the return of the flatterers looking for their gowns and jewels) when, after pelting his false friends with water, Timon pursued the three figures around the stage, ripped off their gowns, pulled down banners, smashed a vase, and vented his rage by desecrating the room that symbolized his past existence. At this moment, with the flatterers leaping for the exits and with strange sounds and music in the background, the entire stage turned, revealing to the audience a stark, unprepossessing wooden configuration – in essence, the backside of the set, the unadorned underpinnings of that world they had been viewing for over an hour. Flavius and his fellows then parted at the foot of this new "set" (4.2) and Turner's first act ended with Timon rising out of the darkness above (still in his distinctive white suit) to deliver over the heads of the audience his tirade against Athens (4.1) while stripping off most of his clothes. At the intermission the viewer was left with one world shattered and lost and a new, unknown arena yet to come.

But this striking and very successful effect had a price tag – the almost total undoing of the Alcibiades plot and the loss of any sense of senate or senators or even Athens. Given an elaborate living room as focus, the first senate scene (3.5), a confrontation between Alcibiades and senators basic to the sub-plot, was inconvenient, since Timon's room presumably could not double as a senate chamber. The director therefore redistributed the lines from this scene, turning most of them into dinner conversation during the first banquet where various guests, rather than the senate, argued with Alcibiades. Later, between 3.4 and 3.6, Alcibiades made a brief appearance alone, reacting to a hand-held paper that called for his banishment. Playgoers unfamiliar with the script were unable to follow the reasons for this banishment (since this production displayed no affront to senate or senators). Similarly, no entity equivalent to "the senate" was established in 3.5 to prepare for the second, parallel confrontation between Alcibiades and Athens in the final scene. With "the senate" thus eclipsed in favor of the director or designer's "room," I came away with a cluster of striking images but no sense of an Athens that drove out both Timon and Alcibiades. Nor did Turner's ending make clear to me whether the senators' capitulation and Alcibiades's consent was desirable or empty. Overall, the gains from the modern villa setting and the visible breaking down of Timon's world certainly outweighed any losses, but I felt a bit cheated when the excitement of 3.6 gave way at the end to an undeveloped Alcibiades and some ill-defined senators, a confrontation that had little relevance to earlier scenes and to the situation in Athens that had caused so much suffering.

A final and highly controversial example of rescripting is provided by Michael Boyd's *Measure for Measure* (RSC 1998). This production was replete with striking visual effects that included elaborate brothel and prison scenes along with plentiful images of cruelty and oppression (as when in 3.2 Lucio stepped on Pompey's fingers and pushed him down into a trapdoor) so as to convey a sense of a police state under Angelo. Such onstage images alone cannot explain the strong and varied reactions to this production, a range of responses evident in the disagreement among reviewers. A positive response was provided by Michael Billington who glimpsed in this show a new RSC aesthetic, "one that may be less than textually pure but that draws on other traditions, including opera and cinema, as a key to the plays' eternal problems. Stratford desperately needs a touch of danger, and in Boyd it has found a director who can supply it." Less sanguine were Charles Spencer who opined that this director "seems more intent on drawing attention to himself than the play" and John Peter who concluded that the "changes and cuts in the text" signal "that the director is imposing a private agenda on the play rather than exploring and resolving its difficulties – which is much harder work." The most extensive critique was provided by Alistair Macaulay who started with a series of options for a director (e.g., "Do you try to turn newcomers into connoisseurs? Or to make the connoisseurs feel like newcomers?"), moved to some pejorative descriptions of Boyd's choices, and concluded that this production "is full of incidental effects that can only confuse people coming to the play for the first time; it casts no valuable new light for those who have seen the play before. It puzzles but it does not interest." In striking contrast to Billington, Macaulay went so far as to suggest that Boyd's production "even confirms the long-growing impression that Shakespeare is the millstone around the RSC's neck. For whom does the director direct? And why?"[8]

Those who did not see this show may well wonder: why all the fuss? A major source of the controversy was signaled by the program note: "The text used in this production is edited by Michael Boyd from the Arden edition." My highly unscientific sampling suggested that many playgoers who did not know the received script well were engaged by this show with its many images evocative of East European power struggles, whereas those familiar with the received text were less sanguine. As might be inferred from the program note, script changes were numerous. The meeting of Isabella, Mariana, and Friar Peter in 4.6 (with its context for the women's testimony in 5.1) was omitted, as were the song that begins 4.1, the duke's explanation of why he withholds from Isabella the news of Claudio being spared ("But I will keep her ignorant of her good,/To make her heavenly comforts of despair/When it is least expected" – 4.3.109–11) and numerous lines in 5.1, including the final couplet.

A mere listing of cuts and changes, however, cannot explain the controversy, for what matters most is the nature of such alterations and their overall effect upon the story being told. Put simply, what made this show so distinctive was its beginning and ending. This *Measure* began with the duke slumped in a chair, an empty gin bottle by his side; without speaking a word this figure then fled up a runway through the audience when Escalus and others punched a hole through the upstage door

(Angelo and his followers arrived later). The duke's speeches that constitute much of 1.1 were then heard on a gramophone, a choice that inevitably involved a great deal of rearranging of the text and elimination of dialogue interchanges. Perhaps most important, 1.1 in this version ceased to be a scene in which the duke effected in public a controlled transfer of power but became something decidedly different – and some playgoers had difficulty finding justification for that difference.

The body of the show then, as already noted, provided some powerful images, but the presentation of the central story involving Isabella, Angelo, and the duke was not all that unusual. Rather, the director's distinctive interpretation became visible again in 4.4 (a key building block in this show) where Shakespeare's dialogue in which Escalus and Angelo puzzle over the duke's return was transformed into a scene that displayed Angelo gathering armed supporters around him for a permanent takeover (the duke's announced return had become a threat), followed by the duke's meeting with Varrius and other allies (Angelo's soliloquy that ends 4.4 was repositioned after this abbreviated 4.5).

The events and dilemmas of 5.1 that traditionalists deem the essence of this problematic script were then presented in somewhat abbreviated form and at times were overshadowed by other highly visible images. For example, the duke's speech to Isabella on the celerity of Claudio's death (389–96) was gone as was much material after Isabella's speech in response to Mariana's plea; in contrast, pride of place was given to the emergence from beneath the stage of the many disheveled prisoners (not just Claudio and Barnadine) blinking in the light. The major thrust of the sequence was the display of a coup and counter-coup. For much of this scene armed soldiers loyal to Angelo were lined up behind him and Escalus while a large number of other figures observed the action from the staircase. Those who started the scene on the stairs were joined by Varrius and others (who at the end of 4.5 had exited at the back of the auditorium), many of whom had rifles concealed under their cloaks, so that when Friar Lodowick was revealed to be the duke, the duke's faction got the drop on Angelo's faction. Guns were plentiful in this sequence, including a pistol Lucio held to the duke's head which the duke appropriated to threaten both Lucio and Angelo (and even Friar Peter had a gun).

Without question, the story being told and the images being set forth were strong and timely: a coup had been forestalled; those imprisoned by an oppressive regime had been released into the light of day. Yet what some readers take to be the heart of this script – Isabella's choice to lend a knee to Mariana and plead for the life of Angelo – seemed somehow diminished, less important, to the extent that one veteran playgoer described this *Measure* to me as a very interesting play – by Michael Boyd. The reviews cited earlier frame the issues well. Do this and comparable productions indeed bring into focus "the plays' eternal problems" by introducing a salutary "touch of danger" (Billington) or is this director "imposing a private agenda on the play rather than exploring and resolving its difficulties" (Peter). Wherein lies an appropriate approach to bringing Shakespeare's scripts to the stage in a new century? What if any boundaries do or should exist in the pursuit of innovation and in-the-theatre excitement for the RSC or any other company? Boyd's choices and changes brought such questions into focus more forcefully than any production I have seen in recent years.

The many examples cited in this chapter cover a wide range of situations that in turn generate provocative questions linked to my recurring emphasis upon price tags and trade-offs. At what point does the solving of a perceived problem (as with the Host–horses–Germans in *Merry Wives*) become a radical change (as perhaps with the omission of Malvolio's "memory")? Are insertions that complete a process left uncompleted in the received text a response to new resources that the King's Men would have used if available, so that the practical theatrical response, then or now, should be: if you have it, use it? Or does the working out of various stories unfinished in Folio *As You Like It* reconstitute the play by providing more closure or reaffirmation than is actually warranted? Whose images are to be most prized? As *who* likes it? In the search for meanings and effects that will connect with today's playgoers, which elements in plays such as *Timon of Athens* or *Measure for Measure* are disposable? At what point does the director take over the function of the playwright? Wherein lies the line between adjustment–improvement and adaptation–translation?

4

Inserting an intermission/interval

"the interim's mine"
Hamlet, 5.2.73

Like most playgoers for years I paid little attention to the twin questions of (1) how many intermissions (US) or intervals (UK) a performance should have and (2) where they should be placed. A series of productions in 1989, however, made me conscious of the often tricky choices that a director must make. At the Oregon Shakespeare Festival I saw a strong production of *All My Sons* in which Miller's three acts were presented with only one break and an even stronger *Cyrano* in which Rostand's three scripted breaks for his four acts were reduced to two. At the National Theatre in London I then saw *Speed the Plow* with Mamet's two intervals reduced to one and *Hedda Gabler* with two intervals rather than Ibsen's scripted three. Then at the Pit I saw *The Man of Mode* with Etherege's three acts presented as two.

The rhythms of all five shows were changed, however slightly, by such adjustments, with the most notable consequences in Howard Davies's *Hedda*. If economy of presentation is the goal, the obvious choice in this four-act script would be to have one interval placed after Ibsen's Act 2, but, in order to set up some special effects (e.g., falling snow during a winter night while Hedda and Mrs. Elvsted awaited the return of Lovborg), Davies ran Acts 2 and 3 together, in the process causing confusion for some playgoers about the passage of time. Moreover, Juliet Stevenson's rendition of the burning of the manuscript-child was so powerful (just before the second interval after Ibsen's Act 3) that, despite more special effects at Hedda's death and superb acting by Stevenson, Act 4 was affected. Inevitably, a play scripted for four acts and three spaces will be changed, however subtly, by presentation in three acts with two spaces.

Comparable problems are generated when Shakespeare's scripts are staged in today's theatres. So far as we can tell, throughout most of his career Shakespeare would have seen his plays performed continuously, from start to finish, with no breaks between acts or scenes. Around 1610, however, the fashion changed, so that performances in the public theatres gradually began to follow the practice of the private theatres in having brief pauses, with musical interludes, between the acts.[1] Elizabethan and Jacobean audiences would therefore have been comfortable with either procedure (continuous flow or act pauses) but would have been surprised by the single fifteen-minute break taken for granted by today's playgoer.

The imposition of such a substantial break upon a dramatic strategy predicated upon a continuous flow of action will therefore introduce changes, undercut linkages, and occasionally create a new set of problems. For example, in making such a decision today's director must not only be concerned with where to stop (some kind of climactic moment) but also where to start up again, for the Elizabethan dramatist, who was not thinking in terms of such a decisive stop and start, did not provide that director with a scene that would re-engage an audience once again settling into their seats after a chat and a drink. To pause in *Julius Caesar* after the mob violence in 3.3 (the usual choice) is to gain a powerful climax (in the RSC TOP 1993 promenade production playgoers leaving for the interval had to walk around the body of Cinna the poet) but to weaken the connection between this single death and the more insidious pricking of names by Antony, Octavius, and Lepidus that begins the next scene, 4.1. As with many comparable trade-offs, a significant gain at the end of 3.3 may be offset by the loss of a potentially meaningful juxtaposition in 4.1.

Not all directors choose to impose such a break upon the script, so that veteran playgoers can provide their own lists of shows with no interruption in the action. Barry Kyle's *Doctor Faustus* (RSC Swan 1989) was presented with no interval (running just over two hours) as were Terry Hands's *Arden of Faversham* (RSC TOP 1982), Sir Peter Hall's *The Tempest* (RNT 1988), various productions of *Julius Caesar* (RSC 1987, RSC 1995, RSC 2001) and *Macbeth* (RSC 1988, RNT 1993, RSC 1999–2000, Globe 2001), and even a recent streamlined *All's Well That Ends Well* (PRC 2001). One of the best productions I have ever seen, Trevor Nunn's *Macbeth* (RSC TOP–Young Vic 1976–78), would have lost much of its intensity if Ian McKellen, Judi Dench, Roger Rees, and company had been forced to suspend operations for fifteen minutes. When he started the Oregon Shakespeare Festival in 1935, Angus Bowmer chose to play the scripts straight through in his outdoor theatre, a practice that was maintained until Bowmer's successor as artistic director, Jerry Turner, introduced an intermission into his production of *Richard II* in 1980. Starting in 1981, such breaks became the norm in the outdoor theatre, as had been the case in the indoor Bowmer Theatre from its inception except for the occasional very short script (e.g., *The Comedy of Errors* in 1976).

The problem and the varying solutions are linked to both directorial strategy and playgoer expectations. Like moviegoers, Ashland regulars up through 1981 were conditioned to expect no intermissions and therefore made the necessary adjustments, so that "Broadway Bladder" was not a factor.[2] Rather, given wide aisles and plenty of light in this outdoor theatre, these playgoers found it relatively easy to move about if necessary, as opposed to those in the Bowmer or any other dark indoor auditorium. For over forty years this part of the unspoken contract for this theatre and its audience *did* work. Granted, some shows seemed interminable, but the successful ones (e.g., Pat Patton's 1976 *King Lear* that lasted well over three hours) posed few problems in terms of perceived time (very different, as we all know, from elapsed time). In contrast, I have seen a *Macbeth* (one of Shakespeare's shorter scripts) at Stratford, Ontario with two intermissions – a choice that led to conjectures about the parlous financial state of the theatre's drink concessions.

If at least one break is deemed imperative, what are the options and what implications follow from those options? In some instances, the choice is fairly obvious. In both *The Winter's Tale* and *Pericles* a large amount of story time elapses between Acts 3 and 4, with Time in the former and Gower in the latter available in 4.1 to note the transition – and in the 1989 OSF production the co-directors switched Pericles actors after the intermission. Similarly, in *King John* the beginning of Act 4 takes us from France to England and clearly starts a new phase of the action. *Twelfth Night* breaks without major disruption after 2.5 (Malvolio's letter scene) as does *Richard III* after 3.7 (the conning of the Mayor and citizens), *The Taming of the Shrew* after 3.2 (Kate and Petruchio's departure after their wedding), *Julius Caesar* after 3.3 (the killing of Cinna the poet), and *Coriolanus* after 3.3 (the title figure's banishment and the plebeians' reaction). In these eight plays the standard act divisions can therefore be taken seriously as potential signals. Other plays have busy ensemble scenes mid way in the progression that usually entail much onstage furniture that then can be removed during the break, so that *1 Henry IV* is often divided after the big tavern scene (2.4), *Macbeth* after the banquet scene (3.4), and *As You Like It* after 2.7 (Orlando's encounter with Duke Senior) where again an onstage banquet can be cleared away. With *2 Henry IV* directors usually pause after 3.1, our first view of the title figure, so as to begin and end their first section with key figures who are visibly sick (Northumberland in 1.1, Henry IV in 3.1). *Love's Labor's Lost* usually is broken after 4.3 (the four lords eavesdropping on each other), *Romeo and Juliet* after 3.1 (the deaths of Mercutio and Tybalt), and *Cymbeline* after 3.4 (Imogen taking on the disguise provided by Pisanio).

Even to these standard choices exceptions can be noted. The decision where to break *The Taming of the Shrew* may vary according to how much if any Christopher Sly material is included, so that directors occasionally stop after 3.1 (Bianca and her tutors – PRC 1989, OSF 1991) – and Baltimore's 1996 Centre Stage production had no intermission at all. Choices for *As You Like It* are usually keyed to the running time of the two parts, so that some productions break at the end of 3.2, the first Orlando-Ganymede scene (ACTER Spring 1991, ACTER Fall 2000) or earlier in this same scene (SFC 1983, SFC 1990, PRC 1997) after Orlando has posted his verses and delivered "Run, run, Orlando, carve on every tree / The fair, the chaste, and unexpressive she" (3.2.9–10) – and the RSC 1989–90 production paused after 2.7, restarted with Orlando's speech, then reverted to 3.1. After witnessing a string of North American *Coriolanus* productions that took an interval after 3.3 (sometimes cutting the final lines so as to end with the protagonist's "There is a world elsewhere" – 135), I have more recently seen a series of United Kingdom productions that broke after 4.2 (the encounter between Volumnia and the tribunes after Coriolanus's departure from Rome). With *Richard III* a few directors (ESC 1988, RSC 1995–96) have paused after the downfall of Hastings (3.4), and Bill Alexander (RSC 1984) stopped not after 3.7 or even after 4.1 but manufactured his own distinctive climax, a wordless coronation scene that included a cadaverous Anne and murder victims such as Clarence and Hastings looking on from the side. Antony Sher's Richard slithered in minus the canes he previously had used, was anointed, slid to his throne, and was raised aloft so that his maniacal look of triumph was the closing image for the playgoer.

Such choices have consequences. In *Romeo and Juliet*, Juliet's speech that starts 3.2 ("Gallop apace, you fiery-footed steeds") can lose some of its immediacy and ironic punch if it is separated by fifteen minutes from Tybalt's death and Romeo's banishment. To break the action in *1 Henry IV* with Prince Hal surveying a sleeping Falstaff is to gain a potentially powerful closing image (as in Pat Patton's 1988 OSF production) but also to diminish the contrapuntal effect in which the Hotspur–Glendower relationship (3.1) comments upon Hal–Falstaff and then the Hal–Henry IV confrontation (3.2) comments upon both. The three scenes are scripted as one continuous sequence, but that sequence is blurred if not eclipsed by the break. Peter Holland notes that the usual choice for productions of *Troilus and Cressida*, after 3.2 (the first meeting of the title figures), "both defines the shaping of the play, framing its two movements with Pandarus's two moments of direct audience-address, and mutes the dramatic sharpness of Calchas's entry to demand the exchange of Cressida viciously hard on the heels of the lovers' one night of love" (3). Such a choice can therefore both heighten a sense of patterned movement or structure and blur a contrapuntal effect basic to this script. Directors who break *Macbeth* after the banquet scene usually choose to start up again with the caldron scene (4.1) with the result that the choric but very useful 3.6 (Lennox and another lord) must be omitted, adapted (as in RSC 1982 where Howard Davies started his second part with a chorus crafted from the 3.6 speeches), or repositioned after 4.1 (OSF 1979, OSF 1986) with the inevitable awkwardness that such restitching involves. *As You Like It*, 3.1 (Oliver's brief interview with Duke Frederick) is also not a promising place to begin again after a pause, especially with the remainder of the play then set in Arden, as is also true of *Richard III*, 4.1 (the unsuccessful attempt to visit the princes in the Tower).

As already noted, to insert a break at an appropriate moment is to make possible the introduction of new business before the play proper resumes and also to allow time for the removal of a set or onstage properties. *As You Like It* playgoers retaking their seats regularly see Orlando posting his verses on Arden's trees; in his RSC 1998 *The Merchant of Venice* Gregory Doran placed his interval after 3.1 (the Shylock–Tubal exchange) so that before the action started again Launcelot Gobbo wandered onstage to inspect the three caskets. In his 1988 RNT Cottlesloe production of *The Winter's Tale* Sir Peter Hall paused not after 3.3 (the finding of Perdita) but after 3.2 (the reading of the oracle and Hermione's apparent death) so that the elaborate platform introduced for the trial could be removed. Peter Holland notes that Stephen Pimlott's 1991 RSC *Julius Caesar* broke after 4.1 at which point the stage crew struck the massive set, but "on some nights the interval lasted forty minutes, longer than the second half of the performance which usually ran for only thirty-five minutes" (3).

Here *The Tempest* provides a particularly good example. With few exceptions (e.g., RNT 1988 with no interval; RSC 1993 where Sam Mendes broke after 3.3) directors pause after 2.2 (the first clown scene), a strong theatrical moment. The build to the interval was one of the high points of Lenka Udovicki's Globe 2000 production, for Jasper Britton's Caliban created a huge ending to the first half of the show by involving first Stephano and Trinculo, then the audience in his "'Ban, 'Ban, Ca-Caliban" song and his "Freedom, high-day!" chant. Here the interactive nature of the distinctive Globe venue (even during a rainstorm when I saw the show) created an unusually lively moment in the theatre. Such was also the case in Nicholas Hytner's 1988 RSC production where John Kane's Caliban energized this moment so as to elicit applause and audience delight at the interval. Hytner then used that fifteen-minute space to change the set (so Caliban's "rock" disappeared) and to remove such items as the wood brought in by Caliban at the beginning of 2.2. Then, in a ploy I have come to expect, before the actual start of 3.1 while the playgoers were still retaking their seats, Ferdinand made a series of trips so as to carry logs and drop them in an open trap. Indeed, I have seen one production (Virginia Stage Company, Norfolk 1987) in which at the end of the intermission Ferdinand made long side-to-side stage crosses with obviously heavy burdens of wood but, while he was offstage after each trip, Ariel scampered back in the opposite direction with what looked like the same logs.

To break *The Tempest* here solves one problem (how do you remove from the stage Caliban's "*burthen of wood*" – 2.2.0) and, as noted, allows for some suggestive business with Ferdinand at the beginning of the next scene (far more than the Folio's simple stage direction: "*Enter Ferdinand bearing a log*"). The trade-off, however, is that the potential parallel between the two log-bearing figures, Caliban and Ferdinand, is diminished or gone, as perhaps is the emphasis upon two distinctively different routes to "freedom" (and here Ariel and others must also be factored in, though not – at least in the Folio – as wood-carriers). As with so many other theatrical choices in interpreting Shakespeare, to raise such a question (where should the interval/intermission come in *The Tempest?*) is to call attention to the many options in how we respond to, value, or trust the signals or strategies in the original scripts.

Once a director has decided upon the point to take such a break, some rescripting may follow to heighten the effect. A likely place for an interval in *The Merry Wives of Windsor* is the end of the first buck-basket scene (3.3), usually a high comic moment. In his 1995 RNT production Terry Hands chose this place to pause and then made some small but telling changes. The Folio ends the scene with three speeches from Parson Evans and Dr. Caius venting their anger at the Host – not the most engaging or laugh-provoking feature of this play. Hands therefore omitted 3.3.238–43, so that his first act ended with a big laugh line from Caius ("If there be one or two, I shall make-a the turd" – 236–37), a brief remonstrance from Evans that was drowned in audience laughter, and a two-word speech from Master Ford not found in the script (a contribution from an actor in a previous production) who, seeing the page and having his jealous suspicions aroused yet again, shouts "Falstaff's page!" The combination in rapid-fire succession of Caius's *turd* and Ford's hysterical jealousy yielded a fine comic climax that sent the audience laughing their way into the aisles.

Similarly, although in a different genre, director Jim Edmondson chose to break his *Henry VIII* (OSF 1984) after a major ensemble scene, 2.4, and then adjusted his script to set up a highly distinctive moment for the title figure. First, he moved the "Break up the court!" that concludes the king's (and the scene's) last speech to a position five lines earlier. Henry's lines revealing his new insight into the cardinals and his yearning for Cranmer's return then became not an aside but a soliloquy delivered from the throne shortly after he had revealed himself as a man tortured by the loss of his infant sons. The director further enhanced the effect by inserting here as the final lines before the intermission the closing lines of 2.2: "But conscience, conscience! / O, 'tis a tender place, and I must leave her" (142–43). Henry's invocation of his "conscience," an invocation many interpreters regard with cynicism, was here presented with striking theatrical force in a climax position – something for playgoers to debate during the break.

Many variations can be noted. *A Midsummer Night's Dream* usually breaks after 3.1 with Bottom being led off to Titania's bed but occasionally after 3.2 with the four lovers asleep. As noted earlier, *Romeo and Juliet* normally pauses after Tybalt's death and Romeo's banishment (3.1) but occasionally (RSC 1980, RSC 1995) after the previous scene (2.6) where the title figures are led off to be married. *Henry V* often breaks at the end of Act 3 after a French scene (3.7) so as to start up again with the chorus to Act 4, but Adrian Noble (RSC 1984) broke at 3.6 (that climaxes with Henry's exchange with Montjoy) as did Michael Kahn (DC 1995) whose playgoers left their seats while Bardolph was still visible hanging onstage (Kahn cut 3.7). *Measure for Measure* usually breaks after Act 3 with some version of the duke's soliloquy in tetrameter couplets (3.2.261–82) but sometimes after the duke's dialogue with Isabella that ends 3.1 (OSF 1986) and less commonly at a climactic moment earlier in the scene (3.1.151) after Isabella's angry rejection of Claudio but before the duke intervenes (PRC 1985). *All's Well That Ends Well* usually breaks after Helena's soliloquy in which she chooses to steal away from Rossillion (3.2.99–129), but exceptions include a break after 3.2, the first

Florence scene (DC 1996), and after 3.4, the Countess's lament over Bertram's and Helena's choices (RSC 1992). In his 1992 OSF production Henry Woronicz set up his intermission by restitching speeches from 3.2–3.3–3.4 so as to intersperse lines from Helena, the Countess, and Bertram who were all onstage at the same time.

David Thacker's *Pericles* (RSC Swan–Pit 1989–90) provides a good example of such an adjustment. After Thaisa's awakening Thacker included the lines up through Cerimon's "Hush, my gentle neighbors" (3.2.106) but omitted the final four lines of the scene (107–10) so that the revived figure remained onstage. Cerimon did continue to speak, but the lines were from 3.4 ("Madam, this letter . . ."), so that all of this short scene (3.4.1–18) was spliced onto the end of 3.2 – Thaisa therefore read her husband's letter while seated in her coffin. At this point, with Thaisa and Cerimon still in view, Pericles, Cleon, and Dionyza appeared above accompanied by Lychorida carrying the infant Marina. Pericles then spoke the final lines of 3.3 ("O, no tears, Lychorida, no tears. / Look to your little mistress, on whose grace / You may depend hereafter" – 38–41), and the interval followed. Given this restitching, the playgoer saw the three members of this divided family at the same time at this center point in the narrative.

Where to break *Richard II* is of particular interest, for I have witnessed four different choices. Atypical is the decision to break after 3.1, the execution of Bushy and Green (OSF 1987), or after 3.4, the garden scene (OSF 1980). The usual choices are to pause after either 3.2, Richard's return from Ireland to receive bad news (SFC 1979, ESC 1988, RSC 2000), or after 3.3, Richard's capitulation at Flint Castle (SSC 1986, RNT 1995, Almeida 2000). Each choice has its advantages. During the interval of Deborah Warner's RNT 1995 show, the playgoer saw a seated queen with her beads and prayerbook; Michael Edwards's SSC 1986 production set up a significant climactic image at the intermission when a principled Bolingbroke clearly not angling for the crown stood flummoxed at Richard's caving in at the end of 3.3. In Jonathan Kent's Almeida 2000 production the interval was necessary to set up the garden scene; the huge stage at the Gainsborough Studios was covered throughout with live grass, but the onstage trees starting in 3.4 after the break had no leaves, a distinction important for the scene and the overall concept. As in *1 Henry IV*, however, something inevitably is lost when the obviously symbolic garden scene loses some of its pivotal position placed as it is between analogous events under one king, Richard II, and under his successor, Henry IV (as when the throwing down of gages in 4.1

clearly echoes the Mowbray–Bolingbroke exchange in 1.1). The notion of the kingdom as garden and the king, whatever his name, as gardener is diminished when the flow of action is interrupted.

Also of interest are the choices facing a director of *Much Ado About Nothing*. Most productions break the action after either 2.3 or 3.1. The former choice sets up a climax at what is often the funniest moment in the show, Benedick's reaction to the news of Beatrice's supposed love for him ("No, the world must be peopled" – 242) and his subsequent encounter with her ("I do spy some marks of love in her" – 245–46). The latter choice sets up the obvious parallel in consecutive scenes when Beatrice, like Benedick moments earlier, believes what she hears and reacts accordingly. Also, a break after 3.1 allows for business during the interval – as in the 1981 Regents Park production where the playgoer witnessed a variety of actions that included Benedick, the scoffer now turned lover, being dressed and shaved. In my playgoing experience, however, the parallel between 2.3 and 3.1 has sometimes turned into a liability, for some directors feel the need to find comic business (e.g., Beatrice falling into a pool of water) to equal or top the previous scene. Although Benedick's scripted reactions in 2.3 to what he hears are indeed very funny, the Quarto provides nothing comparable for Beatrice during the Hero–Ursula exchange; moreover, her coda that concludes the scene (3.1.107–16) is in verse, not Benedick's prose, and is very different in tone and effect, a difference that can be displayed powerfully but can also be blurred or diminished in an attempt to match Benedick in 2.3.

My first memory of a third option is Matthew Warchus's 1993 West End production. By placing the interval after 3.2 rather than after 2.3 or 3.1 (the usual choices), this director in effect called attention to a series of three rather than two cons: that of Benedick by the three men in 2.3, Beatrice by the two women in 3.1, and Claudio–Don Pedro by Don John in 3.2. A few years later in his 1998 Cheek by Jowl production Declan Donnelan also broke the action at this point and, moreover, included a view of the false Hero on a side balcony to reinforce Don John's story. The story line remains the same regardless of when an interval is taken, but, as with *1 Henry IV*, each choice creates a different emphasis, none of which corresponds exactly to the through line scripted in the Quarto.

In such situations the choice of when to pause can reveal something distinctive about the director's interpretation. Should *The Merchant of Venice* be broken after the Shylock–Tubal exchange (3.1) as in Bill Alexander's 1987 RSC production or after the third casket scene (3.2) as in Sir Peter Hall's 1989 West End rendition? Will Shylock or Portia–Bassanio be

granted that climactic position? In *Antony and Cleopatra* at what point in
Antony's tortuous journey (before Actium? after 3.13?) will the production pause? In his OSF 1993 production Charles Towers broke at the end
of Act 3 with Enobarbus's decision to leave Antony and then began his
second part with a reprise of this speech (3.13.194–200). At the Globe in
1999 Giles Block, in deference to the many standees, had two intervals,
with the first after the galley scene (2.7), a choice that allowed the stage to
be cleared of the furniture for the banquet, and the second after Act 3,
whereas Steven Pimlott (RSC 1999) broke after 3.11 (the post-Actium
reconciliation of the title figures). John Caird (RSC 1992–93) took his
interval in the middle of 3.6 as Caesar delivered his account of events in
Egypt while upstage Antony, Cleopatra, and others were seen enthroned
in gold; the final image of the production, again set up by a Caesar speech
delivered downstage, was then a comparable image of the two figures
in death. Similarly, Sir Peter Hall (RNT 1987) broke at the end of 3.6
so as to start up again with 3.7, Antony's choice to fight at sea. This
placement was important for our understanding of Tim Piggott-Smith's
Octavius portrayed in the first half as a caring, duty-bound figure who
hero-worshipped Antony and loved his sister but in the second half as a
brother seeking revenge for the ill treatment of Octavia as revealed in 3.6.

Many of the tragedies pose distinctive problems, so that the choice of
where to pause has much to do with the director's sense of the rhythm
or dynamics of the whole. *Othello* is the least problematic of the major
tragedies with most productions breaking at the end of the temptation
scene with Othello's "Now art thou my lieutenant" and Iago's response:
"I am your own forever" (3.3.479–80). Even here exceptions can be
noted: SFC 1979 with its two intervals after 2.3 and late in 4.2 (so that
the third part began with the Roderigo–Iago exchange that starts at
line 172), and several productions that broke mid way in 3.3 with the
handkerchief lying on the stage floor (RSC Aldwych 1980, RSC TOP
1989, RNT Cottlesloe 1997). At the Aldwych in 1980 Ronald Eyre had his
Emilia staring at the handkerchief as the lights went down; at The Other
Place in 1989 Trevor Nunn chose to start up again after the interval with
a seated Emilia in a quiet moment, smoking a pipe. In Nunn's show,
taking a break mid way in 3.3 provided an opportunity for an attendant
during the interim to pick up the handkerchief (which had fallen on the
floor) and reposition it so that Emilia would readily find it.

Such a placement of the interval will please many devotees of psychological realism who as readers of this script wonder at Othello's rapid
descent into the madness of jealousy during the course of one long scene

(for, even though the handkerchief provided some continuity, the play-goer at The Other Place, given such an interval, had more sense of elapsed time). But something very distinctive in Shakespeare's presentation of Othello's progression or descent is blurred or lost through this choice. To be fair, Nunn's decision was in keeping with this intense, intimate, naturalistic production (most notably Ian McKellen's contained, tightly focused Iago), but here as elsewhere in this show (e.g., 4.1, 5.1) some of Shakespeare's symbolic or imagistic emphases were changed or transmuted.

Typically *Hamlet*, the longest script in the canon, provides the most variations. If a director deems two breaks necessary, the first will likely come after Hamlet's "rogue and peasant slave" soliloquy that ends Act 2 (RSC 1980, Globe 2000) and the second after either 4.3 (Hamlet's confrontation with Claudius) or 4.4 (the first appearance of Fortinbras). A single pause may be placed after Act 2 (SFC 1994), after the nunnery scene (3.1 – RSC 1989, RSC 1997), after Hamlet's "hot blood" soliloquy (3.2 – Donmar 1982, RSC 1984, PRC 1993), after 4.3 (RNT 1989, ACTER Fall 1993) or even as late as 4.4 (Sir Peter Hall Company 1994). As reported to me the interval in SFC 2000 was taken mid way in 3.3 so as to leave the question hanging: will or will not Hamlet kill Claudius in prayer?

Of interest are two 1989 *Hamlet*s. In his RNT rendition (with Daniel Day-Lewis as Hamlet) Richard Eyre used a very full script up through the interval (he did opt for much streamlining thereafter) which was placed after 4.3, 2:25 into the show (the running time of many a complete performance of another script). A more common choice was to be found in the RSC version (with Mark Rylance as Hamlet) where Ron Daniels (who cut approximately 900 lines) broke the action after 3.1 so as to start up again with an ingeniously conceived advice to the players (Rylance played a high-handed director frustrated at his inability to get Lucianus to perform properly the new lines just given him). Wherever one breaks the *Hamlet* (or *1 Henry IV*, *Merchant*, or *Antony*) narrative, something is lost, for each scene feeds upon the previous one, with no "natural" pauses (until perhaps the end of 4.4). Indeed, the act divisions themselves as designated in modern editions can be very misleading given the obvious continuity between the closet scene, 3.4 (where Gertrude does not leave the stage), and 4.1, her exchange with Claudius.

King Lear often is broken after 3.7, the blinding of Gloucester (RSC 1982, RNT 1987, RSC 1990, RSC 1993, Old Vic 1997), a choice that can yield some striking effects harkening back to Peter Brook's landmark

1962 production. Especially if the Quarto's coda with the two servants is omitted (as with Brook), a helpless, bewildered Gloucester can stagger off the stage while the house lights are going up. The Spring 1989 ACTER five-actor production used the Folio script where 3.7 *does* end without the positive words from the two servants. With no attendants available to help him, a whimpering Gloucester crawled off the stage in full light as a climax to what was one of the strongest scenes in this show. Given this break after 3.7, however, the counterpoint with the beginning of 4.1 is changed, so that Edgar's speech (4.1.1–9) no longer serves as a bridge between our two views of the blinded Gloucester, and, as in Nunn's *Othello*, the playgoer gets more sense of elapsed time between the blinding and the reappearance of the helpless figure.

An alternative choice is to break *King Lear* after 3.6, the mock tribunal scene (DC 1991, RNT Cottlesloe 1997). Deborah Warner's first choice (RNT 1990) would have been to take the interval after 3.7, but the length of the show up through the end of 3.6 precluded that option, so she provided a telling climax to her first part that highlighted Lear's neglect or blindness. Brian Cox's Lear and David Bradley's fool were much afflicted with wind and rain, but when Kent arrived in 3.2 to offer some limited help (a garment, some brandy from a flask) the fool was gradually shunted aside (so he reached for but never got any of the brandy) and was then increasingly eclipsed by Poor Tom in 3.4 and 3.6. By the latter scene, the fool was visibly weakening (though only the audience was aware of it), for his few quips were labored and, when it became necessary to cart Lear away, the fool was unceremoniously dumped out of his resting place onto the stage floor. Barely able to raise his head, he delivered his final line but was then left behind by the exiting group, was discovered to be dead by Edgar (who covered him), and remained onstage as the playgoers departed for the interval. By taking the break here with the death of this increasingly eclipsed fool, the first half of the show was given a focus and shape visibly linked to what Lear had lost or destroyed.

This account would not be complete without some attention to choices at the new Globe in London. Theatre historians had hoped that at least some productions would approximate the original playing conditions and therefore not be broken at all, but given the combination of (1) a significant number of standees or "groundlings" and (2) running times of three hours or more such has not been the case (with the exception of Tim Carroll's rescripted and modernized *Macbeth* in 2001). Starting with the 1997 season directors have experimented with alternatives to the single fifteen to twenty-minute break, but the one interval approach appears to

have prevailed: in *A Chaste Maid in Cheapside* (1997) after the christening
scene (3.2); in *A Mad World My Masters* (1998) after the courtesan's faking
sickness (3.2); in *The Honest Whore* (1998) after the abbreviated Part I; in
The Comedy of Errors (1999) after Act 3; in *The Tempest* (2000) after 2.2; in
The Two Noble Kinsmen (2000) after the morris dance (3.5); in *King Lear*
(2001) after the blinding of Gloucester (3.7); and in *Cymbeline* (2001) after
3.4 (Pisanio giving Imogen her disguise).

Choices varied considerably in 1997, the Globe's first full season.
Malcolm McKay's decision to pause after the raucous ensemble christening scene (3.2) in *A Chaste Maid in Cheapside* not only provided a high
comic climax but also enabled the actor who is to play Sir Oliver Kix in
3.3 to take the part of one of the gossips in 3.2. In *The Winter's Tale* David
Freeman provided a ten-minute interval after 4.1 (an unusual placement)
and a second five-minute break after the long 4.4 before the return to
Leontes and Sicilia in Act 5. According to the program, Lucy Bailey's
The Maid's Tragedy was designed for brief four-minute intervals after each
act, but the break after Act 1 was longer owing to the need to clear
away from both the stage and the yard the set for the elaborate masque.
Richard Olivier may have varied his practice for *Henry V*, but when I saw
the show there was a five-minute break after Act 2, ten minutes after Act
3, and five minutes after Act 4. Olivier also provided a shorter and a
longer pause in his 1998 *The Merchant of Venice* (the first after Act 1, the
second after Act 2). Other comparable choices were found in *As You Like
It* (1998) with a longer break after Act 2 and a shorter one after Act 3;
Julius Caesar (1999) with five-minute pauses after each of the first four acts;
Antony and Cleopatra (1999) with a ten-minute break after Act 2 and a five-
minute break after Act 3; and *Hamlet* (2000) with a fifteen-minute break
after Act 2 and a ten-minute break after the first Fortinbras scene (4.4).

Since I have worked closely with the performance history of *Titus
Andronicus*, let me conclude this account of problems and choices with
reference to that script (and here atypically I will draw upon some productions I did not see). A few productions of *Titus* have been played with
no break (OSF 1974, New Jersey Shakespeare Festival 1977 and 1989,
RSC 1981), but, given the expectations of today's audiences, most directors will introduce an interval/intermission after either 3.1 (so that the
closure of Part I comes with the ritual involving hand and heads and
with Lucius's soliloquy) or 3.2 (so that the closure comes after Titus's
attack upon the fly). If the break comes after 3.1, the director will usually make some adjustments so as to smooth over a potentially awkward
transition, for in the Folio at the end of 3.2 Titus leaves the stage with

young Lucius who at the outset of 4.1 enters pursued by Lavinia. As part of the streamlining in his landmark 1955 production, Peter Brook cut the last two speeches of 3.2 (lines 79–85) and the first 29 lines of 4.1, so that Laurence Olivier's Titus moved directly from his gloating over his ability to kill the fly to his question: "How now, Lavinia? Marcus, what means this? / Some book there is that she desires to see" (4.1.30–31). In his 1986 OSF rendition, Pat Patton made fewer cuts but did rearrange some lines from the end of 3.2 and the beginning of 4.1 so as to have Titus start to exit, then sit on the stairs with young Lucius, who is then frightened by Lavinia.

The transition between 3.1 and 3.2 has also been managed in a variety of ways. In John Barton's abbreviated ninety-minute rendition (RSC 1981) with no interval, after Titus put the severed hand in Lavinia's mouth, he and Marcus (carrying the heads) exited with her in a Dance of Death effect with Lavinia leading the way and Titus behind her with his hand on her shoulder (young Lucius was also involved in this procession). The four figures did a half circle and were briefly out of sight behind a screen (so as to drop the heads and hand) during Lucius's speech, then immediately returned for 3.2. Similarly, Deborah Warner (RSC Swan 1987) had her three figures with heads and hand move upstage, put down their objects, stay silent with their backs to the playgoers during Lucius's speech, then turn and return to begin 3.2. To quiet the spectators and bring them back into the mood or flow of the show (no easy matter after the intensity of 3.1–3.2), Warner had her Titus (Brian Cox) in deep concentration start to trudge from side to side upstage while the lights were still up during the interval (which came after 3.2), gradually covering the terrain and moving closer to an audience that, in his self-contained deliberation, he did not acknowledge.

The need for an interval/intermission, along with a potential problem in the transition between 3.2 and 4.1, has therefore led to a series of adjustments. Of the various issues at stake here, perhaps the most interesting is the question of elapsed time. One assumes that when Marcus brings the maimed and ravished Lavinia to Titus in 3.1 that there has been no significant lapse in time between this moment and the end of 2.4, so that Lavinia here is usually presented as we saw her in 2.4. But how much time should be felt to elapse between 3.1 and 3.2 or between 3.2 and 4.1? In such spaces, do the characters (or actors) have an opportunity to wipe off the blood, change to other garments/costumes, and come to terms with some of their woes, or are we meant to feel a thrusting forward of events with no respite? To cite two extremes, in

Jane Howell's version for BBC-TV's "The Shakespeare Plays" Lavinia remained the same bloodied figure from 2.4 through 4.1, so that the viewer got the impression of a continuous, headlong action. In contrast, Mark Rucker and his actors (SSC 1988), keying their sense of elapsed time to Tamora's bearing a child in 4.2 that Saturninus would accept as his own, felt the need for a significant gap between 3.1 and 3.2, so that after the intermission (placed after 3.1) Titus and particularly Lavinia appeared in fresh costumes with bound, unbloodied limbs.

Such choices present to the spectator very different senses of the amount of time taken by Lavinia (and Marcus) to find a way to communicate what has happened and, equally important, the amount of time Titus has been brooding over his wrongs. The Quarto, which lacks 3.2, shows no signs of any space between 3.1 and 4.1; the Folio, where 3.2 first appears, does have an act break between 3.2 and 4.1, but neither Quarto nor Folio would support the kind of decisive punctuation signaled by a fifteen-minute interval. Warner's choice to have a visible pacing Titus was ingenious and, given the intimacy of the Swan, highly effective, but whether in terms of theatrical rhythms or an audience's sense of elapsed time a later playgoing convention has subtly impinged upon the original strategy or effect. Indeed, the more powerful the rendition of 3.1 and 3.2, the more significant (and potentially damaging) is this break in the flow.

Clearly, the interval/intermission issue is linked to a much larger set of recurring problems that arise from the obvious fact that Shakespeare was targeting his scripts not at us but at theatres, players, and playgoers that no longer exist. As a result, all interpretations, especially theatrical interpretations, are acts of translation into our (often unacknowledged) idiom, an idiom that with few exceptions includes the fifteen-minute break somewhere after the midpoint of the action. Given such a theatrical practice (often perceived as a necessity, not an option), ingenious directors will seek ways to use that pause to their advantage and to minimize the side effects, as with the problems that arise when starting up again (hence Warner's choice to have Cox's Titus pace the stage). Meanwhile, only the rare scholarly voice will lament the loss of the original continuity or counterpoint, although that *rara avis* can take comfort from the in-the-theatre example of Angus Bowmer, one of the pioneers and unsung heroes of American Shakespeare.

What's in an ending? Rescripting final scenes

"The end crowns all"
Troilus and Cressida, 4.5.224

For a variety of reasons theatrical professionals continue to be unsatisfied with the closing moments of Shakespeare's plays as scripted in the Folio and the Quartos, so that a playgoer is especially likely to encounter some form of rescripting in Act 5. Many of these cuts and changes go unremarked by reviewers and playgoers; some adjustments have been readily accepted, even welcomed (for example, omitting Fortinbras so as to end *Hamlet* with the death of the protagonist – as in the Olivier movie and RSC 1997); a few, such as Nahum Tate's happy ending to *King Lear*, call attention to themselves like a blinking neon sign.

Often these rescriptings result from the same pressures or rationales described elsewhere in this book. For example, some changes are mandated by the exigencies of a given production. In his tour de force *The Comedy of Errors* (SSC 1988) Danny Scheie used doors, windows, and other tricks of the trade to enable one actor to play both Antipholus twins, a second to play both Dromios, and a third (at 6′4″ and 240 pounds) to play Solinus and a very hefty courtesan. One casualty of this approach, however, was the final ten lines, for, after leaping over a series of seemingly impossible hurdles in high comic fashion, Scheie opted not to attempt the final Dromio–Dromio beat (5.1.415–26) where the two figures elect to depart "hand in hand, not one before another." A familiar and often highly effective interaction and *exeunt* was therefore sacrificed in favor of the overall concept – a trade-off that, in this instance, only a Malvolio among purists would question.

Some directors tinker with an ending to enhance a sense of patterning. As noted in chapter 4, in his *Antony and Cleopatra* (RSC 1992–93) John Caird crafted a final image of the two title figures enthroned in death that echoed what the playgoers had seen just before the interval in the middle of 3.6 when Caesar delivered his account of events in Egypt. Similarly, in his *1 Henry IV* (OSF 1988) Pat Patton set up a suggestive analogue in his final scene by means of a transposition. Like most directors, Patton placed his intermission after the big tavern scene (2.4); moreover, as a final image before this break he had his Prince Hal stand over, touch, and show his affection for the sleeping Falstaff. At the close of the play, Patton then had Hal deliver only the second half of his soliloquy over the dead Hotspur in 5.4 so as to save the first half of this speech for the very end of the show. Thanks to this transposition, the last thing the playgoer saw before the curtain call was Hal for a second time standing over and expressing his appreciation for a prostrate figure, this time Hotspur. In his *Hamlet* (RSC 2001) Steven Pimlott also provided an italicized link by first having a large number of smiling sycophantic courtiers applaud Claudius as their king at the outset of 1.2 and then having the same group in the same fashion applaud Fortinbras at the end of 5.2. To sustain this analogy required some rescripting: Fortinbras entered without any soldiers (so that no bodies were carried off); both Osric and Horatio exited before the final speech; and Horatio's last speech (5.2.391–95) was cut.

Other images or configurations in the received text can also be adjusted to gain a desired effect. In some instances the period before and even after the curtain call can be used for a contribution from the show's clown. In Gregory Doran's *The Merchant of Venice* (RSC 1998) Launcelot Gobbo lingered after the curtain call to pick up golden coins that had been scattered during the trial scene and had remained in view during Act 5. Similarly, in Sandy McCallum's *The Taming of the Shrew* (OSF 1991) Christopher Sly slept through the curtain call only to awake and wander blearily around the stage as the playgoers left the theatre. Directors of *Twelfth Night* often attach stage business to the final song (for example, a departure of Feste and sometimes others from Olivia's house), and at his curtain call Richard Monette (SFC 1994) had Viola shed her Cesario disguise and reappear in a white wedding dress.

Such adjustments to gain a climactic image are not limited to the comedies. The final moments of Bill Alexander's *Cymbeline* (RSC TOP–Pit 1987–88) included not only the re-united royal family but also the white-clad mother and father of Posthumus. In Will Huddleston's *1 Henry VI* (OSF 1975) the fiends who deny Joan's pleas in 5.3 were seen earlier thinly disguised as her servants or torturers; at the end of the show at Suffolk's exit, with midnight tolling in the background, they made a final appearance above to snarl at the audience. Productions of *Macbeth* regularly provide additional figures in the final moments, usually another vision of the witches (as in OSF 1979 and RNT 1993) and less commonly other figures: Gregory Doran (RSC 1999–2000) had as his final image Malcolm and his followers flanked by Fleance and Banquo; David William (SFC 1990) brought onstage not only the witches below but also Lady Macbeth, Lady Macduff, her son, Banquo, and one of Banquo's kingly descendants above. One of the most unusual final speeches in the canon is found in *Troilus and Cressida*, but Trevor Nunn (RNT 1999) crafted a new Epilogue that included not only the scripted speech from Pandarus but also a pastiche of interspersed lines from Troilus (the final couplet of 5.3 and the couplet that precedes the Epilogue – 5.3.111–12, 5.10.33–34), Cressida (her "poor our sex" final lines – 5.2.109–12), and Thersites (on "the Neapolitan bone-ache" and "the dry suppeago" – 2.3.17–20, 74–75). Pandarus still had the final words, but the climactic image for the playgoer, after Thersites had deposited the glove retrieved from Troilus in 5.2, was Cressida alone in the darkness with a hard-to-read expression on her face.

Often final scene changes are designed to change or reinforce a particular sense of an ending. Such alterations are widespread and are to be found in comedies, histories, tragedies, and romances. In the comedies, a director may wish to heighten the "feel-good" appeal of the final moments. Paring back the gibes at "Pyramus and Thisby" in *A Midsummer Night's Dream* can eliminate some obscure puns (e.g., Demetrius and Lysander's *die-ace* exchange – 5.1.307–09) but can also soften considerably the extended attack on Moon (238–61) as in RSC 1999 so as to lighten the tone of the sequence and preserve a more favorable impression of the courtiers. In his *Merry Wives of Windsor* (RNT 1995) Terry Hands made many cuts and adjustments to enhance his comic effects and to streamline what can be an unwieldy script, so that roughly two-thirds of the first thirty-five lines of 1.1 were gone and, as noted in chapter 3, all of the abortive plot against the Host involving Germans and horses was crowded into one scene. To add to the upbeat feeling of the finale some of the gibes directed at Falstaff were cut, and one speech found in the Quarto but not in the Folio was factored in. As a result, in this production some of the build to Ford's "Over and above that you have suffer'd, I think to repay that money will be a biting affliction" (5.5.168–69) was omitted, and that speech was followed not by Page's "Yet be cheerful, knight" but by Mistress Ford's Quarto speech: "Nay husband let that go to make amends, / Forgive that sum, and so we'll all be friends" (G3v).[1] This Falstaff was not as thoroughly chastised by his Windsor tormentors and then did not have to repay the twenty pounds, an omission and insertion that enhanced the affirmative tone.

A far more extensive reconception of a scripted ending was provided by Bill Cain in his Victorian music hall *Twelfth Night* (OSF 1988). Most of the darker tinges were gone from this crowd-pleasing show; rather, Feste and Sir Toby epitomized good cheer and festival, to the extent of leading the audience at the outset in a sing-along version of "O Mistress Mine." In contrast, a killjoy Malvolio broke off this festive singing and later, to stop the revelry in 2.3, destroyed an onstage piano. This director, moreover, resolved "the Fabian problem" (why does this figure suddenly appear as one of the eavesdroppers in 2.5?) by eliminating Fabian as an independent entity and giving his lines to Feste.

In the final sequence, Cain then made some distinctive choices. Toby appeared in 5.1 with no visible wound or blood – and the Dick Surgeon passage (197–201) was gone. Having no Fabian to deliver the reconciliation speech to Olivia (355–68), Cain had Maria deliver the opening lines ("Good madam, hear me speak") and then had Feste/Fabian pick up with "Maria writ / The letter." This Feste/Fabian, moreover, did not imitate Malvolio's voice in his reading of the letter and then at Olivia's request did read it properly (so the same actor did both the Feste and Fabian readings). After his "whirligig of time" speech (370–77), Feste/Fabian extended his hand in a gesture of peace to a Malvolio who paused noticeably before delivering his "I'll be reveng'd on the whole pack of you" (378). With the two figures telescoped into one, any distinction in the Folio script between Feste-revenge and Fabian-reconciliation was therefore gone.

During the final song, the audience saw a priest blessing three couples (Toby and Maria were also kneeling onstage) with rice being thrown from above by Andrew and Antonio. Feste moved to stage right for the latter part of his song, with the onstage group singing the last verse in unison, so that the whole moment was prettified, with the actual words being sung about swaggering, wiving, and drinking now irrelevant. At the curtain call, moreover, the audience was encouraged to join in the final singing of "O Mistress Mine" (the words were scrolled down from above behind the actors), and Malvolio was pushed forward from the semi-circle of actors to join in. One had to be a killjoy playgoer (or someone who liked the mixed tone of the Folio version) not to participate in the singing and sense of holiday. Here and elsewhere, the effect was musical and upbeat, with few if any shadings (although in 1.2 Viola *had* twice been threatened with rape by the sailors). To get that warm and fuzzy effect, however, Cain chose not to dig into the original script but rather opted to eliminate any elements that did not fit neatly into his interpretation and to manufacture a Feste/Fabian figure that blurred various distinctions present in the Folio.

Most final scene changes are not this drastic. In her *Twelfth Night* (SSC 1986), Marcia Taylor sent off her Cesario just after the climactic meeting with Sebastian to have him/her return as Viola before the final Malvolio sequence, a change that necessitated some rewriting of Orsino's final speech. This rescripting both provided the spectator with a striking image only anticipated in the script and changed the dynamics of the final moments. Similarly, few directors of *As You Like It* can resist making minor changes in Rosalind's epilogue, a speech that only makes full sense if delivered by a boy actor, especially "If I were a woman" (Epilogue. 18), but Anne-Denise Ford (OSF 1986) tinkered elsewhere as well. For example, the second son of old Sir Roland who delivers the news of the bad duke's conversion was replaced by Le Beau; Hymen became a bumbling Corin who forgot his lines. Then, after an early exit by Rosalind and Orlando, the final moments were devoted to a display of dancing couples, with a long lingering view of Celia and Oliver – to the point that some members of the audience, perceiving what they took to be signals for closure, started to applaud. But Rosalind then appeared, with Orlando in the background, wearing his trousers – so that presumably the point was being made that this marriage had already been consummated – perhaps the logical and emotional consequence to Orlando's "I can live no longer by thinking" (5.2.50).

Such choices inevitably bring with them consequences both obvious and subtle. At the point when Malvolio learns about the two nearly identical handwritings, the audience at Santa Cruz did not have before them two nearly identical twins, so no such analogy was readily available. In the Folio, moreover, the appearance of Viola "in other habits" as "Orsino's mistress, and his fancy's queen" is dependent upon retrieving her "maid's garments" from the captain "in durance, at Malvolio's suit" (5.1.274–77, 381–88). After the steward's revengeful exit, Shakespeare has Orsino add: "Pursue him, and entreat him to a peace; / He hath not told us of the captain yet," thereby reminding us that the Orsino–Viola union is, to some extent, contingent upon the good will of Malvolio. To display Viola in those maid's garments is then to diminish greatly the impact of this disgruntled steward upon the ending and to soften and perhaps oversimplify the final effect.

As with Viola's maid's garments or Rosalind's trousers, directors regularly craft their own images in the tragedies and histories to gain a desired effect. A good example is the penultimate scene of *2 Henry IV*, a moment that has received little attention from critics and is sometimes cut in performance. Here one or more beadles drag onstage Doll Tearsheet and Mistress Quickly, with the accusations against Doll that "There hath been a man or two kill'd about her" and "the man is dead that you and Pistol beat amongst you" (5.4.6, 16–17). Though Doll rages and the Hostess invokes the name and supposed influence of Falstaff, these two figures are arrested, as we are reminded in the next scene (5.5.31–39). Of special interest here is the claim from an apparently pregnant Doll: "and the child I go with do miscarry, thou wert better thou hadst strook thy mother, thou paper-fac'd villain" and the beadle's response: "If it do, you shall have a dozen of cushions again; you have but eleven now" (5.4.8–10, 14–15). The "child," it appears, is only a cushion, another Falstaff-like trick comparable to those used against the Lord Chief Justice, Prince Hal, Justice Shallow, or Mistress Quickly to sidestep authority.

Recent directors have tended to include rather than omit the comic anarchy of this scene albeit with some adjustments. In particular, both Michael Bogdanov (ESC 1988) and Michael Attenborough (RSC 2000) had their arresting officers brutally manhandle Doll and Quickly to convey a sense of an oppressive police state. To gain this effect, however, both directors cut the beadle's "you shall have a dozen of cushions again" speech; moreover, Bogdanov's Doll was not visibly pregnant whereas Attenborough's Doll was truly pregnant rather than faking that condition. Apparently, a quip about cushions, easily missed by an auditor, was deemed disposable in order to set up an evocative image of two or more men striking and hauling away the two women.

What then is lost or diminished in this rescripting? Throughout his history plays Shakespeare regularly focuses upon children, heirs, and descent, with Prince Hal and his brothers being but one of many such sets reaching back to the sons of Edward III. Part II starts with the reported death of a son, Hotspur, that elicits a reaction from his father that has ominous implications for the future health of the kingdom, and is followed by the appearance of the son of Richard II's Mowbray, a figure who through his presence and pointed comments (see especially 4.1.111–27) recalls the conflicts still simmering from Bolingbroke's past, and by the appearance of a crown prince who waits in the background and discusses his problematic status with Poins in 2.2. Related references recur in the dialogue, whether in the rebels' concern "that our hopes (yet likely of fair birth)/Should be still-born" (1.3.63–64), Mowbray's allusion to the lives that have "miscarried under Bullingbrook" (4.1.127), or the account of fearful omens that include "unfather'd heirs and loathly births of nature" (4.4.122).

The most revealing passages are linked to the rhetoric of rebellion. In one of his major speeches the Archbishop analyzes the awkward dilemma of the king who "hath found to end one doubt by death/Revives two greater in the heirs of life" (4.1.197–98). In this view, each corrective action by Henry IV or his agents instead of providing a solution only adds to the problem, as epitomized by the onstage presence of a second Mowbray. The Archbishop then sums up the dilemma of a king whose kingdom "like an offensive wife/That hath enrag'd him on to offer strokes, /As he is striking, holds his infant up" so that "resolv'd correction" is prevented (202–12). Similarly, just before the rebels accept John's "princely word," Hastings predicts that if this rebellion fails, others will "second our attempt," and, "If they miscarry, theirs shall second them," so that, in his terms, "success of mischief shall be born, /And heir from heir shall hold his quarrel up/Whiles England shall have generation" (4.2.44–49).

Doll's claim of pregnancy in the raucous penultimate scene is then a climax to a series of rebel allusions to heirs and unborn children, most notably the Archbishop's image of a wife who holds her infant up to avoid correction. However, both here and with Falstaff in 5.5 such stratagems do not work. In the context established by the imagery in the rebels' speeches, not only are Doll and her accomplices arrested in the legal sense, as the rebels were arrested or attached by Westmoreland (4.2.106–9), but their way of life and, even more important, their seeds for the future are also being brought under control. Both Doll and Falstaff, the epitomes of the diseases and subterfuges of the world under Henry IV, are here being exposed, arrested, and metaphorically denied any progeny. In imagistic terms, an answer is being acted out to Hastings's prophecy that "heir from heir shall hold his quarrel up/Whiles England shall have generation," for, in the Archbishop's terms, "resolv'd correction" has transcended the threat of the infant hostage or the continuing problem posed by "the heirs of life." Admittedly, 5.4 is comic, even anarchic in its language and action, but there is a logic to both the arrest and the exposure of the false pregnancy that defines the "new" world under Henry V. To eliminate the officer's "you shall have a dozen of cushions again" speech is then not merely to streamline the scene by removing an obscure joke but to reconfigure a climactic image.

A comparable situation is found at the outset of the final scene of *Romeo and Juliet* where the First Quarto stage directions spell out what is implicit in the Second Quarto dialogue. First: *"Enter County Paris and his Page with flowers and sweet Water"*; *"Paris strews the Tomb with flowers"* (I4v); the Q2 speech that accompanies the latter action begins: "Sweet flower, with flowers thy bridal bed I strew" (5.3.12). Next, according to Q1, Romeo and Balthasar enter *"with a torch, a mattock, and a crow of iron,"* with those implements cited in both Quartos' dialogue ("Give me that mattock and the wrenching iron" – 22). In a major speech, Romeo then lies about "Why I descend into this bed of death," threatens Balthasar if he returns ("I will tear thee joint by joint, / And strew this hungry churchyard with thy limbs"), and characterizes "The time and my intents" as "savage-wild, / More fierce and more inexorable far / Than empty tigers or the roaring sea" (22–39). The contrast between the two lovers of Juliet, one with flowers and sweet water, the other "savage-wild" with mattock and crow of iron, could hardly be more striking.

Playgoers, however, rarely get to see this sequence as scripted – unless once includes the wildly hilarious version presented in the RSC *Nicholas Nickleby*. To eliminate Paris's *"sweet"* or perfumed water should not surprise us and may not make a significant difference to an interpretation, but the absence of Romeo's mattock and crowbar is another matter entirely. Indeed, to pursue the possible function of these two tools is to open up a series of theatrical and scholarly questions that defy easy answers. Initially, such answers seem self-evident to the reader with a naturalistic bent who imagines a verisimilar tomb that must be pried open by "real" tools. However, in the 1590s both Paris and Romeo may have entered on a bare apron stage *as [if] in a graveyard*, so that a sense of "the tomb" would be conveyed not by a physical structure thrust onto the stage but by dialogue references ("thy canopy," "this vault," "The stony entrance of this sepulchre" – 13, 86, 141) accompanied by gestures to a stage door or trap door. Paris's flowers and sweet water, as objects that would be carried by a conventional mourner, would then have further established a sense of place as would the digging or prying implements brought in by the inexorable, savage-wild Romeo. In those first performances, the latter's highly visible properties may therefore have functioned not as tools to be used for "real" prying but rather as part of a theatrical shorthand to convey a sense of a tomb. Just as a playgoer in the 1590s knew it was "dark" when figures on a fully lit stage could not see each other or inferred "in prison" when manacled figures were accompanied by jailers wearing keys, that playgoer recognized "a tomb" when figures entered with accoutrements appropriate to a graveyard.

Such an historical rationale, however, carries little weight with directors today who have their own notions of how to present the Capulet tomb or monument. Playgoers therefore usually get to see some kind of onstage structure that serves as the tomb and rarely see the mattock and crowbar. My goal here is not to sing hymns to the virtues of the original staging (which is by no means certain)[2] but rather to note the consequences of omitting Romeo's tools. When watching the conflict between Paris and Romeo the playgoer is presented with two contrasted lovers or sets of values, with one of them literally and symbolically destroying the other. To cut the mattock and crow of iron today is to sustain a "romantic" view of Romeo that is undercut or qualified by the signals in the Quartos. With such tools in hand, Romeo's speech addressed to "Thou detestable maw, thou womb of death," can take on added meaning, especially: "Thus I enforce thy rotten jaws to open, / And in despite I'll cram thee with more food" (45–48). The metaphoric emphasis here is upon a forcing open, a violation, associated with Death and Appetite, for Romeo is forcing open the "jaws" and cramming himself into the "maw" that will devour him (and Juliet). Here Romeo is not merely performing an action necessary to the story (opening the tomb to reach Juliet) but, more important, is acting out his tragic error by breaking open what should be inviolate and thrusting both himself and, unknowingly, Juliet into the maw of death (with overtones perhaps of violated virginity), a choice presented in terms of savage-wild appetites out of control (a maw gorged with morsels, "cram thee with more food," "hungry churchyard"). In a curious fashion, however, post-1590s scholarly and theatrical emphasis upon a verisimilar tomb has pulled attention away from what does emerge as the most distinctive (and unusual) "image" in this particular tomb scene – the savage-wild lover using a mattock and crow of iron to rip open whatever separates him from his beloved while also dispatching his more conventional rival wooer, whether by means of a sword or, more savagely, by means of his prying tools – a strident and, for me, highly disturbing image.

Romeo's tools may regularly disappear from today's productions with few playgoers aware of their absence, but far more distinctive was Michael Boyd's rescripting of the play's final moments (RSC 2000). Boyd made several of the standard cuts (e.g., Peter and the musicians in 4.5) and actually included the chorus to Act 2, but the notable feature of this production was the reappearance of the various figures who die during the action: Mercutio, Tybalt, Paris, and eventually the two title figures. This show started with the usual build to a brawl, but at the height of the fray all the onstage figures froze and Romeo (or Romeo's ghost) appeared to deliver the Prologue. The bulk of the action that followed was not unusual until the end of Act 4 when, after Juliet drank her potion, the ghosts of both Tybalt and Mercutio appeared, exited, and reappeared above to watch the rest of the performance. Tybalt did not participate in the subsequent action, but Mercutio in 5.1 helped the apothecary hand down the packet of poison to Romeo and in 5.2 delivered Friar John's lines and displayed the undelivered letter to Friar Lawrence (perhaps giving added force to Mercutio's earlier "A plague a' both your houses!" – 3.1.106). After his death Paris too appeared above (Romeo had placed his body in the tomb represented by an open trapdoor). Juliet then stabbed herself while embracing the dead Romeo and slid out of sight into the trap.

What followed became the conversation piece of the RSC 2000 season. As the reconciliation was taking place between the two feuding families, Romeo and Juliet silently emerged from their tomb unseen by those on stage and slowly departed through the theatre audience by means of the runway that linked the stage and the audience left aisle. Their departure *was* eventually seen by the friar who was the only other figure to exit in that direction. The suggestion was of a union in afterlife if not on earth watched over by a Mercutio and Tybalt who were no longer enemies. An obvious price tag for Boyd's concept was the elimination of the two bodies as the play's central focus during the final sequence, so that the cost of the feud – and the image of Romeo's dagger mis-sheathed in Juliet's bosom (5.3.203–5) – were played down in favor of the director's otherworldly vision.

Elsewhere in the tragedies directors often experiment with ways of emphasizing the presence (or "spirit") of Julius Caesar in Act 5. Terry Hands (RSC 1987) had his Caesar literally walk the stage during the battlefield scenes. In contrast, director Michael Edwards (SSC 1988) included no such supernatural manifestation but did have the same actor who had played Julius Caesar reappear first as Pindarus, then as Strato – although a helmet blurred the effect so that one had to consult the program to catch it. In this interpretation Brutus was correct in more ways than one when he stated: "O Julius Caesar, thou art mighty yet! / Thy spirit walks abroad, and turns our swords / In our own proper entrails" (5.3.94–96), for the Caesar actor, if not Caesar himself, held the swords that killed both Cassius and Brutus. Having the Caesar actor play Strato (as also in Globe 1999) may not be an unusual choice, but director Michael Kevin (OSF 1991) went a step farther. When his Brutus sought help in his suicide, he was first rejected by two figures who revealed themselves to be the actresses who had played Portia and Calpurnia; the actual death blow was then provided by a Strato played by the Caesar actor.

Of the tragedies perhaps the most likely to undergo final scene rescripting is *Othello*, because, for a variety of reasons, the title figure's weapons and several related passages as scripted in the Quarto and Folio have not fared well in recent productions. Harold Scott (DC 1991) omitted both Othello's major speech comparing his heroic past to his diminished present that starts with "Behold, I have a weapon" (5.2.259) and his confrontation first off, then onstage with Gratiano. This Othello therefore did not lose two weapons during 5.2, so that "I am not valiant neither, /But every puny whipster gets my sword" (243–44) as delivered here was greatly diminished in its impact as was the build to the third weapon of the scene to be used in the suicide, a weapon whose nature and genesis remained unclear in this production. Weapons were also a major casualty in Brian Bedford's production (SFC 1994). Here Othello did find a sword in his chamber with which to challenge Gratiano and did wrest a sword from a guard with which to commit suicide, but in deference to the 1940s setting most of the other plentiful references to swords were gone. In 5.2 Othello did not have a sword when accosting Desdemona, Emilia (who did not say "I care not for thy sword" – 165), or Iago ("*The Moor runs at Iago*" – 235); this Othello therefore did not comment that "every puny whipster gets my sword."

Michael Attenborough (RSC 1999) made some comparable choices. According to the program the director cut 250 lines from the received text. Many of these cuts were familiar to me (e.g., 3.1; 3.2; 3.4.1–22; chunks of 1.3 including the reference to Marcus Luccicos); as many reviewers noted, Othello's reference to his age ("I am declin'd/Into the vale of years" – 3.3.265–66) was gone in deference to the age of actor Ray Fearon as was Iago's "praise" of women in 2.1. Given the many elisions I was surprised to witness Othello's rarely included appearance in 5.1 to cheer on the murder of Cassio, though typically this scene overall was pared back.

The effect of such streamlining was most evident in the final scene. Some of the director's omissions are standard practice (Desdemona's references to Othello's rolling his eyes and gnawing his lip and the interjections that interrupt Othello's final two speeches – 5.2.37–38, 43, 357).

With no bed curtain Lodovico's "The object poisons sight, / Let it be hid"
(364–65) was omitted, as was a chunk of Gratiano's report of Brabantio's
death (206–09), Othello's "every puny whipster gets my sword" (244),
and much of the recounting of events before the suicide speech – and
"when we shall meet *at compt*" was changed to "meet *again*" (273). Othello
did say "I have another weapon in this chamber" but not "It was
a sword of Spain, the ice-brook's temper" (252–53). Most distinctive
was the omission of the beginning of Othello's "I have seen the day"
speech, his account of the previous use of the weapon he is brandishing. This Othello spoke the first half-line ("Behold I have a weapon" –
259) but then moved immediately to "But (O vain boast!) / Who can
control his fate?" (264–65), so that omitted were the praise of the weapon
("A better never did itself sustain / Upon a soldier's thigh") and the subsequent comparison of heroic past and diminished present: "I have seen the
day / That with this little arm, and this good sword, / I have made my way
through more impediments / Than twenty times your stop" (261–64).
Also omitted from this speech was "Man but a rush against Othello's
breast, / And he retires" (270–71). At stake here was not narrative efficiency but a potential anomaly given the Edwardian setting of this
production wherein swords were primarily ceremonial.

   Such cuts and changes carry a price tag. The failure of Othello's sword
in 5.2 after Desdemona's death, as heightened by "every puny whipster
gets my sword" and "Man but a rush against Othello's breast, / And he
retires," charts the end of a process that starts in Acts 1 and 2, where, with
or without a weapon of his own, the protagonist stops potential brawls by
his mere presence (1.2, 2.3) and impresses the duke, senators, and usually
the playgoers with his arias in 1.3. The emphasis on weaponry therefore
spans the play, but whether one interprets Othello's transformation in
phallic or chivalric terms, the pay-off was greatly diminished in all three
of these productions.

   Consider, as another revealing example, *Coriolanus*, where directors
often rewrite the last scene to gain a desired effect. Indeed, rare is the production that plays the Folio as scripted, particularly the climactic image
of Aufidius standing upon the body of Coriolanus: "*Draw the Conspirators,
and kills Martius, who falls; Aufidius stands on him*" (5.6.130). Jerry Turner
(OSF 1980) not only ignored the Folio signal for Coriolanus's death but
rewrighted the scene. The Folio calls for three groups of figures for this
final confrontation: Aufidius and his conspirators who actually commit
the murder; the commoners who enter with Coriolanus ("*Enter Coriolanus
marching with Drum and Colors, the Commoners being with him*" [69]); and the

lords of the Volscian city. In the Oregon production, however, most of the lords' lines were cut (a few were given to the conspirators). Then Coriolanus was stabbed repeatedly (six or seven times) by conspirators *and* commoners, giving Denis Arndt as Coriolanus the opportunity to act as an almost superhuman figure who, although given a series of mortal wounds, kept getting up, kept moving on, and eventually in high heroic fashion leapt to his death – choosing his own moment to die rather than being brought down by lesser men, no matter how many. Meanwhile, the voices of restraint or the comments upon the murder provided by the lords (110, 123–27, 130, 141–46) were eliminated. Rather, the spectators at this production saw *everyone* onstage pitted against one heroic individual who stood and fell alone and thereby greatly enhanced his stature – an effect undercut by the Folio stage direction that sets up the image of Aufidius standing or treading upon the prostrate body.

Given Arndt's bravura performance, this death scene was a superb theatrical experience and helped to elicit standing ovations. But to gain this heroic ending, note what had to be sacrificed. As I understand Shakespeare's strategy here, this final scene sets before us in a Volscian city the same elements (lords, conspirators, commoners) that Coriolanus had faced in Rome between 2.1 and 3.3 (patricians, tribunes, plebeians), a confrontation that, despite the support of one group (the patricians), had led to his banishment, his "I banish you," and his "There is a world elsewhere" (3.3.120–35). To include the same elements in the final scene in the Volscian city, again, with one of the groups – the lords of the city – supportive, is to act out the obvious fact that there is no world elsewhere, that the hero's second confrontation with such a city leads to a second defeat, this time his death – and an ignominious death for the conquering war machine of Act 1. The ironies and deflation of the Folio ending (as I read it) have therefore been traded off for an heroic climax that appealed to a post Viet Nam audience in 1980 – at the risk of rewrighting the play or translating it into a new language or idiom.

A different approach was taken by David Thacker (RSC Swan 1994) who not atypically developed a homo-erotic bond between Coriolanus and Aufidius, most notably in 4.5, where during his long speech Aufidius slowly embraced a still Coriolanus, and the final scene. The adjustments made for the latter were then particularly suggestive. As is usually the case, Thacker did not adhere to the Folio signal that directs Coriolanus to make his last entrance with drums and colors, *"the Commoners being with him"* (an echo of his comparable arrival in triumph in 2.1). Toby Stephens's Coriolanus then had no illusions about what was coming and even encouraged it, perhaps as a form of suicide, to the point of providing a slight motion to Aufidius at the end, as if to say "do it now." The actual murder was committed by a large group, not solely by Aufidius and his conspirators; Aufidius then did tread upon the body albeit not violently or savagely.

What was particularly noteworthy came next. The crowd backed off, the lords exited, and others slipped away, leaving Aufidius on the ground holding Coriolanus in an embrace. At this point in the Folio, Aufidius has the play's final speech (5.6.146–54) that starts with "My rage is gone" and moves to a series of commands ("Take him up. / Help, three a' th' chiefest soldiers . . . Beat thou the drum . . . Trail your steel pikes"); after he promises that, despite the injuries he has caused, Coriolanus "shall have a noble memory," Aufidius ends with the command "Assist" followed by the stage direction: "*Exeunt, bearing the body of Martius. A dead march sounded.*" In this instance, the words were there, but Thacker did not adhere to the Folio stage direction. Rather, in what emerged as one of the most powerful moments in the show, Aufidius's "assist" was resisted or ignored, so that the body was *not* borne off the stage. Instead, a different climactic final image was crafted in which Aufidius, deserted by the other Volscians, was left alone cradling the dead Coriolanus, either as a lost lover or as the only opponent worthy of him or as some combination of the two. Again, a strong image in the Folio (of Coriolanus being carried off by the Volscians) was superseded by an equally strong image more in keeping with today's values and agendas.

Brian Bedford (SFC 1981) made many cuts (4.2, 4.3, the officers' choric beginning to 2.2, the latter part of 3.1, the servants' dialogue in 4.5, Aufidius's aside in 5.3, the senator's speech as Volumnia passed over the stage in 5.5), but of special interest were some omissions in the final scene. The Folio stage direction that calls for "*great shouts of the people*" (5.6.48) was ignored and the subsequent dialogue that describes Coriolanus's triumphant return accompanied by a crowd "Splitting the air with noise" (49–51) was cut. Rather, Coriolanus entered above and the already hostile commoners filed in silently to form a semicircle facing him on the lip of the stage below. Aufidius then stabbed Coriolanus who fell and was apparently devoured by the mob below. The final image was then a dead, broken body on the stage floor encircled by the commoners as if it had been digested by the many-headed monster (and here the playgoer did get to see Aufidius put his foot on his antagonist's chest). The image was striking, but to achieve it the director had to pare back elements of the scene, especially the shift in allegiance of the Volscian citizens.

All three of these directors succeeded in their goal of providing a powerful final image for their playgoers even if that goal meant adjusting or eliminating elements scripted in the Folio. Clearly, any director seeking a heroic sendoff for a superhuman figure will not welcome the image set up in the Folio stage direction of Aufidius standing upon Coriolanus's body; to pit the title figure against everyone onstage, to isolate him with Aufidius, or to have him devoured by the populace is to close with a powerful image that resonates with today's playgoers. Sometimes such decisive changes in an ending grow out of design choices, as when an emphasis in the dialogue upon swords in *Othello*, 5.2 jars with a transposition into a later period. If *Troilus and Cressida* is transposed to the 1850s (RSC 1985) or *Coriolanus* to the 1980s (RNT 1985), we should not be surprised if Hector and Coriolanus are gunned down by riflemen – although how Hector and Coriolanus die, choose to die, or blunder into dying is no small matter in any setting or interpretation. Such changes raise a recurring question: where does "Shakespeare" end and "interpretation" begin? What price "good theatre" or standing ovations?

The most visible proponent of such reconceiving of Shakespeare's strategies for closure is Michael Bogdanov. In his 1986 RSC modern-dress production of *Romeo and Juliet* Bogdanov had his Romeo inject rather than drink the apothecary's poison; he then cut the final 140 lines. Rather, after Juliet's death the stage was darkened; when the lights came up, the audience saw the prince reading most of the opening choric sonnet (switched to the past tense) from note cards while standing in front of two golden statues. When this Mafia don finished, photographers ran down the theatre aisles, snapping pictures first of him, then of Montague and Capulet shaking hands, then of various combinations involving the wives (so Lady Montague was not dead), the friar, the nurse, even the apothecary, so that what we saw was a press conference and photo session after an unveiling. After some perfunctory mourning and laying of flowers, the final image was that of Benvolio going off alone, disconsolate (the only show of real emotion). This production therefore ended with our actually seeing the two golden statues promised in the script, with the emphasis not upon reconciliation of the feud but upon phoniness and exploitation, an emphasis and set of images that dominated the final moments. Clearly, this Verona had not been changed for the better by the deaths of the young lovers or by the handshakes of the former enemies.

Bogdanov's rescripting had an electric effect upon the matinee audience that watched this show with me – and since many readers and playgoers are less than enthusiastic about the 140 lines between Juliet's death and the prince's final couplet, especially the friar's long speech that recounts what we already know, the omission produced few cries of outrage. But the golden statues, although cited in the script, are yet to come in Shakespeare's version; rather, they represent something promised, a fulfillment of a pledge. In contrast, the climactic image in the Quarto is the *one* joining of hands by the two fathers ("O brother Montague, give me thy hand, / This is my daughter's jointure" – 5.3.296–97), a handshake that is somehow generated by the friar's lengthy speech. Shakespeare's strategy therefore allows for a growing awareness in these final moments, especially by Capulet, of the cost of the feud and his peremptory behavior in Acts 3 and 4. To substitute the golden statues and the photo session handshakes for Shakespeare's single climactic handshake is to reinforce one possible interpretation at the expense of a simpler, less cynical solution linked to the evidence found in the Quarto.

In his English Shakespeare Company seven-play rendition of the two tetralogies Bogdanov also made major adjustments. Since the three parts of *Henry VI* were refashioned into two plays, the many changes, especially in Parts I and II, came as no surprise (see chapter 7). More interesting to the student of Shakespeare's endings are the adjustments Bogdanov made elsewhere. As noted in chapter 3, he and Michael Pennington (his co-director and lead actor) felt the need at the end of *1 Henry IV* for some additional justification for the split between Prince Hal and his father that the playgoer will encounter in Part II, so that they moved Falstaff's claim to have killed Hotspur from the end of 5.4 to the end of 5.5 so as to be overheard and in part believed by Henry IV. Similarly, to undercut what might otherwise be seen as an upbeat climax to *Henry V* Bogdanov included the Dauphin, conspicuously absent in Shakespeare's version, in the French entourage of the final scene. Pennington's Henry V then labored noticeably in his attempt to woo the princess and create harmony between England and France and, along with everyone else on stage, was nonplused when the Dauphin stormed off just as the treaty was being announced and celebrated. In this instance, a figure that Shakespeare, for whatever theatrical or political reason, chose not to include made perhaps the strongest statement in the scene.

Most striking among the various endings was the climax of Bogdanov's *Richard III*. In this seven-play cycle the director had been using costumes, props, and other choices to move the playgoer forward in time, so that this, the final play, was in 1980s dress and decor, with the emphasis upon the boardroom not the council chamber, gangland rivalry not medieval warfare – and if you have always wondered what happens to the wine Richard calls for in 5.3, the tuxedoed ghost of Clarence drinks it. In the final battle sequence the famous "A horse! a horse!" (5.4.9) line was delivered offstage, and then, in striking contrast to the consistent 1980s look and to the accompaniment of Barber's "Adagio for Strings," two helmeted figures in bulky medieval armor, one golden and one dark, fought a graceful, highly stylized battle with huge swords, a fight that exuded a weariness that epitomized the long sequence of battles and squabbles. As in his *Romeo and Juliet*, the stage was then darkened; when the lights came up, we heard and watched Richmond deliver his closing lines in a modern television studio with overhead TV monitors, technicians, cameramen, and even a make-up person who curtsied to Princess Elizabeth. Gone, however, with a 1980s victorious Richmond the sole speaker and primary focus, was Derby-Stanley giving the crown to Henry VII (the crown as image was almost completely gone from this show), so that this rendition omitted the punch line for the Stanley strand of the plot, an element that, however interpreted, can be a major part of the overall effect. Gone too was any mention of George Stanley, so that Bogdanov's audience was given no resolution of that figure's fate and therefore was left in the dark about the full price tag for the victory. The medieval battle followed by the modern television victory speech was a powerful theatrical climax to the seven-play sequence, but the price tag, in terms of what was or had to be omitted, was high.

Although many European directors go much farther, relatively few United States, Canadian, and British directors reshape and reconceive Shakespeare's endings in Bogdanov's fashion. Rather, what is more often at work behind the various changes and adjustments is a director's sense of economy or climax. As productions approach or exceed the three-hour mark, theatrical professionals get impatient with speeches or beats that seem to them excrescent or redundant and therefore often resort to the blue pencil in Act 5, especially in a long final scene or sequence – as in Adrian Noble's 1988 RSC *Macbeth*, presented without an interval, where Macbeth's encounter with young Siward was included but the subsequent dialogue in which old Siward learns about and reacts to his son's fate was gone. In particular, to a nuts-and-bolts director speeches in which an onstage figure recounts events already witnessed by the playgoer seem redundant and hence cuttable. Notable examples include the speeches of Marcus and Lucius after the four deaths in *Titus Andronicus*, 5.3; Iachimo's narration of past events during the complex final scene of *Cymbeline*; and the friar's speech (and indeed the entire 140 lines) after the death of Juliet.

For many interpreters of *Titus*, the play is "over" at the death of the title figure, so that most of the productions I have seen have made significant adjustments to the 135 lines after the murders. Pat Patton (OSF 1986) not only cut many lines but also rearranged various elements so as to end his show with a coda from Marcus patched together from earlier speeches on putting the pieces of Rome back together again. Mark Rucker (SSC 1988) kept the sequence of events in the script but made selective cuts. For example, since this director had no acting area "above" in his outdoor theatre, his Marcus did not offer to leap to his death hand-in-hand with Lucius if the Romans so willed. In both Rucker's and Deborah Warner's (RSC 1987) productions, moreover, the post-murder lines from Marcus and Lucius that recount events already witnessed by the audience, with their emphasis upon the horrors perpetrated upon the Andronici, were directed not at fellow actors but rather at the playgoers who here served as "Romans," an effect enhanced at the 1988 version of Warner's show at the Pit where actors were seated on the steps in the aisles. Lost in all three shows was any sense that the speeches of Marcus and Lucius are directed at onstage figures who, as we watch, have to decide whether to hail Lucius as the new emperor (the eventual decision) or condemn him as a murderer who is no improvement on Saturninus – one possible interpretation of the Roman lord's response to Marcus's first speech after the murders, a response often reassigned to Marcus by modern editors (see chapter 9). Especially in Patton's production, a modern sense of closure (or economy) led to a reshaping of the Quarto script.

A comparable effect was provided by Gregory Doran in his 1995 RNT Cottlesloe production that originated in South Africa. Again, the final 135 lines in 5.3 after the murders were greatly reduced and played in a different order. Lucius kissed the dead Titus and gave thanks to Aemilius and the Romans, then referred to Aaron's child; Aaron was brought on to give his defiance, receive his sentence, and be taken off along with Tamora's body. The show ended with a stripped down version of Marcus's earlier speeches, so that the final lines were: "O, let me teach you how to knit again / This scattered corn into one mutual sheaf, / These broken limbs again into one body" (5.3.70–72). Given a very positive view of both Marcus and Lucius and given the many links to contemporary South Africa, this climactic appeal had a distinctive power (akin to a positive reading of the Capulet–Montague handshake at the end of *Romeo and Juliet*). The production as a whole but particularly the rescripted ending packed a strong punch.

Also in bad repute among interpreters of Shakespeare is the final scene of *Cymbeline*. Sir Peter Hall (RNT Cottlesloe 1988) moved his actors around like pieces on a heavily raked chessboard so that figures on all parts of the crowded stage could be seen clearly and each new situation could be showcased appropriately. Many of the revelations and interactions here seem overdone to modern eyes and ears, particularly Iachimo's speeches (5.5.141–46, 147–49, 153–68, 169–209) that, as with the comparable speeches in *Titus*, recount what we already know. Hall did cut about 20 lines here, but he and his Iachimo (Tim Piggott-Smith) found the theatricality in this moment so as to demonstrate forcefully that it is by no means redundant. During Iachimo's account, Fidele was in clear view of the audience stage right and Posthumus was on the ground downstage center, so the playgoer could see both their faces. Much of the point of the speech was therefore its effect not upon us (we know the story) but upon the onstage auditors (who do not). We therefore listen to Iachimo but watch Innogen (Hall used the Folio spelling) and especially Posthumus whose reaction begins the next movement.

Here and in other segments of this often maligned scene, Hall and his actors demonstrated that this final sequence *is* crafted shrewdly, especially if the playgoer is encouraged (or allowed) to hear and watch not only the series of revelations but, equally important (as in *Titus*, 5.3), the impact of those revelations upon the key figures. One result of such a process is to establish the centrality of Cymbeline himself as the figure who has most to learn and by the end has changed the most. For example, the barbarism he enunciates early in 5.5, in which the onstage prisoners to their horror discover that they are to be killed in order to appease the souls of the English dead (69–74), gives way to the final section in which "Pardon's the word to all," Rome and Britain are reunited, and the final word is "peace" (422, 459–65, 485).

A comparable example is provided by Henry Woronicz's *Romeo and Juliet* (OSF 1988). Rather than cutting most or all of the 140-line stretch after the death of Juliet as had Bogdanov, Woronicz quickly filled his stage to overflowing with the prince, the parents, and many of the servants and supernumeraries who had populated 1.1 and 3.1. As staged here, the interaction between old Montague and old Capulet inflamed the passions of the feud once again, so that for a third time representatives of the two families were squaring off to do battle. Clearly, a highly volatile situation was about to explode yet again. In this rendition, the often maligned friar's speech was therefore necessary, even crucial, to the resolution, especially as delivered in passionate, soul-searching terms by Jim Edmondson whose Friar Lawrence confessed his own failings but also indicted the two families, especially the Capulets.

When the prince finally turned to the two old men with his telling question: "Where be these enemies?" (5.3.291), a chastened Capulet stood, gave his hand to his wife, and, after a glance between them and a pause, offered his hand to "brother Montague." Montague's response was slow and grudging, even painful, so that his taking of Capulet's hand and his offer of the golden statue were not merely a whitewash of the various deaths (or a PR stunt as in the Bogdanov interpretation) but clearly acted out a difficult choice, a theatrical closure that was *earned* by bitter experience (and generated primarily by Edmondson's rendition of the friar's speech). The feud, as presented here, could *only* be stopped from the top, by these two old men, now scarred by tragedy, for, as Woronicz had demonstrated, without this choice the fighting would erupt again within moments. In this rendition, the final 140 lines were neither unwieldy or excrescent but were an essential part of the tragedy – again (as in *Titus* and *Cymbeline*) in large part owing to the interplay between a speaker (the friar, Marcus–Lucius, Iachimo) and an onstage audience (Montague–Capulet, the Romans, Posthumus–Innogen).

A comparable effect was provided by Jim Edmondson in his *Henry VIII* (OSF 1984). This show had earlier displayed in 2.4 a Henry obsessed with male issue (see chapter 4) so that the director could build upon this concern by means of two significant choices in Act 5. First, when the old lady brings tidings of the child born to Anne, Henry asks: "Is the Queen delivered? / Say ay, and of a boy" (5.1.162–63). In Edmondson's rendition, the old lady's initial response ("Ay, ay, my liege, / And of a lovely boy" – 163–64) produced hysterical joy from the king and for a moment completely stopped the flow of action and dialogue. The old lady's subsequent lines ("The God of heaven / Both now and ever bless her! 'tis a girl / Promises boys hereafter" – 164–66) then produced an equally hysterical reaction from Henry who had to be restrained by Suffolk from throttling the oblivious bringer of bad tidings. The king then did not exit at line 170 but remained on his throne, so that after the old lady's departure the spectator saw him muse in stony silence, then repeat her line ("'tis a girl / Promises boys hereafter"), and finally smash anything within reach. Obviously, this Henry was *not* reconciled to the birth of a daughter.

These choices then set up what for me was the high point of this production (and a moment otherwise very hard to realize for a modern audience). Critics, editors, and historical scholars who comment on the final scene can describe the likely effect of Cranmer's prophetic speeches upon the original audience and perhaps how a reader should react, but playgoers today, although enjoying the pageantry of the christening, usually do not respond well to the vision and certainly see no parallel to the final scene of *The Winter's Tale*. Here, however, the director and his Henry found a human or personal focus to climax their production. At the outset this king was not fully involved in the ceremony but rather listened halfheartedly to the expected praise of the infant Elizabeth and of England while the baby was held by a neutral figure (and with the "shades" of Buckingham, Wolsey, Katherine, and Anne on the fringes silently observing). But as Cranmer proceeded with his speech, the intended audience became not us but Henry, who as he listened ("Thou speakest wonders" – 5.4.55) gradually became reconciled to this infant girl and, at the climax of the speech, took the baby in his arms, recapitulating an earlier image, a cradling of his imagined dead male child in 2.4. In a script in which continuity and through-lines are often hard to find, this director and this Henry found a meaningful and theatrically exciting climax that successfully knit together various strands and left the spectator with a sense of Henry's growth and new understanding as epitomized in his reconciliation to the baby Elizabeth.

In his *Richard III* (RSC 1995–96) Steven Pimlott did much streamlining: the first two ghosts in 5.3 (Henry VI, Prince Edward) were omitted, though the often cut Vaughan appeared here and earlier; Buckingham, Hastings, and Stanley lost a lot of their lines, so that these figures along with the political dimensions of the script (e.g., in 3.5, 3.7, 5.1) were pared back in favor of David Troughton's distinctive jester-like Richard. Especially noteworthy were the changes in 5.3 and what follows. The battle at Bosworth Field metamorphosed into a dining table covered in white within a white box where figures congregated around a seated Richard and Richmond. Before the appearance of the nine ghosts Richard did move into the downstage area to put his dagger in the ground, break bread, and sip wine so as to suggest a communion, but he returned to his chair for the rest of this extended sequence. After the appearance of the ghosts and a slightly pared down version of Richard's soliloquy (lines 196–99 and 204–06 were cut) came the most obvious directorial move, for the subsequent Richmond and Richard beats were broken up into smaller units that were then restitched so as to alternate (with Richmond eventually moving above for his oration and Richard remaining below). No onstage fights were displayed; rather, with the ghosts and Margaret visible above, Richard moved into the downstage audience left area and tried unsuccessfully to reprise some of his earlier speeches such as the opening lines of 1.1 or the "All the world to nothing!" speech of 1.2. With Richard retired to the side of the stage, Richmond had his final speech which was punctuated by Richard's ironic clapping.

Another provocative choice was provided in Robin Phillips's *The Winter's Tale* (SFC 1978). Particularly striking here was Martha Henry's Paulina, a crusty, iron-willed, forbidding figure who dominated the stage in her key scenes in Acts 2, 3, and 5. Indeed, this figure proved such a force to be reckoned with that the actress and director concluded that she would never have consented to the marriage with Camillo thrust upon her in the closing moments by Leontes (5.3.135–46), so that these lines were omitted and no such marriage was included.

Several related problems converge here. First, theatrical professionals, like all interpreters of Shakespeare, build their interpretations upon the signals provided in the script. However, to reason that Paulina would never have subjected herself in this manner to Leontes's will is to indicate that the actor's or director's concept of such a figure is in conflict with the facts supplied in the Folio where such a marriage (and, presumably, Paulina's acquiescence) *is* established as part of the final ordering. In this instance, something basic to many modern interpretations, whether our sense of psychological realism or our assumptions about individual independence in marital choice, is in conflict with something apparently taken for granted by the original dramatist and audience (e.g., a sense of a cycle to be completed or of kingly prerogatives), to the extent that the original signals here were rejected or suppressed. The interpretative choices in the SFC production therefore highlight a revealing gap between modern psychological or cultural reasoning and the interpretative logic of Shakespeare and his audience.

Another potential part of the original theatrical logic for such a moment may also be at work here, a feature even more alien to us today. Speculating about the doubling of parts in the original productions of Shakespeare's plays (a practice basic to stage presentation then but easily ignored today) both Stephen Booth and John C. Meagher[3] single out this scene and suggest that (1) the boy actor who played Mamillius in the first two acts reappeared as Perdita in the last two acts and (2) the same actor who played Antigonus in Acts 2 and 3 also played Camillo in Acts 1, 4, and 5. Especially for playgoers who would already "know" the actors (a situation possible today with any company that maintains some of its personnel over a period of time), various speeches could have a somewhat different meaning or effect, as when Paulina laments the absence of "My mate (that's never to be found again)" and Leontes rejoins: "I'll not seek far /(For him, I partly know his mind) to find thee /An honorable husband" (5.3.134, 141–43). Such speculations cannot be "proved" (no such casting list survives for a Shakespeare play), but our predominantly psychological approach to such a choice or overall situation (would such a figure as I understand her from previous moments in the play have acted this way?) may, in the original production, have been overshadowed or conditioned by another principle linked to a sense of patterning in both the story and the theatrical personnel. The SFC choice to omit this moment may then signal a revealing gap between then and now, a gap that, in turn, demands some mental adjustments on the part of the modern interpreter. What indeed would be (or would have been) the effect if both Paulina and the audience recognize in Camillo an Antigonus "reborn" in the sense of the same actor playing the mourned for husband and the new mate? How would such a metatheatrical element fit with our working assumptions about psychological realism and dramatic narrative?

Ironically, rescripting of final scenes is not common practice in the so-called problem plays. Rather, directors can realize a wide range of effects without altering the received text, most notably at the end of *Measure for Measure* where either on the stage or on the page an interpreter must fill in the blank space left in the Folio as to how Isabella is to react to the duke's proposal of marriage. Directors of *Troilus and Cressida* regularly tinker with the battle sequence, especially if their production is set in a later period, but Trevor Nunn's refashioning of the final speech noted earlier was an exception for that play, as was Laird Williamson's insertion of sonnet 109 as Bertram's final speech in *All's Well That Ends Well* (see chapter 3). Two final examples can conclude this treatment of rescripted endings.

Of the many items that make up the much discussed climax of *All's Well* perhaps the least explored is Bertram's patch. At the end of Act 4 Lavatch describes the arrival of Bertram "with a patch of velvet on's face," adding: "Whether there be a scar under't or no, the velvet knows, but 'tis a goodly patch of velvet. His left cheek is a cheek of two pile and a half, but his right cheek is worn bare." Lafew's comment ("A scar nobly got, or a noble scar, is a good liv'ry of honor; so belike is that") then elicits Lavatch's rejoinder: "But it is your carbonado'd face" (4.5.94–101). The exchange prepares the playgoer for something soon to be seen and provides in advance three different ways to evaluate that image. Most obvious is Lafew's inference that the velvet patch worn by "the young noble soldier" (103) covers "a noble scar" or "a good liv'ry of honor," a worthy emblem of heroic deeds (the kind of scar one associates with Coriolanus). In contrast, Lavatch's cynical reference to "your carbonado'd face" suggests that under the patch lurks a scar of less worthy origins, an incision "made to relieve syphilitic chancres."[4] The third possibility is supplied in the clown's comment: "Whether there be a scar under't or no, the velvet knows, but 'tis a goodly patch of velvet." Bertram's left cheek, like his right, may be bare of any scar at all.

This exchange in 4.5, albeit difficult for an auditor to follow (and hence often cut), is linked to major images in this script. Parolles, under extreme pressure, describes Bertram as "a dangerous and lascivious boy, who is a whale to virginity" and is "very ruttish" (4.3.220–21, 215–16) but does not associate him with venereal disease. Lafew's "noble scar" is in keeping with Bertram's martial exploits in Florence, but the verbal emphasis, starting in 2.3, has been upon the comic hero's less than honorable behavior. In a major speech after Bertram's rejection of Helena, the king comments at length upon "dropsied honor" (2.3.128), while the countess notes that her son's "sword can never win/The honor that he loses" by deserting Helena (3.2.93–94). Repeatedly, Bertram's honor is called into question in Act 4, especially in his dialogue with Diana about the ring that is associated with "an honor 'longing to our house,/Bequeathed down from many ancestors,/Which were the greatest obloquy i' th' world/In me to lose" (4.2.42–45). Note too that Parolles, who is associated with "snipt-taffata," "villainous saffron" (4.5.1–2), scarves, and fashions, tries to fake an honor he has not earned: "I would the cutting of my garments would serve the turn, or the breaking of my Spanish sword" (4.1.46–47). Both the general comments on honor and the specific analogy to Parolles preclude Lafew's generous inference about the velvet patch and rather suggest a Bertram who is using that patch to direct attention away from his shameful treatment of Helena and his loss of the ring.

At the end of 4.5, before we see the returning Bertram, Shakespeare signals the presence of a velvet patch and provides three possible interpretations, one of which (that it, like Parolles's scarves and military bearing, covers nothing of substance) follows from a well-developed cluster of images. But no further mention of patch or scar is to be found in the Folio. As a result, critics and editors rarely comment upon the patch's presence or function in the final scene. Directors in turn eliminate the exchange in 4.5 (as in DC 1988), include some or all of the lines but ignore the patch in 5.3 (the usual choice), or provide some token resolution (the SFC 1977

Bertram wore a tiny black spot the size of a "beauty mark"). In his two-hour streamlined production (PRC 2001) David Hammond provided Bertram with a prominent scar as early as 3.3 and then retained the 4.5 lines devoted to that scar with no reference to a patch. Given the silence in the Folio after 4.5, one can appreciate the in-the-theatre decision to cut the Gordian knot by omitting or adjusting the 4.5 exchange, but the question remains: what if Bertram *is* wearing such a patch, particularly a patch large enough to recall Parolles's blindfold of Act 4? If then at some point during the climactic scene that patch should fall off or be taken off (by Bertram, by Helena, by someone else) to reveal no scar beneath, this loss of the last symbol of "dropsied honor" would be juxtaposed with the "new" Bertram who accepts Helena and transcends his former self, just as Parolles's blindfolded state, once transcended, had led to new insight and new status. The loss of the patch, moreover, would be offset by the regaining of the ring, the symbol of true, lineal honor, and with the restitution of Helena as wife, undoing the sin against honor that, as noted by various figures, had offset any chivalric gains (so I can envisage Helena putting the ring on Bertram's finger and taking off the patch). Reunion with Helena, not a velvet patch covering a non-existent scar, brings honor back to Bertram. An italicized presence and removal of such a patch can reinforce key images, ideas, and analogies and buttress the change in Bertram that troubles so many readers.

Discussion of the rescripting of final scenes would not be complete without at least some attention to *Measure for Measure*. Michael Boyd's controversial choices were treated in chapter 3, but also of interest was Steven Pimlott's production (RSC 1994–95), a show that had the distinction of presenting an Isabella who in the final moments first slapped and later kissed the duke. Pimlott made a variety of cuts (for example, Pompey's soliloquy that begins 4.3), but two struck me as particularly provocative. First, all the appearances of Friar Peter in 4.5, 4.6, and 5.1 were gone. To dispense with this friar's lines in the complex final scene (see 5.1.137–62) is to save some running time at the expense of narrative continuity and theatrical rhythm, a trade-off not of monumental importance to most playgoers. An unexpected result of Friar Peter's erasure, however (as pointed out to me by Homer Swander), was to change radically the terms of Barnadine's pardon. In Pimlott's version, the duke's initial lines to Barnadine were included ("Thou'rt condemned, / But for those earthly faults, I quit them all, / And pray thee take this mercy to provide / For better times to come" – 5.1.482–85) but, for obvious reasons, what follows was cut: "Friar, advise him, / I leave him to your hand"

(485–86). With no visible churchly presence in this Vienna after Friar Lodowick is gone, Barnadine gets the kind of carte blanche mercy associated with the previous sixteen years under the duke or with Escalus's failed handling of Pompey in 2.1 rather than being left, not a completely "free" man, in the care of the friar so that he can come to terms with heavenly matters. Barnadine may not be a central concern to many playgoers, but Pimlott's change significantly affected any evaluation of the duke's judgment which as played here represented a step backwards rather than forwards.

Even more telling was the omission of an exchange between the quirky, troubled duke and Isabella, a passage that clearly stood in the way of the desired interpretation but one that for me serves as a litmus test of any reading of this difficult scene. Between the departure of Angelo and Mariana to be married (380) and their return (399) the duke explains to Isabella why he allowed Claudio to die (supposedly "the swift celerity of his death" forestalled his efforts), a sequence that builds to "But peace be with him!/That life is better life, past fearing death,/Than that which lives to fear. Make it your comfort,/So happy is your brother" to which she responds "I do, my lord" (394, 396–99). As played here, these lines were linked to a growing anger on Isabella's part, including an obvious irritation at "Make it your comfort" that eventually led to her ripping a crucifix from his costume and the slap. Earlier in this same beat, however, in response to the duke's "I am still /Attorneyed at your service," the Folio has her reply: "O, give me pardon,/That I, your vassal, have employ'd and pain'd/Your unknown sovereignty" to which he responds: "You are pardon'd, Isabel" (384–87).

For whatever reason, this begging and granting of pardon were gone. After all, what woman of spirit (and Isabella is surely that) would not bridle at "comfort" from a supposed authority figure who was too slow on the uptake to save her brother? Why should she, the injured party, ask for pardon for employing and paining his sovereignty, known or unknown? But the "Make it your comfort" line (treated negatively by this Isabella) is a clear echo of the lengthy "Be absolute for death" speech Friar Lodowick delivers to Claudio in 3.1 and has a sound theological basis that would be fully apparent to a would-be nun. Moreover, although many 1990s readers and playgoers may disapprove, Shakespeare's Isabella clearly does beg pardon, an action that conveys something significant, however interpreted, about deeply ingrained assumptions about hierarchy and authority. Isabella may still end up hostile to or ambiguous about the duke's offer of marriage, but, as with the suppression of Paulina's marriage to Camillo, how are we to assess an interpretation (or a build to the slap) that can only be sustained by eliminating a significant piece of evidence?

Admittedly, the final scene of this play is replete with pregnant silences that continue to generate controversy among both academics and general playgoers so as to lead interpreters in very different directions. Pimlott's changes, however, linked as they are to the gender politics of the 1990s, strike me as belonging to a different category. Again, I return to my series of linked questions. How should playgoers view improvements in the received texts that make possible an interpretation more suitable to today's prevailing sensibilities? Are such directorial choices a sign of creative energy and ingenuity in combating the ravages time has wrought on historically specific onstage situations? Or do such choices display a lapse in creative imagination wherein a thesis takes precedence over the evidence, a situation not unknown in the scholarly world? Is the marriage arranged for Paulina or Isabella's request for pardon a throwaway item easily discarded by the director-as-playwright or is it an essential ingredient for any interpretation? Who is to decide?

Rescripting stage directions and actions

"with a quaint device the banquet vanishes"
The Tempest, 3.3.52

From the eighteenth century to the present the editors of Shakespeare's plays have treated the stage directions found in the Folio and the various Quartos with considerably less respect than the dialogue. In his landmark 1790 edition Edmund Malone decided "that the very few stage-directions which the old copies exhibit, were not taken from our author's manuscripts, but [were] furnished by the players" and therefore announced: "All the stage-directions therefore throughout this work I have considered as wholly in my power, and have regulated them in the best manner I could."[1] Although recent editors may not be as openly scornful, in today's editions the original signals are regularly moved, adjusted, or reconfigured. In an influential essay E. A. J. Honigmann has justified such a practice by arguing that, since "Shakespeare was careless about stage-directions," the editor or reader "cannot avoid giving a higher authority to the 'implied stage-directions' of the dialogue than to directions printed as such," for "our general understanding of a character . . . or of what can and cannot be done successfully in the theatre . . . must always override the printed stage-directions." Honigmann concludes: "We have a great opportunity, and a great responsibility: to see the plays, not as editors direct, but as we would wish to direct them ourselves."[2]

Given such views in the editorial and scholarly community, playgoers should not be surprised to find directors ignoring or adjusting stage directions found in the editions they use and substituting onstage effects of their own devising for properties, costumes, and actions specified or clearly implicit in the received texts. A variety of often overlapping imperatives lie behind such adjustments. Most obvious are the problems caused by new settings or design choices, especially when scripted signals for weaponry jar with a reconfiguration to a later period. Also subject to change are those onstage images whose rationale eludes today's theatrical professional or whose meanings conflict with a desired interpretation. Of particular interest is a third category where scripted signals for supernatural events are superseded by an emphasis upon verisimilitude or psychological realism.

CHANGING THE PERIOD

To move a play's action to a later historical period is to make various elements in the original script irrelevant or anomalous. Typical is the moment in *Richard III* when, to justify to the Mayor and to the world Hastings's rapid execution, Richard and Buckingham enter "*in rotten armor, marvellous ill-favored*" (3.5.0 – the Quarto specifies only "*in armor*"). This signal is regularly ignored even in productions that retain period costume (e.g., OSF 1978, RSC 1984), but if the choice is modern dress obviously the armor will disappear. The Folio's outlandish costume, however, can have a significant effect upon the subsequent scene, for the more bizarre the appearance of Richard and Buckingham, the more of a sardonic twist is given to their scarcely believable claims about Hastings and to the intimidated Mayor's acceptance of "all your just proceedings in this cause" (66). Moreover, this ungainly armor, mockingly thrust on against non-existent enemies in Act 3, reappears in Act 5 as the armor that does not or cannot protect Richard (who appears "*in arms*" – 5.3.0) against Richmond. Like many other images in this play, the rotten armor has an immediate and distinctive impact upon the tone and meaning of 3.5 (where Richard appears to be in total control, able to dare other figures not to believe him) but takes on a far different meaning when the opponent is not Clarence, Hastings, the Mayor, or the two helpless princes but the untainted Richmond, God's captain (5.3.108), who fills the moral and political vacuum in which Richard has thrived.

As noted in chapter 5, productions of *Othello* are regularly transposed to a later period and therefore likely to undergo rescripting of weapons that can be integral to major effects, particularly in the final scene. The Quarto signal, "*The Moor runs at Iago*" (5.2.235), makes little sense in a production featuring rifles and revolvers; however, to substitute knives for swords drastically changes the image of the protagonist and subverts some key lines ("every puny whipster gets my sword"; "I have seen the day / That with this little arm, and this good sword..." – 5.2.244, 261–62) that must then be sacrificed. In Brian Bedford's production

(SFC 1994) set in the 1940s the brawl in 2.3 that climaxes with the fight between Montano and a drunken Cassio involved much punching and kicking but no swordplay; the result was to diminish the sense of danger in the violence – and at his subsequent entrance Othello too did not have a weapon. In 5.1 Iago handed Roderigo a knife (and had one of his own as well), but Cassio had no weapon, so that he had to wrest one from his assailant. Swords were not visible in 1.2 when Brabantio's group squared off against Othello's men, so that Othello's "Keep up your bright swords, for the dew will rust them" (59) was cut. Bedford's Othello (Ron O'Neal) did not have the opportunity to build upon this line, a defining moment for other actors who have used it to set up a hero who, when faced with armed men, can stop a brawl merely with his tone of voice or a weaponless gesture.

Such transpositions to later periods inevitably have an impact on battle scenes. A major moment early in *Coriolanus* is the abortive one-on-one combat between the title figure and Aufidius: "*Here they fight, and certain Volsces come in the aid of Aufidius. Martius fights till they be driven in breathless,*" at which point Aufidius, denied any closure with his enemy, states: "Officious, and not valiant, you have sham'd me / In your condemned seconds" (1.8.13–15). In David Thacker's Napoleonic dress production (RSC Swan 1994) the Volscians carried rifles with bayonets and then rescued their leader by pointing their weapons at Coriolanus. The choice made immediate sense – unless one paused to wonder why this all-conquering Roman had not been shot down at any previous point during the conflict. Similar questions were raised for me in 1985 when within forty-eight hours I saw both Hector (RSC) and Coriolanus (RNT) gunned down from a distance by riflemen – and in Howard Davies's *Troilus and Cressida* set in the 1850s Hector did not pursue and win a sumptuous armor as a prelude to his fatal encounter with Achilles and the Myrmidons. Can one-on-one chivalric combat or chivalry in general co-exist with rifles?

Similar problems arose in Michael Edwards's modern dress *1 Henry IV* (SSC 1984) where the battle scenes featured army fatigue uniforms rather than knightly armor. The price tag in this instance was a diminution of Shakespeare's emphasis upon counterfeit kings in the climactic vignettes of 5.3 and 5.4, as when Douglas challenges Henry IV: "What art thou / That counterfeit'st the person of a king?" (5.4.27–28). In this production both Sir Walter Blunt and Henry IV in their encounters with Douglas were dressed as five-star generals, but, with Blunt not wearing a visored helmet to conceal his identity, the confusion for Douglas and for the spectator about many marching in the king's coats or of various counterfeits "Semblably furnish'd like the King himself" (5.3.25, 21) was considerably diminished. Here at least one of Shakespeare's images was lost or buried. Other adjustments had to be made in the final scenes when the battles, staged with great energy and verisimilitude in the woods and terrain around this outdoor theatre, were carried out with rifles, uzis, pistols, and bayonets rather than with swords, daggers, and shields. As with comparable moments in *Coriolanus* and *Troilus and Cressida*, at least some sense of the individual prowess and chivalric ideals of a Hotspur or Douglas was lost in such a trade-off.

The 1980s setting of this production did provide one richly suggestive moment. In one of the many battlefield vignettes that constitute 5.3 and 5.4 the Quarto has a weaponless Hal ask Falstaff "lend me thy sword" three times (5.3.40, 43, 49), with Sir John refusing and offering instead his supposed pistol. Hal looks in Falstaff's case, finds not a weapon but a bottle of sack, and, with the line "What, is it a time to jest and dally now?", "*throws the bottle at him*" (55). If, as most interpreters agree, sack epitomizes the carefree world of the tavern, Hal's action as signaled in the script constitutes a clear rejection not only of Falstaff as individual at this moment but also of that way of life in which jesting, dallying, and idleness ("What, stand'st thou idle here?" – 40) take precedence over a different sense of time and responsibility. The potential meanings here are manifold.

In the SSC modern-dress production, Shakespeare's images and actions underwent a sea-change. Hal pulled out of the case and brandished not a bottle of sack but a can of Budweiser; he then started to throw the can at Falstaff, checked himself, and eventually carried it off with him. Shakespeare's symbolic action as specified in the Quarto was therefore suppressed. In response to my query, however, the Prince Hal actor (Paul Whitworth) argued that the greater punishment to Falstaff in this instance would not be to throw the can at him but to take it away and deprive him of it. More important, moments later this same can of beer became a meaningful symbol not of the tavern world but of a momentary bond between Hal and Hotspur. Alone on stage after much fighting and running, a bedraggled Hal paused to drink the beer appropriated from Falstaff, only to be surprised by a Hotspur who held a pistol on him. Unabashed, Hal took another swig of the beer and then tossed the can to Hotspur, who drank some, poured the rest on his head to cool himself off, and then threw his pistol away in order to engage Hal in single and equal combat. A clear sense was conveyed here, albeit without the trappings of chivalry, of something shared between the two warriors, an unspoken code that, in modern as well as in Elizabethan terms, may be

archaic and unrealistic, especially in the presence of high-powered auto-
matic weapons and with a kingdom at stake, but is nonetheless appealing
and moving. On the one hand, I missed the throwing of a bottle-can at
Falstaff (one of Shakespeare's summary images), but I would not have
wished to lose this moment where the imagery set up by the actors and
the director clarified and developed something very important in the
script that can easily be blurred in any production.

Such trade-offs need not be limited to battle scenes. As noted in
chapter 5, a major proponent of updating Shakespeare's plays to a later
period is Michael Bogdanov. In Act 5 of his modern-dress *Romeo and
Juliet* (RSC 1986) Romeo got a packet, not a cup or vial from the apothecary and, despite the latter's instructions in the script ("Put this in any
liquid thing you will / And drink it off" – 5.1.77–78), used a needle to
administer the poison. Here then was a striking image for a contemporary audience: a desperate young man injecting drugs in order to destroy
himself. But this image in turn generated new problems. Some spectators were troubled by Romeo's expertise with the needle (are we to infer
a previous habit?). Even more formidable were the problems posed for
the auditor listening to Juliet's final speeches (e.g., "O churl, drunk all,
and left no friendly drop / To help me after?" – 163–64). Watching this
production, are we to understand her as being deceived by appearances
so as to make a false deduction (so that Juliet here is comparable to
Romeo moments earlier thinking she is dead?), or is this error to be ignored? Since so much of Juliet's speech depends upon Romeo's *drinking*
the poison ("I will kiss thy lips, / Haply some poison yet doth hang on
them, / To make me die with a restorative" – 164–66), this rescripting is
not inconsequential. Indeed, this change in the build to Juliet's death can
weaken what is potentially the most moving line in the play: "Thy lips
are warm" (167). Moreover, to eliminate the image of Romeo drinking
the poison is to eliminate a possible visual link between his death-choice
and Juliet's choice to drink the friar's potion in 4.3, a built-in comparison
that can reveal much about their respective statures and tragedies. This
change, presumably to add immediacy to Romeo's death, therefore can
significantly affect the dynamics of *both* suicides.

CHANGING THE IMAGE

The most revealing rescripting of stage directions is linked to imagery –
more specifically images or effects clearly signaled in the original scripts
but deemed inappropriate, unacceptable, or impractical today. Typical as

already noted is the final configuration in *Coriolanus* where directors seeking a more heroic or upbeat ending resist having a triumphant Aufidius stand on the body of the title figure: "*Draw the Conspirators, and kills Marcius, who falls; Aufidius stands on him*" (5.6.130). Both Quarto and Folio *King Lear* direct the bodies of Goneril and Regan to be brought onstage (5.3.238) before Lear appears with the dead Cordelia (and such a reappearance can help to establish an echo of the configuration in 1.1 with the father and his three daughters), but for practical reasons, given the many ins and outs in this sequence, that signal is regularly ignored in the theatre. In a different vein, serious or troubling moments were diminished in Judd Parkin's fast-paced farcical *The Taming of the Shrew* (OSF 1978); in particular, gone were Kate's blow to Bianca ("*Strikes her*" – 2.1.22) and the latter's tied hands ("Unbind my hands" – 2.1.4).

Another approach is the elimination or alteration of scripted properties as a solution to problems. In Ian Judge's *Troilus and Cressida* (RSC 1996) Cressida gave Troilus as a token not a glove (4.4.71) but a scarf, a property which Troilus discarded in 5.2 so that it ended up in the hands of Thersites. In Tim Albery's *Macbeth* (RSC 1996) the witches in 4.1 were operating with most of the Folio lines but with no caldron; also cut were the leafy boughs Malcolm calls for from Birnam and orders thrown down (5.4.4–7, 5.6.1–2) and the severed head in the final moments (not an unusual omission). The latter problem was "solved" by turning Macduff's "Behold where *stands* / Th' usurper's cursed head" (5.9.20–21) to "Behold where *lies*" with the actor then pointing to Macbeth's body. Perhaps to speed up the action the servants and dishes specified in the stage direction that begins 1.7 were ignored, so that Macbeth was already visible onstage by the end of 1.6. Most curious was the omission of a series of lighting implements specified in the stage directions. One oddly shaped lantern was present at the murder of Banquo (3.3), but the scripted torches were gone from 2.1 as was Lady Macbeth's candle in 5.1 (she entered lighting matches). Since the action from 5.2 on took place in front of a painted backdrop with burning haystacks, the play's "fire" or "light" was in the scenic design rather than in a series of handheld properties, a choice that affected "out, out brief candle" among other passages.

1 Henry IV provides an unusual array of distinctive stage directions that do not fare well in today's productions, even when a change in historical period is not at issue. Like Michael Edwards, Adrian Noble (RSC 1991) adjusted the Quarto stage directions for the Hal–Falstaff interaction in 5.3, albeit for different reasons. Here, when offered a bottle of sack in place of a sword, the prince did not throw the bottle at Falstaff but handed it back to him. This small alteration helped to sustain an overall interpretation in that it forestalled a more decisive rejection of Falstaff, sack, and the world of the tavern, a toning down also evident in this Hal's soft rendering at the end of the tavern scene of the final two words of "I do, I will" (2.4.481) and his muted delivery of "Peace, chewet, peace!" (5.1.29). In addition, the Quarto directs Falstaff to pick up the dead Hotspur (*"He takes up Hotspur on his back"* – 5.4.129), a signal rarely observed in the theatre for practical reasons (just as some King Lears do *not* carry in Cordelia at the end of 5.3). Robert Stephens did not pick up and eventually carry off Hotspur's body; instead, this Falstaff cradled the dead Hotspur in his arms and descended on the lift by which he had entered in 1.2 and 3.3.

Michael Attenborough (RSC Swan 2000) also tinkered with the Quarto stage directions – although Desmond Barrit was only the second Falstaff in my playgoing experience actually to pick up and carry off Hotspur's body. However, for practical rather than conceptual reasons (as I was told), the playgoer saw Falstaff pull the bottle from his holster but not deliver it to Hal who therefore did not throw it back. Also re-scripted was the unusually elaborate signal in 2.2 for the re-robbing of the robbers at Gadshill which starts: *"As they are sharing, the Prince and Poins set upon them"* (2.2.101). As presented at the Swan, the four robbery victims carried a large rectangular bag which, in a fine bit of comic business, was flipped from one fearful figure to another like a hot potato until the last of the four tossed it to Falstaff and fled the stage, whereupon Falstaff, surprised by the two figures in buckram, flipped it to Hal and also fled. For me, the *"As they are sharing"* signal suggests that the four scripted figures (in this production reduced to three with Gadshill's lines going to Peto) are prematurely dividing up their spoils, a prefiguration of the four figures in 3.1 (Hotspur, Glendower, Mortimer, and Worcester) who are displayed prematurely dividing up the map of England, with Hal the pivotal figure in forestalling both attempted robberies – as signaled in Hotspur's death speech: "O Harry, thou has robb'd me of my youth!" (5.4.77).

For any director significant problems are posed by *3 Henry VI*, 2.5 which displays Henry VI along with *"a Son that hath kill'd his father"* and *"a Father that hath kill'd his son, at another door, bearing of his son"* (2.5.54, 78). This scene was conceived for an expansive 1590s platform stage, but, if you are director Katie Mitchell (RSC TOP 1994), how do you present blood, bodies, and highly rhetorical speeches in the intimate confines of The Other Place? In a large Elizabethan theatre sustaining the illusion that the father and the son can speak aloud but not be aware of each other is much easier. Mitchell's actors delivered their lines full front to the playgoers, with no attempt to conceal the artifice. Rather, the major choice here was to forgo the two scripted bodies and instead have the father and son each carry in a small object wrapped in a white handkerchief that, when uncovered and addressed as if a body, turned out to be a rose. That link between body and rose, moreover, was sustained by the placement upstage of roses upon crosses that accumulated during the final scenes.

Of particular interest are rescriptings of stage directions that may have set up meaningful effects then but seem obscure, intrusive, or irrelevant today. A good example is the practical joke played upon Francis the drawer by Prince Hal at the outset of the famous tavern scene in *1 Henry IV*. Whether owing to a sense of dramatic economy or a distaste for such pranks, this moment is often pared back or omitted in performance, even though readers have responded to Poins's query ("But hark ye, what cunning match have you made with this jest of the drawer? Come, what's the issue?" – 2.4.89–91) with a variety of answers (e.g., that the dialogue with Francis is an index to the prince's own uneasiness about his truancy or apprenticeship).[3] What most concerns me here is the stage direction at what I take to be the climax of the trick: "*Here they both call him; the drawer stands amazed, not knowing which way to go*" (2.4.79), a highly visible onstage image (what I term theatrical *italics*). What if the frenzied movement of Francis, as he responds alternatively to Poins's offstage calls and the prince's onstage questions, that climaxes in this amazed state visibly echoes onstage activity already seen (e.g., of Hotspur in the previous scene) or soon to be seen (e.g., of Falstaff confronted with the truth about his flight at Gadshill)? As I understand the scene, Shakespeare is here setting up for the playgoer a paradigm of the controller and the controlled, the puppetmaster and the puppet, so as to encourage us to recognize what makes Hal so distinctive. That interpretation may or may not satisfy other readers or viewers, but the episode, especially the theatrical punch line signaled in the stage direction and reinforced by Poins's question, cries out for *some* kind of explanation on the stage or on the page.

A similar effect is generated by Romeo's attempted suicide in 3.3 where the Second Quarto provides no stage direction, but the First Quarto (perhaps based upon an actor's memory of some production) provides: "*He offers to stab himself, and Nurse snatches the dagger away*" (108). Some editors incorporate the q1 signal into their texts, but Arden 2 editor

Brian Gibbons rejects the Nurse's intervention as "neither necessary or defensible." Rather, for this editor "this piece of business looks like a gratuitous and distracting bid on the part of the actor in the unauthorized version to claim extra attention to himself when the audience should be concentrating on Romeo and the Friar" (p. 180). On stage today the Nurse does occasionally intervene (RSC 1986, ACTER 1995), but usually she assists the friar (RSC Swan 1989, RSC 1991–92) or the friar acts alone (OSF 1988, RSC 1995, RSC 2000).

But what if the strategy behind Q1's stage direction is to call attention not to the actor but to the onstage configuration (as with the amazed paralysis of Francis the drawer), a configuration that in turn epitomizes images and motifs enunciated in the dialogue? After Mercutio's death, Romeo had cried out: "O sweet Juliet, / Thy beauty hath made me effeminate, / And in my temper soft'ned valor's steel!" (3.1.113–15). Then, after Romeo's aborted attempt at suicide, the friar's long moralization begins:

> Hold thy desperate hand!
> Art thou a man? Thy form cries out thou art;
> Thy tears are womanish, thy wild acts denote
> The unreasonable fury of a beast.
> Unseemly woman in a seeming man,
> And ill-beseeming beast in seeming both
>
> (3.3.108–13)

The playgoer who sees Romeo's self-destructive violence interrupted (surprisingly) by the Nurse and then hears the friar's terms (e.g., "Art thou a man?"; "Thy tears are womanish"; "Unseemly woman in a seeming man") is therefore encouraged to consider: what kind of "man" *is* Romeo at this point in the play? What by one kind of interpretative logic may seem "gratuitous and distracting" or "out of character" or "unbelievable" may, in the terms of a different logic or vocabulary, prove imagistically or symbolically consistent or meaningful. Indeed, how better act out the ascendancy of the "womanish" or unmanly side of Romeo and call that ascendancy to the attention of a first-time playgoer?

Several moments in *Titus Andronicus* (e.g., the *exeunt* in 3.1 that includes Lavinia carrying Titus's hand in her mouth, Tamora's appearance in 5.2 as Revenge) have troubled readers, editors, and playgoers and therefore have often been blurred or eliminated by directors. Of interest is the signal for Titus to appear "*like a cook, placing the dishes*" (5.3.25), an odd costume immediately called to our attention by Saturninus's question: "Why art thou thus attir'd, Andronicus?" (30). Titus's answer ("Because

I would be sure to have all well,/To entertain your Highness and your empress" – 31–32) has not satisfied subsequent theatrical professionals, so that today's productions often do not present here a decidedly different image of the revenger. For the original audience, moreover, such a costume (along with "*placing the dishes*") would have served as part of a theatrical shorthand to denote the "place" (a banquet room) and would have suggested (wrongly) a subservient Titus debasing himself in degree in order best to serve his emperor and empress.

But to ignore this distinctive costume (OSF 1986) or to play it for laughs (RSC 1987) may be to blur a climactic image that brings into focus various motifs in the play linked to appetites, feeding, and revenge. The Folio stage direction for 3.2 calls for a banquet (3.2.0), but Titus opens that scene with the order: "So, so, now sit, and look you eat no more/Than will preserve just so much strength in us/As will revenge these bitter woes of ours" (1–3). By the end of the play, however, revenge has become linked not to abstinence but to feeding and appetite, usually in dangerous or self-destructive terms. For example, in her overconfident claims to Saturninus, Tamora promises to "enchant the old Andronicus/With words more sweet, and yet more dangerous,/Than baits to fish, or honey-stalks to sheep"; the fish, she notes, "is wounded with the bait," and the sheep "rotted with delicious feed" (4.4.89–93). The most potent orchestration of "appetite" or feeding is found in Titus's long speech at the end of 5.2 where the revenger first torments the muted Chiron and Demetrius with a detailed account of what he is going to do to or with them (e.g., "I will grind your bones to dust,/And with your blood and it I'll make a paste"), then promises to "make two pasties of your shameful heads," and finally announces that he will "bid that strumpet, your unhallowed dam,/Like to the earth swallow her own increase" (186–91). After his command that Lavinia "Receive the blood" and a second reference to paste and heads, Titus "*cuts their throats*" and announces "I'll play the cook" so as "To make this banket, which I wish may prove/More stern and bloody than the Centaurs' feast" (197–205).

When Titus enters to set up the banquet in 5.3 (with or without a cook's costume), the spectator is therefore well prepared. The savage ironies in his lines, moreover, are anything but subtle, for he starts with "Although the cheer be poor,/'Twill fill your stomachs, please you eat of it" (5.3.28–29); builds to "Will't please you eat? will't please your Highness feed?" (54); and, in response to the emperor's command to fetch Chiron and Demetrius, climaxes with: "Why, there they are, both baked in this pie;/Whereof their mother daintily hath fed,/Eating the flesh that she herself hath bred" (60–62). Indeed, these lines and the overall effect have seemed excessive to many directors and readers.

But what would have been the effect if Titus *does* appear "*like a cook*" (as predicted in the closing lines of 5.2) and, in this odd costume, does call emphatic attention to his culinary role as he hovers around the banqueters? In imagistic terms, what has so far been primarily verbal or aural (animals "rotted with delicious feed") now is being displayed visually, not only in the pasties being consumed by Tamora and others but also in the purveyor of such delicacies, Titus, who sets up the feeding of (and himself feeds on) his enemies so as to become a visible part of the appetitive revenge process (just as Tamora had "become" Revenge in 5.2). The image of the revenger as cook builds upon what has gone before and, especially as italicized here by both the costume and Saturninus's question, brings to a climax the feed-and-be-fed-upon imagery earlier linked to the hunt and to the "wilderness of tigers" (3.1.54), a wilderness in which *both* families have now become prey. The same man who in 3.2 had urged his family to refrain from eating now sets up the meal for others and feeds upon his revenge. Moreover, if Aaron or Tamora's body is placed in the trap door, this cook–revenger has generated a feast that parallels and supersedes the "detested, dark, blood-drinking pit" and "fell devouring receptacle" (2.3.224, 235) that had claimed Bassianus, Quintus, and Martius. In short, at the climax of this revenge process, "*Titus like a cook*" makes very good sense indeed.

Much of the effect of such italicized moments, whether Francis standing amazed, the Nurse snatching the dagger, or Titus as cook, lies in their surprise value or initial illogic, a surprise that is designed to call attention to that moment and, ideally, to tease the playgoer into thought, into making connections. That effect, however, can be undermined, even eliminated entirely, if a director resists such images or such logic of illogic, so that a provocative signpost (at least for the 1590s) is then lost. In such cases, to de-italicize is to diminish the range of possibilities, to weaken the signals, so as to preserve a post 1590s sense of decorum or verisimilitude, principles Shakespeare was aware of but was willing to strain, even violate, to gain his effects.

RESCRIPTING THE SUPERNATURAL

The same problems and trade-offs can regularly be seen in moments that involve magic or the supernatural. Occasionally, a director will insert additional supernatural figures, as already noted in the final sequence of

Michael Boyd's *Romeo and Juliet*. In some productions of *The Winter's Tale*, when Antigonus recounts his dream or vision (3.3.16–37), the Hermione actress stands silently upstage (Globe 1997), delivers the words attributed to her (RSC 1986, ACTER 1989, RSC 1992), or, with a hand extended forward (to prefigure the posture of the "statue" in 5.3), whispers the name "Perdita" at line 33 (ACTER 2001). The more common practice, however, is to pare back such moments or eliminate them entirely. Typical is *The Two Noble Kinsmen* (Globe 2000) where Tim Carroll chose not to follow the Act 5 signals that spell out the responses of Mars, Venus, and Diana to various offerings, in particular the latter's response to Emilia who offers a silver hind which "*vanishes under the altar, and in the place ascends a rose tree, having one rose upon it*" with that rose then falling from the tree (5.1.162, 168). The Globe Emilia did carry a flower, but no attempt was made to deal with the hind or the vanishing effect, so that the role of the gods in the denouement was much diminished.

A comparable situation is Queen Katherine's final scene in *Henry VIII* (4.2) where the sleeping figure has a "vision" (so termed in the heading to the long Folio stage direction) involving dancing figures "*clad in white robes*" with "*golden vizards on their faces*" and bearing a garland. According to the Folio, the figures in the vision bow to Katherine, dance, and take turns holding the garland over her head, while she, still in her chair, "*makes (in her sleep) signs of rejoicing, and holdeth up her hands to heaven*" (4.1.82). During this action, moreover, as confirmed in the ensuing dialogue, Griffith and Patience are onstage but see nothing.

For a variety of reasons, the elaborate signal in the Folio creates difficulties for modern actors and directors. Gregory Doran (RSC Swan 1997) provided no such group of figures but had a dozing Katherine react to something not seen by the playgoer. Howard Davies (RSC 1983) brought in the dancing figures, and Katherine rose from her chair, danced *with* them, and remained standing when the lights returned to normal. As a spectator, I got the impression of a dream rather than a vision, an effect enhanced by the dimmed lighting and perhaps keyed to Griffith's reference to "such good dreams" (93). In contrast, Jim Edmondson (OSF 1984) reduced the Folio's group of vizarded dancers to one figure dressed in white that came to a dozing Queen who, with half-opened eyes, was vaguely aware of her women (also in white costumes) winding sheets. In this rendition, the spectator was left with the sense of an hallucination, not a transcendental vision – and lost too was any link to either the vizarded group of masquers led by the king in 1.4 or the very different coronation of a Queen in 4.1. Similarly, to emphasize the dream and to have the queen rise and actually join the dance, as in RSC 1983, is also to diminish the visionary or transcendental nature of this moment, especially when one remembers that in the original production, where the King's Men had no variable lighting, the spectator would have been conscious of Griffith and Patience onstage impervious to the vision (what Katherine refers to as "a blessed troop" – 87). As I have argued elsewhere,[4] this combination of seeing and not-seeing figures recurs in Jacobean drama, so that the changes made by all three directors signal the presence of a stage convention available at the Globe for presenting a transcendental moment but deemed to lack efficacy today.

Another visionary moment rarely played as scripted is the appearance in *Cymbeline* to a sleeping Posthumus of first the ghosts of his father, mother, and two brothers and then, in response to their complaints, Jupiter who "*descends in thunder and lightning, sitting upon an eagle*" and "*throws a thunderbolt*" (5.4.92). The usual procedure in my playgoing experience is to omit the brothers and their lines (5.4.52–57, 69–80) so as to present two rather than four ghosts (RSC TOP–Pit 1987–88, PRC 1996, RSC 1997) and then, with the notable exception of Sir Peter Hall (RNT 1988) and Mike Alfreds (Globe 2001), to find a way to present a distinctive Jupiter minus the eagle. Hall provided a spectacular effect, an actual descent on a golden eagle; Alfreds, in a production with only six actors, had the Jupiter actor move downstage while the four actors playing the ghosts suddenly flanked him with their arms extended so as to suggest the eagle's wings. Adrian Noble (RSC 1997) had his Lucius actor appear above with a golden mask and descend far enough to hand down the tablet with his prophecy to Posthumus's father. Tazewell Thompson (PRC 1996) had his Guiderius actor appear above in native American dress with an eagle headdress, but this figure did not descend, so that the reference to the tablet ("This tablet lay upon his breast" – 109) was cut, as were the lines after Jupiter's departure (114–22).

Of the many adjustments to this sequence perhaps the least successful was Bill Alexander's cutting not only Jupiter but all the spoken lines (RSC 1989). Alexander had recently directed a small theatre production of this script (RSC TOP–Pit 1987–88) in which the playgoer had not seen Jupiter but had heard the lines and had seen a shadow of the god and his eagle. In the main house production, however, the two brothers of Posthumus were eliminated in a first round of cuts, other compressions followed, and finally, with the show running very long during previews, *all* of the lines in the sequence were cut. The father and mother of Posthumus were still included and were credited in the program but now had no lines, so they merely entered, deposited the tablet with the prophecy on their son's chest, and departed. According to my exit polling, this appearance of Sicilius Leonatus and "*an ancient Matron, his wife*" (from the Folio stage direction at line 29) mystified many playgoers (one waggish reviewer referred to the couple as two well-dressed prison visitors). Moreover, the daunting final scene of this romance cannot be fully realized without this vision, not only because the playgoer loses the genesis of the tablet-prophecy (as well as another view of "family reunion") but also because of the omission of Jupiter's richly suggestive lines: "Whom best I love, I cross; to make my gift, / The more delay'd, delighted" (101–02). However interpreted, something essential to romance in general and this romance in particular was absent from this production.

THE TEMPEST

The two plays that pose the greatest problems in staging the supernatural are *The Tempest* and *Macbeth*. In her program note to *The Tempest* (Globe 2000) Lenka Udovicki calls attention to the special problems of staging "magic" at a reconstructed Globe Theatre: "It's a great challenge to stage a play which contains so many moments of magic and to do so without theatrical lighting, smoke machines and other tricks of the theatre. One has to think through action, through the actors themselves, and trust the imagination of the audience." In her production in what has become a standard move she factored Ariel into the opening scene, so that the storm was displayed by means of ropes and a sail dropped from above, the boatswain at a wheel, the master above, the frenzied movement of the other actors, and, most important, Ariel in distinctive white costume and make-up carrying a small boat that she manipulated so as to cause those on board to lurch and sway accordingly. Similarly, inserted into the next scene was an appearance upstage of first Antonio, then Alonso to mime various actions during Prospero's long narrative to Miranda. In the final scene Prospero's magic circle ("*They all enter the circle which Prospero had made, and there stand charm'd*" – 5.1.57) was not drawn on the ground but was formed by the whitened bodies of six "spirits" stretched out on the stage floor.

The two magical moments that provide major hurdles for any production of *The Tempest* are the disappearing banquet in 3.3 and the masque of 4.1.[5] The Folio stage directions for the former are unusually elaborate – to the point that some scholars have argued that they are elaborations by scrivener Ralph Crane rather than part of Shakespeare's manuscript.[6]

Alonso and his courtiers first hear "_Solemn and strange music_"; then "_Enter several strange Shapes, bringing in a banket; and dance about it with gentle actions of salutations; and inviting the King, etc., to eat, they depart_" (3.3.17, 19). As Alonso is about to eat: "_Thunder and Lightning. Enter Ariel, like a harpy, claps his wings upon the table, and with a quaint device the banquet vanishes_" (52). After Ariel's long indictment of the "three men of sin" (53–82), "_He vanishes in thunder; then, to soft music, enter the Shapes again, and dance, with mocks and mows, and carrying out the table._" For the "_quaint device_" at the Globe or Blackfriars Andrew Gurr suggests "a kind of reversible table-top with dishes fastened to one surface and the other bare – in which case the banquet would certainly have been brought out already fastened to the table."[7] The combination of such a reversible table, the harpy's wings to cloak the device, and some misdirection of the playgoer's attention could have produced the desired effect.

Sometimes a director (e.g., Sir Peter Hall in RNT Cottesloe 1988) will include all the elements of the scene so that "_several strange Shapes_" do indeed bring in a table covered with food, that food does disappear by means of "_a quaint device_," and the spirits re-enter to take away the table. Nicholas Hytner (RSC 1988) provided a variation wherein six blue-faced spirits (one for each courtier) brought in closed transparent globes containing visible food (so six devices rather than one) that flipped at the key moment to show nothing inside (though the first time I saw this production one of the six did not work properly). Adrian Noble (RSC 1998) had his shapes, wrapped in blue cloth (two reviewers compared them to tea-bags), bring in not a table but two large pots heaped high with food and also distribute candles placed in bowls. At the key moment came an explosion accompanied by puffs of smoke so that the food disappeared; with Prospero standing invisible in the midst of the courtiers, Ariel as harpy descended from above with huge red wings and an amplified voice.

In my playgoing experience, however, directors have more often adjusted or ignored the Folio signals. One approach is to set up a trick disappearance but eliminate the spirits or shapes. Tazewell Thompson (PRC 1998) had his banquet rise from below through a trapdoor and later descend, so that he omitted the now unnecessary table-carrying spirits (lines 20–49 were cut) – and, in this rewrighted show, Prospero did not appear in the scene. The shapes or spirits and the lines describing them were also gone from Charles Towers's production (Virginia Stage Company 1987) where several very colorful pedestal-like objects emerged from the stage floor, then disappeared quickly as a harpy's head dropped from above so that Ariel could stand behind it and deliver her indictment. In contrast, David Thacker (RSC Swan 1995) kept Ariel and two spirits onstage for the entire performance; in 3.3 the previously invisible spirits, now seen by those onstage, pantomimed placing food at the courtiers' feet, so that, with the food imagined rather than real, nothing had to be brought on and off the stage. Another variation was provided by Richard E. T. White (DC 1989) who had his spirits initially appear with mirrors so that the courtiers could look at themselves; he then dropped sheets from above on which were projected images of food, fruit, and also people. With Ariel suspended from above and Prospero watching from an aisle in the auditorium, these images, rather than a tangible banquet, disappeared.

Another choice is not to have the banquet disappear but rather to keep it visible to the playgoer and have it carried off at the end of the scene (RSC 1982). In Michael Addison's production (OSF 1978) the disappearance of the banquet (two bowls of fruit) was eclipsed by the reappearance of the "island spirits" (so noted in the program), huge Easter Island-like figures who stole in silently and towered over the courtiers. In Udovicki's Globe production, Prospero led onstage two female figures clad in white gowns carrying the banquet table (accompanied by two additional figures in veils who tangoed with two of the courtiers). At the key moment the two gowned figures dropped the table on the floor, but the food remained visible. Ariel then emerged from underneath not as a winged harpy but as a black-clad terrorist or partisan wearing a bandoleer of cartridges, so that, as with other elements in this show, a key image (here Ariel as threat) was reconfigured in modern Balkan terms.

Similarly, rather than having his spirits carry the banquet onto the stage, Sam Mendes (RSC 1993) opted for stage magic by having them hold a cloth so that a table formed under it, but again the banquet did not disappear so that no vanishing occurred here or in the masque of 4.1. As harpy, moreover, Ariel changed from a blue to a white suit with blood on the front and sported golden claws but had no wings or any distinctive headdress (he did react with red streamers from his hands after the three men of sin drew their swords). James Macdonald (RSC 2000–01) provided not a vanishing banquet but his own alternative image. Upstage the black clad spirits seen throughout the show (as opposed to "*several strange Shapes*") brought in a table and a three-tiered cake with a glazed cherry on the top (for Sebastian to sample) while the courtiers looked out over the heads of the audience and described what they saw. Ariel as winged harpy then appeared and stamped on the cake which collapsed into a pile of ugly compost.

Each of these choices has consequences. Admittedly, a harpy may not be a meaningful entity for today's playgoers (as already noted, the harpy's wings probably served a practical purpose in helping to conceal or facilitate the "*quaint device*"), so that a director's re-imaging of such a figure is understandable. Nonetheless, various things easily get lost or blurred when the banquet does not disappear so as to surprise both the courtiers and the playgoers. In particular, without such a distinctive action or image, gone is any symbolic sense of evanescence or impermanence in an apparently substantial object that melts "into air, into thin air" to "Leave not a rack behind" (4.1.150, 156). If this scripted moment is deficient in "magic," a major building block that helps to set up the breaking of the masque in 4.1 and other subsequent images is eliminated.

As noted in the discussion of Marston's *The Fawn* in chapter 2, Jacobean masques pose major problems for today's theatrical professionals and playgoers. Directors have therefore tried just about every conceivable variation on the Folio signals that include entrances for Iris, Ceres, and Juno (who is directed to descend at 4.1.74 but does not speak until line 103), then the appearance of nymphs and reapers who join "*in a graceful dance, towards the end whereof Prospero starts suddenly, and speaks; after which, to a strange, hollow, and confused noise, they heavily vanish*" (138). As with the 3.3 banquet, some directors try to reproduce the effect signaled in the Folio. Adrian Noble (RSC 1998) presented the three goddesses behind a scrim followed by three nymphs and three reapers who kept dancing even after Prospero's first attempt to break off their dance, so that he had to struggle to get their attention.

To keep all the elements in the script, however, is unusual. Some directors take the Gordian knot approach and eliminate the masque entirely. Charles Towers (Virginia Stage Company 1987) began his scene with the Ariel–Prospero exchange about Caliban that starts at line 164; Prospero's "Our revels now are ended" speech (148–58) was then re-inserted later as a reaction not to the disappearing goddesses and dancers but to the "*divers Spirits in shape of dogs and hounds*" (254) who pursue the clowns. Richard E. T. White (DC 1989) provided his own rewrighted version: Iris, Ceres, Juno, nymphs and reapers were gone; rather, in lieu of a marriage masque the playgoers were presented with sonnet 116 ("Let me not to the marriage of true minds / Admit impediments") along with projections on a screen of images of Ferdinand and Miranda, flowers, and stars. Prospero did retain some of his lines, though I could not follow to what he was referring in his "These our actors" (148). White provided a striking moment with noise, then a sudden removal of the screen and a change in lighting, but what emerged was a very different sense of exactly *what* was being broken or violated. This show was strong on visual images or tricks but consistently omitted or transformed scripted images (logs, dogs, the disappearing banquet, the masque, the chess set).

More common is the choice to include some but not all of the elements scripted in the Folio. James Macdonald (RSC 2000–01) included Iris, Ceres, and Juno but no nymphs and reapers; rather, Ferdinand and Miranda were given magical shoes and did an elaborate and crowd-pleasing dance. Sam Mendes (RSC 1993) had his Prospero hand Ariel a small box that opened to reveal Pollock's Toy Theatre, and then a full-scale replica dropped from above. The subsequent action included the three goddesses and three sicklemen (with hats covering their faces) but not the nymphs and the dance; rather, Prospero started suddenly, and the middle reaper was revealed to be a menacing Caliban. The result was to highlight Prospero's state of mind or psychological process but also to eliminate all of the associations linked to the dance of paired figures and its interruption. Similarly, Terry Burgler (Theatre Virginia 1987) had three children play the three goddesses and had Ariel, placed behind them, speak a streamlined version of their lines in three different voices and then, in lieu of a dance, sing "It was a lover and his lass" from *As You Like It*; the interruption of this song then generated Prospero's revels speech. Tazewell Thompson (PRC 1998) provided three elaborately costumed goddesses upstage but no nymphs and reapers, so that the goddesses danced with each other, then Ferdinand and Miranda rose to join them to be interrupted by Prospero. Both Prospero's nature–nurture speech (188–93) and his "Our revels now are ended" (148–58) were gone (the latter speech was moved to the end to replace the Epilogue), so that the interruption of the masque had no particular meaning or special quality.

Clearly for a variety of reasons the Folio signals in 4.1 are difficult to realize today – hence the varied responses. Nonetheless, exactly what fails in this scene so as to generate Prospero's justly famous revels speech is no small matter. A final example is David Thacker's production (RSC Swan 1995), a show, as already noted, with limited resources, so that the goddesses were three spirits draped in white sheets who delivered the lines, and the nymphs and reapers were eliminated. The breaking of the masque or dance, however, was as successful as I have seen it done and was for me the high point of this production. With Ariel presiding, the dance started with two of the spirits who were joined by Ferdinand and

Miranda, then other spirits, then the courtiers who had been sleeping up-stage, then the two clowns. What initially had been stately music became increasingly raucous; Caliban then appeared on an upstage trunk, gesturing and shouting, so that the music became his music, out of Ariel's or Prospero's control (comparable to the end of 2.2 where Caliban's "Freedom, high-day!" chant had a similar effect on the spirits). Standing in the midst of this frenzied activity, Prospero broke off the dance, so that this "vanity of mine art" or "most majestic vision" (4.1.41, 118) had been destroyed, never completed. Paul Jesson's delivery of the revels speech was then impassioned, anything but a set piece, a reaction to what had just happened or not happened, and therefore provided a genesis for the anger at Caliban in the subsequent nature–nurture speech.

MACBETH

Similarly, the supernatural dimension of *Macbeth* is often rescripted, whether owing to difficulties in staging the apparitions in 4.1 or to a desire to sustain an intense psychological emphasis that may not mesh comfortably with Banquo's ghost or other effects signaled in the Folio. As with comparable moments in *The Tempest*, choices vary widely in these two scenes. For the banquet scene the Folio clearly signals two entrances for the ghost: "*Enter the Ghost of Banquo and sits in Macbeth's place*"; "*Enter Ghost*" (3.4.36, 87). The original strategy thereby called for Macbeth and the playgoers, but not Lady Macbeth and others onstage, to see the apparition. However, to stress the psychological rather than the super-natural some directors do not have the Banquo actor visible to the spectators (RSC TOP–Young Vic 1976–78, RSC 1982, RSC 1988). Gregory Doran (RSC Swan–Young Vic 1999–2000) provided a variation (that, I confess, puzzled me) wherein no visible figure appeared for the ghost's first scripted entrance (Antony Sher's Macbeth directed his speeches at a figure not seen by the playgoer), but for the second appearance the Banquo actor, with no visible blood, moved quickly over the stage and exited, so that for a second time a key speech ("What man dare, I dare . . . I am a man again" – 98–107) was directed at empty space.

When the ghost is visible to the playgoers, the effect can vary considerably. Jim Edmondson (OSF 1987) provided an unusually active ghost by employing two actors wearing identical bloody masks, so that one could exit above and the second could immediately re-enter below. The Folio places the ghost's first entrance after Lady Macbeth's "You do not give the cheer" speech (31–36) and just before Macbeth's "Sweet remembrancer!" but both editors and directors have tinkered with this placement. Some directors, like editor Kenneth Muir in his influential Arden 2 edition, prefer the irony of having the ghost enter a bit later at Macbeth's "Were the grac'd presence of our Banquo present" (40) so that he appears unwittingly to be invoking the apparition. In Richard Eyre's production (RNT 1993) after the murder of Banquo in 3.3 the body remained downstage; at Macbeth's hypocritical wish for Banquo's presence, the corpse got up, walked upstage to the empty seat at the banquet table, sat, and then turned to keep facing Macbeth (the ghost's second appearance was effected by means of a shadow that kept getting larger).

More common is to have some form of stage trickery or misdirection for this first appearance so that the Banquo actor is already in place at the table for Macbeth's "The table's full" (45). Indeed, in my playgoing experience actually to see the ghost enter at "Sweet remembrancer!" and sit "*in Macbeth's place*" is rare. A related choice is somehow to include the witches here (and elsewhere where they are not scripted) whether as servants, companions for the thanes, or some combination of the two (SFC 1978). David Wheeler (PRC 1995) provided ubiquitous witches: all three were present in 3.4; one reappeared as the nurse in 5.1 (and smiled wickedly on her way out); another appeared in the England scene (4.3) with wine for Malcolm only to depart when his confession of depravity proved to be a ruse.

To have Macbeth confront something not visible to the playgoer can yield a very powerful effect, most notably in Trevor Nunn's production (RSC TOP–Young Vic 1976–78), by far the most successful rendition of this script that I have seen, where Ian McKellen's Macbeth was reduced to sub-human status by the confrontation. Nonetheless, my theatre historian gene strongly supports the Folio reading. Any interpretation of the differences between the two approaches will depend upon one's reading of other parts of the play (e.g., the witches). My own formulation is keyed to what I take to be a defining moment, Macbeth's "What man dare, I dare" speech (3.4.98–107) which for me boils down to the statement: I can handle anything but this sight ("Take any shape but that" – 101). The question then follows: what exactly is it that Macbeth cannot face?

Not surprisingly, directors, actors, and students today are most comfortable with some form of psychological realism, an approach in this instance keyed to a Macbeth who is wrestling with what appear to be internal demons rather than a Macbeth who is confronted with a supernatural entity. When asked to choose, the majority of my students prefer a ghost only visible to Macbeth so that the X which he cannot face is something within himself, a reading that fits neatly with other passages in the script – for example, "To know my deed, 'twere best not know myself" (2.2.70). The Folio, which signals two entrances for the ghost, clearly calls for an actor to play a visible and usually bloody Banquo ("never shake / Thy gory locks at me" – 3.4.49–50) who takes Macbeth's seat once and sometimes twice. An onstage ghost does not rule out a psychological reading but, unlike a figure only seen by Macbeth, can allow or encourage a sense of a supernatural entity in keeping with the witches, the apparitions, and a possible satanic pronunciation of S-E-Y-T-O-N. The key question for me is then: is Macbeth unable to confront something in himself (or what he has become) or is he unable to confront something that exists outside the world of man and therefore beyond the capabilities of even a hero who can triumph over "the rugged Russian bear, / The arm'd rhinoceros, or th' Hyrcan tiger" (99–100)? Statements such as "What man dare, I dare" and "I am a man again" clearly echo other passages in the tragedy that link manhood with *dare-do-deed* and, at least with Macduff, with feeling ("But I must also feel it as a man" – 4.3.221). McKellen's presentation of a Macbeth who was sub-human, something less than a man, at the climax of this speech set up powerfully how far he had descended and fit smoothly with a ghost linked to his internal demons, but the alternative reading can be just as powerful and meaningful if what the tragic protagonist cannot combat comes from an otherworldly visitation.

Similarly, the apparitions in 4.1 are rarely presented as scripted in the Folio which calls for "*an armed Head*," "*a bloody Child*," and "*a Child crowned, with a tree in his hand*" (4.1.68, 76, 86), directs each to descend (72, 81, 93), and, after calling for "*Hoboys*" (106), specifies "*A show of eight Kings*," the eighth "*with a glass in his hand, and Banquo last*" (111). Although not signaled in a stage direction, the caldron is mentioned repeatedly in the dialogue. Theatre historians suggest that it would have been placed over a trap door so that the three apparitions could rise from beneath it and descend accordingly.

Directors, however, resist such an approach, so that playgoers rarely get a chance to see what may have been the original version of the scene. The prophecies provided by the apparitions ("Beware the Thane of Fife," "none of woman born / Shall harm Macbeth," "Macbeth shall never vanquish'd be until / Great Birnan wood to high Dunsinane hill / Shall come against him" – 72, 80–81, 92–94) are crucial to the events that follow but can be delivered by the witches or some other mechanism (and here the absence of skilled child actors available to the King's Men is also a factor). Directors therefore regularly pare back or eliminate the three apparitions (SFC 1978). Tom Haas (PRC 1979) provided no caldron or images, only Banquo in his army costume of 1.3, and presented the prophecies by means of a disembodied voice (this production depended heavily upon electronic music and sounds for its witchly effects). Howard Davies (RSC 1982) cut the first two apparitions and had Fleance appear as the third. Trevor Nunn (RSC TOP–Young Vic 1976–78) had the witches deliver the speeches and focused Macbeth's and the playgoer's attention upon three objects or fetishes that resembled voodoo dolls which Macbeth then kept with him and interacted with for the rest of the show.

When apparitions are included, they can vary widely. Adrian Noble (RSC 1988) cut 3.5 and 3.6 so that the place remained the same from the banquet scene through the Lady Macduff scene (4.2); he then did use child actors for the 4.1 apparitions with those actors becoming the Macduff children in the following scene. Joe Dowling (DC 1995) had no caldron, so that the witches deposited imaginary ingredients at the base of an onstage tree. The apparitions were oversized images in vaults that were wheeled onto the stage; the kings were an upstage procession in white with a bloody Banquo above. At the other extreme are productions that provide a special effect in lieu of the scripted action. Pat Patton (OSF 1979) had the apparitions projected onto the bared chest of the male first witch; similarly, Gregory Doran's images (RSC Swan–Young Vic 1999–2000) were shapes projected on the back wall. In both instances from where I was seated at the Bowmer and the Young Vic I could not make them out. Jim Edmondson (OSF 1987) provided not just a head but a corpse with an armed head, then an aborted bloody baby, and finally a child carrying a tree; all three figures were held by mummy-like figures placed in front of a slab that rose from below (and in this production Banquo's line of kings was visible). David Wheeler (PRC 1995) had his witches throw "real" objects into the caldron and then pull the apparitions (a helmet, a bloody babe, a figure with a tree) out of the trap; the procession of kings was represented by crowns dropped from above.

Such effects can become very elaborate. David William (SFC 1990) presented his playgoers with three monster figures in armor with bishop's mitres, one with a crocodile tail, bizarre figures that carried the specified apparitions. Given the wealth of personnel available, moreover, the director had no shortage of actors to play the shield and mirror-bearing kings (with Banquo above looking on). However, of those Folio images to which the prophecies are keyed only the third was easy to see (and even here the bough and crown were very small). The second figure held up a bloody babe on its way out (so the playgoer got at least a flash of that image); the armed head was there with the first but hard to make out. Richard Eyre's "ring of fire" production (RNT 1993) provided a series of fiery circles that climaxed in a caldron-less caldron scene where Alan Howard's Macbeth carefully set the chairs and table from the banquet scene inside the circle, then sat and slumped over. The witches entered, did their chanting (but had no "real" objects with no caldron in which to throw them), with each going to the table inside the circle, then retreating outside before the flames arose, with the emergence of those flames keyed each time to "fire *burn*." After the initial effect, I confess to watching the choreographed movement (and musing about faulty timing and toasted witch) rather than listening to the words. Again, with no caldron the apparitions (Macduff, Lady Macbeth, and Malcolm holding the appropriate objects) emerged from upstage trees; after glimpses of the procession of kings (mostly seen as shadows), Banquo entered to sit by Macbeth so that they almost touched heads as if he was challenging Macbeth for his place.

Here, as in *The Tempest* and comparable scenes elsewhere in the canon, directors must deal with playgoers who have been conditioned by cinema and television to expect convincing special effects and therefore may not be in tune with the supernatural elements as originally scripted. In such instances the gap between then and now can be a chasm. In my playgoing experience, however, productions of *Macbeth* often have faltered in the caldron scene when the apparitions did not come across as eerie or forbidding and did not seem integral to the rest of the play. Some of the elaborate or "maximal" effects described above therefore proved to be less telling than a simpler rendition of the images as scripted in the Folio. Especially if boy actors are available, a rendition of the Folio apparitions ("*an armed Head*," "*a bloody Child*," "*a Child crowned, with a tree in his hand*") can set up links to subsequent moments, whether Macbeth's severed and helmeted head, the bloody murders of young Macduff and young Siward, or the crown and boughs linked to Malcolm. At stake here, as with Francis standing amazed, the Nurse snatching the dagger, Titus as cook, and the disappearing banquet, are scripted images that have a rationale or pay-off that may still be accessible today.

RICHARD III

A particular challenge is posed by the eleven ghosts in *Richard III* that appear to Richard and Richmond before the battle at Bosworth field: Prince Edward; Henry VI; Clarence; Rivers, Grey, and Vaughan; the two young princes; Hastings; Anne; and Buckingham. Television or cinema renditions such as Jane Howell's rendition for the BBC-TV series can readily turn the ghosts' appearance into a dream sequence, but, although an occasional stage production will include all eleven (OSF 1978), directors faced with a shortage of personnel usually pare down the ghosts to nine or fewer (e.g., RSC 1984, RNT 1990, RSC TOP 1992). Such streamlining makes sense in practical terms, for often Vaughan has already disappeared from the acting script, and Henry VI and his son Edward (both of whom die in *3 Henry VI*) do not make an appearance in this play (unless one counts Henry as corpse in 1.2).

More significant than the number of onstage ghosts included is how their speeches are presented. The basic effect as scripted is reasonably clear: with both combatants asleep onstage in their visible or to-be-imagined tents, each ghost or set of ghosts enters, delivers first a speech to Richard that climaxes with "Despair and die!", then an encouraging speech to Richmond. What is less clear, however, is when these figures depart, for, curiously, although each entrance is noted, neither Quarto nor Folio marks an *exit* or *exeunt* for any of the ghosts. Editors regularly provide such exits after each speech to Richmond and some directors follow suit, so that the standard choice is to have each figure enter or otherwise appear, give its speech, and then exit or otherwise disappear.

What seems fairly straightforward on the pages of many editions, however, does not necessarily translate directly to the stage. Steven Pimlott (RSC 1995–96) had the ghosts of murdered figures, starting with Clarence, congregate and remain visible in a downstage area, so that in this production a ghostly presence was not limited to Act 5. As noted in chapter 5, rather than having tents, the action in 5.3 centered around a table within a white box, with the sequence of ghosts addressing both seated figures. Before the dream sequence Richard moved downstage to the ghost area, put his dagger in the ground, broke bread, sipped wine, and moved back to his chair for the visit of nine ghosts (no Henry VI and Prince Edward). Sam Mendes (RSC TOP 1992) also had his ghosts address both Richard and Richmond but restitched this sequence (and also some previous and subsequent material) so as to have considerable back and forth movement between the two antagonists. The six ghosts (Clarence, Rivers, Hastings, Anne, Buckingham, and an actor who spoke no lines) delivered abbreviated versions of their speeches to Richard, then even briefer versions to Richmond.[8]

An alternative choice is to omit all the speeches to Richmond and have the ghosts only address Richard, an approach that can better preserve a sense of Richard's dream or nightmare as opposed to a supernatural manifestation. As the climax to his seven-play cycle, Michael Bogdanov (ESC 1988) provided ten ghosts (all except Vaughan) who addressed a Richard sitting or lying in his bed (the speeches to Richmond were cut): Henry VI in white stabbed Richard; a tuxedoed Clarence drank the wine Richard had called for; Rivers and Grey appeared above; Hastings carried the satchel that had held his head in 3.5; Anne sat on the bed, fondled Richard, and spat; and Buckingham fired a pistol at which point the lights came up suddenly to end the dream. Richmond retained his speech about "their souls whose bodies Richard murther'd / Came to my tent and cried on victory" (5.3.230–31), but the playgoer did not see that tent or hear any such speeches directed at him. Comparable effects were provided by Richard Eyre (RNT 1990) who set up a tent for Richard but not for Richmond; rather, the latter exited at the end of his speech before the appearance of the first ghost (5.3.108–17) only to re-enter as a part of Richard's dream. As in Bogdanov's production, what followed was a series of bizarre nightmare images: Clarence forced wine down Richard's throat; Anne danced with Richmond; the two boys played keep-away games; Buckingham provided a crown of thorns; and a smiling (and younger) Margaret roamed the stage (one fellow playgoer quipped that the credits should include "dream sequence by David Lynch").

To have the ghosts only address Richard is to tame a 1590s sense of the supernatural (unless one can imagine parallel concerted dreams) and also to eliminate an option left open in both Quarto and Folio. In both manuscript and printed play texts of the period mid scene exits are regularly omitted, so that having no such signals for the series of ghosts here is not unusual. Nonetheless, although these figures clearly enter individually or, in two cases, in groups, the possibility exists in both the Quarto and the Folio that they depart together, all eleven at one time. Moreover, if such an option is exercised, exactly when they leave is up for grabs and can make a *very* big difference.

In case such a group departure sounds absurd, I can offer three such instances from plays later in the period, two of which are rip-offs of the scene in *Richard III*. In none of these groups do the ghosts actually speak to the figure being visited, but all come and go as a group. In Richard Brome's *The Queen's Exchange* (1631) the group of six is friendly, not hostile to Anthynus, the sleeping figure, so that he is equivalent to Richmond rather than Richard. These ghostly kings like Banquo's progeny in *Macbeth* depart hand-in-hand in sequence; the last one then *"takes up"* the recumbent figure *"and leaves him standing upright"* so that there is some interaction between ghosts and sleeping figure. In Nathaniel Richards's

Messalina (1635) the eleven ghosts enter, surround the villainous title figure (who is not asleep) *"with their Torches,"* and *exeunt* as a group. The pre-battle situation in Thomas Goffe's *The Raging Turk* (1618) is closest to *Richard III*, for here the seven ghosts, each with *"a sword and burning Tapers,"* are *"led in"* by an eighth figure, Nemesis, and *"encompass Bajazet in his bed."* After a speech from Nemesis, the ghosts *"one after another strike at Bajazet with their swords"* (although the blows are forestalled by Nemesis) and then *"exeunt in a solemn dance."* After another Nemesis speech, a furious Bajazet wakes up, rejects what he has seen, and soon goes off to his doom. Also worth noting is a moment near the end of George Chapman's *The Revenge of Bussy D'Ambois* (1610) where, after the death of Montsurry, *"Music, and the Ghost of Bussy enters, leading the Ghosts of the Guise, Monsieur, Cardinal Guise, and Chatillon; they dance about the dead body, and exeunt"* (5.5.119).[9]

None of these scenes is an exact analogue to the situation in *Richard III*. In none do the ghosts address the figure involved (and Messalina is not asleep); in none is there a second figure equivalent to Richmond. Still, all four groups, whether five, six, seven, or eleven figures, perform some concerted action such as *"a solemn dance"* or an encircling of the villain with torches and weapons (and here the dying Katherine's vision in *Henry VIII* may be relevant). The question then arises: given the absence of individual *exits* or a group *exeunt* for the comparable ghosts in *Richard III*, what would be the effect upon our sense of this elaborate visitation if the eleven figures accumulate onstage and at some point *exeunt* together, perhaps in a solemn dance or some impressive fashion?

I do not claim to have a neat answer to this question; moreover, to have each ghost or group depart after giving its speech, as is usually done, makes good theatrical sense – and I see no evidence in the script for a solemn dance, a brandishing of weapons, or even a use of torches. But the possibility does exist that, as with the ghosts in the later plays, the eleven figures congregate somehow around the sleeping Richmond, so as to form a group of twelve – which is the number appropriate for a jury. The latter part of Richard's soliloquy (5.3.193–99) focuses upon conscience that "condemns me for a villain," cites perjury and murder, and pictures his accumulated sins that "Throng to the bar, crying all, 'Guilty! guilty!'" The imagery of a trial or courtroom is *very* audible here, though the indictment comes not through the normal channels of justice but from within Richard (his conscience) or from whatever forces lie behind the ghosts. To keep the ghosts onstage during this soliloquy is possible in the Quarto and Folio, and the configuration of eleven plus one as a jury seems to me a distinct possibility, one that would reinforce in an obvious way a major image in this part of the play. Again, no firm evidence survives for the staging of these eleven ghosts, but an obvious, jury-like configuration just before or even during Richard's soliloquy could have provided the kind of italicized moment that would make major motifs in the language of the text much more audible and visible. To what extent have both the editorial and theatrical approach to the ghosts' exits eclipsed this option?

ANTONY AND CLEOPATRA

Comparable questions are generated by another moment that bedevils directors today, the puzzling sequence in *Antony and Cleopatra* where Antony's sentries *"place themselves in every corner of the Stage"* and then *"Music of the hoboys is under the stage"* (4.3.8, 12). This signal is linked to a performance on the rectangular Globe platform but, for a variety of reasons, has not fared well in today's productions. Jack Landau (Stratford, Connecticut 1960) provided a noise to startle the sentinels that turned out to be a raiding party from Caesar's camp. Charles Towers (OSF 1993) cut the entire scene and substituted a moment in which Antony, alone onstage and with a tinkling sound in the background, paused. The goal, I was told, was to suggest the hero's meditation on what he had been (an effect repeated by Cleopatra in 5.2), but, without any spoken words, what came across to me was a gap in the action. Other directors have included the scene and the sound under the stage (RNT 1987, RSC 1999) to no particular effect. John Caird (RSC 1992–93), who elsewhere emphasized the supernatural elements in the script (as in his enhancement of the soothsayer noted in chapter 1), provided a cluster of soldiers in the middle of the stage but no four corners effect and no special quality. Giles Block (Globe 1999) did place his guards at the four corners of the Globe stage but used offstage music because, I was told, his musicians decided that there was not enough room for them in the crawl space under the stage. In my playgoing experience this moment has therefore not emerged as an eerie or distinctive event, whether because of an instrumentation problem (today's hoboys–oboes do not do the job), a placement problem (our acoustics or theatrical configurations are not suited to under-the-stage effects), a historical–cultural gap between then and now, or, as is most likely, some combination of all three.

Is this scene then a lost cause or can some of the original point or force still be achieved? Again, I can provide similar directions from two contemporary plays, both connected to the four winds: *"Enter at four several corners the four winds*" who are then presented to Neptune as his subjects (Heywood, *The Golden Age* [1610]); and from a masque-within-a-play "*Enter four at several corners, address'd like the four winds, with wings, etc. and dance all to the drum and fife*" (Middleton, *No Wit, No Help Like a Woman's* [1611]).[10] I am not suggesting a connection between Shakespeare's scene and the four winds, although both Heywood and Middleton *are* presenting an image of something all-encompassing that spans the world. Rather, the key to Shakespeare's scene lies in the combination of the eerie noise ("*Music of the hoboys is under the stage*"), the configuration of the sentries, and the second soldier's suggestion: "'Tis the god Hercules, whom Antony lov'd, / Now leaves him" (4.3.12, 16–17).

Why fuss over this moment which, it could be argued, can be dispensed with little loss to the main action? If the music and the overall configuration set up for the playgoer in 4.3 constitute a one-shot image, applicable only to this scene, then it is of interest primarily as a curiosity, a bit of Jacobean stage iconography that had some kind of meaning for the original playgoers but can be ignored today. My sense, however, is that this image of Roman soldiers in the four corners of the stage is meant to recur so as to enhance some major motifs in this complex play. The conflict (however defined) between Rome and Egypt is at the basis of many, even most interpretations of this tragedy, with Egypt linked to sensuality, idleness, the supernatural, mystery, and Cleopatra's infinite variety in contrast to Rome's reason, practicality, honor, duty, business, following rules, and keeping one's square. Starting in 1.1, Roman viewpoints, often expressed through Roman soldiers or spokesmen such as Philo and Demetrius, frame the actions and speeches of the two title figures, so that the Roman point of view is carefully and repeatedly defined and refined by such figures as Octavius, his advisers, and Enobarbus and is internalized in Antony himself. Some of these Roman frame scenes, starting with 1.1, *could* be staged with Romans in the four corners, but I see no real evidence for that particular configuration before Act 4.

What is especially expressive about the situation in 4.3 is that the onstage Romans are faced with something that they cannot explain in terms of their distinctive real world logic. Something inexplicable is happening here, something mysterious, something "strange" (a word repeated twice – 19, 22) that elicits the obvious question "What should this mean?" (15). Roman soldiers in the four corners are seemingly in control of the stage and the situation, but something is happening in their midst that cannot be contained or explained by means of their reflexes, their way of looking at the world.

Without indulging in overly ingenious speculation, I see two likely analogues to this moment in the remainder of the play. The first is linked to Enobarbus's death, a scene that begins *"Enter a Sentry and his Company. Enobarbus follows"* (4.9.0). The *"Company"* here involves a minimum of two soldiers, for the sentry and two others speak in the subsequent scene – and earlier the *"company of Soldiers"* (4.3.0) that had no *"Sentry"* involved four speakers who managed to speak to each other even though placed at the corners of the stage. The placement of the three or more figures in 4.9 is not specified (they *could* remain together as a group), but what happens if, as in 4.3, they position themselves at the corners and then, in their midst, something happens that again is "strange"? If Enobarbus stabs himself, the effect is interesting but limited in scope; but if Enobarbus dies from no visible cause (with a broken heart as a likely reason), for a second time something happens within a Roman frame that defies Roman real world logic, with "Come on then, he may recover yet" (4.9.33) as the sentries' final word. I cannot prove that in the original production the soldiers in 4.9 were placed *"in every corner of the Stage"* as in 4.3, but to do so is to set up a clear, even italicized parallel between two moments, both of which depict both a "Roman" frame and something that cannot be contained or explained within it.

The richest moment in my hypothetical sequence would then come at the very end of the play after the deaths of Iras, Cleopatra, and Charmian. The operative direction here is *"Enter Caesar and all his Train, marching"* (5.2.332) so that the stage is to be swelled with Romans looking at the three dead Egyptian women. What follows, along with Caesar's closing epitaph, is another odd sequence that is regularly pared down or omitted (as in OSF 1993 where the last spoken line was "A way there, a way for Caesar!" – 333) wherein, in a fashion comparable to Sherlock Holmes or medical examiner Kay Scarpetta, three Romans deduce what we as playgoers already know – how Cleopatra managed to kill herself. Once accomplished, Octavius assumes that he understands what has just happened, just as he thought he had understood Cleopatra at the end of their previous interview.

What is the effect, then, if four members of Caesar's *"Train"* place themselves in the four corners of the stage so as, for a third time, to suggest something not contained within the frame of Roman logic, the Roman point of view, another "mystery" that the Romans cannot fathom or handle? In general terms, there is the mystery of Cleopatra's appeal, her special status or stature, even for Dolabella. More specifically, the Romans here satisfy themselves as to how Cleopatra and her women had killed themselves ("This is an aspic's trail" – 351), but what if we have seen Iras die for no apparent reason (like Enobarbus in 4.9) so as to elicit her mistress's "Have I the aspic in my lips?" (293). The Holmes-medical examiner deductions by the Romans tame the mystery so as to bring it back into their (and our) world of logic-rule-square-cause-and-effect, but the playgoer's sense of what has happened need not jibe with that neat, reasoned formulation. This tragedy is "about" many things, but both the assets *and* the limits of "Roman" thoughts or thinking are one major focus, an emphasis that can be enhanced by some distinctive staging of one, two, perhaps three moments building to this final coda. The play ends with Romans in Roman costumes dominating a stage that contains the bodies of three Egyptian women; the "Roman" world of Octavius with its universal peace now reigns supreme (and given the Jacobean way of establishing place onstage, Roman costumes suggest "Rome" even if the narrative places the scene in Egypt). But the eerie noise under the stage, the death of Enobarbus after making a reasoned "Roman" choice to leave Antony, and the inexplicable death of Iras suggest qualities in both Antony and Cleopatra that cannot be contained or explained in the Roman scheme of things, which, as I understand the play, is also *our* scheme of things.

As a theatre historian highly conscious of how few stage directions actually survive (the norm is silence), my goal is to get as much mileage as possible out of the available evidence in an effort to recover what happened in those first performances. Not surprisingly, today's theatrical professionals often take a very different approach and, especially when moving the action to some later period, do not feel constrained by effects targeted at the original playgoers and playhouses but prefer to eliminate anomalies and dampen supernatural elements that seem to jar with today's assumptions or agendas. Particularly in *The Tempest* and *Macbeth* the transformation of the original stage directions and implicit actions can therefore provide prime examples of the price tags and trade-offs in the rescripting process.

7

Compressing Henry VI

"Commanded always by the greater gust"
3 Henry VI, 3.1.88

When dealing with Shakespeare's *Henry VI* on the page or on the stage, a critic, an editor, or a director immediately confronts the question of the integrity of the three plays as they have survived in the 1594 Quarto of Part II and the 1595 Octavo of Part III (among the earliest of Shakespeare's works to appear in print) and the First Folio (where Part I first appears). Since the eighteenth century, scholars and theatrical professionals have shown little confidence in or enthusiasm for these histories as intact entities, worthy of analysis as discrete units, but rather have either lumped them together as one item that can be dealt with summarily or raided them so as to appropriate detachable elements that suit the interpreter's agenda. As noted in chapter 3, directors often graft Richard of Gloucester's speeches from Part III onto *Richard III*; several scholars have written tellingly about Joan de Pucelle;[1] and other distinctive parts have been singled out for attention or analysis, with one line ("The first thing we do, let's kill all the lawyers" – Part II, 4.2.76–77) achieving a cult status. Admittedly, starting in the 1960s and 1970s a few academic critics have argued forcefully in behalf of thematic or imagistic integrity;[2] at least three directors (Terry Hands, Jane Howell, Michael Boyd) have treated the scripts with respect. But for the most part both scholars and theatrical professionals, weaned on standards and assumptions derived from subsequent plays in the canon, have had only intermittent interest in this trilogy other than as context for *Richard III*.

The reasons for such neglect or atomization are no secret. For the academic critic, the interpretative tools that for generations have worked well for later Shakespeare plays, whether for analysis of "character," imagery, or structure, do not provide satisfying results when applied to *Henry VI*. As to the latter, the Elizabethan fondness for episodic structure or multiple unity here collides with a post-Elizabethan prizing of concentration and subordination of elements – as seen also in comparable discomfort among critics with the rebel scenes in *2 Henry IV* or the Aumerle rebellion in *Richard II*. Despite a long series of apologias (starting in the early 1950s with H. T. Price),[3] interpreters have therefore sensed formlessness rather than coherence in this trilogy – a problem only "solved" with the emergence of Richard of Gloucester as a focal figure.

Such an introduction, as a reader of scholarly prose will recognize, is a prelude to The Answer, a formulation that will set the record straight now and forever so that The Problem will no longer bother future readers. Sadly (for I would be delighted to set things aright), such is not the case, for I lack the insights that would enable me to descend from Mount Sinai to deliver the reader of these plays to the promised land. Rather, I offer a paradox linked to a closed loop, a version of the infamous hermeneutic circle. Perhaps more than with any other group of Shakespeare plays, the key to each of the three parts of *Henry VI* as a discrete unit, a play with its own distinctive shape and rationale (regardless of the interpretation eventually to be drawn from that shape and rationale), lies in the play as an onstage event, the play-as-seen-heard rather than the play-as-read (and few will quarrel with the limitations of this trilogy as plays-to-be-read). Such a claim, in turn, usually leads to a paean in behalf of performance-oriented interpretation. That approach, however is keyed to often unexamined assumptions drawn from twentieth-century theatre, whereas the rationale behind Elizabethan staging (especially in the early 1590s when that rationale was still taking shape) can be different, in ways both subtle and obvious, from what readers, playgoers, and theatrical professionals take for granted today. In my terms, Shakespeare, his fellow players, and his playgoers shared a theatrical vocabulary accessible, even obvious, then but easily blurred or eclipsed today.

Paradoxically, one consequence of this situation is that the staging of these three plays in our theatres rather than helping to bridge this gap in our understanding can instead widen it so as to become part of the problem rather than part of the solution. When treating these plays as playscripts to be enacted by modern actors before today's audiences, directors inevitably make many adjustments that in turn eliminate or blur elements important for the original strategy. My point is not to fault actors and directors (who to survive must take into account the theatrical vocabulary they share with their paying customers and whose negative attitude towards these plays has been heavily conditioned by critics, scholars, and editors) but rather to lament that what can be a valuable tool for investigating other scripts – seeing the play-on-the-page come to life on the stage – is often denied the would-be interpreter of *Henry VI*.

Three recent and highly visible productions can serve as instructive paradigms. Michael Bogdanov (ESC 1988), Adrian Noble (RSC 1988–89), and Pat Patton (OSF 1991–93) elected to present the first tetralogy to their audiences by condensing four plays into three, with *Richard III* standing alone and the three parts of *Henry VI* compressed into two plays (the ESC plays were entitled *The House of Lancaster* and *The House of York*; the RSC *Henry VI* and *The Rise of Edward IV*; the OSF, presented a year apart in summer 1991 and summer 1992, *1 Henry VI* and *The Conclusion of Henry VI*). The choices made when setting up such compressed versions of event-filled history plays can then be instructive – what is deemed essential versus what is treated as disposable? – especially in the context of the commercial and artistic success of the RSC's 1977–78 Terry Hands *Henry VI* trilogy (played "warts and all" with few cuts), the significant achievement of Jane Howell's first tetralogy for BBC-TV's "The Shakespeare Plays" (one of the most successful items in that series), and the positive reception of Michael Boyd's sequence (RSC 2000–1). The plays *are* do-able, as demonstrated by Hands (along with Alan Howard, Helen Mirren, Emrys James, Peter McEnery, Julian Glover, and others),[4] Howell, Boyd, and Pat Patton (whose part III in 1977 was one of the strongest shows I saw in twenty years of playgoing at the Oregon Shakespeare Festival).

As experienced directors, both Bogdanov and Noble were much concerned with the commercial as well as the artistic advantages of presenting three rather than four plays, so that the choice to streamline the received script came easily (as one who had already mounted Part III successfully, Patton's decision was more grudging). Some of Noble's rationale is set forth in the preface to the printed edition of his script where he describes himself as continuing a process started by Shakespeare. For example, Shakespeare saw "the dramatic advantages of shape and focus achieved by running several events into one," a process, Noble observes, "which we have taken further." In his conclusion, moreover, he notes: "We all had to learn to value narrative over 'character moments' and to value story-telling over psychology."[5] Clearly, a different rationale is at work behind these plays, one that demands some adjustments from both today's theatrical professional and playgoer. Moreover, any compression of three event-filled plays into two is going to necessitate major omissions and adjustments ("running several events into one").

All three adaptations of the *Henry VI* material, in turn, followed the same general pattern. The material from Part I was allotted roughly ninety minutes so as to be completed by the first interval/intermission; the second half of the first play then contained the first three acts of Part II; the last two acts of Part II and the first two acts of Part III (with much restitching of elements) occupied the pre-interval section of play number two; the remaining three acts of Part III then finished the job. Patton and script consultant Hilary Tate used the printed version of Noble's adaptation as their point of departure, but they factored in material omitted by Noble (e.g., the confrontation between Gloucester and Winchester at the Tower in Part I, 1.3; the exposure of Simpcox in part II, 2.1; and the capture of Henry VI by the Yorkists in part III, 4.8).

Given such a master plan, certain problems emerge, problems that, in turn, can provide some insights into distinctive features of the three plays. First and perhaps most important, the structural integrity of Shakespeare's Part II was undermined. For example, the prophecies of 1.4 were not fulfilled. All three directors cut the prophetic references to Walter-water (part II, 1.4.32–33, 64–65); indeed, Noble cut the entire Suffolk death scene (4.1), so that, even though his head did appear in Margaret's hands, the playgoer had no clue as to how he died (the plot summary in the program informed the reader that Suffolk "is murdered aboard ship as he leaves England"). Somerset, moreover, whose death is also predicted (1.4.34–37, 66–69), died in the next play (in Oregon a calendar year after the prediction) with no reference to castles or alehouse signs. The kind of implicit structure provided by the working out of prophecies or riddles (best seen in *Macbeth*) was therefore gone.

The same was true for the genesis of the Cade rebellion. Noble provided a powerful image to open *Edward IV*, with the Cade supporters rising from grated traps and filling the stage, but this subterranean emergence meant something very different at the outset of a new play as opposed to being experienced in 4.2 of a continuum. Similarly, Bogdanov began his second play with a train station scene to show York's return from Ireland (5.1), then switched to a Cade meeting hall rally (4.2). Gone from all three productions was any link between this new force unleashed upon England and the deaths of Gloucester, the Cardinal, and Suffolk or the earlier machinations of York; gone as well was any analogy to *Julius Caesar* where again a major political murder at the center of the play comparable to the assassination of Gloucester opens the way to violence and war. To look closely at such compressions is therefore to bring into focus Shakespeare's sense of structure or cause-and-effect.

All three versions amalgamated the scenes that end Part II and those that begin Part III. One result was to conflate two important political scenes (Part II, 5.1; Part III, 1.1) so as to produce more than a little confusion (e.g., about the two Cliffords). Another consequence was to economize on battle scenes in play two so as to combine the first battle of St. Albans that ends Shakespeare's part II with the battles that begin his part III (and this alteration necessitated a host of other significant changes).[6] The most telling effect of this compression was that a high percentage of the violence in Shakespeare's Parts II and III was now concentrated in the ninety-minute segment that began play 2, for this stretch contained all the violence of Part II: the Cade scenes (done by Noble with many onstage decapitations and a host of severed heads on poles); York versus Clifford; Richard versus Somerset; and then most of the violence in Part III: the battles of Acts 1 and 2; the murders of Rutland and York; the death of young Clifford. At the interval of Noble's production, one observer (who did not know Shakespeare's script) asked me: "What are we watching – a Renaissance *Full Metal Jacket?*" In this segment controlled use of onstage violence in the original scripts metamorphosed into theatrical overkill.

Clearly, some advantages do follow from this compression. Patton was faced with the added problem that his 1991 Oregon playgoers had to wait until summer 1992 to see the second play, as opposed to Bogdanov and Noble's playgoers who could see the two shows on consecutive evenings or sometimes on the same day. He therefore made a strenuous and often successful effort to find an integrity and continuity so that each play-and-a-half could stand on its own legs as a discrete unit. For example, the first meeting of Margaret and Suffolk (Part I, 5.3) now occurred in the same play as their parting (Part II, 3.2), a link enforced in this production by some analogous staging – in both scenes Suffolk kissed Margaret and then lifted her off the ground in a distinctive fashion. The increased pace and the many cinematic crosscuts (wherein one part of the stage was darkened so that other figures could appear above or on a set of stairs) heightened the many divisions among the English in play one (e.g., Gloucester versus Winchester, Somerset versus York), a process aided by Patton's adept use of banners, roses, color-coded maps, and other aids for the United States playgoer unfamiliar with British history.

Given a stopping point mid way in Shakespeare's Part II, Patton's solution to the problem of closure is of particular interest, for his production ended with a coda composed of lines spoken by Margaret (holding Suffolk's head and repeating "Think therefore on revenge" – 4.4.3),

Henry VI (repeating "And God shall be my hope" – see 4.4.55), and York. The latter had the final speech, for, standing above with the three spirits from 1.4 in the background, he delivered: "Whiles I in Ireland nourish a mighty band, / I will stir up in England some black storm / Shall blow ten thousand souls to heaven or hell" (3.1.348–50) and planted his sword in the railing just before "or hell." As an admirer of Part II I missed the thrust forward into the Cade scenes and the Lancaster versus York confrontation in Act 5, but Patton's conclusion did convey a distinctive force and logic of its own.

For Noble and Patton, the radical compression of the materials that constitute Part I necessitated a different sequence of scenes. Instead of the Folio progression, a series of "England" scenes were grouped together at the beginning (1.1, 1.3, 2.4, 2.5, 3.1), followed by a sequence of "France" scenes (1.2, 1.4, 1.5, 2.1, 3.2, 3.3). One price tag therefore was the elimination of the Folio's alternation of episodes, so that the 1590s juxtaposition of English and French elements was scrapped in favor of two longer sustained sequences that nonetheless contained within them an onstage equivalent to cinematic cross-cuts wherein figures in different locales were visible at the same time, a different yet comparable 1990s effect. A later theatrical logic or continuity therefore superseded the original; concern for ease of access for the playgoer, a major strength of both shows, led to a valuing of one sense of narrative over another. Other economies also came at a price. In Patton's reformulation one Salisbury died in Part I (1.4), but to avoid confusion a second and more important Salisbury (the father of Warwick), who has some potentially significant moments in Part II (in 2.2, 3.2, and especially 5.1 in his confrontation with Henry VI), was eliminated. Obviously, many lines had to be sacrificed, including one of the most admired speeches of Part I – Joan's "Glory is like a circle in the water" (1.2.133–39).

The trade-off was that all three shows provided inventive and theatrically exciting moments. My favorite OSF 1992 moment came in *3 Henry VI*, 5.1 when Richard convinced Clarence to forsake Warwick and rejoin his brothers by carefully placing on the stage floor a distinctive property, the napkin stained with Rutland's blood that had been used to torment York in 1.4 and in this production had also been italicized in 2.1 and 3.2. Elsewhere, Patton displayed his mastery of banners on the large outdoor stage: to simulate battles and processions; to facilitate exits and entrances; and to conceal bodies or groups of upstage figures (e.g., the Yorkist army during Margaret's return in Part III, 5.3) who could be frozen in place during a cross-cut scene downstage, an efficient exit-saving technique that made it possible to include more segments from the three plays. The feather shown and discussed by Henry VI (Part III, 3.1.84–89) was established as a significant image, as were the three properties (or trademarks) introduced in a brief prologue in 1992 that echoed the 1991 closure: Suffolk's head cradled by Margaret, a sword brandished by York, and a rosary fingered by Henry VI.

Bogdanov and Noble also provided many distinctive images and strong visual links between episodes. Noble had Margery Jordan's death at the stake (in his play 1) repeat the fate of Joan (events divided between Shakespeare's Parts I and II); also in play 1, the first meeting of Margaret and Suffolk (just before the interval) was echoed in the play's final moments when Margaret cradled Suffolk's severed head. Twice, moreover, Noble found significant images (albeit in two different plays) to convey the price to be paid to gain the power associated with the throne. First, the dead Mortimer (at the end of Shakespeare's Part I, 2.5) descended in his cage-prison, an object then replaced with Henry VI's golden throne (a disturbing and effective juxtaposition). Then, at the end of play 2 the body of the murdered Henry VI descended in similar fashion, to be replaced by a throne inhabited by Edward. In both instances, the image of a body under the throne was strong and meaningful.

Of the many changes and elisions several small choices had a disproportionally large impact. Bogdanov pared down considerably the "common man" scenes from the first two acts of Part II (although, unlike Noble, he and Patton did retain the Simpcox episode), so that Peter and his master Horner disappeared from view. No charge of treason was therefore brought against York by means of Horner's reported comments, so that, in turn, no particular reason remained for choosing Somerset over York as Regent of France (Gloucester recommends to the king that Somerset get the regency "Because in York this [Horner's comment] breeds suspicion" – 1.3.206). Bogdanov's King Henry, moreover, not Gloucester, provided "This doom" (204). Although on the surface only an innocuous series of cuts and changes, such giving of the decision to Henry had a significant effect upon the portrayal of three major figures. First, Henry appeared much more decisive as a politician than was the case anywhere else, a shift that set up a very different progression to his one assertive moment when, after recovering from his swoon at the news of Gloucester's death, he banished Suffolk in 3.2. Second, Gloucester lost one of his two highly visible judgments (the other coming with Simpcox) and hence some of his special stature, a diminution that contributed to one of the weak spots in this production. Third, an insight into the danger posed by York was eliminated, as was also true in other cuts made by Bogdanov (most notably the elimination of York's speech that ends 1.1 and the paring down of Gloucester's final speech in 3.1, including his reference to "dogged York, that reaches at the moon, / Whose overweening arm I have pluck'd back" – 158–59). Having Henry deliver the "doom" therefore had a significant impact upon three of the key figures in this play and upon the dynamics of Part II as a whole.

Comparable small but telling changes can be noted in Noble's production. In both Shakespeare's Part III (4.8.38–50) and Noble's adaptation, Henry VI has a speech in which he naively concludes that, because he has been mild and merciful, the people will support him rather than Edward in the coming conflict. In Noble's version, Henry exited after this speech so that some playgoers were surprised to see him turn up in prison a few scenes later; in Shakespeare's scene, however, he is immediately confronted and arrested by the Yorkists (whom the people *have* supported) so that Henry's speech serves as the first half of a one-two punch – with the second element, the deflation, gone from Noble's version (Patton factored this arrest back in). Similarly, in Shakespeare's Part III, a Henry VI anxious to relinquish kingly power gives over his political authority to both Warwick and Clarence (4.6), but in Noble's version only Warwick was so designated. Shortly thereafter (5.1) Clarence arrives at Coventry where his brothers are besieging Warwick and decides to change sides, forsaking Warwick in favor of the Yorkist cause. Does it not make a difference to our understanding why Clarence makes this switch whether he is or is not a sharer in kingly power? At the least, a figure who has left his brothers in order to gain half a kingdom (however provisionally) is not faced with the same choice as a figure who has played second fiddle to an older brother and now is to be second again to Warwick (as in Noble's stripped down version).

Such choices and resulting problems may be inevitable given the squeezing of three plays into two, but that three-into-two choice is itself a product of a series of assumptions, both aesthetic and commercial, about the dramaturgy and coherence of these early Shakespeare plays. What if, in contrast, these histories do have a distinctive theatrical shape or logic (as suggested above in my account of the prophecies and the role of Gloucester's assassination in Part II), albeit one not as accessible today as that found in later comparable plays?

To pursue such a defense of the integrity of these plays I will focus upon a few distinctive and revealing configurations. My emphasis will be upon scenes and images (1) that, although easily blurred for a reader today, would be hard for a playgoer in the 1590s to miss; (2) that depend more upon visual–theatrical than upon poetic–verbal effects (or are underdeveloped in poetic–verbal terms); and (3) that were omitted or blurred significantly in the three productions (and, in a few instances, were realized meaningfully in other productions).

Let me start with one of the least discussed moments in the most maligned of the three plays, *1 Henry VI*. At the nadir of her fortunes just before her capture by York, Joan de Pucelle appeals for help to a group of onstage "*Fiends*" (5.3.7), but in response these fiends, according to the Folio stage directions, "*walk, and speak not*," "*hang their heads*," "*shake their heads*," and finally "*depart*" (s.d.s at 12, 17, 19, 23). This exchange has not fared well on the page or on the stage, for to deal with this script is inevitably to run afoul of this scene and this appeal–rejection that in several ways tests the reflexes of today's interpreters. The Folio's call for fiends and for specific reactions is unusually clear (and presumably would have posed few problems in the 1590s for playgoers attuned to *Doctor Faustus*), but, as noted in chapter 6, Elizabethan onstage presentation of the supernatural repeatedly strains "our" paradigms of credibility (and canons of taste), with this moment a particular challenge.

Directors have therefore tinkered with the Folio signals. In Howell's rendition for television, Joan speaks her lines while staring at the camera so that no supernatural entities are in sight to walk, refuse to speak, hang their heads, and eventually depart. In Noble's rendition, various onstage corpses from the previous battle rose as if animated to provide an onstage audience but without the reactions to Joan's pleas specified in the Folio. In the Hands production, amid the onstage cannons that dominated the battlefield set Joan offered herself to the fiends who appeared suddenly "looking like gas-masked soldiers from the French trenches of the First World War."[7] Bogdanov cut the fiends and altered the text, so that, alone on stage and looking at the audience, his Joan directed her appeal not to any diabolic entities but rather to the Virgin Mary, a change that eliminated any infernal climax for this sequence.[8] Both Will Huddleston (OSF 1975) and Pat Patton did stage the rejection and both got a great deal of mileage out of the supernatural events overall. As noted in chapter 5, Huddleston had the fiends appear elsewhere thinly disguised as her servants or torturers and as a final image placed them above to snarl at the audience. Patton staged Joan's standoff in combat with Talbot in 1.5 so that she avoided an apparent defeat by a magical touch, then kissed him, and, after her unsuccessful appeal to the fiends, had these bizarre figures (like Banquo's ghost unseen by those onstage) surround her during a spectacular burning at the stake.

Even to a casual reader the interaction between Joan and the fiends leaps off the page in vivid (and to many, offensive) fashion – a good example of theatrical *italics*. What if Joan and her devils are not a one-shot effect but rather the climactic example of a larger progression of images and moments that starts in Act 2? From her first appearance Joan has claimed supernatural powers (see 1.2.72–92), a claim tested in the first meeting between Joan and Talbot that results in a stand-off; still, Joan scorns his strength (1.5.15) and leads her troops to victory at Orleans. Moments later, Talbot, aided by Bedford and Burgundy, scales the walls and regains the town, so that a united English force wins back what had just been lost. The three leaders working together therefore accomplish what Talbot, facing Joan alone, could not.

Shakespeare then provides a gloss on both this victory and the larger problem of unity–disunity by means of Talbot's interview with the Countess of Auvergne (a scene omitted in all three productions). Her trap for Talbot fails, as he points out, because she has only caught "Talbot's shadow," not his substance. The set of terms is repeated throughout the remainder of the scene (e.g., "No, no, I am but shadow of myself. / You are deceiv'd, my substance is not here") and is explained by the appearance of his soldiers, at which point he points out: "Are you now persuaded / That Talbot is but shadow of himself? / These are his substance, sinews, arms, and strength, / With which he yoketh your rebellious necks" (2.3.45–66). The individual standing alone, no matter how heroic (one thinks of Coriolanus), is but a shadow without the substance of his supporters, his army, his country.[9]

As two generations of critics have reminded us, however, *1 Henry VI* is about division, not unity, a division that has already been displayed in the split between Winchester and Gloucester and widens in the Temple Garden scene (that immediately follows Talbot's lecture to the countess), with its symbolic plucking of red and white roses. The figures who had joined Talbot in the victory at Orleans, moreover, soon disappear (Bedford dies, Burgundy changes sides). Factionalism thrives, to the extent that the division between York and Somerset (unhistorically) undoes Talbot himself. When the hero is "hemm'd about with grim destruction" (4.3.21), Sir William Lucy appeals in Talbot's behalf to York (4.3.17–23) and then to Somerset (4.4.13–28), but neither of these rivals provides the necessary timely support. Lucy can only point to "the vulture of sedition" that "Feeds in the bosom of such great commanders" and lament that "Whiles they each other cross, / Lives, honors, lands, and all, hurry to loss" (4.3.47–53). Lucy's listing of Talbot's titles (4.7.60–71) can then be mocked by Joan as "a silly stately style indeed," for "Him that thou magnifi'st with all these titles, / Stinking and fly-blown lies here at our feet" (72, 75–76). In the terms of 2.3, Talbot has been denied his substance and, along with his son, must face death as a shadow of his heroic self.

Joan's scene with her devils follows less than a hundred lines after her exchange with Lucy. With the French forces fleeing the conquering York, all Joan can do is call upon her "speedy helpers" or "familiar spirits" to help with their "accustom'd diligence," but neither the offer of her blood, with which she has fed them in the past, a member lopped off, her body, or even her soul will gain the needed support. She therefore concludes: "My ancient incantations are too weak, / And hell too strong for me to buckle with: / Now, France, thy glory droopeth to the dust" (5.3.1–29).

No one makes grandiose claims for the imagery of this sprawling play. But a verbal patterning involving shadow and substance is clearly set forth in Act 2 and echoed thereafter (see Alençon's speech 5.4.133–37); moreover, Talbot eventually falls (and France ultimately is lost to England) because of divisions whereby "substance" is denied and the hero must stand alone as shadow of himself. In her scene with the fiends, Joan too is deserted, denied by those who formerly supported her. Like Talbot, her heroic status cannot exist alone, so that she becomes a mere shepherd's daughter, not the figure who raised the siege at Orleans and was a match for Talbot in battle. The denial by the fiends is here the equivalent to the denials by the squabbling York and Somerset that undo Talbot, a link that can be reinforced through the staging. What if the fiends' scripted reactions to Joan's offer echo similar walking apart, hanging and shaking of heads, and departures by York and Somerset in their responses to Lucy's pleas in behalf of Talbot? Although not specified in the Folio, such iterated actions would highlight for the playgoer two or three parallel failures by first Lucy and then Joan, rejections that visibly set up the deaths of the two previously unbeatable or heroic figures. Just as Lucy fails to get the necessary support, a failure that means Talbot must give way to the new factions, so Joan fails to get the support she too desperately needs and must give way to the third Frenchwoman, Margaret, who appears immediately upon Joan's exit with York. However interpreted in theological or political terms, the highly visible fiends can reinforce an ongoing pattern of images or configurations linked to the central themes of the play.

Of the three plays, Part I has been the most disparaged, but in all of the three-into-two adjustments Part II suffered the greatest damage because its elements were split into two separate plays (and, in Patton's version, two different summers). As noted earlier, such a split calls attention to the different kinds of through-lines or pay-offs set up in earlier scenes and realized later (as is most obvious with the prophecies). Other cuts and changes made by the three directors call attention to comparable links and images. For example, Noble manufactured a fresh image in 4.2, for his Cade not only knighted himself (119–21) but also knighted Dick the Butcher, underscoring even further the indictment of titles and hierarchy. As part of his streamlining of Act 5 of Part II, however, Noble cut Henry VI's knighting of Alexander Iden (5.1.78); in play 1 he had also cut Henry's grant of a dukedom to a kneeling Suffolk as a reward for bringing Margaret as bride (Part II, 1.1.63–65). Shakespeare's own sequence of giving new titles to kneeling figures was therefore gone, with two instances of number two in the series but no number one and no number three.

All three plays but particularly Part II gain much of their distinctive shape from such visible repetitions, but with many of these elements eliminated, transposed, or located in two different plays (and hence two different evenings or even two different years) much of that rationale was gone. For example, Gloucester tells his wife that "I must offend before I be attainted," for his foes, no matter how powerful, "could not procure me any scathe / So long as I am loyal, true, and crimeless" (2.4.59, 62–63). Two acts later, Lord Say tells the king and Buckingham: "The trust I have is in mine innocence, / And therefore am I bold and resolute" (4.4.59–60). At their next appearances, however, both figures are accused and swiftly convicted by their enemies and are murdered shortly thereafter with Gloucester's body and Say's head subsequently brought onstage. If such elements, however, are (1) pared down or cut completely and (2) placed in two separate plays, no such analogy or structural link is available, whatever interpretative spin one chooses to place upon it. In Noble's script, moreover, the arraignment and arrest of Gloucester (Shakespeare's 3.1) *preceded* the scene with Eleanor (Shakespeare's 2.4). An actor or playgoer can readily accept a Gloucester who exhibits naive blindness in 2.4 and then is chopped down in 3.1, but how is the actor or playgoer to deal with the same Gloucester speech ("I must offend before I be attainted") *after* he has already been shocked by the turn of events at court? Is Noble's Gloucester the same shrewd figure who saw through Simpcox and kept York in check?

Part III suffered the least from adaptation and compression, for several clearly linked moments were retained and were in the same play. In Shakespeare's Act 1 the Lancastrians led by young Clifford kill a Yorkist child (Rutland) and the symbol of the Yorkist cause (Richard); in Act 5 the Lancastrians do the same: the three brothers kill Prince Edward, and in the following scene Richard of Gloucester murders Henry VI in the Tower. In Patton's OSF 1977 production a highly visible detail added to this patterning, for Margaret's taunting of York with the napkin bearing Rutland's blood left blood on Richard's face. Such a bloody face was then seen again on the father contemplating the son he has killed (2.5) and most tellingly on Margaret herself after she had kissed her murdered son Edward (5.5).

The streamlining occasioned by three-plays-into-two, however, did take its toll. Indeed, what may seem to the adapter redundancies and hence cuttable episodes looked at another way can add up to a distinctive feature of this play. For example, in his speech to his captors in 3.1 (pared down in all three versions) Henry VI first raises questions about oaths and obedience but then laments the frailty of human nature:

> Look, as I blow this feather from my face,
> And as the air blows it to me again,
> Obeying with my wind when I do blow,
> And yielding to another when it blows,
> Commanded always by the greater gust,
> Such is the lightness of you common men.
> But do not break your oaths . . .
>   (3.1.84–90)

Many disparate episodes in the next two acts provide demonstrations of this thesis – that, regardless of their pretensions about oaths and principles, feather-like men and women are "commanded always by the greater gust." In the next scene (3.2) that greater gust is King Edward's lust for a beautiful widow that takes precedence over political allegiances, most notably his bond with Warwick; that turnabout is quickly paralleled in Warwick's rapid switch in reaction to this disgrace in which he tells his hated enemy Queen Margaret "let former grudges pass, / And henceforth I am thy true servitor" and she responds: "Warwick, these words have turn'd my hate to love, / And I forgive and quite forget old faults" (3.3.195–201). The most obvious example comes when Clarence, who marches in ready to fight against his own brothers in behalf of Warwick, with little ado throws his red rose at his former ally and rejoins the

Yorkists (eliciting Richard's delicious line: "Welcome, good Clarence, this is brother-like" – 5.1.105).

Easily lost in this sequence of events, however, is 4.7, a scene omitted by Noble, Bogdanov, and Patton in 1977 (in 1992 he cut the first section with the Mayor) but one of the gems of Howell's television rendition. Here Edward gains access to the city of York by vowing that he has come as duke, not as a would-be king ("I challenge nothing but my dukedom, / As being well content with that alone" – 23–24), but the arrival and threatened departure of Sir John Montgomery ("Then fare you well, for I will hence again, / I came to serve a king and not a duke" – 48–49) puts Edward on the spot (in a manner that closely parallels the dilemma faced by Edward's father in 1.2 – whether to keep his bargain with Henry VI or seek the crown now). In the spirit of "like father, like son," Edward quickly caves in to the urgings of Richard and Hastings, so that, in Howell's rendition, with drums sounding in the background, the Mayor (rather than a soldier) shakily reads the proclamation of Edward's kingship, and Montgomery, visibly itching for action, stands by impatiently, snatches away the paper, and offers his open challenge to single combat. The rapidity of Edward's switch in his professed intentions yields both dark comedy and a telling insight into the value of oaths and protestations in this political jungle.

In the spirit of Henry's speech on "the greater gust," the sequence of turnabouts by key figures such as Edward, Warwick, and Clarence heightens the uncertainties and lack of any firm principles or beliefs in this Darwinian society and, if played in full, helps to explain the rise of Gloucester and the genesis of Richard III and *Richard III* (the first, longest, and most famous of Gloucester's speeches is positioned just after Edward's decision to marry his widow in 3.2). The streamlined versions tell the same story (often with considerable panache), but the repeated betrayals or apostasies (like the recapitulation in Act 5 of the brutal killings of Act 1) are the bones and sinews from which this play takes its distinctive shape. To cut the Countess of Auvergne, Peter-Horner, and Sir John Montgomery is to economize on time and personnel so as to enhance the narrative pace but also to eliminate paradigms that, if attended to, can call attention to central themes and images. Whether with shadow-substance in Part I, the many analogous situations in Part II, or the action following Henry's feather speech in Part III, the repetitions, even apparent redundancies (according to today's sensibilities), *are* the essence of the plays.

In calling attention to such losses, my goal is to bring into focus a broader and deeper interpretative problem. The stage directions for the fiends' reactions to Joan's pleas are unusually explicit, but the absence of any comparable signals for the reactions of York and Somerset to Lucy's pleas for help makes any claims about linkage between the two moments conjectural. Such lack of specific signals, however, is the norm in the extant playscripts, for in most cases clear indications of stage business or properties have not survived. Such gaps in our knowledge of what may have been obvious in the 1590s are compounded by the changes in theatrical vocabulary between then and now, for inevitably our inferences about how an Elizabethan company would have staged X are heavily conditioned by how *we* would stage X.

A particularly useful example is the moment in Part III when Edward IV, having been surprised and captured by Warwick and Clarence, is carried onstage "*in his gown, sitting in a chair*" (4.3.27). In the Howell television rendition, Edward is bound to his chair so that the image for the spectator is that of a prisoner (comparable to Gloucester in the blinding scene of *King Lear*). Howell's choice makes immediate sense to a viewer today, but it may also blur a distinctive effect keyed to the original stage conventions.

For what is easily missed today is that, in the age of Shakespeare, bringing a figure onstage in a chair was the primary way of signaling "*enter sick*" or "*as if sick*." To cite only a few of the many examples, in *Westward Ho* Mistress Tenterhook, pretending to be sick, calls for "a chair, a chair"; a companion says "she's sick and taken with an Agony." In *Othello*, after "finding" the wounded Cassio, Iago cries "O for a chair / To bear him easily hence!" (5.1.82–83) and mentions the chair twice more (96, 98); when the chair arrives, he adds: "Some good man bear him carefully from hence, / I'll fetch the general's surgeon" (99–100) and "O, bear him out o' th' air" (104); the 1622 Quarto (but not the Folio) then directs Cassio in the next scene to be brought in "*in a Chair*" (5.2.282). Elsewhere in Shakespeare's plays, chairs are specified for sick or dying figures in *1 Henry VI* (2.5.0, 3.2.40), *2 Henry VI* (2.1.65), and *King Lear* (4.7.23). Examples are also plentiful in the plays of Fletcher and Brome and can be found as well in Peele, Chapman, Dekker, Heywood, Marston, Massinger, Markham, Haughton, and Ford and in many anonymous plays.[10]

To return to the scene in Part III, when Edward is carried onstage "*in his gown, sitting in a chair*," the initial signal for the original spectator would have been that this figure is entering "*sick*" or "*as sick*." In this instance, however, the signals would be misleading, for Edward is embarrassed and vulnerable but not sick. But significantly this play starts and ends with throne scenes, with that royal seat a symbol of the disorder in a kingdom in which three different figures are seen sitting upon the English throne. Indeed, in the opening scene the titular king, Henry VI, comes onstage to discover Richard of York seated upon his throne, an initial usurpation that typifies what is to follow. The presence of a king (or pseudo-king) brought onstage in what appears initially to be a sick-chair is therefore more than a momentary trick played upon the spectator. Rather, that initial confusion of throne-chair and sick-chair calls attention to an important set of associations that links disease to kings and power-brokers, associations reinforced by the unkinging, rekinging, and unkinging of Henry VI in the last three acts. Memories of both the opening confusion about the throne and the momentary sick-chair image of 4.3 should then inform the final moments, where the surface order assumed by Edward ("Now am I seated as my soul delights, / Having my country's peace and brothers' loves" – 5.7.35–36) is undercut by a continuing sense of the kingdom's diseases, as typified in Richard's asides (e.g., "I'll blast his harvest" – 21). The momentary effect with Edward in his chair therefore reinforces a potentially meaningful iterative pattern that links disease imagery to the throne and to the larger political concerns of the play.

Nor is this sick chair–royal chair image limited to Part III. Squabbles in the presence of Henry and his throne are a major symptom of what is wrong in Part I, so that in Howell's production Exeter delivers his choric speech on "this base and envious discord" (and recalls the prophecy "That Henry born at Monmouth should win all, / And Henry born at Windsor lose all") while pointing to the empty throne (3.1.186–200). The scenes that precede and follow this chaotic activity around the boy-king seated on his throne are instructive. First, Shakespeare presents the plucking of red and white roses by Suffolk and York in the Temple Garden scene (2.4), a symbolic beginning to the divisions to come. Moments later, Mortimer, who is "*brought in a chair*" by his jailers (2.5.0), provides a long disquisition to Richard about the Yorkist claim to the throne. This claim, passed from this dying figure to the up-and-coming Richard, is linked visually to a figure in a sick-chair. Mortimer's ominous laying on of hands (see lines 37–38) is immediately followed by our first view of the young Henry VI, presumably on his throne, who is unable to control the squabble between Gloucester and Winchester or the fight, offstage and then onstage, between their servingmen. The one action this vulnerable king does take, however, is to restore Richard to his dukedom, so that the figure bequeathed a claim to the throne in the previous scene by a figure in a sick-chair is now given status and power by a demonstrably weak occupant of the royal seat. This sequence is then extended in the next scene where, during the loss and recapture of Rouen, the dying Bedford is "*brought in sick in a chair*" (3.2.40) to witness Falstaff's cowardice and then the English victory. At the climax of this action, "*Bedford dies, and is carried in by two in his chair*" (114), though Patton's Bedford (OSF 1991) had his throat cut by the French.

Throughout the play, Henry's "throne scenes" act out his inability to control internal divisions and hence England's diseases, but his first appearance in 3.1, sandwiched between scenes displaying figures dying in their sick-chairs, neatly sums up the problems to come, problems linked both to the Yorkist's claim to the throne (symbolized by Mortimer) and to the dying off of that loyal older generation devoted to the good of the country rather than factional interests (symbolized by Bedford). As with Joan's fiends and Talbot's shadow versus substance, much of the theatrical coherence of this episodic play arises from such linked images and configurations. If the final scene also has an onstage throne (as in Part III), Suffolk's convincing the king to take Margaret as his bride (made ominous by Suffolk's closing reference to Paris and the implicit analogy between Margaret–Helen and England–Troy) enacts a climactic link between the royal chair and potential diseases to come. Again, even in this early play, a set of associations made accessible by conventional theatrical practice (*enter sick*) can be used to italicize important meanings and effects.

In Part II, such chair–throne patterning is present but less emphatic, for Shakespeare uses violent deaths and the Cade rebellion to highlight the kingdom's diseases. The dead or dying Gloucester and Winchester are displayed onstage but (apparently) in sick-beds rather than sick-chairs. The impostor Simpcox, however, enters "*between two in a chair*" (2.1.65) in front of a weak king who, early in the same scene, is unable to control the quarrel between Gloucester and Winchester. Humphrey's uncovering of Simpcox's fraud acts out his important role in keeping some semblance of order in England, but, owing to Elinor's disgrace and his own naivete, Humphrey's position is soon undermined. Simpcox in his chair therefore prepares us for a hapless Henry on his throne who is unable to protect Humphrey or Lord Say (the latter linked to the palsy and "full of sickness and diseases" – 4.7.89, 93); this king is therefore vulnerable to an obvious fraud (Cade) in Act 4 and defenseless against a formidable opponent (York) in Act 5 (so that, as a result, Henry finds York seated in his throne in the first scene of Part III). When the inevitable confrontation does come,

York's critique pinpoints the vulnerability of Henry as possessor of the royal seat, for he begins "No; thou art not king," then cites the attributes of kingship ("That head of thine doth not become a crown: / Thy hand is made to grasp a palmer's staff / And not to grace an aweful princely scep-tre"), and concludes: "Give place! By heaven, thou shalt rule no more / O'er him whom heaven created for thy ruler" (5.1.93, 96–98, 104–5). As in the other two plays, such powerful accusations are enhanced by even a subliminal memory of the purportedly lame Simpcox exposed as a fraud and forced by the beadle to "give place" from *his* chair (and leap over a stool). The whole may be greater than the sum of its parts, but first an interpreter must have all the parts and some sense of how they might work.

The productions cited in this chapter provided a great deal of narra-tive excitement so as to engage and entertain playgoers (and television viewers) unfamiliar with the scripts. The many cuts and transpositions (along with the telescoping of disparate figures into one to economize on personnel) could be seen as the price tag for mounting *Henry VI* at all (although the RSC 1977–78 and 2000–01 renditions provide testi-mony that three-into-two is not the only available route). As in previous chapters, in singling out some representative choices, my purpose has not been to mount an indictment of the director-as-vandal. Rather, I have sought to bring into focus both the assets and liabilities of such modern onstage interpretations as a tool for understanding the original dramaturgy, theatrical vocabulary, and potential meanings. For the the-atre historian, the changes made by Bogdanov, Noble, and Patton can be especially revealing when the original onstage logic (whether linked to analogical thinking, distinctive images, or signifiers in an lost vocabulary) is no longer seen or appreciated, so that directorial adjustments serve as signposts that point to differing notions of how a play works or how that play is (or should be) put together. Such signposts can be particularly revealing in productions of *Henry VI* where the overall shape or sense of organization may be more in tune with Spenser's *The Faerie Queene* or Sidney's *Arcadia* than with *Henry V* or *Hamlet*.

The changes made by the three directors can therefore serve as a use-ful window into an Elizabethan theatrical logic, linked to a 1590s sense of analogy, imagery, and onstage story-telling, that is difficult, at times impossible, to recapture today. Some directorial decisions or adjustments can produce considerable theatrical excitement – and in this area I have not done justice to any of the productions. Other changes, however, fail to achieve the intended goal, a graceful elision of three long, ungainly plays, but rather constitute radical surgery or, for a different metaphor, provide not an adaptation but a translation into a new and different theatrical language. The many virtues of these productions and the various commercial advantages of slimming *Henry VI* into two items must therefore be weighed in a scale that takes into account the evisceration of Part II and other diminutions or losses – and that three major renditions of this trilogy in the late 1980s and early 1990s took this route should give us pause. Both Talbot's lecture on shadow versus substance and Henry VI's lament about the feather commanded by the greater gust should serve as chastening thoughts for interpreters of this trilogy on the stage or on the page.

8

The tamings of the shrews: rescripting the First Folio

"They sit and mark"
The Taming of the Shrew, 1.1.254

Any play in the Shakespeare canon is a candidate for rescripting or rewrighting, but a playgoer is most likely to encounter substantive alterations in a production of *The Taming of the Shrew*. A variety of reasons underlie such decisions. As might be expected, some elements in the Folio text (the role of Hortensio, the final couplet) are regularly adjusted or improved. More tellingly, the availability of additional Christopher Sly material in an alternative 1594 version of the taming story has provided an irresistible temptation for some directors. Perhaps most significant, discomfort with the Folio's final sequence, particularly Katherine's long speech and related stage business, has led to a wide variety of adjustments and some rewrighting. The goal of this chapter is to call attention to a range of in-the-theatre choices, to link those choices to an ongoing scholarly debate about rival texts, and to call attention to the price tags and trade-offs for such rescripting.

To start with some textual history, printed in 1594 and reprinted in two subsequent quartos (1596, 1607), *The Taming of a Shrew* (hereafter referred to as *A Shrew* or 1594) is the version of the Katherine story known to readers during the 1590s and early 1600s.[1] Today's reader, however, is familiar with *The Taming of the Shrew* (hereafter referred to as *The Shrew* or 1623), the play as printed in the First Folio of 1623. Playgoers of the period may have seen either or both versions. Playgoers today regularly see neither. And thereby hangs my tale.

Scholars have offered a variety of explanations for the existence of two comparable but discrete stage versions of this taming story. The 1594 edition could be an attempt to cash in on the box office success of *The Shrew* by offering a play with a virtually identical title (albeit set in Athens, not Padua, with only Katherine having the same name as the counterparts in 1623) that actually had been written or staged earlier. In this formulation, *A Shrew* would therefore be a previous theatrical version of the story and hence a source for Shakespeare, as with comparable situations found with *The Troublesome Reign of King John/King John* and *The Chronicle History of King Leir/King Lear*. *A Shrew*, however, could equally well be a "bad quarto"[2] (although an unusual, atypical one) – an adaptation of a previously existing *The Shrew* generated perhaps by one or more actors involved in a production (a process scholars term *memorial reconstruction*). This latter position has been advanced forcefully by a phalanx of scholars that includes Samuel Hickson, Peter Alexander, G. I. Duthie, Richard Hosley, and, more recently, editors Brian Morris, H. J. Oliver, Ann Thompson, and Stephen Roy Miller.[3]

Proponents of *A Shrew* as the earlier "source" play have been largely silent over the last fifty years, for "bad quartos," memorial reconstruction, and related arguments have dominated the field. However, even for this book with its focus on today's in-the-theatre choices, the debate over 1594 versus 1623 warrants some attention. What difference does the decision about the status of *A Shrew* ("bad quarto" versus source versus some other option – e.g., that both 1594 and 1623 draw upon some common *ur*-version) make for interpreters of the Folio script who are *not* editors or scholars with a large investment in these competing narratives? To what extent does one's sense of the 1594 Quarto affect how one reads, interprets, or stages what has survived in the Folio? To invoke those two immortal words, *so what?*

To start with one of the many interpretative implications linked to the two (or more) options: if *A Shrew* is deemed a memorially reconstructed text that was concocted *after The Shrew*, it provides a flawed report that, unlike other supposed "bad quartos," was in turn tinkered with by an adapter. If this chronology is accepted, the 1594 script could therefore serve as a comment upon, even an interpretation of, 1623, so as to provide us with *The Shrew* as seen through the eyes and ears of X and Y. For example, such an after-the-fact adaptation could demonstrate how someone (reporter, adapter, compositor) reacted to the taming as revealed in the Christopher Sly coda and other features distinctive to 1594. In contrast, if in the version that survives in the Folio Shakespeare was building upon an earlier play, the interpreter today can, as with other situations where the source material is fairly certain (for example, the history and Roman plays), gain some insights into the 1623 version by attending to what was kept, what was adjusted, what was inserted, and what was further developed, so as to gain a better sense of the overall design or strategy.[4]

Admittedly, to tackle this problem yet again is to risk immersion in details and intricate paths of reasoning that can frighten away everyone except editors and the most intrepid readers. Nonetheless, to revisit this quagmire might be worthwhile if questioning again the relationship between 1594 and 1623 leads to some insights into the moot questions that swirl around this script, especially in the last scene, so as to arrive at a formulation of value to a director or a critic not vitally interested in *A Shrew* or the competing scholarly narratives. My goal therefore is to explore the differences between 1594 and 1623 with the *so what?* question in mind. When are the differences telling or revealing? What difference does or should the precedence of one or another version make to interpretation today on the page or on the stage? Of particular importance to this book, how have directors used material from *A Shrew* and what are the implications of those choices?

Given such questions, many differences between the two texts are of potential interest. To avoid obfuscation (or sinking into the quagmire), I will concentrate on three discrete yet related elements: (1) the Sly material; (2) Lucentio and especially Hortensio as opposed to the roughly comparable figures in 1594; and (3) the final sequence.

SLY MANEUVERS

My point of departure is the Christopher Sly material unique to 1594, the feature of that script that has received the most attention by far and in turn has had the greatest impact upon interpretation today on the page and especially on the stage. The first two scenes of both versions (often referred to as "The Induction" but not cited as such in either script) are different in various details yet roughly analogous, but the Folio Sly is not referred to again after the stage direction at the end of 1.1 (*"They sit and mark"* – 254). In obvious contrast, the 1594 Sly has several scripted interjections after this point (3.309–16; 11.78–79 and 12.1; 13.45–54), falls asleep (13.127–33), is reclothed offstage, and is finally placed onstage so that his awakening in the presence of the tapster provides a coda or epilogue that ends the comedy (15.1–23). The three scholarly editions of *The Shrew* from the early 1980s (Arden 2, Oxford, and Cambridge) reprint the Sly material unique to 1594 as an appendix so as to provide a do-it-yourself-kit for that reader or director who feels that the Sly story as set forth in the received text (that is, the Folio) is somehow incomplete – a position endorsed as well by various critics.[5]

Such a do-it-yourself-kit approach to the Sly episodes, however, has its pitfalls. For example, the most striking penetration of Sly into the play proper comes in the 1594 equivalent to 5.1 when Sly reacts strenuously when a group of figures is threatened with prison. What is instructive here is the difference between 1594 and 1623 as to who is in trouble and why. In 1594 Sly intervenes not to save the equivalent to the true Vincentio (the figure threatened with prison in Folio 5.1) but rather to prevent the arrest of the two plotters (Valeria/Tranio and Phylotus/Pedant) who do not have the success of their analogues in 1623 and are easily cowed by the father of Aurelius/Lucentio. Indeed, the entire sequence is distinctively different, for after the duke (the equivalent to the true Vincentio) rejects Phylotus (the substitute father), his son Aurelius (onstage already, not initially offstage as is Lucentio) kneels and begs to be heard, whereupon the duke reacts: "Peace villain. / Lay hands on them and send them to prison straight," at which point *"Phylotus and Valeria runs away Then Sly speaks"* (13.43–44).

For a director today to insert the 1594 Sly interruption into a production of *The Shrew* (as in SFC 1981 and OSF 1991) is therefore to rescript the scene in more ways than one. Although the threat of prison may motivate Sly's interruption in both scenes, the threat to the true Vincentio (1623) is very different in tone and kind from the threat to the two fleeing tricksters – and the subsequent arrival of Lucentio in 1623 yields a very different pay-off. As noted by editor Stephen Roy Miller (p. 113) the 1623 line, "he shall not go to prison" (5.1.95) is spoken not by Sly (who has long been silent or has disappeared) but by Gremio who quickly backs down and is overruled by Baptista ("Away with the dotard, to the jail with him!" – 106–07). An objection to someone being sent to prison therefore *is* to be found in 1623 but from a different speaker, directed at different figures, and with a very different impact. What seems to the casual reader simple and straightforward when the "additional" Sly passages from 1594 are printed as an appendix to 1623 in the Arden, Oxford, or Cambridge editions (just plug them in) is, in fact, far more tangled, so that, as with the two versions of *King Lear*, a third conflated version of 5.1 can emerge that corresponds to neither *A Shrew* or *The Shrew*.

Such qualifications have had little effect upon theatrical practice, for directors, confronted with what appears to be an incomplete Sly narrative, have responded with a wide range of solutions. Least common in my playgoing experience is to play the Folio version in which the Lord sets up Sly and his "lady" as observers of the events of 1.1 and 1.2 but at some point these Induction figures disappear or fade into the background. In

1623 what starts as a play-within-a-play by visiting players apparently becomes the play proper directed not at Sly but at the playgoers in the auditorium. In roughly twenty productions, I have seen the Folio version only once (Santa Barbara 1991) where Homer Swander set up the first two Padua scenes (1.1, 1.2) as entertainment directed at an onstage audience, and then, in response to Tranio's invitation to "quaff carouses to our mistress' health, / And do as adversaries do in law, / Strive mightily, but eat and drink as friends" (1.2.275–77), had Sly descend from above so as to join the exiting group in search of a drink and disappear from the play. According to my highly unscientific exit poll, the Santa Barbara audience was not troubled by this supposedly aborted version of the story.

A noteworthy (and controversial) variation was Michael Bogdanov's choice (RSC 1978) to start with Sly not as being ejected from a tavern but as a drunk in the theatre aisle arguing with an usherette ("no bloody woman's going to tell me what to do...go on, you go and get the police...don't you talk to me like that, you bloody cow"). To the dismay of many playgoers (who were ready to call the police) he then climbed onto the stage and ripped down the flimsy old-fashioned set (one of the items cited in the promptbook is a "*Romeo and Juliet* balcony") to reveal a bare stage with metal stairs, scaffolding, and catwalks. He was restrained by actors playing stage personnel and fell asleep to be found by the Lord and his huntsmen who bathed and reclothed him. As Graham Holderness notes (p. 79), initially Sly responded to the Lord and his servants (Induction.2.1) in the original "demotic idiom" ("Hey, what's going on?...Just get me a pint of bitter, would you?"), but gradually "the deceptive strategies of the Lord are powerful enough to transform Sly's earthy contemporary patois into the mellifluous cadences of Elizabethan blank verse," starting with a version of lines 68–69: "Am I a lord, and I've got such a lady? / Or do I dream? or have I dreamed till now?" Sly and his "lady" then watched the beginning of the Padua narrative, but during 1.1 he left his position as observer to follow Kate (played by the actress who had been the usherette) and therefore did not observe the subsequent action. Rather, the actor (Jonathan Pryce) reappeared as Petruchio.

To play the Folio as scripted, however, is rare, even perhaps daring. More common is the Gordian knot approach: eliminate Sly and the Lord completely (from what already is one of the shortest plays in the canon) and start with the entrance of Lucentio and Tranio that begins 1.1 (OSF 1984, RSC 1987, Centre Stage Baltimore 1996). As noted in chapter 3, such a production may actually begin before the first line is spoken with an ensemble street scene that involves the entire cast (what OSF director Pat Patton termed "Times Square") or some other inserted material, as when Judd Parkin (OSF 1978) started not with Sly but with a Punch and Judy show with much pounding and thwacking, an accompanying song about a husband and his shrewish wife, and a meeting between Kate and Petruchio punctuated by a blow.

If some Sly material *is* to be included, a director may resort to a variety of options. One obvious choice is to use the Folio Sly scenes and then plug in the readily available material from *A Shrew* – as in SFC 1981 where Peter Dews placed his Sly above for most of the performance, included the various interjections (including "we'll have no sending to prison" – 13.45), and concluded with the 1594 coda. More expansively, Sandy McCallum (OSF 1991) chose to factor in the additional Sly material from *A Shrew* but with his own twists and additions. The early Sly/Lord encounters for the most part followed the Folio, although the arriving players *were* aware of the trick, so that one of those players (as in *A Shrew*), rather than Bartholomew the page, became Sly's "lady." Sly observed the play from a special place above from which he made the interjections scripted in 1594 (e.g., "when will the fool come again?" [3.309] was inserted before 2.1) along with others invented for 1991 purposes (e.g, to set up an intermission after 3.1, Sly said "Bid the players tarry, for I must make water before I burst"). After the intermission, the Lord and Sly re-entered without the "lady" (with such lines as "I cannot find my wife"; "your wife is not well"; "will they play again"; and "please you to attend"). When Gremio cited Petruchio's " 'A health!' quoth he" (3.2.170), Sly responded "I'll drink to that"; when after the wedding Petruchio drew his sword to "defend" Kate, Sly interjected "lay on Petruchio!"; and just before 4.1 he queried: "Be they married now?"

In the final scenes of this production Sly had a major moment in 5.1, where, as scripted in *A Shrew*, he descended, objected strenuously to the true Vincentio being sent to prison, was reassured, and then fell asleep on a bench. But unlike *A Shrew*, this Sly was not taken offstage at the Lord's direction but stayed onstage, asleep, for the remainder of the show. Moreover, McCallum did not include 1594's closing interchange with the hostess where Sly announces that he will apply to his own wife the lesson he has supposedly learned about how to tame a shrew. Rather, this Sly did not wake up until after the curtain call, at which point he wandered around in a stupor while the playgoers departed from the theatre. The director also cut the final couplet shared by Hortensio and Lucentio (5.2.188–89), so that the show ended with Petruchio's "God give you good night!" (187) addressed not to the onstage auditors but to the playgoers. This director's closure therefore corresponded neither to the Folio nor to *A Shrew*.

Of particular interest are three further variations on the framing action which in turn had a significant effect on how a playgoer understands the climax of the comedy. Two of these rescriptings presented the Padua events as Sly's dream (a concept also part of Bogdanov's strategy in 1978 albeit one not understood as such by most reviewers or playgoers). First, David Hammond's Sly (PRC 1989) was discovered by a Lord who resembled a Mafia don (with a notable scar) and his two "huntsmen," two gun-toting capos or hoods. The subsequent trick concocted at Sly's expense seemed a bit odd coming from this sinister figure, especially the iterated "Carry him gently" or "do it kindly" lines (Induction.1.46, 66, 72), but the first scene did make good sense, as did the conning of Sly in the next scene. Hammond cut various speeches (e.g., the comparison of hounds at the outset, the Lord's instructions to the players about Sly's possible reaction to the play), but the first three scenes (the two Induction scenes and the first Padua scene), although updated to the 1980s, were played straight with no major adjustments.

But starting with what is 1.2 in modern editions Hammond made some distinctive choices. As noted earlier, after the last Sly interlude in the Folio (at the end of 1.1 in our editions) the stage direction reads: "*They sit and mark*." Not so here. Rather, to the accompaniment of juggling and clowning by the "players," Sly, his "lady," and the features that had signaled the Lord's house (an ornate red couch with an erotic sculpture, bawdy hangings) were taken away; in their place, the ensemble rolled a canvas across the stage, and a curtained Padua set appeared upstage, so that the play-within-the-play of 1.1 became "the play." The actor who had played Sly then appeared on a motorbike with his Grumio to begin 1.2, and the audience was encouraged to make the connection and to see the play from this point on as Sly's dream (the Lord and his servants had hit the various "dream" lines very hard at the outset, and Sly had provided some significant yawns).

Much of what followed starting in 1.2 was not greatly affected by this "dream" approach, for the staging of the Petruchio–Kate scenes, although energetic and successful, was not strikingly different from other productions. An exception came just before the intermission when at the end of the wedding scene (3.2) the Lord–don appeared above to throw down colored confetti on those below, perhaps as a reminder of his controlling presence, but at least up through 4.3 (the second of the two scenes at Petruchio's house) the "dream" concept or the Sly/Petruchio doubling did not appear to be a major factor.

But interesting things started to happen in 4.5. The sun–moon exchange proceeded as usual, but the climax of Kate's process – the "budding virgin" passage (27–49) – was delivered not to a traditional old "true Vincentio" but to a Vincentio played by the Lord–don who here entered (in his original mafioso costume) what had originally been a play-within-a-play presented to him and who was accompanied by his two gunsels who reflexively reached for their guns when accosted by two seemingly mad strangers (and later in 5.1 grabbed and threatened Tranio, Biondello, and the Pedant). Then, in a curious and very suggestive move, after the "budding virgin" exchange Petruchio offered his arm to Kate, but she instead took the arm of Vincentio/Lord and exited, leaving behind a puzzled Petruchio to finish the scene with Hortensio. As context for this moment I should note that when the players arrived at the outset of the show the two actresses who were to play Kate and Bianca had embraced the Lord as old "friends" who knew where the power or money was to be had, so that this exit by Kate could be seen either as a tit-for-tat response to the "taming" or as a signal of what was to come – the "players" recognizing the ultimate ascendancy of the Lord over a Petruchio who eventually must revert to being Sly.

The last scene reinforced the latter possibility by having a tipsy, sleepy Bianca spend some time in Vincentio/Lord's lap, again suggesting where the real authority lay. In the wager and the famous speech that followed, Petruchio and Kate played their lines forcefully with no winks and no special effects, building eventually to a climactic kiss. Then, as the lighting started to change, an upstage Hortensio and Lucentio delivered the play's final lines slowly and knowingly while the rest of the cast disassembled the Padua set by rolling up the stage cover and removing the hangings at the rear. During this long kiss, Kate began to unbutton Petruchio's distinctive shirt, so that with the actors departed and with the stage cleared of its Padua covering, the playgoer saw the actor who had been playing Petruchio stripped to his undershirt and hence back to the initial image of Sly when first discovered by the Lord. At the same time, the set itself had reverted to the image at the outset, so that once again a downstage metal ladder descended from above to suggest an alley, waterfront, or some other non-privileged space. With the Lord above, looking down, a bewildered Sly was then dragged back into this non-magical, non-comedic space by the two hoods. Unlike the comparable figure in *A Shrew*, this Sly had no lines and therefore drew no moral from his experience (e.g., "I know now how to tame a shrew"; "I'll to my wife presently, / And tame her too, and if she anger me" – 15.16, 20–21). Rather, all this confused, helpless figure on the stage floor could do was reach out his hands imploringly to the Lord above or anyone else for help. The dream was clearly over.

This provocative ending left open a variety of interpretations. Clearly, the kind of moral or lesson found by Sly in *A Shrew* (a do-it-yourself-kit for dealing with a shrewish wife) was not applicable here. Rather, as my informal exit polling confirmed, some feminists in the audience (who had not been looking forward to the patriarchal terms of Kate's final speech) could conclude after this coda that the taming plot, the wager, and especially Kate's forty-four lines could be written off as no more than a drunken male fantasy. At the least, the sense of triumph and mutuality in the closing moments as detailed by many academic critics was strongly conditioned if not undermined by the return not just to a morning-after Sly (as in *A Shrew*) but to an ascendant Lord and a groping, confused Sly/Petruchio. Again, Hammond's solution to "the Sly problem" corresponded neither to the Folio nor to *A Shrew*. The Sly/Petruchio doubling is not possible in the Folio script given the entrance of Petruchio immediately after "*They sit and mark*" (although a Lord/Petruchio double *is* possible). Moreover, to make the players a knowing part of the trick on Sly (as in *A Shrew*) Hammond had to cut the Lord's lines to them in the opening scene wherein he describes Sly as an eccentric lord who has "never heard a play" before (Induction.1.93–99). Nonetheless, Hammond's use of the two significant doublings (Sly/Petruchio, Lord/Vincentio), the coda, and several other distinctive moments (e.g., Kate's exit with Vincentio/Lord in 4.5) produced a distinctively different perspective on a vexed and vexing set of problems. Whether drunken male fantasy or shattered romantic vision, Hammond's ending provided much food for thought.

Comparable was the approach taken by Gale Edwards (RSC 1995). According to the program, 175 lines had been cut, but such figures can be misleading. A director can omit a significant number of lines (as did John Barton in 1980 when he cut 900 lines from *Hamlet*) but still retain all the scenes and segments, indeed the essential shape and thrust of the script. However, to cut the final ten lines of the Folio *Shrew*, the first of which is "Why, there's a wench! Come on, and kiss me, Kate" (5.2.180), may be (according to some theatrical professionals who bent my ear on this subject) to create a new play co-authored by William Shakespeare and Gale Edwards. This production therefore raised some provocative questions about directors' concepts and the original scripts.

Veteran *Shrew*-watchers may disdain reading the plot summary in a program, but such advance preparation was useful for this show. The reader was informed that Sly falls asleep after "arguing late at night with his wife who finally, in despair, returns home without him" and then "in his dream a lord appears with his fellow huntsmen, discovers the poor creature on the ground and decides to play a trick on him." Moreover, "as part of his dream, Sly will play the hero of his own fantasy, a cavalier fortune hunter called Petruchio. The dream world set up by the players is that of Padua." At the end, during Katherina's big speech "Petruchio slowly realizes what he has been attempting to do to Katherina in the name of love," so that "his dream has become a nightmare, and he is back asleep where he began. Christopher Sly awakes."

Presenting this narrative, however, posed problems. Some onstage (as opposed to program) signals are needed to establish that Sly is "dreaming" first the Lord and then the Padua events. The only such clue I received as a playgoer was the very deliberate, even stilted delivery of the Lord's initial lines, a phenomenon that some playgoers interpreted as bad acting. The director's approach therefore raised some intrusive questions. Why should Sly dream the Lord and his trick as opposed to the Kate story and does not such a strategy make the Bianca-related events even more than usually irrelevant? Moreover, as Michael Billington noted shrewdly in his review (*The Guardian*, April 24, 1995), if the "play" is indeed Sly's "wife-taming fantasy," "You'd expect Sly to imagine himself as a swaggering hero" rather than "a nervous windbag who is easily outsmarted by his servant Grumio." For Billington, Edwards "tries to have it both ways: to present the action as a male dream and, at the same time, to cut Petruchio down to size," so that the director's "natural feminist instinct runs counter to the structure she has devised."

Much depends, of course, upon the punch line, the handling of the final moments. Despite various cuts and alterations, the presentation of the Kate–Petruchio story was by no means unusual for the bulk of this production. Michael Siberry's Petruchio was clearly a fortune hunter at the outset (so that to stake him in 1.2 the three suitors to Bianca threw money on the stage floor), but his first meeting with Josie Lawrence's Kate in 2.1 was funny and lively, with moments of rapport between the two. At the end of 4.1 Petruchio delivered his falconry speech slowly and clearly, at which point an exhausted Kate entered to sit upon an upstage chair and stay in sight during 4.2 so as to display more fully the "taming" effects upon her and to build sympathy. The sun–moon–budding virgin tests in 4.5 were presented in the usual fashion and led to a huge kiss at the end of 5.1, in this production the apex of the Kate–Petruchio story, though Petruchio's final couplet (149–50) was cut, including "Is not this well?" Meanwhile, sporadic appearances of the Lord and his men presumably reminded the playgoer of the dream or the concept.

The wager set up in 5.2 then placed heavy emphasis upon the money, so that a large number of bills was again thrown onto the floor to be picked up by the winner, with the echo of 1.2 suggesting that Petruchio was still a fortune hunter and had changed little – and this Petruchio was anything but certain he was going to win the bet. After Baptista wrote his check for the additional 20,000 crowns, Petruchio visibly decided to push matters further, so thence followed the command for Kate to discard and tread upon her hat (she complied, but only after a long pause) and the command that elicits the infamous speech (preceded by her even longer pause). That speech, some of it very emotional, was then directed not at the other two women, who became increasingly irrelevant as this scene progressed, but at Petruchio and was keyed in part to the money on the floor which Kate saw and reacted to (is that what all this has been about?). Her final words were then the final words spoken in this scene ("My hand is ready, may it do him ease" – 179) as she knelt and laid her hand upon the floor.

What followed was the director's sense of an appropriate ending. A shaken Petruchio crossed the stage, knelt, but, realizing how badly he had erred, said nothing. The rest of the actors gradually faded away; given his prolonged silence, Kate rose and backed off, leaving him alone on the floor. He slept and became Sly again; the Lord and his men entered, reclothed Sly (with some dialogue inserted from *A Shrew*), and left. This production had begun with an angry Sly–Mrs. Sly encounter in lieu of the Sly–Hostess exchange in the received text. When Sly awoke, his wife (the Kate actress in a black cloak) came downstage, so that he ended the show at her feet, silently abasing himself, with the final image offering a hint of an embrace and a reconciliation (so Petruchio has gone too far and blown it, but Sly can still make amends). Presumably, an unacceptable 1590s ending has herein been made palatable for the 1990s, although to achieve this effect the director had to introduce a new figure (Mrs. Sly) because the received text found in the Folio or the Riverside was inadequate for her purposes.

For Edwards (according to various interviews) Sly/Petruchio's macho dream or fantasy turns a rebellious Kate into a subservient woman, but that dream turns into a nightmare: watching Kate deliver her final speech causes him to question whether breaking her spirit was something he really wanted or had the right to do. Is the play as presented here then (in reviewer John Peter's terms) "a piece of theatrical marriage counselling" (*The Sunday Times*, April 30, 1995)? Other productions of this script have omitted the final two lines (so that Kate and Petruchio do not *exeunt*, thereby leaving everyone else behind), but most of those renditions still provided a contrast between their relationship as it has evolved and those of Bianca–Lucentio and Widow–Hortensio. In this version, however, those other figures seemed superfluous by the end of the show so that a playgoer might well wonder what all the fuss had been about. In addition, much of the director's concept was linked to silences and mimed actions rather than to dialogue, so that key signals, starting with the Lord's delivery at the outset, were fuzzy. Are indeed the final ten lines in the received text negligible or dispensable? What price taming the Folio version of *The Shrew*?

An even more elaborate and inventive reformulation of the Christopher Sly story, albeit one not set up as Sly's dream, was provided by Bill Alexander (RSC 1992). In his program note Alexander noted that the lines spoken by Sly and others in his production were "adapted" from *A Shrew*, a text that, "in terms of the relationship of the Sly story to the Shrew story, represents Shakespeare's original schematic intention." To restore what he termed "the full scheme of the play" Alexander chose to follow "the structure of the Quarto text while remaining faithful to the 1623 Folio for the Shrew story itself." Since the frame for this production was set in the present, this choice entailed finding 1992 equivalents for Sly, the anonymous Lord, and the visit of the players, choices that in turn set up what amounts to a new plot line that involved a sexist and manipulative Lord Simon Llewellyn and his entourage that included several women who made their bids for "freedom" by the end of the performance.

Alexander's version of "Shakespeare's original schematic intention" started with Sly being ejected from a pub (The Ugly Duckling) and found by Lord Simon and his modish 1990s retinue. Gone therefore were all the references to the hunt; gone too were the caring qualities of the Folio Lord, for Alexander's Simon pushed women around and took advantage of everyone. As Peter Holland notes, the director's "extensive rewriting of the Induction was not only about updating to the 1990s" but "was also an attempt to see the frame as an exercise in class mockery"[6] so that Alexander provided such lines as "Leave him alone, Simon. Don't touch him. He's disgusting; probably working-class" and the response: "The drunk needs teaching a lesson, so we'll mess around with his mind for a bit." Except for the coda, the remainder of the show took place in a posh drawing room where a younger brother, not Bartholomew the page, became Sly's lady. The aristocratic group and Sly (with whom the playgoer was encouraged to sympathize) then watched "the play," with the players occasionally inviting a bystander to handle a minor role (and Holland notes the anomaly of the actors playing "to the theatre audience with their backs to the group that had ostensibly commanded and paid for their performance" [p. 131]).

A key scene for this concept was then 4.1 where Petruchio and his fellow players conscripted the onstage observers to play first Curtis, then the other servants; the aristocrats were handed scripts, subjected to Petruchio's whims, even given blows, so that they were vulnerable to an extreme version not only of Kate's early behavior but also of Lord Simon's (at one point, Petruchio threw a chair at Simon who kicked it back). In addition, most of the props in this scene were make-believe, not real, so that the playgoers saw no actual fire, water, dog, or meat – though Petruchio delivered "real" blows.

After the interval (placed after 4.1) the two groups (aristocrats and players) watched "the play" together. When Vincentio was threatened with prison, Sly came forward with a broken bottle only to be calmed by Petruchio (or actor Anton Lesser) with "It's all right. It's only a play." The prolonged Kate–Petruchio kiss at the end of 5.1 then generated comparable kissing among the onstage audience (one of the most successful moments in this concept) – and here even Sly took the hand of his "lady." In 5.2 one of Lord Simon's ladies was pressed into playing the Widow and, to the amazement of all, did so without access to a script (so that she either already knew her lines or chose to improvise). Kate's final speeches and her story overall then appeared to have less impact upon the Padua figures than upon the aristocratic group where various new relationships were suggested at the end, most notably the shunning of Lord Simon by the lady he had earlier dominated, so that, in Holland's terms, the Kate–Bianca stories "became a pedagogic device, changing the onstage audience" (131). The production closed with the reawakening of Sly who caught a glimpse of the actors who had put on "the play."

In these rescripted productions directors have drawn upon the Folio Induction and the additional "frame" material in *A Shrew* so as to provide a "new" story, much onstage excitement, and an adjusted ending deemed more suitable to today's sensibilities. In particular, the changes made by Hammond, Edwards, and Alexander were linked to the gender politics of the 1980s and 1990s and to fears that the received text might prove offensive or unacceptable to many in a given audience. The decision to factor *A Shrew* material into *The Shrew* so as to "complete" what is "missing" – or the alternative move, to dispense with the Sly story altogether – means in turn that a playgoer rarely if ever gets to see the Folio version performed (and directors never have to decide what to do with Sly after "*They sit and mark*"). The Folio Shrew, like *2 Henry VI* (as noted in chapter 7), therefore has almost ceased to exist as a current theatrical entity.

Such a situation raises yet again my recurring question: how should playgoers view "improvements" in the received text that make possible an interpretation more suitable to today's prevailing sensibilities? Taming a script has distinct advantages, both for theatrical professionals and their playgoers, but the price tag can be high – in this case a rewrighting of the ending of an innovative early comedy wherein, subtly or overtly, the now "completed" frame shifts the focus at the climax away from a contrast between Kate–Petruchio and the rest of Padua. Does the existence of *A Shrew* provide a model for resolving an anomaly or has it become a blank check for adaptation at the pleasure of a director? Here as elsewhere, playgoing (to borrow from Brutus) "craves wary walking" (2.1.15).

UNSUCCESSFUL TAMERS: HORTENSIO, POLIDOR, AND SLY

Such rescriptings of Sly and the framing story are the most visible adjustments to this script, but directors also, in response to other perceived anomalies, tinker with the role of Hortensio, a feature of the Folio version that has played a part in various scholarly debates. Readers who argue that the 1623 text is flawed or incomplete build upon the fact that Hortensio is not included or is somehow forgotten in the negotiations over Bianca (2.1) and is absent from the wedding scene (3.2) where Tranio/Lucentio seems to be taking over Hortensio's role as an old friend of Petruchio (for example, when Tranio says " 'Tis some odd humor pricks him to this fashion; / Yet oftentimes he goes but mean apparell'd" – 72–73).[7] Bill Alexander's solution (RSC 1992) to the latter problem was to allot his Hortensio many of Tranio's lines in 3.2 to or about Petruchio (e.g., "Though he be blunt, I know him passing wise"; "Go to my chamber, put on clothes of mine" – 24, 113). In a very different approach to Hortensio, Sandy McCallum (OSF 1991) cut

Tranio's speech to Bianca on Petruchio's taming-school (4.2.54–58), so that his Hortensio was not present for Katherine's encounters with the meat, haberdasher, and tailor in 4.3 (Grumio took on some of his lines and function) and did not observe the sun–moon–budding virgin interchanges in 4.5. As a result, this Hortensio did not have his coda to 4.5 ("Have to my widow!" – 77–79), so that the charting of his course to marriage was gone. By omitting this speech, cutting Gremio's presence in 5.1, and moving the initial Lucentio–Bianca–Biondello segment of 5.1 to the end of 4.4, McCallum moved directly from the Vincentio–Petruchio–Kate meeting in 4.5 to Vincentio's arrival at Baptista's house, so that 4.5–5.1 became one continuous unit. A consequence of such streamlining, however, was a considerable diminution of both Hortensio and the taming–education motif.

Admittedly, the Hortensio story may not be a primary concern for many readers, but this part of the narrative is affected in interesting ways by the various adjustments made by directors to the Sly frame. Here attention to the distinctions between 1594 and 1623 is useful. Polidor, the suitor roughly comparable to Hortensio in 1594, is a scholar and a friend of Ferando/Petruchio who courts and wins (without a Gremio or other rivals) Emelia, the youngest daughter of Alfonso; meanwhile, another suitor, Aurelius (Lucentio), son of the duke of Sestos, woos Alfonso's middle daughter, Phylema. The most interesting parallel between Hortensio and Polidor is that both end up with "untamed" shrews, as revealed by the brief but highly charged one-scene appearance of the Widow in 5.2 of *The Shrew* and by the final beat of *A Shrew* (the last interchange before the Sly coda), where Polidor, "in a dump," tells his new bride "I say thou art a shrew" and Emelia responds: "That's better than a sheep" (14.157–59). The coda–epilogue that immediately follows the Polidor–Emelia exchange, moreover, also focuses upon the supposed lesson learned by Sly that, according to him, will lead to a yet-to-be-attempted taming of *his* wife. The 1594 version therefore peaks with its equivalent to the Petruchio–Kate resolution and *exeunt*, a climax followed by comments from Aurelius and Alfonso about the departed couple, the Polidor–Emelia exchange in which a new shrew is revealed, and the Sly coda with its lesson drawn by one onstage observer from what the playgoer has just witnessed and a goal of taming enunciated although not completed or actually staged.

Despite the limits of the verse and overall execution, the 1594 resolution has its own distinctive advantages, but, as I read it, it offers an unambiguous "taming" of Katherine without irony or mutuality that is

played off against a new Kate-like role for Emelia and a linked resolution
from Sly. Although anathema to many sensibilities today, such a package
or strategy seems to me of considerable theatrical interest. This version,
moreover, was *Shrew* as known to the reading public up through 1623 in
three quartos, whereas plays such as *Love's Labor's Lost*, *2 Henry IV*, and
Much Ado About Nothing never made it to a second quarto (whatever that
statistic means).

That clearly defined strategy in 1594 should then lead to a reconsideration of the very different strategy in 1623 – and here is where both
sources and "bad quartos" can be stimuli in causing an interpreter to
see more clearly the distinctive choices in the script under investigation.
Clearly, the absence of a continuing Sly story denies any obvious closure
for the Folio narrative, but, equally important, that silence means that
no moral is drawn, however baldly, by an onstage observer who plans to
put that "lesson" into practice. Rather, the rhythm in 1623 takes us to
the Kate–Petruchio climax and then winds down after their *exeunt* in a
couplet shared by Hortensio and Lucentio. With reference to today's productions, moreover, note that neither 1594 or 1623 ends with Petruchio's
lines; rather, both call for the final lines to be delivered by those who constitute the world left behind. Today's director who lets Petruchio have
the last word (as in OSF 1984 and OSF 1991) so that "God give you good
night!" is directed to the playgoers is therefore going against *both* scripts
on a strategic choice of some consequence.

To return to Hortensio (and Lucentio), what I had missed, until encouraged by the 1594 strategy to rethink matters, is the very different
story or rhythm generated by Hortensio in 1623. In the 1623 version of
4.2, Hortensio, unlike Polidor, is soured on his first love interest, a younger
sister of Kate, after he sees her kissing and courting what he thinks is a
mere scholar (Polidor *is* such a scholar in 1594). He therefore refers to
Bianca as "this proud disdainful haggard" (4.2.39), a clear echo (for the
playgoer) of Petruchio's falconry speech at the end of the previous scene,
and decides to go to what Tranio describes as "the taming-school" where
Petruchio as schoolmaster "teacheth tricks eleven and twenty long, / To
tame a shrew and charm her chattering tongue" (54, 57–58). As a failed
tutor of Bianca, Hortensio heads off for teacher-training.

Unlike the playgoer, however, Hortensio has not witnessed 4.1 and, despite his use of "haggard," has not heard either of Petruchio's soliloquies
on his methods (2.1.168–80, 4.1.188–211). Somehow in 4.3 he participates
in the denial of meat (though the stage business is not clear) and later
is asked by Petruchio to pay the tailor and so ameliorate the situation.

Significantly, at the end of this scene his reaction to Petruchio's "It shall be what a'clock I say it is" is no more informed than Kate's ("Why, so this gallant will command the sun" – 4.3.195–96), so that apparently Hortensio like Kate has not caught on to what underlies Petruchio's method. Rather, during the climactic sun–moon debate he urges Kate to comply ("Say as he says, or we shall never go" – 4.5.11) not out of any understanding of "taming" or insight into Petruchio's procedures but as a weary traveller who wants to get on with it (enough is enough). Once Kate acquiesces, Hortensio observes: "Petruchio, go thy ways, the field is won" (23). At the end of this scene, he then draws a moral in his terms: "Well, Petruchio, this has put me in heart. / Have to my widow! and if she be froward, / Then hast thou taught Hortensio to be untoward" (77–79), so that the next time we see him he is married to his formidable Widow.

What is of particular interest when invoking 1594, then, is that in that version it is not Hortensio but Sly who, at the very end, after the finish of the Petruchio–Kate story, draws the moral ("I know now how to tame a shrew" and "I'll to my wife presently, / And tame her too, and if she anger me" – 15.16, 20–21). The verbal links between this passage and Hortensio's speech at the end of 4.5 may not be that close, but the sentiments and the announced purpose are the same, with both the 1594 Sly and the 1623 Hortensio supposedly learning from Ferando/Petruchio "how to do it" ("I know now how to tame a shrew"; "and if she be froward, / Then hast thou taught Hortensio to be untoward") and then going off "to do it" ("I'll to my wife"; "Have to my widow!").

The parallels and distinctions can be pursued further. The play-goer must imagine the confrontation between the 1594 Sly and his wife (though that playgoer does witness the final confrontation between Polidor and Emelia). However, Hortensio's declaration of what he has supposedly learned comes at the end of 4.5, so that, in keeping with the emphasis throughout *The Shrew* upon failed education (as in 3.1 with Bianca's rival tutors), the playgoer sees the results of Hortensio's course at The Taming School in 5.2 where he is cowed by his Widow who serves as the Folio's highly entertaining equivalent to Polidor's Emelia and Sly's wife. As a teacher–tamer–educator, Hortensio therefore fails twice with two very different women.

To look closely at the Hortensio story is then to raise some provocative questions about the competing narratives that purport to explain the relationship between 1594 and 1623. Would a putative reporter or adapter move from the 1623 Hortensio's decision in 4.5 and subsequent confrontation with the Widow in 5.2 to the 1594 strategy involving

Polidor/Emelia and Sly's coda? Such a progression (or perhaps regression) seems to me possible but unlikely. Rather, in this instance I find it more likely that Shakespeare, in building upon some version of 1594, scrapped the Sly-coda and the third daughter, set up the rivalry over Bianca (that heightens both the education motif and the mercantile view of this Padua), and developed Hortensio and the Widow as a replacement for the *A Shrew* material (along with Bianca too as a significant presence in 5.2).

What are the consequences of such weighing of the options? So what? If even some of my argument about the 1623 Hortensio versus his 1594 equivalent has merit, then tacking on the 1594 Sly coda to a production of the Folio script is comparable to conflating the two versions of *King Lear*, indeed is more suspect given the substantive differences between 1594 and 1623. Rather, if the Sly coda is included in a rendition of the 1623 script, the playgoer will witness *both* the lesson drawn by Sly *and* the lesson drawn in 4.5 by Hortensio, two components that do not co-exist in *either* play.[8] The two versions of *Shrew* do cover much analogous ground on taming, shrews, and lessons, but they do so in a very different fashion and with a decidedly different theatrical rhythm or strategy – as is especially noticeable when one looks closely at what follows the Ferando–Kate *exeunt* in the last scene. Indeed, 1594 ends with a focus upon four marriages, perhaps four different directions to pursue (although little is done with Aurelius–Phylema). At stake therefore are two very different trajectories or strategies that cannot be conflated, with the differences having considerable interpretative significance. To conflate them (as in SFC 1981) is, even more than with the conflated *King Lear*, to create a third entity that corresponds neither to version one nor to version two.

TO COME OR NOT TO COME AT *"THEIR HUSBANDS' CALL"*

Such concerns about the Sly material and Hortensio, needless to say, are of less concern to would-be interpreters of *The Shrew* than the many distinctions, small and large, between Kate–Petruchio in 1623 and Kate–Ferando in 1594. For example, the 1594 version of 2.1, their first meeting, is much shorter and less complex, with no initial soliloquy from Ferando and with no clear indication that the father, Alfonso, is to leave the stage during the interview. When offered Ferando's hand, moreover, *A Shrew*'s Kate, unlike her 1623 counterpart, has an angry speech but then says *aside*: "But yet I will consent and marry him, / For I methinks have lived too long a maid, / And match him too, or else his manhood's good" (3.169–71).

Other 1594 speeches and sequences also differ in suggestive ways, whether in the marriage scene (Folio 3.2) or the taming scenes in Act 4. For example, in the former, *A Shrew* supplies a specific rationale for Ferando's red cap and outlandish marriage costume ("She's such a shrew, if we should once fall out / She'll pull my costly suits over mine ears. / And therefore am I thus attired awhile" – 4.115–17), but has no equivalent to Petruchio's "To me she's married, not unto my clothes" (3.2.117). In the latter, Ferando has a simpler version of the 1623 falconry speech (the comparison between the two versions of this speech is basic to the "bad quarto" argument); the sequence of ordeals for Kate is then basically the same albeit shorter, simpler, and more violent, with no Hortensio present and no lengthy sequence involving Sander/Grumio and the tailor. In 1594, Kate and Ferando are not observers during the equivalent to 5.1 and therefore do not remain onstage after the departure of the ensemble for a kiss "in the midst of the street" and Petruchio's "Is not this well?" (5.1.144, 149). Although rarely cited in the "bad quarto" debate, this last distinction strikes me as significant, for I find it difficult to conceive of a putative reporter who would forget or omit this highly charged and highly memorable theatrical moment.

As already noted in the discussion of both Sly and Hortensio/Polidor, the differences between the two final sequences can be particularly instructive. Overall, the last scene in *A Shrew* has the same general shape as its counterpart in 1623 but, as with other comparable moments, is shorter and simpler. Unlike 1623, the women in 1594 are not onstage at the outset, so that no bantering takes place before the wager. Kate here does provide a major speech on wifely obedience (14.114–42) but one composed of different elements with more emphasis upon biblical material, especially Eve's sins. Her final lines focus upon women's duty to obey, love, keep, and nourish their husbands, "Laying our hands under their feet to tread" to procure their ease; as a precedent she announces: "I'll first begin, / And lay my hand under my husband's feet" (139, 141–42). The text then supplies a stage direction not spelled out as such in 1623: "*She lays her hand under her husband's feet*," to which Ferando responds: "Enough sweet, the wager thou hast won, / And they I am sure cannot deny the same" (143–44). At this point Alfonso gives a hundred pounds (not 20,000 crowns) – "Another dowry for another daughter, / For she is not the same she was before" (148–49) – so that the father's providing of a second dowry comes *after* Kate's big speech, not before it as in 1623.

With the *so what?* question in mind, of particular interest is a phrase in another stage direction unique to 1594 which specifies the nature of Kate's entrance with the two recalcitrant wives. First, Ferando comments: "For see where she brings her sisters forth by force"; then the stage direction reads: "*Enter Kate thrusting Phylema and Emelia before her and makes them come unto their husbands' call*" (99). The final phrase – "makes them come unto their husbands' call" – refers back to the wager and the failure of the first two wives (in either version) to respond. No such specific wording, however, is to be found in the Folio.

In itself this 1594 phrase is unremarkable – apparently merely a "fictional" signal that provides little if any insight into the original staging but merely enhances the narrative for a reader.[9] But when linked to other passages, most notably Ferando/Petruchio's falconry speech, "makes them come unto their husbands' call" sets up an imagistic and conceptual link otherwise easy to miss, one that can have a fruitful pay-off in both versions of the story (and therefore can be operative whether the 1594 adapter read *The Shrew* in such terms or whether Shakespeare developed such a motif after he encountered it in his source).

What is at stake here is the relationship between (1) the rationale behind the taming process, as enunciated by both Ferando and Petruchio in their respective falconry speeches, and (2) the wager and its aftermath. In 1594 (6.37–47) Ferando announces that to tame his shrew he plans to use various denials ("curbs of hunger, ease and want of sleep") so as to "mew her up as men do mew their hawks / And make her gently come unto the lure." No matter how stubborn Kate proves, "Yet would I pull her down and make her come / As hungry hawks do fly unto their lure." In 1623 Petruchio notes that his falcon, Kate, "now is sharp and passing empty, / And till she stoop, she must not be full-gorg'd, / For then she never looks upon her lure" (4.1.190–92). He then describes how he will deny her sleep, with these devices summed up as "Another way I have to man my haggard, / To make her come, and know her keeper's call" (193–94). Both Ferando and Petruchio therefore specify that the shrewish wife, like a falcon or haggard, must be trained to look upon or "gently come unto" her lure; Petruchio, moreover, invokes the same phrase that turns up in the 1594 stage direction and dialogue when he states that a major goal of the "taming" process is to make the wife-haggard "come, and know her keeper's call."

To my knowledge, few interpreters have linked these falconry speeches to the wager and the final sequence, but such links are potentially there and can be meaningful, particularly if the interpreter views Petruchio's

1623 reference to "her keeper's call" in the context of the terms provided in the 1594 final scene. In the less familiar sequence as scripted in *A Shrew*, the scene opens with the three husbands and their servants (the brides' father, Alfonso, joins them a bit later), but does not include either the three women or the equivalents to Vincentio and the Pedant. Aurelius/Lucentio proposes a "trial of our wives; / Who will come soonest at their husbands' call" (14.3–4) and comparable locutions pepper the subsequent discussion ("For he may call, I think, till he be weary, / Before his wife will come before she list"; "my wife comes as soon as I do send"; "whose wife soonest comes when he doth call" – 6–7, 13, 21). After the two refusals, Ferando bids his servant Sander "Command your mistress to come to me presently" (75); when she complies ("Sweet husband, did you send for me?" – 81), he orders her to take off her cap and tread upon it; the stage direction reads: *"She takes off her cap and treads on it"* (86). To "try her further" (90), Ferando then asks about Kate's two sisters and then orders: "Fetch them hither, and if they will not come, / Bring them perforce and make them come with thee" (93–94) thereby setting up the stage direction: *"Enter Kate thrusting Phylema and Emelia before her and makes them come unto their husbands' call."* What follows is some bickering among the two couples who have lost the wager, Ferando's order to "tell unto these headstrong women, / What duty wives do owe unto their husbands" (112–13), a shorter, highly orthodox version of Kate's speech, her laying of her hand beneath his foot, and the final speeches from Ferando and Alfonso (as described earlier).

The scene as scripted in *The Shrew* is richer and more complex but still has a comparable shape. Initially, a much larger group is onstage (the three couples, the two fathers, the Pedant, Gremio, and the three servants). A great deal of banter is provided before the women *exeunt*, in part to introduce the Widow (and establish a rivalry with Kate) but also to set up Bianca as a bird ("Am I your bird? I mean to shift my bush" – 5.2.46), albeit not a falcon but one that is the object of pursuit. After more hunting talk, again with a focus upon Bianca as "This bird you aim'd at, though you hit her not" (50 – and with the emphasis upon dogs, not haggards), the wager is proposed (by Petruchio rather than Aurelius–Lucentio) without any reference to *husbands' call* but in simpler terms: "Let's each one send unto his wife, / And he whose wife is most obedient, / To come at first when he doth send for her, / Shall win the wager" (66–69). What follows is basically the same as in 1594, although (1) Baptista provides the second dowry with Kate offstage; (2) Kate throws her cap "under-foot" (122) in the presence of the other two wives; and

(3) the Widow provides some strong resistance to Petruchio not found in *A Shrew*. As in 1594, however, Petruchio's initial order conveyed by Grumio is "Say I command her come to me" (96) as opposed to Lucentio's "bid" (76) and Hortensio's "entreat" (86). Similarly, with regard to the other two wives, he tells Kate "Go fetch them hither. If they deny to come, / Swinge me them soundly forth unto their husbands. / Away, I say, and bring them hither straight" (103–05); when she returns, he notes: "See where she comes, and brings your froward wives / As prisoners to her womanly persuasion" (119–20).

In both versions, then, Kate distinguishes herself from the other two wives by (1) coming at her husband's command; (2) throwing off and treading upon her cap; (3) fetching the wives after they had refused to come at the bidding or entreaty of their husbands; and (4) providing a long speech to "these headstrong women" about "What duty they do owe their lords and husbands" (130–31). Admittedly, Kate is not a falcon-haggard (or a hound-retriever) and therefore possesses language, a mind, autonomy, and many strengths that stretch the analogy beyond the breaking point. Nonetheless, as an integral part of the final sequence in both scripts, Ferando/Petruchio (1) "commands" her to come; (2) sends her back to bring–swinge–fetch the other two women; and (3) orders her to perform two other distinctive actions. Meanwhile, Bianca is set up metaphorically not as a falcon linked to the will of a master-husband but as a bird ("Am I your bird . . . shift my bush") that is a prey or a target for men ("you hit the white" – 186).

To come or not to come at their husbands' call is a locution that is spelled out in 1594 but is less audible in 1623. However, owing to the far better developed "education" motif, the distinctions among the routes taken by Petruchio, Lucentio, and Hortensio in *The Shrew* are clearer and more meaningful than the fates of the comparable figures in *A Shrew*. In both instances, moreover, the wager and its aftermath constitute the final field-testing of the approach to taming and education enunciated earlier by both Ferando and Petruchio in their falconry speeches. In 1623 if not in 1594, Kate is far more than a trained bird (or hound) being put through her paces, but there *is* a logic underlying 5.2 in which the formerly "headstrong" independent shrew now comes at her husband's call-command, fetches objects to that trainer–husband, and performs a highly visible action and gives a lengthy speech as instructed. Such a bald formulation of the links between the falconry speeches and the wager runs the risk of flattening out many significant qualifications that critics and theatrical professionals have found in the Kate–Petruchio relationship. Nonetheless, the wording of the 1594 stage direction and speeches does bring into sharp focus a strategy or relationship that has significant implications for any interpretation of this final sequence.

Such interpretations will continue to vary widely. As a final response to my *so what?* question, note that in 1594 Sly is not present during the wager and its aftermath; nonetheless, the lesson he learns from the rest of the Kate–Ferando story is simple and blunt ("I know now how to tame a shrew"). The absence in the Folio, however, of (1) this after-the-fact drawing of a "lesson" and (2) any specific signal that Kate "*lays her hand under her husband's feet*" leaves open a space that is closed down in 1594. In today's productions, after enjoining the wives to "vail your stomachs . . . / And place your hands below your husband's foot," Kate often starts to do so, but her actual lines read: "In token of which duty, if he please, / My hand is ready, may it do him ease" (5.2.176–79). Given the specific stage direction, the 1594 Kate and Ferando have few options at this point, but the 1623 Petruchio ("Why, there's a wench! Come on, and kiss me, Kate!" – 180) can prevent Kate from completing or even starting this action ("My hand is ready" can be played with no more than a small gesture with that hand). Indeed, Homer Swander (Santa Barbara 1991) had his Petruchio, after lifting Kate's hand from the floor, place *his* hand in the same spot.

That space left open for interpretation in 1623 but not in 1594 should be factored into the "bad quarto" versus source controversy. If *A Shrew* is indeed the later version, then those responsible for the adaptation remembered, read, or interpreted the final sequence of *The Shrew* in a manner consistent with the Sly coda and Kate's placing her hand beneath Ferando's foot. In this formulation, at least one set of interpreters of the Folio version of this comedy understood the taming story in such straightforward, hierarchical, patriarchal terms. On the other hand, if *The Shrew* is the later version, Shakespeare adapted the raw materials found in *A Shrew* so as to complicate a simpler narrative, eliminate any unambiguous lesson enunciated by Sly, and leave open the disposition of Kate's hand and Petruchio's reaction. If *A Shrew* is deemed a memorially reconstructed "bad quarto," the reader today with a patriarchal bent can argue that the reporters responsible for the 1594 text are remembering accurately the original stage business; in the terms of this narrative, when Shakespeare's *The Shrew* was staged in the 1590s, Kate put her hand beneath her husband's foot. However, if *A Shrew* is deemed a source, the reader today with a penchant for mutuality or irony can argue that such a disposition of the wife's hand was acted out in an earlier, cruder version of the taming story but was softened or eliminated completely in Shakespeare's adaptation. In this formulation, either the 1623 Kate did not complete such a submission or the 1623 Petruchio did not allow it. In short, the various elements that constitute the basis for the "bad quarto" versus source debate need not provide fodder only for editors and bibliographers but can have major consequences for the ideological wars that arise out of this controversial scene.

To return to my beginning, my fresh look at some of the facets of the competing narratives that purport to explain the relationship between *A Shrew* and *The Shrew* has yielded no definitive answers. Admittedly, in a few instances I find the prevailing account (which would place the 1623 version earlier) unsatisfactory, for I cannot imagine a theatrical adapter forgetting or cutting the Kate–Petruchio kiss at the end of 5.1 (a high point in many productions today) or turning Hortensio–Bianca–Widow into Polidor–Emelia. Such doubts, however, may complicate rather than disprove the prevailing narrative and certainly do not provide a telling blow in this combat.

What does emerge, however, is the value of attending closely to the evidence provided by 1594 as a window into a better understanding of 1623. The "completed" Sly story in the former may appeal to many readers of the latter frustrated by an apparent lack of closure, but, upon investigation, the carefully wrought closure in 1594 calls attention to a distinctively different and in its own terms compelling strategy in 1623. Both plays, in fact, present multiple "shrew" stories, so that the 1594 title, with its emphasis upon "a" shrew, may signal a deliberate ambiguity that can encompass Kate, Emelia, and even Sly's wife. Admittedly, many of the differences between the two versions (I have omitted numerous examples) result not from conceptual or strategic choices but from differing levels of execution, but some features of the Ferando–Kate material unique to 1594, the very different trajectories for the non-Kate material, and the variations in the placing of Kate's hand beneath her husband's foot are significant and worthy of our attention. Not to take such evidence into account is then to indulge in yet another taming – this time a diminution of the Folio's *The Shrew* into one or another rigid category that cannot do justice to its richness and complexity.

9

The editor as rescripter

"Here's a change indeed!"
Othello, 4.2.106

In the process of rescripting directors often take on the role of editors, whether to reconfigure the horse-courser scene in *Doctor Faustus*, the Christopher Sly material in *The Taming of the Shrew*, the final scenes of *Othello* and *Coriolanus*, or supernatural elements in *Macbeth* and *The Tempest*. Conversely, an editor wrestling with a problematic passage or stage direction may consciously or inadvertently take on the role of a director and make choices according to a sense of how X could be, should be, or would have been staged. As noted in chapter 6, E. A. J. Honigmann has argued in favor of an editor's prerogative to make necessary changes in stage directions in keeping with the "responsibility: to see the plays...as we would wish to direct them ourselves."[1] Clearly, decisions *must* be made: that is what editors do and what many readers want. The danger is that in seeking to clarify a situation for a first-time reader that editor may in fact be closing down an equally valid option, especially for a potential user in the theatre.

In the past many editors may have ignored or even scorned the theatrical facets of their work, but more recent practitioners are far more knowledgeable and sympathetic about such matters. Indeed, in the 1980s and 1990s one sub-group of editions exhibits a performance orientation by including accounts of production choices, photographs, stage history, additional stage directions, and other ancillary material to enhance a reader's awareness of a theatrical dimension that extends beyond the printed page.[2] Such new attitudes, however, can bring with them new problems, especially in an age when facsimiles of the First Folio and the various Quartos are widely available to actors, directors, and in-the-theatre textual advisers or dramaturgs.

The editorial process can therefore provide a form of rescripting or, in some instances, what might be termed *unscripting*, the turning of a playscript, a blueprint designed to be read by knowledgeable theatrical professionals of a distant period, into a literary text designed to be read by students and general readers more familiar with prose fiction than plays. In making hundreds of decisions about words, punctuation, stage directions, locale, speech prefixes, and other elements, editors (often unconsciously) invoke their sense of what is logical, realistic, or "Shakespearean" and in that process make adjustments and filter out particles. Eliminated by that editorial filter, along with obvious errors and inconsistencies, are various items that can be of interest or value to today's theatrical professionals. In addition, the interpolation of many necessary stage directions (especially exits) absent from the original printed texts can also complicate matters, for to insert such signals today is to introduce an editorial or theatrical logic that may or may not be in tune with the original vocabulary.

A full review of editorial practice, a focus of much attention in recent years, is far beyond the scope of this book, but discussion of some representative examples can call attention to the problem. In the highly selective account that follows my examples are drawn from items I have invoked in other contexts, scenes that were the focus of workshops done with actors, and problems brought to my attention by other scholars.

SMALL MATTERS

In the preceding chapters I have noted a wide range of instances where directors have changed the received text provided in today's editions. Given the availability of facsimiles of the original Quartos and First Folio, however, the reverse is sometimes the case wherein a theatrical professional will bypass an editor's choice and instead revert to the reading found in the unedited early printed version. For example, in every modern edition of *Titus Andronicus* I have checked, when Lucius confronts the captured Aaron his speech reads: "First hang the child, that he may see it sprawl – / A sight to vex the father's soul withal. / Get me a ladder" (5.1.51–53). Most editors insert a stage direction here (for example, in the Riverside: "*A ladder brought, which Aaron is made to ascend*"), and Aaron responds "Lucius, save the child." In all the Quartos and the Folio, however, the line reads: "*Aaron*. Get me a ladder, Lucius save the child" so that in all the early printed editions Aaron is the speaker of both phrases. To editors since the eighteenth century the attribution of the entire line to Aaron has seemed an obvious error, hence the emendation. But in Mark Rucker's production (SSC 1988) Bruce A. Young (an actor who regularly consulted the early printed texts) chose to play the line not as emended (with Lucius saying "Get me a ladder") but as scripted in the Quarto, so that his Aaron said (in keeping with the scansion): "Get *me* a ladder" (i.e., "get a ladder and hang *me*"). Played in this fashion, the phrase became an important part of Aaron's appeal that Lucius hang him but spare the child ("Touch not the boy, he is of royal blood" [49] is his previous line). The passage made perfect sense to the Santa Cruz auditors who were not mystified by the Quarto version and indeed were unaware of the originality of this reading. Such a theatrical choice does not wipe out three centuries of editorial tradition but does highlight the difficulties of making in-the-study judgments about what works or does not work on the stage.

What is at stake here and elsewhere can be summed up by the question: what constitutes an error or inconsistency that warrants editorial intervention in behalf of a reader? The early printed editions do contain many outright errors, even though actorly ingenuity may occasionally make sense out of some of them (as with comic turns drawn from *pood pasture* and *Butonio* cited in chapter 1). Still, as with "Get me a ladder," the editorial desire to correct, clarify, and regularize may filter out particles that may have been part of the original strategy and could still make sense in the theatre today.

Sometimes even the most minuscule of changes or adjustments can have significant implications on the stage. A good example is the presence or absence of one typographical space in *A Midsummer Night's Dream*. In modern editions (including the Wells–Taylor Oxford old spelling edition), in her final interchange with her ass-headed lover Titania tells Bottom: "Sleep thou, and I will wind thee in my arms," and then tells her attendants: "Fairies, be gone, and be all ways away" (4.1.40–41). The Arden 2 editor then glosses "be all ways away" as "Be off in every direction" (p. 88). Wanting to be alone, this Titania sends her fairies off every which way – presumably using all the available stage doors or exits.

But in all the Quartos and all the Folios Titania's line reads: "Faieries be gon, and be alwaies away" (Q1, F3r). When spoken, the sound of the two alternative phrases, of course, is the same; the difference apparently is a mere space on the page (as seen most clearly in the Oxford old-spelling rendition of "al waies" – 1481). But Homer Swander (Santa Barbara 1990) had his Titania deliver the line with great force so as to convey that she meant not "in every direction" but *always–forever*, for this Bottom had permanently superseded Mustard, Cobweb, and the others. This interpretation of the line was then reinforced by the shocked expressions on the faces of the exiting fairies as they made a hasty and disorganized departure. Titania's "dotage" was therefore more extreme in this production than in any other I have seen, a strong theatrical choice that in turn set in motion other effects to follow in this scene. The same sounds may be linked to both the Quarto and the emended line, but the theatrical options encouraged by "alwaies" are lost when the original word (and potential signal) is screened out by the editor (and the New Cambridge edition does not list this change in its textual notes – see p. 106, though the Riverside does so and puts "all ways" in square brackets).

A comparable problem is to be found in the deposition scene of *Richard II*. Except in old-spelling editions (see Wells–Taylor, 2023), in today's texts Richard's response to Bolingbroke's "Are you contented to resign the crown?" reads: "Ay, no, no, ay; for I must nothing be; / Therefore no no, for I resign to thee" (4.1.200–2). But in the two late Quartos (where this sequence first appears) and in the Folio the passage actually begins: "I, no; no, I" (TLN 2122). Admittedly, throughout the period *ay* often *is* printed as *I*; as with *alwaies/all ways*, moreover, the words as spoken sound the same. But is a yes-no-no-yes rendition on the page an accurate transcription or is it a translation? Especially with the first *I*, an actor then or now could easily signal the first person I/me by a gesture, even an intonation, a signal that in turn can affect much of the major speech of unkinging that follows (with its repeated emphasis upon "I"). As with *alwaies/all ways*, to make this seemingly self-evident change is, perhaps, to close down a valid theatrical option.

Another tiny change regularly made by editors that forestalls an interesting option is found in a pivotal speech in *The Winter's Tale*. In the Folio Paulina's key speech (5.3.94–97) reads:

> It is requir'd
> You do awake your Faith: then, all stand still:
> On: those that think it is unlawful Business
> I am about, let them depart.
>   (TLN 3300–03)

Leontes responds: "Proceed: / No foot shall stir." At line 96, the Riverside atypically provides "On;" whereas most other editors smooth out the passage by substituting "Or" and eliminating the Folio colon. In his 1996 Oxford edition Stephen Orgel renders the passage: "Then all stand still – / Or those that think it is unlawful business / I am about, let them depart" and notes that an earlier editor's emendation of *On:* to *Or* "has been generally accepted" (p. 228). In support of this change the Arden 2 editor (J. H. P. Pafford) argues: "In manuscript *n* and *r* could be similar, and a broken flourish at the end of either could be like a colon" (p. 158).

The emended passage is the one familiar to most readers and theatrical professionals, but versions of the stand-alone "On" construction are not hard to find in the early printed texts of Shakespeare's plays. To his comment above Pafford adds: "It must however be recorded that *On* is often used with the sense of 'Let us proceed', 'Come on'" equivalent to Leontes's usage that immediately follows Paulina's speech. He cites two comparable uses of *On* in this play (Polixenes's "On, good Camillo" [1.2.411] and Hermione's "then on" [2.1.29]) as well as Antony's "On:" (*Antony and Cleopatra*, 1.2.96) and Henry VIII's "But on;" (*Henry VIII*, 1.2.192). Noteworthy too is Cleopatra's exit line after Antony has departed to battle: "Then, Antony – but now – Well, on" (4.4.38). Paulina's usage, especially following her "all stand still" command, may then indicate some implicit action. Pafford may conclude that "a three-fold shift 'Stand still: Proceed: Depart' would surely leave an audience puzzled as to what such instructions intended," but should such a judgment about what is puzzling to a reader close down what may be a fruitful option for actors and directors? Could Paulina here make a gesture, perhaps to start some ritual? Or could her previous reference to a possible accusation of her being "assisted / By wicked powers" (90–91) and her mention here of "unlawful business" have triggered a movement by someone onstage to exit ("let them depart"), thereby setting up Leontes's command to "Proceed." To substitute *Or* is to keep the sense of the passage intact, but to retain *On:* is to open up a space that in turn generates one or another in-the-theatre decision.

SPEECH PREFIXES

In chapter 1 I provided examples of directors reassigning speeches, whether to economize on personnel, clarify a murky situation, or enhance a through-line (as with Jim Edmondson's Gardiner in his *Henry VIII* or Seyton in his *Macbeth*). Editors too encounter speech prefixes in the early printed texts that appear to warrant adjustment, for, especially in supposed "foul papers" plays that are purportedly at one remove from a Shakespeare manuscript, situations recur where the designation of the speaker of a speech is murky or clearly wrong, whether as a result of haste in composition or the compositor's difficulty in reading Shakespeare's hand. Some speech prefixes are obvious errors: no one argues that Adam rather than Orlando should deliver "Why, whither, Adam, wouldst thou have me go?" (*As You Like It*, 2.3.29) as in the Folio (TLN 733). Others cry out for some kind of resolution, so that the editor of *Coriolanus* must puzzle over which citizen speaks which lines in 1.1. Some adjustments reflect the editor's bias, as with the now unusual but once fairly common choice to reassign to Prospero the "Abhorred slave" speech directed at Caliban (1.2.351–62) because such angry comments were "out of character" for Miranda, the speaker in the Folio (Prospero did speak these lines in RSC 1982, Virginia Stage Company 1987, and PRC 1998).

As with other categories addressed in this chapter, I will forgo the extended treatment that this topic deserves and focus instead on several examples from one play. The 1600 Quarto of *Much Ado About Nothing* provides plentiful examples of questionable speech prefixes, as with the assignment of speeches to the Watch in 3.3 (E3r–F1r – see Riverside 3.3.37, 44, 49, 54, 67, 88, 96, 106, 125, 164, 166, 169, 175) or the designation of the masked figure who speaks with Margaret in 2.1 as *Bene.* (B4r–B4v – for the five speeches the Riverside substitutes [*Bora*] – 2.1.100, 103, 105–6, 108, 111). Because confusion *can* be detected in such situations, editors find more justification for emending speech prefixes that *could* be correct but, at least to some readers, sound wrong.[3]

In editions of *Much Ado* two speeches in 5.4 are regularly taken away from Leonato, with the first (I3v) given to Antonio ("This same is she, and I do give you her" – 54), and the second (I4r) to Benedick ("Peace, I will stop your mouth" – 97). As F. H. Mares notes in his New Cambridge edition (p. 143), "some business could be made" to suit the first speech to Leonato so that emendation "seems unnecessary." The second, however, has seemed a Benedick line to most editors (including Mares), so that the Arden 2, Pelican, and Riverside editors make the change and add "[*Kisses her*]" or "[*Kissing her*]." Here again the "foul papers" or early draft status of the manuscript that stands behind the printed text makes such an emendation even more plausible.

But what happens if the second line remains Leonato's? To have a third party take control at this climactic point would at first seem odd (Mares finds it "hard to think of any argument that could justify this speech in Leonato's mouth" – p. 144), but that is exactly what happened earlier when Beatrice played this role for Claudio and Hero: "Speak, cousin, or (if you cannot) stop his mouth with a kiss, and let not him speak neither" (2.1.310–11). As Edward Berry notes, the emendation in the final scene (like reassigning Miranda's speech to Prospero) relies not upon textual evidence but "upon a critical judgment, that it makes more sense for Benedick to initiate his own kiss than for Leonato to bring the two lovers together." Berry goes on to note that "if anyone needs silencing at this moment, it is probably Benedick, who is preparing the next attack in a skirmish that threatens to become another war"[4] – and as an analogue note the aggressively witty behavior of the men in the final moments of both *A Midsummer Night's Dream* and *Love's Labor's Lost*. Given the tit-for-tat wit combat in evidence since 1.1, should Benedick here have the last word so as to silence Beatrice or should they end this last round as equals, brought together in a climactic kiss by a third party, Leonato? Clearly, the climax of this beat is silence and a kiss, but does the reassignment of this speech to Benedick make better sense of this moment or does it close down other equally valid and interesting options for actors and readers?

A comparable example is provided by the penultimate "monument" scene, 5.3 (I2v) where again editors regularly add to or emend the Quarto's attribution of speeches. As in other plays (for example, *As You Like It*) the question of who sings a song is left open in the Quarto, so that Claudio gives the order "Now, music, sound, and sing your solemn hymn" (11), with Balthasar, the designated singer of 2.3, the practical choice. Trickier and far more interesting in interpretative terms is who should speak the epitaph that ends with the indented couplet: "Hang thou there upon the tomb, / Praising her when I am [dumb]" (9–10 – *dombe* is the Folio reading as opposed to Q1's *dead*) and who should deliver "Now, unto thy bones good night! / Yearly will I do this rite" (22–23) – the latter speech is assigned to *Lo.* or a lord in Q1, presumably the same *Lord* who speaks line 2. Up to line 29 ("Good morrow, masters") the Quarto specifies the *Claudio* speech prefix only for the opening question ("Is this the monument of Leonato?") and "Now, music, sound," but editors, starting with Capell in the eighteenth century, have weighed heavily the "I" in lines 10 and 23 and accordingly have assigned both the epitaph and the lord's line to Claudio (so to the Arden 2 editor "it seems natural that Claudio should himself deliver the epitaph" – p. 210). Given the presence of "I" in both passages ("when I am dumb," "yearly will I do this rite") "obviously" the lines are to be spoken by Claudio. Here, moreover, is another example of where the foul papers status of this document can encourage adjustments of "errors" linked to haste in composition or lack of polishing.

But what if a major thrust of this moment is that Claudio is again working through a proxy (as with Don Pedro's wooing in his behalf in 2.1) rather than speaking for himself (as he must do in 5.1 and 5.4)? To the literalist "yearly will I do this rite" may only make sense coming from Claudio, but what is the *theatrical* effect if this line, like the epitaph ("Praising her when I am dumb"), is spoken by "*Lord–Lo.*," thereby appropriating the first-person voice that *should* be Claudio's? In his note to line 12 (p. 211) the Arden 2 editor dismisses as "too sophisticated a response" the interpretation of critics who find in the song " 'extravagance and insincerity', even 'something of comedy', as signs of Claudio's deluded sentimentality," but some such negative effect is far more likely if the playgoer is aware of an anonymous figure uttering lines in Claudio's behalf. Or one may prefer a more positive reading of the same evidence – that a detached Claudio, watching and hearing the lines spoken rather than delivering them himself, can show *more* rather than less heartfelt emotion (the interpretation preferred by the actors who experimented with the Quarto version in an ACTER workshop).

The key question remains: what is the function of this brief but puzzling scene? Is the playgoer to see a "new" Claudio (repentant, coming to terms with death and loss, as a preparation for regaining Hero) or is that image–interpretation to a greater or lesser extent a result of editorial intervention and modern staging? Is or is not the playgoer to sense something phony in these rites (e.g., that Claudio is going through the motions of penance, just as he is going through the motions in his wedding in 5.4)? Perhaps most important (since obviously this short scene is not an end in itself), if we follow the Quarto's version of 5.3 as opposed to the editorial text, is there a different pay-off in 5.4, perhaps an altered progression to the unveiling of Hero? Is there perhaps a significant price tag for such emendations?

REFASHIONING STAGE DIRECTIONS

As noted in chapter 6, to aid first-time readers editors often tinker with the stage directions in the Quartos and Folio and insert new ones, so that these adjusted signals can influence how theatrical professionals approach their scripts. Occasionally, directors resist such adjustments. A good example is one of the many powerful scenes in Deborah Warner's *King John* (RSC TOP 1988), the death of Count Melune (5.4). Warner was using as her script R. L. Smallwood's useful and well annotated New Penguin edition, but the format of that series precluded square brackets to distinguish between stage directions in the Folio and those inserted by the editor (the Riverside stage direction cited earlier that calls for

Aaron's ladder *was* placed in square brackets). Near the end of this scene Salisbury says to the dying Melune "My arm shall give thee help to bear thee hence" (58), a line that is readily interpreted as "I will help you off the battlefield." Smallwood therefore ends his scene with the [unbracketed] stage direction: "*Exeunt, giving assistance to Melun*" (p. 146 – the Riverside provides "*Exeunt [leading off Melune]*" – 61). But, to create *her* climax to this scene, Warner's Salisbury, cradling the dying Melune, reached back one hand in which Pembroke placed a dagger, so that "My arm shall give thee help to bear thee hence" became a quiet, almost loving blow, a mercy killing, that fit beautifully with the mood established by an impassioned, very convincing Melune. Not limited by the editorial stage direction, Warner and her actors created a fine theatrical moment (a choice, I should note, that Smallwood himself endorsed).

As is often the case, the issue at stake in both the New Penguin and Riverside insertions is not "which answer is correct?" but "what is the function of such a signal?" and "who is the intended audience for it?" One technique, as evidenced in the Riverside approach to "My arm shall give thee help to bear thee hence," is to use square brackets or some comparable on-the-page signal to distinguish between what was in the Quarto or Folio text and what has been added or adjusted by the editor. An alternative (and controversial) approach found in the Stanley Wells–Gary Taylor Oxford University Press edition warrants some discussion.

In his carefully reasoned rationale Wells announces a working principle in his Oxford edition – to be "rather bolder than most of us have been about acting on our own judgement, without requiring editorial precedent." He therefore begins with "the basic premise that the editor needs to identify points at which additional directions, or changes to those of the early texts, are necessary to make the staging intelligible, and that he should make the additions and changes irrespective of what earlier editors have done."[5] Underlying this formulation, then, is the assumption, noted by Margaret Jane Kidnie, "that the responsible editor of modernized editions will necessarily adopt an interventionist approach to staging."[6]

As part of her analysis Kidnie singles out the Oxford editors' approach to the killing of Mutius in *Titus Andronicus*, 1.1 where Wells argues that, as "an oddity of the stagecraft" according to the extant stage directions, the "body has had to remain, ignored, onstage throughout the upper-level episode." The anomaly can be resolved, according to Wells, "if we make the quite reasonable assumption that Mutius' body should not remain on stage, but should be dragged off by Lucius after the killing" and be "carried back again by Marcus, or by one or more of the sons." In this solution, the line "O Titus, see! O, see what thou hast done!" (1.1.341) "would gain immeasurably in effectiveness if Marcus were not pointing to a body which had been lying around the stage throughout the previous episode" but rather were "carrying his nephew's corpse as Lear, later, was to carry the dead Cordelia" (p. 103). Kidnie notes that "the scene may well have been originally staged as Wells suggests," but "however effective the proposed solution to the perceived problem, it is not the only answer available." She also questions: "*is* it that unusual for a corpse, in a scene of heightened activity, to lie onstage, unnoticed?"[7] For Kidnie, "This proposed editorial intervention" falls "somewhere between unnecessary tidying and subjectively imposing staging on a dramatic text." Here an editor "is constructing the staging that he thinks would be the most effective in performance, but once the editor's assumptions about performance are encoded into the script, it becomes difficult to historicize this intervention for the reader as a matter of debate and contested interpretation" (468).

Wells also announces that, as part of his approach to such interventions, "We shall not print square brackets to signal alterations or additions to directions when we believe that they are indisputable: when they merely regularize names, for instance, or when they indicate action which is indisputably required by the text" (78). Here the issue becomes what is and is not "indisputably required by the text." A test case is an inserted stage direction in an important in-the-theatre moment singled out in chapter 8, the brief Kate–Petruchio exchange at the end of 5.1. Left alone onstage, he asks for a kiss, she is "asham'd to kiss" in public, he responds "Why then let's home again," and she acquiesces: "Nay, I will give thee a kiss; now pray thee, love, stay" (5.1.142–48). The scene then ends with his couplet: "Is not this well? Come, my sweet Kate: / Better once than never, for never too late" (149–50).

Here the issue is not *what* happens (clearly this sequence builds to a kiss) but *when* it happens. The Folio provides no stage direction, and the Riverside, Pelican, Arden 2, and single volume Oxford editors do not provide one. The Wells–Taylor edition, however, inserts "*They kiss*" after her "I will give thee a kiss; now pray thee, love, stay" and before his "Is not this well?" with that signal *not* placed in square brackets. Presumably, the inserted "*They kiss*" falls into the category of signals that "indicate action which is indisputably required by the text," and, moreover, the placement of the insertion is so obvious as not to require any indication of such editorial intervention (and, as critics of this edition have often noted, the editorial apparatus is in a separate volume).

But is the situation that obvious? Need the kiss come as indicated by Wells–Taylor – so that she kisses him, he reacts "Is not this well?" – or, in contrast, is "Is not this well?" (addressed to the playgoers) a response to her verbal acquiescence so that he kisses her after his question and before "Come, my sweet Kate." Yes, a kiss takes place; yes, an editor may wish to help a first-time reader visualize that kiss. But no, the timing of that moment is by no means so self-evident as to be inserted without brackets, a signal in the Riverside and other texts that an editor is reproducing what is in the Folio. Is this insertion indeed in the same category as a signal such as "*Enter Lucentio as Tranio*" (also presented without brackets) that helps a reader visualize the reappearance of a newly disguised figure?

A related problem is linked to what is and is not to be labeled an *aside* in today's editions (a term apparently not in Shakespeare's working vocabulary though widely used by his contemporaries).[8] E. A. J. Honigmann has argued: "Modern editions of Shakespeare contain many more asides than are found in the Folio and quartos, as often as not a legacy from eighteenth-century editors who maimed and deformed where they undertook to cure." Honigmann then uses examples from *1 Henry IV*, *Timon of Athens*, and *Hamlet* to argue shrewdly against the assumptions that lurk beneath many editorial choices. For example, he notes that by inserting *aside* an editor "often implies that the speaker would not have dared to utter the same words openly," but "if the situation includes an impudent speaker or an inattentive listener the case for an aside is weakened." For Honigmann, Hamlet's "A little more than kin, and less than kind" (1.2.65 – designated [*Aside.*] in the Riverside) "expresses the riddling impudence that is characteristic of all of his exchanges with Claudius before Act V"; why then "assume that he would not have dared to speak out loud, and that the only alternative is an aside?" Another alternative is "that Hamlet, the arch-soliloquiser, not infrequently mutters to himself and cares not a rap whether or not others catch his words," but "Such opportunities are lost if the editor prints '*Aside*'" (176–78).

My own pet example is to be found at the end of the caldron scene where Macbeth, although onstage with Lennox, devotes 12 lines (4.1.144–55 – also labeled [*Aside.*] in the Riverside) to his plans against the Macduffs and his innermost thoughts. Most editors treat this passage as an aside and have Macbeth address Lennox again only in the final line and a half of the scene – a choice that does work effectively in today's productions. But, like Honigmann's Hamlet, Macbeth by this point may not care who knows what he is thinking or planning or, as an alternative, may be so rapt in his little world of man (as in 1.3) that he is momentarily unaware of Lennox's presence. As with Honigmann's examples, to mark this speech as an *aside* is to enforce upon the unsuspecting reader one choice at the expense of other equally interesting options. For example, Jim Edmondson (OSF 1987) provided a rationale for the appearance of the "messenger" who, after the departure of Rosse, appears with a warning for Lady Macduff (4.2.65–73) by having that figure overhear Macbeth's "The castle of Macduff I will surprise" comment (4.1.150–53).

ENTRANCES AND EXITS

Clearly in some instances the placement of a stage direction or an action can make a significant difference to the onstage effect. Honigmann calls attention to a group of signals "misplaced" in the Quartos and Folio (170–74) and argues in favor of more "textual tidying" than is currently the practice, particularly with "see where he comes" directions where the placement may vary before or after the spoken line. Editors, he notes, "know that Elizabethan dramatists and copyists were careless about the precise placing of stage-directions" and "usually prefer to leave well alone, if they think they can get away with it." However, Honigmann, like Wells, argues in behalf of more rather than less intervention, for "by moving a stage-direction a line or two we can quite often improve the sense or stage-effect, and so we must ask ourselves whether there is any real need to follow the first Quarto or Folio" (172). He then provides a series of examples where such repositioning would make "the actor's task" easier.

As Honigmann notes, some signals may be misplaced in the early printed texts, but others may be keyed to onstage effects lost or blurred by such adjustments. Relevant here is one of the best-known comic moments in all of Shakespeare, the entrance of a smiling Malvolio in yellow stockings and cross-gartered (*Twelfth Night*, 3.4). Except for the Riverside, all the modern editions I have consulted place that entry just before Olivia's "How now, Malvolio?" (16), so that she and the playgoer see the entering figure at the same time. In the Folio, however, Malvolio is directed to enter two lines earlier (14, TLN 1535), just after Olivia's "Go call him hither," so that in the only authoritative early printed text of this comedy Malvolio is onstage for her "I am as mad as he, / If sad and merry madness equal be" (14–15).

To some readers the difference may seem unimportant; to Honigmann and most editors the Folio placement appears illogical or impractical.

Given the preferred staging today, moreover, to follow the Folio is to run the risk of drowning Olivia's lines in the audience laughter at Malvolio's new look and bizarre behavior. But this Folio placement is but one of many that fall into the category of what I term "early" entrances[9] in which the original printed text brings in figures one or two or even ten lines before they actually speak or are noticed by those already onstage (as in the Second Quarto of *Romeo and Juliet* where Romeo enters eight lines before he addresses the friar at 2.3.31). Some of these early entrances may be the result of errors or sloppiness by author, scribe, bookkeeper, or compositor; many (like Malvolio's) have been filtered out of the editions we use.

But what happens if we take this placement as seriously as any other bit of evidence in the Folio *Twelfth Night*, a clean orderly text that has no other such anomalous placements? What would be the effect upon Malvolio if at his entrance he overhears Olivia talking about her own madness? Could such words reinforce in his mind the evidence gained from the letter in 2.5 and therefore serve as another building block for the cross-purposes and comic delusion that follow? Or would a playgoer who sees Malvolio enter while at the same time hearing Olivia talk of her own malady be more likely to see an analogy between the two instances of comic madness or self-delusion? In procedural terms, should not this apparent anomaly at such a rich moment be field-tested in the theatre as opposed to being rejected out of hand? Should not a director at least know of the option, particularly if this moment is but one example of a larger family of comparable entrances scattered throughout the canon?

A comparable example at another high comic moment is found near the end of the first Kate–Petruchio scene where the Folio directs Baptista, Gremio, and Tranio to enter not at "Here comes your father" (2.1.279, TLN 1159) but three lines earlier (TLN 1155), just before "For I am he am born to tame you, Kate" (2.1.276). In this play and throughout the canon, a "here comes" line is normally preceded or followed by the appropriate stage direction, but exceptions such as this one test the rule. The scene *can* be played effectively with the signal as repositioned in the Riverside and roughly half of the editions I consulted, but the earlier entry, especially if Petruchio is immediately aware of the observers, provides some rich comic possibilities. For example, the actor can change his tone and posture, visibly adjusting his role for the benefit of such an onstage audience. Or, to gain a broader effect, the three entering figures, fearful of Kate's wrath, may tiptoe onto the stage, setting up a decided contrast to Petruchio's bold lines.

Such effects are not limited to the comedies. *Troilus and Cressida* provides a provocative early entrance that is rarely encountered by the reader
unfamiliar with facsimiles of the original texts. In both the Quarto (D2v)
and the Folio (TLN 1082–83) Cassandra erupts into the Trojan council
scene ("*raving*" in the Quarto, "*with her hair about her ears*" in the Folio)
before her first speech. Of the editions I have consulted, only the Signet
keeps this Quarto–Folio placement. Rather, most readers of this scene
will find "*within*" inserted before her first two speeches ("Cry, Troyans,
cry!"; "Cry, Troyans!" – 2.2.97, 99) and her entrance moved so as to
follow Hector's "It is Cassandra" (100) and precede her third speech.

The placement of Cassandra's entrance raises some provocative questions. Should she be onstage or *within* for her first two cries? To keep her
offstage until her third speech may increase the scene's verisimilitude,
for to many readers Troilus's "I do know her voice" (98) suggests that he
hears but does not see her. But, in defense of the Quarto–Folio choice, this
play offers repeated examples of figures who cannot or do not see or
hear what should be apparent to them. This scene in particular, with its
exploration of the Trojan code of honor and value, develops at length
the distinctive myopia linked to Troilus and Hector. Again, to delay
Cassandra's entrance is to offer a smoother, less jolting experience for
the reader or playgoer, but what if the placement of her appearance (in
this instance, found in both Quarto *and* Folio) is a calculated effect designed to ensure that the playgoer cannot miss the faulty seeing of the
Trojan council that here is deciding the fate of their city ("Troy burns,
or else let Helen go" – 112)? What if Priam and his sons, facing us, do
not deem it worth the effort to turn and look at this intruder who bears
what *we* know to be a true vision of the fate of Troy, particularly if these
figures in this scene decide to keep Helen? Cassandra's early presence
strikes me as richly suggestive, both for 2.2 and for the play as a whole, to
the extent that any tinkering with the original strategy needs more justification than an additional dollop of verisimilitude for some readers.

This same script provides an intriguing problem linked not to an
entrance but to an *exeunt*. In 4.5 in the Greek camp neither the Quarto
nor the Folio provides an entrance for Cressida and Diomede, so that
editors can choose according to their view of the staging or timing. The
Riverside is then typical in having these two figures depart at line 53
just before Ulysses's scathing comments on Cressida (54–63). However,
for their departure the Quarto has no designated *exit*, and the Folio
provides one at line 63 (TLN 2620) so that (1) Diomede and Cressida
are in sight during Ulysses's speech and (2) the first spoken line after

Cressida's exit is "The Troyans' trumpet" which, as is often noted, can sound like "the Troyan strumpet." As with Malvolio–Olivia, what is the effect if a beleaguered Cressida, who has just fought back verbally after undergoing a kissing gauntlet, hears Ulysses classify her among the "sluttish spoils of opportunity/And daughters of the game"? Ian Judge (RSC 1996) did play the scene so that Cressida heard the speech; her troubled reaction helped the playgoer better understand why in 5.2 she forsook Troilus and instead chose Diomede as her protector.

A series of similar editorial problems are found in *As You Like It* where many mid scene exits are omitted in the Folio (for example, for Jaques in both 3.2 and 4.1), a common phenomenon in early printed texts. In addition, several *exits* that have interpretative significance are changed by editors to *exeunts* and vice-versa. The reader of the Folio cannot rule out the possibility that the *exit–exeunt* distinction was not rigorously observed by Shakespeare, a putative scribe, or the compositor, but the terms do vary and often those variations are adjusted by editors.

The most interesting and complex problem linked to *exits* and *exeunts* is generated by the play's final couplet before Rosalind's Epilogue. Both of the duke's lines (5.4.197–98) have been tinkered with by editors starting with Theobald in the eighteenth century, whether to adjust the scansion of "Proceed, proceed: we'll begin these rights" (TLN 2774) or to move the comma in "As we do trust, they'll end in true delights" (2775). But most troubling to editors and other interpreters are the three *Exits* (5.4.196, 198; Epilogue.23): for Jaques (2774), the duke (2776), and Rosalind (2796), with no *Exeunt* specified for the large number of other figures in this ensemble scene. Should the duke's *exit* be converted to an *exeunt*, perhaps after some onstage dancing, as in the Riverside ("*[A dance.] Exeunt [all but Rosalind]*") or the Pelican ("*Exit [in the dance]*")? Or should Rosalind's *exit* be converted to an *exeunt* so that the entire ensemble is onstage during her epilogue? The Second Folio, to which editors grant little or no authority, *does* make the latter change, so that the duke has no *exit* and all *exeunt* after the Epilogue. The Arden 2 editor comments (p. 130): "F2 improbably implies the presence of the rest of the cast while she speaks, by emending *Exit* to *Exeunt*," but modern productions regularly do it this way, so that Rosalind comes forward from the group of dancers or revellers and, with a full stage behind her, delivers her appeal for applause so as to set up the curtain call.

The issues here are many and tricky. Should there indeed be an onstage dance? The duke has called for such festivities, only to be stayed by Jaques; his "Proceed, proceed" would seem to re-initiate what had been interrupted, but the music and dance *could* be offstage so that "Proceed, proceed" sends the ensemble off to complete "these rites." If the *exit* after the duke's couplet is taken at face value, moreover, he could depart through the same stage door just used by Jaques, thereby indicating that two figures rather than one have forsaken the festivities. The merriment and dancing could then be onstage or offstage. If the former, the dancing should somehow generate the Epilogue so that the *exeunt* for the revellers would be in keeping with the Second Folio emendation; if the latter, the dancers would depart (with or without the duke) through the door not used by Jaques, leaving Rosalind alone for her final speech.

The Folio as we have it does not work, for somehow a large group of people who are either dancing or about to dance must leave the stage, but no such departure is signaled. Either the duke's or Rosalind's *exit* can be changed to an *exeunt*, but the effect is very different. To end with a dance and a stage full of happy revellers is to enhance the Epilogue and provide an upbeat conclusion (again, a standard in-the-theatre choice today). To have the duke follow Jaques and have the revelry offstage is to provide a somewhat darker ending, with more emphasis upon elements not woven into the spirit of comedy, an interpretation more often associated with *Twelfth Night* than with this play. Choices must be made. But on what basis and by whom?

MASSED ENTRIES AND "*SILENCE*" IN *THE WINTER'S TALE*

Five of the plays in the "Comedy" section of the First Folio exhibit features that scholars link to the work of the scribe Ralph Crane. In three of these plays (*The Merry Wives of Windsor*, *The Two Gentlemen of Verona*, and *The Winter's Tale*) the reader encounters "massed entries" – in which all the figures who are to appear in a scene, no matter when, are listed in the initial stage direction[10] – as opposed to normal practice wherein characters are cited only at the point at which they enter. Few readers, however, are aware of this practice, because editors pare down that inclusive initial grouping and then insert subsequent entrances for figures who arrive during the course of the scene. Although most of these editorial adjustments are straightforward, even obvious, interesting problems are generated by the massed entries in *The Winter's Tale*.

The Folio text of *The Winter's Tale* contains more stage directions than *Two Gentlemen* or *Merry Wives* but still very few (apart from scene headings, only forty-three), with many necessary exits and entrances missing. In thirteen of the fifteen scenes, moreover, all the characters to appear throughout the subsequent scene are massed in the initial heading. The Arden 2 editor, J. H. P. Pafford,[11] therefore distinguishes among three categories: (1) scenes that follow "normal" practice (4.3, 5.2) so as to have various figures (the clown, the old shepherd, Paulina's steward) enter as needed with no initial massed entry; (2) scenes that provide a massed entry that makes no difference (1.1, 3.1, 4.1, 4.2, 5.3) in that no figures arrive after the initial entrance; and (3) scenes that provide a massed entry and need adjustment because some figures in the initial Folio stage direction do not appear until later (1.2, 2.1, 2.2, 2.3, 3.2, 3.3, 4.4, 5.1). Like other editors Pafford sees little difficulty in distinguishing the third group of eight scenes from the second group of five scenes (only one of the second group, 5.3, has more than two figures) and alters his text accordingly.

Some of these adjustments are indeed obvious: for example, 2.3 (where the initial entry includes Paulina who clearly is to arrive later); 3.3 (where the massed entry includes not only Antigonus, the baby, and the mariner but also the shepherd and the clown); 4.4 (where Autolycus is cited at the outset); and 5.1 (where the opening stage direction includes not only Leontes and his court but also Florizel and Perdita). Nonetheless, for several scenes in this group of eight the massed entries *could* work as printed. For example, Leontes and his lords *could* be onstage from the outset of 2.1 observing Hermione, Mamillius, and the ladies as he had observed Hermione and Polixenes in the previous scene – again, the Folio provides no *enter* for Leontes and his group.

To those accustomed to "our" version of this play, such an alternative may appear strained or quirky, but to assume too much about massed entries may be to run the risk of blocking out possible options left open in the Folio but closed down in modern editions. *If* doubt does exist about some of the initial stage directions in Pafford's third group or *if* the Folio version of one or more of those scenes can be played with no loss (and indeed with some gain or special force), is emendation indeed necessary or obligatory? To what extent has the obvious presence of massed entries in *some* scenes and in two other Folio plays become a blank check that has led to a blurring of Jacobean stage practice?

At the risk of appearing overly ingenious, I will focus upon two scenes. At first look, the opening stage direction for Folio 2.3 (TLN 898–99) *seems* to be an obvious massed entry ("*Enter Leontes, Servants, Paulina, Antigonus, and Lords*"), for (1) Paulina and servants are included at the outset (though, unlike 3.3, the baby is not mentioned) and then (2) the Folio provides "*Enter Paulina*" (TLN 928, 2.3.26) with the baby and "*Enter a Servant*" (TLN 1126, 2.3.193) with news of Cleomines and Dion.

The Folio, however, signals no comparable entrances for the first servant, who, in response to Leontes's "Who's there?", brings news of Mamillius at 2.3.9, or for Antigonus and the lords, who first speak after Paulina's entrance at line 26.

Given the delayed arrival of a Paulina who is cited in the initial stage direction, editors have tinkered with the entire entry. The Riverside initially provides "*Enter Leontes; Servants* [*keeping the door*]," then at the servant's first line (9) places [*Advancing*] next to the speech prefix, and subsequently signals "*Enter Paulina* [*with a child*]; *Antigonus and Lords* [*endeavoring to hold her back*]" (26). In his 1996 single volume Oxford edition, Stephen Orgel signals at the outset "*Enter Leontes*," then "*Enter a Servant*" (9) and "*Enter Paulina with a baby, Antigonus, Lords and Servants*" (26), and, in keeping with the Wells–Taylor "Editorial Procedures" (p. 85), provides no square brackets "where the specified action is clearly implied by the dialogue." In his note (p. 131) Orgel observes that the massed Folio signal "simply indicates the personnel of the scene," that some early editors did make "Leontes' first speech an extended aside with Antigonus and the Lords on stage," but that Capell and others "had Antigonus and the Lords enter later with Paulina, and saw the opening speech as a soliloquy." This editor concludes: "In terms of dramatic logic the latter seems the preferable alternative."

In support of this emendation an editor can also cite the ordering of the named figures, for if Antigonus and the lords are placed after Paulina in the massed entry then, presumably, they do not precede her onto the stage but arrive with her or trailing after her. But why then does the Folio's "*Enter Paulina*" include no mention of the men? Why signal her arrival but not theirs? Why, moreover, provide an entrance for one servant at the end of the scene (with news of the oracle) but not for another (perhaps the same) servant at the outset of the scene (with news of Mamillius)?

Here and in comparable moments in this script what is easily missed or blurred for a reader is the potential theatrical effect of figures who are onstage but silent (though possibly active). Whether in 2.3 or earlier with Camillo ("What? Camillo there?" – 1.2.209), Leontes's "Who's there?" or "What . . . there?" lines need not necessarily be directed at an offstage figure but could instead be designed to call forth an attendant already onstage but standing in the background, especially on a wide, deep stage. Whether the figure is on or offstage, the same response ("Ay, my good lord" – 1.2.210; "My lord?" – 2.3.9) would be appropriate.

The question then follows: what if Paulina is the only figure in the massed entry for 2.3 who does not belong there? In this reconstruction (chosen by editors such as G. L. Kittredge, Peter Alexander, Baldwin Maxwell, and Frank Kermode), Antigonus, the lords, and a servant would be onstage from the outset, watching Leontes from a distance, and would then try to intercept Paulina. Their presence, visible to the playgoer, would then be signaled by Paulina's jibe that "'Tis such as you, / That creep like shadows by him, and do sigh / At each his needless heavings" (2.3.33–35), for if the lords do not enter struggling with Paulina (and no such group entrance is signaled), they could be in our view (creeping and sighing?) until her arrival.

What are the consequences of such an interpretation? This staging, endorsed by the Folio stage direction, which now becomes accurate *except* for the inclusion of Paulina, would make Leontes's "Nor night, nor day, no rest" speech (1–9) not a soliloquy but an extended Macbeth-like "rapt" delivery in which the speaker is oblivious to his surroundings. Such an interpretation could be reinforced if the actor is wearing a nightgown that in Elizabethan theatrical terms can denote not only sleeplessness but also a troubled or tortured mind[12] – as reinforced by the servant's lines ("he hath not slept to-night") and Paulina's response that "I come to bring him sleep" and rather it is the lords who "Nourish the cause of his awaking" (2.3.31, 33, 36). More context would therefore be provided for Paulina's critique of the lords and a greater contrast between her forceful behavior and that of the courtiers. To have the lords onstage from the top therefore both changes the nature or value of Paulina's entrance and emphasizes Leontes's self-absorption, so that instead of witnessing a soliloquy the playgoer sees a figure who has isolated himself from a visible human community.

More telling are the problems or options found in a pivotal scene, Hermione's trial in 3.2, where the editor or director must again decide: who is on stage and when? That some doubt about the opening stage directions in 2.1, and 2.3 (massed entries versus accurate signals) *may* exist helps to set up the highly problematic status of 3.2 where the scene as printed in the Folio makes very good sense indeed, especially when seen in the context of a comparable moment in *Henry VIII*. The Folio's opening signal reads: "*Enter Leontes, Lords, Officers: Hermione (as to her trial) Ladies: Cleomines, Dion*" (TLN 1174–75, 3.2.0). Editors, who assume this stage direction to be a massed entry, divide it into three sections as signaled by the colons (as also in 2.1), so that Hermione and her ladies appear after lines 9–10 (the officer's statement that "It is his Highness' pleasure that the Queen / Appear in person here in court"). The Riverside therefore begins the scene with "*Enter Leontes, Lords, Officers*" and then provides

"[*Enter*] *Hermione (as to her trial*), [*Paulina, and*] *Ladies* [*attending*]" (3.2.0, 10); Orgel provides essentially the same signals minus the square brackets. Later, when a lord says: "therefore bring forth,/And in Apollo's name, his oracle" (117–18), editors insert a stage direction (in both the Riverside and Orgel "[*Exeunt certain Officers*]") so as to have Cleomines and Dion (the oracle-bearers) escorted in at line 123, the end of Hermione's "The Emperor of Russia" speech. In another related emendation, most editors change *Silence* of line 10 from a stage direction (as printed in the Folio) to a word spoken by the officer. The New Penguin editor (p. 185) notes that *Silence* "would be a very unusual stage direction but is a traditional law-court cry. The entry of Hermione may be supposed to cause some stir in the court, which must be silenced before the indictment can be read" (see also Pafford, p. 56). In his production, moreover, Nicholas Hytner (RNT 2001) not only treated *Silence* as a word to be spoken but moved it earlier to be the first utterance of the scene.

The scene as emended, with three inserted stage directions and "Silence" as a word to be spoken, is the scene most of us know. In defense of such altering of the Folio one might ask: if massed entries are prevalent elsewhere, why not here also? If Hermione is already onstage, why would she be formally ordered to "Appear in person here in court"? As to the two oracle-bearers, Pafford notes (p. 60): "It is not strictly necessary to assume that Cleomenes and Dion are off stage. They could quite well have been in the Court from the outset and be simply brought forward at 123." He concludes, however, that "there is perhaps greater dramatic and stage effect . . . in bringing them in with some ceremonial at 123 than in having them on stage all the time."

But despite such arguments and despite the presence of massed entries in five, perhaps seven other scenes, Hermione, Cleomines, Dion, and the packet containing the oracle, in keeping with the only extant theatrical signal, *could* be on stage from the outset. For just such a moment, moreover, one can turn to *Henry VIII* where Queen Katherine, not only onstage but also, like Hermione, the focus of attention, is nonetheless called to "come into the court" (2.4.10–11). Obviously, as used here "into the court" has a formal, procedural meaning as opposed to "bring her to this room from some other place." Moments earlier, in response to a parallel call ("Henry King of England, come into the court"), the king, without moving from his throne, had responded: "Here" (6–9). At least in *Henry VIII*, 2.4, "to come into the court" is formally to acknowledge one's presence rather than to *enter* from offstage. Admittedly, the two situations are similar, not identical, but the presence of Katherine from the outset, despite the call for her to "come into the court," points to the possibility, even the likelihood, that Hermione too is present from the beginning – as would be the case if we take the Folio stage direction literally rather than as a massed entry.

More potential insights into the situation in *The Winter's Tale* then follow, for a stage direction spells out Katherine's response to "come into the court": *"The Queen makes no answer, rises out of her chair, goes about the court, comes to the King, and kneels at his feet; then speaks"* (12). That Katherine *"goes about the court"* provides further context for the call for Hermione to appear "in court," for, as is clear in context and in the Holinshed passage upon which this scene is closely based, *"the court"* consists of some but not all of the figures onstage so that the queen must bypass this group in order to reach the king.[13] More important, the signal in *Henry VIII* that *"The Queen makes no answer"* suggests that *"Silence"* in *The Winter's Tale*, 3.2 may not be an error, as is assumed when editors turn it into a spoken word at the end of the officer's speech, but rather is a signal that Hermione initially should not speak (presumably, an appropriate response would have been: "Here") and thereby like Katherine does not recognize the authority of Leontes's court.[14]

The same logic pertains to the oracle-bearers. Indeed, despite Pafford's conclusion about the "greater dramatic and stage effect," which is more "theatrical": to bring the two figures in during the "Emperor of Russia" speech ("with some ceremonial") or to have them in sight, waiting, during the entire scene, with the eventual answer or vindication visible in a distinctive casket or scroll? The latter option, with the playgoer conscious of something important not yet seen or addressed by those onstage, can be highly theatrical if it generates for the playgoer a growing tension or anticipation. The Folio version, with the oracle in view from the outset, *could* provide a potent stage effect.

Also in terms of theatrical effect, let me return to the question: is *Silence* a stage direction or a word to be spoken? If Hermione, like Katherine, is onstage during the officer's appeal for her to appear "here in court," a total silence from her (when all eyes are riveted upon her) could be a highly "theatrical" response. In such situations, "Silence" in the theatre can be electric. What follows *Silence*, if it *is* treated as a stage direction, is Leontes's "Read the indictment" (11) which then can emerge not as a mere pro forma comment but rather as an act of frustration after her non-response or non-compliance if she initially refuses to appear or respond as requested (i.e., no "Here" here). The *Silence* problem becomes more interesting, moreover, when one thinks forward to the famous final scene. Would a conspicuously silent Hermione in 3.2 prepare us more tellingly for the "statue" later (and for Paulina's "I like your silence, it the more shows off / Your wonder" – 5.3.21–22)? Similarly, would the highly visible onstage presence of the oracle in some distinctive package or container, here and in 3.1, somehow link up with two other significant properties: the baby of 2.3 and 3.3 and the fardel of 3.3 and 4.4? What "images" or building blocks does the Folio version establish or italicize at the beginning of 3.2?

Such questions and conjectures cannot be easily resolved, nor do my various claims about the theatrical effectiveness of several entries as printed in the Folio necessarily undermine the more familiar editorial choices. Nonetheless, the massed entries as printed in this Folio play *are* demonstrably inconsistent as opposed to the nearly uniform procedures in the other Crane plays. Need we therefore automatically assume that 3.2 begins with a massed entry that must then be emended, especially if that initial stage direction *can* work as written for Hermione and the oracle-bearers and if, given the model provided in *Henry VIII*, "*Silence*" *can* make good theatrical sense for a Hermione already onstage?

The choice as to who is onstage and when – in 3.2 but also in 2.1 and 2.3 – has major interpretative consequences in the theatre, so that any emendations of Folio stage directions should be made cautiously and judiciously, with full awareness of the theatrical implications. Those who do puzzle over the massed entries in this play may end up siding with Pafford and with the traditional choices (though editors *are* divided on how to treat the beginning of 2.3). But various questions do (and should) persist. In particular, have all the options, particularly for potential in-the-theatre effects, been given full consideration? Whose sense should prevail of what is "the greater dramatic and stage effect" or "the preferable alternative" according to "dramatic logic"?

RESCRIPTING *TITUS ANDRONICUS*, 5.3

Another pivotal scene that regularly undergoes editorial rescripting or unscripting is *Titus Andronicus*, 5.3, where, given the dearth of stage directions, the problem of how to stage the action after the various deaths is compounded by what appears to be a textual muddle. In the Quarto (κ3r) Lucius's couplet that accompanies his killing of Saturninus is followed, with no intervening stage direction, by a six-line speech from Marcus (67–72). In the Arden 2, Pelican, and single volume Oxford editions, however, that speech extends for another 23 lines, until Lucius speaks ("Then, gracious auditory"), with line 72 beginning "lest Rome."

But in the Quartos and the Folio, a new speaker takes over after the six lines from Marcus (*"Roman Lord"* in the Quartos, *"Goth"* in the Folio), and his speech begins "Let Rome." Again, after Aemilius has called for Marcus to descend with Lucius, the Arden 2, Pelican, and Oxford editors along with the Riverside give "Lucius, all hail, Rome's royal Emperor!" and "Lucius, all hail, Rome's gracious governor!" to *"All"* or *"Romans"* (141, 146). The Quartos and the Folio, however, give both "all hail" lines to Marcus as part of one continuous speech (Arden 3 editor Jonathan Bate gives the first "all hail" to Marcus but the second to *"All Romans"*).

The editors of three important texts of this tragedy have thereby taken out a *"Roman Lord"* where Shakespeare put him in and then put in *"Romans"* at a later point when Shakespeare gave the lines to one speaker, Marcus. Such changes: (1) reconstruct the role of Marcus (see the Oxford editor's long note on p. 189), both giving and taking away lines; (2) complicate decisions about staging (e.g., when Marcus should move above); and (3) close down some meaningful options about the reactions of "the Romans" to what has happened. Although these changes seem to smooth out rough spots in the play as presented in the Quarto, they may instead blur distinctive effects. If a Roman lord (Aemilius in the Riverside) does intervene after Marcus's first speech, the latter has time to ascend (and perhaps, offstage, collect Aaron's child) so as to set up the climactic speech (119–36) that builds to the "hand in hand" image. Moreover, at the outset of the Roman lord's speech the "let" need not be emended to "lest" (see the Riverside, New Cambridge, and Arden 3 editions) if the lines as printed in the Quarto are understood as one bystander's angry reaction to the murders and to Marcus's first attempt at a resolution.

Here then is a reconstruction of the scene as found in the Quarto with no editorial intervention. Titus kills Lavinia, then Tamora; Saturninus kills Titus; Lucius kills Saturninus. Four bodies (and the remains of the pie) are somewhere onstage. The same Marcus who in 1.1 spoke in behalf of the senators and tribunes makes his first attempt at ordering the chaotic situation (67–72) by addressing "You sad-fac'd men, people and sons of Rome, / By uproars sever'd" and offering his alternative: "O, let me teach you how to knit again / This scattered corn into one mutual sheaf, / These broken limbs again into one body." The "this" and "these" can refer specifically to the four bodies, for, in his first six-line speech, Marcus with a gesture may be offering a response to the still visible onstage carnage. If the speech prefix attributing the next passage to a Roman lord (or a Goth) is eliminated and "let" changed to "lest," the next four lines (73–76) then spell out Marcus's vision of the consequences should the Romans not heed his advice, for he would be saying, in effect, let us knit things back together "lest Rome herself be bane unto herself" and, in the process, "Do shameful execution on herself." The passage, as emended, does make sense, for Marcus, speaking in behalf of the "new" post-Saturninus Rome, would be pleading: listen to me, help put things back together, lest Rome destroy herself.

But what happens when we follow the Quarto? Here Marcus's first attempt to provide an answer ("O, let me teach you") is rejected by Aemilius or some other figure who cries out angrily: "Let Rome herself be bane unto herself, / And she whom mighty kingdoms cur'sy to, / Like a forlorn and desperate castaway, / Do shameful execution on herself" (73–76). If the speech reads "let Rome" rather than "lest Rome," Marcus, an obvious part of the family involved in this yet-to-be-explained blood-shed, is not accepted as a source of answers or alternatives (as opposed to the outset of 1.1). Rather, the Roman lord's sentiments would be: if this kind of carnage is what Rome has been reduced to, then let Rome go ahead and destroy itself. Why should we try to preserve such a society? Let it go down the drain. The subsequent lines from this Roman lord are then less angry, more sorrowful or bewildered, as would be expected from someone who had just heard about the rape and mutilation of Lavinia, is not yet privy to the plotting of Aaron and Tamora, and is reacting primarily to the murders and to the revelation of the presence of Chiron and Demetrius in the meat-pie. That lord then turns not to Marcus, who, for all this Roman knows, may have been an integral part of these events, but to the banished Lucius ("Rome's dear friend" and "Rome's young captain") for an explanation ("Tell us what Sinon hath bewitch'd our ears" – 80, 94, 85).

Lucius, who has had time to move above, now delivers a twenty-three line speech (96–118) that, like Friar Lawrence's comparable long speech at the end of *Romeo and Juliet*, recounts what the audience already knows. But both of these climactic speeches are directed not at us but at the on-stage figures, here the "Romans" not involved in the plots and counter-plots. To complete the case in behalf of the Andronici, Marcus speaks for a second time (119–36), using as a symbolic property Aaron's child. In this version, Marcus's first attempt to knit things back together was rejected by the angry Roman lord, but his second attempt is buttressed first by the revelations provided by Lucius and then by the presence of the child ("The issue of an irreligious Moor, / Chief architect and plotter of these woes" – 121–22). In his final twelve lines, Marcus hammers home his message. First, he sums up: "Now judge what cause had Titus to revenge / These wrongs unspeakable, past patience, / Or more than any living man could bear." Then, given the evidence presented, he asks: "Now have you

heard the truth, what say you, Romans?/Have we done aught amiss"?
Shall we, he goes on, at your command "hand in hand all headlong hurl
ourselves" on the stones below so as to "make a mutual closure of our
house"? He concludes (perhaps holding the baby in one hand, Lucius's
hand in the other): "Speak, Romans, speak, and if you say we shall, / Lo
hand in hand Lucius and I will fall."

It is to this second speech by Marcus that Aemilius responds: "Come,
come, thou reverent man of Rome, / And bring our Emperor gently in
thy hand, / Lucius, our Emperor, for well I know / The common voice do
cry it shall be so" (137–40). That confidence is reinforced by editors who
reassign the next line ("Lucius, all hail, Rome's royal Emperor!" – 141)
and the similar line 146 to "*Romans*" or "*All*." But if both "all hail" lines
are spoken by Marcus (perhaps as cheerleader), various interpretative
options follow for the other "Romans" on stage (some of whom may still
be in shock from all the revelations), options that are precluded by the
editorial choice to redistribute the lines. The effect *could* be the same as
that desired by the editors, but, conceivably, the Romans could respond
not to the first but to the second "all hail" from Marcus or could respond
feebly to both. In the theatre, Lucius's "Thanks, gentle Romans" (147)
can be played a variety of ways, depending upon the strength or weakness
of the reaction from the onstage crowd. Given the range of options in
the Quarto, the *user* of these modern editions should ask: is making such
a choice – on the page, without the benefit of the trial-and-error of
rehearsal – the function of the editor? Where does "editing" end and
interpretation or rescripting begin?

At the risk of trying the patience of the reader, let me note one more
emendation, for of those editors who do retain the Quarto's "*Roman
Lord*" (rather than Marcus) and "let Rome" (rather than "lest Rome"),
some (Riverside, New Cambridge) print as the speech prefix not "Roman
Lord" but "Aemilius." For reasons of economy and efficiency such an
equation makes good sense, for Aemilius *is* set up as an independent figure in 4.4 and 5.1 as go-between between Saturninus and Lucius and is
therefore clearly identified as a respected figure – the only such "named"
Roman available as a non-aligned spokesman. Nonetheless, several interesting theatrical options follow if "Roman Lord" and "Aemilius" are
not conflated if: (1) that lord is identified only by costume so as to be a
representative Roman voice, someone not associated with the Andronici
or Saturninus/Tamora; (2) he says "let Rome," not "lest Rome" in an
angry fashion; (3) another figure, Aemilius, *not* this anonymous Roman
Lord, then calls for Marcus to descend with the new emperor, Lucius;
and (4) both "all hail" lines are spoken by Marcus, not by "*Romans*" or

"*All*" as in most modern editions (including the Riverside which has Aemilius–Roman Lord, not Marcus, give the earlier speech).

What is the difference? The answer lies in the new *theatrical* question: how does the previously angry unnamed Roman lord react (1) to Aemilius's decision in behalf of him and the other Romans (e.g., what if Aemilius is played as a time-server, an Osric or a Rosse?); (2) to Marcus's first all hail; (3) to Marcus's second all hail (for me, the presence of the *two* "all hails," both spoken by Marcus, carries considerable theatrical potential)? When Aemilius "orders" the events by naming Lucius as the successor to Saturninus, is the "Roman" response (1) quick and firm; (2) gradual; (3) grudging or (4) do some onstage Romans remain dubious? No "right answer" is to be found in the Quarto; indeed, a strong case can be made, given one interpretation of the climax, for assigning the "Roman Lord" speech to Aemilius. But do students, critics, actors, and directors want from their editions (that are to serve as playscripts) a plausible but iffy decision that may in turn close down equally valid or theatrically interesting options of which the reader is no longer aware? For me, the most fruitful answers will arise not from editors working on the page but rather from "field-testing" the script that survives in the 1594 Quarto.

Given the many virtues of today's editions, my highly selective discussion of editorial interventions may appear churlish. Moreover, as Honigmann rightly observes, in many respects the Elizabethans were far more casual than today's editor in matters of detail, a situation that encourages much tidying up. Nonetheless, Honigmann's arguments and the working practice of many editors raise some troubling questions about the tangled links between editing and interpretation, particularly when the product of such efforts serves as the basis for a production. At what point does appropriate intervention to "improve the sense or stage-effect" (Honigmann) or provide "greater dramatic and stage effect" (Pafford) or set up a moment that "would gain immeasurably in dramatic effectiveness" (Wells) end and rescripting begin? If, as I assume, Shakespeare and his colleagues knew what they were doing in theatrical terms, what is the price tag for such improvement or standardization by a scholar who, although an expert on matters bibliographical and compositorial, may or may not be in tune with the logic of today's theatre, much less the onstage vocabulary of the 1590s or early 1600s? I agree with Honigmann that "we must ask ourselves whether there is any real need to follow the first Quarto or Folio" ("reason not the need"?), but my own response can best be summed up in the vernacular: "If it ain't broke, don't fix it."

Conclusion: what's not here

"Let every eye negotiate for itself"
Much Ado About Nothing, 2.1.178

By this point readers will be well aware of the many items and issues not pursued in this book, but, at the risk of belaboring the obvious, I will conclude with a brief explanation of my rationale for inclusion and exclusion. First and most important, this study has not been intended as a comprehensive approach to the performance history of Shakespeare's plays over the last twenty-five years, a daunting task far beyond my reach. A host of pertinent studies already exist and have been cited along the way, many of them devoted to productions of a single script.[1]

Rather, I have concentrated on stage productions I was able to see and for which I have reliable notes.[2] Based in the United States I have managed to see a large number of United Kingdom shows starting in 1978 but have been limited to RSC, RNT, Globe, Almeida, and other productions available during my annual two or three weeks in London and Stratford, as has also been true for my encounters with productions in Oregon (between 1974 and 1993), Ontario, and other venues. I do not claim to have noted everything of significance in these productions, but especially over the last fifteen years I have sought to keep track of directors' choices – and have taken much flak from theatrical professionals, academic colleagues, and fellow playgoers for my note-taking habits at intervals or after shows. Ironically, some of my favorite productions are poorly represented in this book even though I have made a conscious effort to squeeze them in because they lacked significant rescripting outside of minimal cuts.

In addition, I have made sparing use of comments from directors, although a wealth of such information is available, especially for highly visible United Kingdom productions in London and Stratford where media attention is intense. Such comments can often be revealing, particularly about a concept or line of interpretation, and can also provide fodder for an academic to dissect, even pillory (a stance I have sought to avoid). However, over the years I have encountered disparities between what directors say in response to interviewers' questions and what actually happens under the pressures of time, budget, and rehearsal room interactions, so that I have chosen to concentrate on actual choices that I have witnessed. In taking such a route I have in mind two passages: D. H. Lawrence's dictum: "Never trust the artist. Trust the tale";[3] and my reformulation of Matthew 7:20: "by their cuts ye shall know them."

I have also made sparing use of theatre reviews, even though such material for United Kingdom productions is available in *Theatre Record* (although not included in that publication are items from *TLS* and Shakespeare journals). Reviewers writing for potential purchasers of tickets, as opposed to "for the record," must work with a broad brush so as to react swiftly and selectively to what they have seen (and I have great respect for how much some of these reviewers can accomplish in a short space and under a severe time limit). However, what is of necessity omitted from such accounts is attention to the script alterations central to this book. In chapter 3 I singled out a distinctive choice by the director of the DC 1996 *All's Well That Ends Well* (the insertion of sonnet 109 to bolster Bertram's notoriously brief "Both, both. O, pardon!"), but neither the local print reviews nor a review for the record in *Shakespeare Bulletin* (Fall 1996, 22–23) mentioned this directorial move. Had I not seen the show myself I would not have been aware of this significant item. In such situations I see no alternative to Claudio's admonition (which he himself fails to follow): "Let every eye negotiate for itself, / And trust no agent" (*Much Ado*, 2.1.178–79).

When taking on a director's choices, an academic, especially a critic or teacher with an investment in a given play, can easily slip into an attack mode. Accounts of productions in scholarly journals often provide a professorial grade sheet or scorecard (usually with the emphasis upon errors rather than hits) and can leave the impression of the expert having the last word, an academic version of Falstaff wounding a dead Hotspur in the thigh. Obviously, I am not immune to such tendencies and cannot avoid bringing my own value judgments to bear on individual productions, but I have made a strenuous effort to minimize such reactions in favor of what I hope will be seen as a fairminded account of price tags and trade-offs. Neutrality on such matters may be a fiction, but I wish to avoid the stance of a colleague who, just after the conclusion of a performance of Michael Boyd's RSC 2000 *Romeo and Juliet* (with the inserted ghosts noted in chapter 5), was apoplectic to the point of speechlessness.

Similarly, my goal has not been to push my idiosyncratic readings of various moments (e.g., in chapter 6 Prince Hal and Francis the drawer or the ghosts in *Richard III*). Rather, my concern has been with elements that arguably could or should be significant for any interpretation on page or stage. What exactly *is* a disposable item or one inconsequential enough that it can be translated without loss into today's idiom? When are the original signals irrelevant or intrusive or just plain silly? What role should historical knowledge of what happened in the first performances play in any evaluation of current theatrical practice? As to the latter question, after nearly thirty years of struggling with the available evidence, I am painfully aware of the theatre historian's dirty little secret – how little we actually know about how these plays were first conceived and performed. Nonetheless, at various points I have played the historical card in the hope of providing the reader with a perspective on problems and issues prevalent today.

As some readers will have noted, I have made no attempt to theorize my approach or offer a master narrative to encompass my findings (e.g., the elevation of the psychological over the supernatural noted in chapter 6), a task I leave to others. Moreover, rather than providing definitive conclusions I have repeatedly adopted an interrogative mode. In chapter 7 I quoted a snippet from John Peter's review of Gale Edwards's *The Taming of the Shrew* (RSC 1995). At the outset of that review Peter raised the same questions to which I keep returning: "how many liberties can you take with a play in order to interpret it? What is the difference between interpreting a play and making it say what *you* want it to say? Do dead playwrights have rights?"[4] Similarly, in an essay on production choices Stanley Wells asks: "where does the borderline come between interpretation and fresh creation?"[5] Clearly, concern with rescripting and rewrighting, price tags and trade-offs, is not mine alone. Moreover, answers to my many questions are not readily available.

Rather than claiming to provide such answers or attempting to theorize the situation, my goal has been to provide multiple examples from England and North America so that readers interested in such questions, whatever their background (academic, theatrical, or none of the above), can either work out their own standards for evaluation or at least be better aware of the many problems. My hope is that readers will be able to beef up my various categories and distinctions with comparable examples from their own playgoing, either from the many shows I have not seen or even from material I managed to miss in shows I did see. What is provided here is a beginning, a framework, not a final formulation etched in stone on Mount Sinai.

Raising questions about rescripting inevitably gets the scholar or teacher involved with murky editorial and textual problems that have been noted but not fully developed in the preceding chapters. I confess that as a teacher I have not had great success, at least with undergraduates, in dealing with the instabilities in various Shakespeare texts, whether the two versions of *King Lear* or the vagaries of *Hamlet* or *Othello*, an area of investigation that appeals to me but not to my clientele. Moreover, my students, who are anything but textual purists, often approve of directors who take liberties with the original words and sequence of scenes and therefore *prefer* cinematic versions such as the Oliver Parker *Othello* (with Laurence Fishburne and Kenneth Branagh) or the Kenneth Branagh *Much Ado About Nothing* which streamline the original playscripts and invoke various television or cinematic conventions with which they are familiar. To such students a focus on what has been omitted, transposed, or inserted can seem artificial or, in a pejorative sense, "academic."

My response is to invoke something akin to truth in advertising. I, for one, will pay close attention to any theatrical interpretation that is based on a reading of the received playscript, but, in the spirit of consumerism, I return to my series of questions. What is or should be the appropriate stance for evaluating stage or cinematic productions of Shakespeare's plays? More specifically, how are we to evaluate a reading or staging that to sustain its interpretation must omit or ignore a significant part of the original text? On a spectrum that ranges from the Second Quarto of *Romeo and Juliet* to *West Side Story* at what point does one move from interpretation to rewrighting? Should we, as teachers and students, care about such matters? If not us, then who?

As noted in chapter 1, I have no interest in what I think of as the Blame Game, the academic process of fault-finding wherein the director becomes a vandal sacking the sacred text. Rather, my goal has been to single out directorial or actorly choices and then explore the implications of those choices for interpretation. Since Shakespeare did not script his plays with us in mind, such an approach is inevitably intertwined with cultural difference in one form or another, whether those differences are attached to assumptions about ghosts and the supernatural, narrative form, or the role of poetry and iterative imagery. To focus on elements that are absent from a production (or transposed or inserted) is to flirt with various dangers (e.g., academic snideness, artificiality) and to run the risk of turning the playgoing experience into a search for flaws and anomalies, an anti-director form of "Gotcha!" I do not recommend such a negative stance to others, but for my purposes not to explore such avenues, to borrow from Mark Antony, would be "the most unkindest cut of all" (*Julius Caesar*, 3.2.183).

A final provocative example is provided by one of the most daunting staging problems in the Shakespeare canon – how to raise a dying Mark Antony to Cleopatra, Charmian, and Iras placed above: "*They heave Antony aloft to Cleopatra*" (4.15.37). Steven Pimlott (RSC 1999) provided no visible monument but rather placed Antony in a chair center stage and had the three women, far downstage and facing the audience, pull on imaginary ropes and move backward until level with him. In Giles Block's Globe 1999 production (with an all-male cast), Paul Shelley's Antony managed to dampen the laughs often elicited by the botched suicide (e.g., at "How, not dead? not dead?" – 4.14.103) or his subsequent question to Cleopatra's messenger ("When did she send thee?" – 119). In contrast, the strenuous physical effort needed to hoist Antony up (and the length of time consumed doing so) evoked titters from some Globe playgoers – and the image presented included not only Charmian and Iras struggling in the background but Mark Rylance's Cleopatra hauling on a rope while standing on the railing of the above. What was most revealing to me was that such laughter was not damaging but was integrated into a larger, inclusive effect. The key to this effect was getting the audience back into the proper mood for Antony's death and Cleopatra's epitaph (preceded by Rylance's cry of despair), and here the actors succeeded, with the mood enhanced by the visible presence of four Romans waiting silently below. Overall, the physical difficulty of the hoisting became central to the imagery or ironies of the scene so as to provide an important context for the death and the reaction to that death. As staged here, the awkwardness was essential so that it could be transcended.

As many doubters have noted, staging Shakespeare's scripts on a reconstituted Globe stage certainly does not serve as The Answer to All Problems, with or without strictures from the Authenticity Police. Nonetheless, I found the RSC versus Globe approaches to Cleopatra's monument particularly instructive. As a great believer in the role of an audience's "imaginary forces," I am more than ready to participate in the stage conventions crafted by a director, whether with dead figures who walk off the stage (a device invoked by Pimlott in his production) or a height that is to be imagined rather than enacted. Nonetheless, some practical theatrical choices have significant and sometimes unforeseen interpretative consequences so as to become an integral part of the imagery or tone of a key scene. As with so many directorial decisions cited in this book, to reconceive or streamline such a moment is to chart a smoother journey for today's playgoer at the risk of eliminating something integral to the play.

Like the Egyptian women and Roman soldiers whom the Folio directs to "*heave Antony aloft to Cleopatra*," all interpreters of these scripts in the theatre must struggle with daunting problems and flirt with potential disasters. Theatre historians can set up hypotheses or point to the virtues in the original scripts with no particular damage done if their arguments fail to convince (other than a rejection slip from a journal or university press), but a director will not stay a director for very long if he or she misjudges the economics of the situation or the tastes of the targeted audience. To rescript is to cut the Gordian knot so as to save running time, economize on personnel, and make Elizabethan–Jacobean language, culture, and onstage conventions more accessible to today's playgoers. Is this process inevitable? When is the price tag too high? Are there gradations to be observed, as when Trevor Nunn (whose work I much admire) distinguishes between "a fundamentalist" fidelity to the text and a less rigorous but principled "loyalty to the text"?[6] Should playgoers prize directors who follow their own vision as urged by Polonius ("This above all: to thine own self be true") or should those playgoers invoke Paulina's injunction ("It is requir'd / You do awake your faith")? In every theatrical venue, now and in the future, the purchasers of tickets ultimately will decide – and this book is my attempt to lay the groundwork for informed decisions.

Appendix: productions cited

In this list I provide the date, venue, and director for stage productions included in this book. Unless otherwise noted, references to the Royal Shakespeare Company are to productions in the two large theatres (the Royal Shakespeare Theatre in Stratford, the Barbican in London) as opposed to the Swan, The Other Place (TOP), and the Pit. I do not distinguish between Oregon Shakespeare Festival productions at the Elizabethan Stagehouse and the Bowmer, Royal National Theatre productions at the Olivier and Lyttleton, and Stratford Festival Canada productions at the Festival Theatre and the Avon. When I supply two consecutive years for a RSC production (*Richard III*, 1995–96), the later date refers to a remounting at the Barbican in London or on tour which was the version I actually saw. Not included in this list are (1) several shows to which I refer but did not see (for example, the Peter Brook 1955 *Titus Andronicus*); (2) Jane Howell's productions of the *Henry VI* plays and *Titus Andronicus* for BBC-TV's "The Shakespeare Plays"; and (3) several movies cited in passing.

SHAKESPEARE'S PLAYS

All's Well That Ends Well

1975	OSF	Jon Jory
1977	SFC	David Jones
1988	DC	Michael Kahn
1989	RSC	Barry Kyle
1992	OSF	Henry Woronicz
1992	RSC Swan	Sir Peter Hall
1996	DC	Laird Williamson
2001	PRC	David Hammond

Antony and Cleopatra

1960	Stratford, Conn.	Jack Landau
1987	RNT	Sir Peter Hall
1992–93	RSC	John Caird
1993	OSF	Charles Towers
1999	RSC	Steven Pimlott
1999	Globe	Giles Block

As You Like It

1978	SFC	Robin Phillips
1983	SFC	John Hirsch
1983	PRC	Greg Boyd
1985	RSC	Adrian Noble
1985	ACTER	No director
1986	OSF	Ann–Denise Ford
1989–90	RSC	John Caird
1990	SFC	Richard Monette
1990	University of the South	David Landon
1991	ACTER	No director
1992	OSF	Jim Edmondson
1998	Globe	Lucy Bailey
1999	New Jersey Shakespeare Festival	Scott Wentworth
2000	ACTER	No director

The Comedy of Errors

1976	OSF	Will Huddleston
1988	SSC	Danny Scheie
1999	Globe	Kathryn Hunter
2000	RSC	Lynne Parker

Coriolanus

1980	OSF	Jerry Turner
1981	SFC	Brian Bedford
1985	RNT	Sir Peter Hall
1994	RSC Swan	David Thacker
2000	Almeida	Jonathan Kent

Cymbeline

1987–88	RSC TOP–Pit	Bill Alexander
1988	RNT Cottlesloe	Sir Peter Hall
1989	RSC	Bill Alexander
1996	PRC	Tazewell Thompson
1997	RSC	Adrian Noble
2001	Globe	Mike Alfreds

Hamlet

1980	RSC	John Barton
1982	Donmar	Jonathan Miller
1984	RSC	Ron Daniels
1989	RSC	Ron Daniels
1989	RNT	Richard Eyre
1993	PRC	David Hammond
1993	ACTER	No director
1994	SFC	Richard Monette
1994	West End	Sir Peter Hall
1997	RSC	Matthew Warchus
2000	Globe	Giles Block
2001	RSC	Steven Pimlott

1 Henry IV

1979	OSF	Peter Moss
1979	North Carolina Shakespeare Festival	Louis Rackoff
1984	SSC	Michael Edwards
1988	ESC	Michael Bogdanov
1988	OSF	Pat Patton
1991	RSC	Adrian Noble
2000	RSC Swan	Michael Attenborough

2 Henry IV

1982	RSC	Trevor Nunn
1988	ESC	Michael Bogdanov
1989	OSF	Henry Woronicz
2000	RSC Swan	Michael Attenborough

Henry V

1977–78	RSC	Terry Hands
1984	RSC	Adrian Noble
1988	ESC	Michael Bogdanov
1995	DC	Michael Kahn
1997	Globe	Richard Olivier

1 Henry VI

1975	OSF	Will Huddleston
1977–78	RSC	Terry Hands
1988	ESC	Michael Bogdanov
1988–89	RSC	Adrian Noble
1991	OSF	Pat Patton

2 Henry VI

1976	OSF	Jerry Turner
1977–78	RSC	Terry Hands
1988	ESC	Michael Bogdanov
1988–89	RSC	Adrian Noble
1991–92	OSF	Pat Patton

3 Henry VI

1977	OSF	Pat Patton
1977–78	RSC	Terry Hands
1988	ESC	Michael Bogdanov
1988–89	RSC	Adrian Noble
1992	OSF	Pat Patton
1994	RSC TOP	Katie Mitchell

Henry VIII

1983	RSC	Howard Davies
1984	OSF	Jim Edmondson
1997	RSC Swan	Gregory Doran

Julius Caesar

1968	University of Wisconsin	Edward Amor
1978	SFC	John Wood

1987	RSC	Terry Hands
1988	SSC	Michael Edwards
1991	OSF	Michael Kevin
1991	RSC	Steven Pimlott
1993	RSC TOP	David Thacker
1995	RSC	Sir Peter Hall
1999	Globe	Mark Rylance
2001	RSC	Edward Hall

King John

| 1988 | RSC TOP | Deborah Warner |

King Lear

1976	OSF	Pat Patton
1982	RSC	Adrian Noble
1987	RNT	David Hare
1989	ACTER	No director
1990	RSC	Nicholas Hytner
1990	RNT	Deborah Warner
1991	DC	Michael Kahn
1993	RSC	Adrian Noble
1997	Young Vic	Helena Kaut-Howson
1997	Old Vic	Sir Peter Hall
1997	RNT Cottlesloe	Richard Eyre

Love's Labor's Lost

| 1980 | OSF | Dennis Bigelow |

Macbeth

1976–78	RSC TOP–Young Vic	Trevor Nunn
1978	SFC	Robin Phillips and Eric Steiner
1979	OSF	Pat Patton
1979	PRC	Tom Haas
1982	RSC	Howard Davies
1987	OSF	Jim Edmondson
1988	RSC	Adrian Noble

1990	SFC	David William
1993	RNT	Richard Eyre
1995	DC	Joe Dowling
1995	PRC	David Wheeler
1996	RSC	Tim Albery
1999–2000	RSC Swan–Young Vic	Gregory Doran
2001	Globe	Tim Carroll

Measure for Measure

1972	Milwaukee Repertory Company	Nagle Jackson
1977	OSF	Jerry Turner
1985	PRC	Greg Boyd
1986	OSF	Jim Edmondson
1994–95	RSC	Steven Pimlott
1997	ACTER	No director
1998	RSC	Michael Boyd

The Merchant of Venice

1986	CSC, New York	James Simpson
1987	RSC	Bill Alexander
1989	West End	Sir Peter Hall
1991	OSF	Libby Appel
1993	RSC	David Thacker
1998	Globe	Richard Olivier
1998	RSC	Gregory Doran

The Merry Wives of Windsor

1978	SFC	Peter Moss
1980	OSF	Jon Cranney
1990	DC	Michael Kahn
1995	RNT	Terry Hands

A Midsummer Night's Dream

1970–71	RSC	Peter Brook
1979	OSF	Dennis Bigelow
1990	Santa Barbara	Homer Swander
1999	RSC	Michael Boyd

Much Ado About Nothing

1981	Regents Park	Ian Talbot
1989	OSF	Pat Patton
1990	RSC	Bill Alexander
1993	West End	Matthew Warchus
1998	Cheek by Jowl	Declan Donnelan

Othello

1979	SFC	Frances Hyland
1980	RSC Aldwych	Ronald Eyre
1980	RNT	Sir Peter Hall
1989	RSC TOP	Trevor Nunn
1991	DC	Harold Scott
1994	SFC	Brian Bedford
1995	PRC	David Hammond
1997	DC	Jude Kelly
1997	RNT Cottesloe	Sam Mendes
1999	RSC	Michael Attenborough

Pericles

1989	OSF	Jerry Turner and Dennis Bigelow
1989–90	RSC Swan–Pit	David Thacker

Richard II

1979	SFC	Zoe Caldwell
1980	OSF	Jerry Turner
1986	SSC	Michael Edwards
1987	OSF	Jerry Turner
1988	ESC	Michael Bogdanov
1995	RNT Cottlesloe	Deborah Warner
2000	RSC TOP	Steven Pimlott
2000	Almeida	Jonathan Kent

Richard III

1977	SFC	Robin Phillips
1978	OSF	Pat Patton
1984	RSC	Bill Alexander
1988	ESC	Michael Bogdanov

1990	RNT	Richard Eyre
1992	RSC TOP	Sam Mendes
1993	OSF	Jim Edmondson
1995–96	RSC	Steven Pimlott

Romeo and Juliet

1975	OSF	Jim Edmondson
1980	RSC	Ron Daniels
1986	RSC	Michael Bogdanov
1988	OSF	Henry Woronicz
1989	RSC Swan	Terry Hands
1991–92	RSC	David Leveaux
1995	ACTER	No director
1995	RSC	Adrian Noble
2000	RSC	Michael Boyd

The Taming of the Shrew

1978	OSF	Judd Parkin
1978	RSC	Michael Bogdanov
1981	SFC	Peter Dews
1984	OSF	Pat Patton
1987	RSC	Jonathan Miller
1989	PRC	David Hammond
1991	OSF	Sandy McCallum
1991	Santa Barbara	Homer Swander
1992	RSC	Bill Alexander
1995	RSC	Gale Edwards
1996	Centre Stage, Baltimore	Jackson Phippin

The Tempest

1978	OSF	Michael Addison
1982	RSC	Ron Daniels
1987	Virginia Stage Company, Norfolk	Charles Towers
1987	Theatre Virginia, Richmond	Terry Burgler
1988	RSC	Nicholas Hytner
1988	RNT Cottlesloe	Sir Peter Hall
1989	DC	Richard E. T. White

1993	RSC	Sam Mendes
1995	RSC Swan	David Thacker
1998	RSC	Adrian Noble
1998	PRC	Tazewell Thompson
2000	Globe	Lenka Udovicki
2000–1	RSC	James Macdonald

Timon of Athens

| 1978 | OSF | Jerry Turner |

Titus Andronicus

1974	OSF	Laird Williamson
1981	RSC	John Barton
1986	OSF	Pat Patton
1987	RSC Swan	Deborah Warner
1988	SSC	Mark Rucker
1995	RNT Cottlesloe	Gregory Doran

Troilus and Cressida

1985	RSC	Howard Davies
1996	RSC	Ian Judge
1999	RNT	Trevor Nunn

Twelfth Night

1986	SSC	Marcia Taylor
1988	OSF	Bill Cain
1992	PRC	Martin Platt
1994	RSC	Ian Judge
1994	SFC	Richard Monette
1998	Lincoln Center	Nicholas Hytner
1998	Young Vic	Tim Supple

The Two Gentlemen of Verona

| 1987 | Regents Park | Ian Talbot |
| 1989 | OSF | Bill Cain |

The Two Noble Kinsmen

| 2000 | Globe | Tim Carroll |

The Winter's Tale

1978	SFC	Robin Phillips
1981	RSC	Ronald Eyre
1986	RSC	Terry Hands
1988	RNT Cottlesloe	Sir Peter Hall
1989	ACTER	No director
1990	ACTER	No director
1992	RSC	Adrian Noble
1997	Globe	David Freeman
2001	ACTER	No director
2001	RNT	Nicholas Hytner

PLAYS BY SHAKESPEARE'S CONTEMPORARIES

Arden of Faversham

1982	RSC TOP	Terry Hands

Beaumont and Fletcher, *The Maid's Tragedy*

1981	RSC TOP	Barry Kyle
1997	Globe	Lucy Bailey

Brome, *The Jovial Crew*

1992	RSC Swan	Max Stafford-Clark, adapted Stephen Jeffreys

Dekker, *The Honest Whore*

1998	Globe	Jack Shepherd

Dekker, *The Shoemakers' Holiday*

1987	OSF	Jerry Turner

Ford, *The Broken Heart*

1994	RSC Swan	Michael Boyd

Ford, *'Tis Pity She's a Whore*

1981	OSF	Jerry Turner

Heywood, *A Woman Killed With Kindness*

1991–92	RSC	Swan–Pit Katie Mitchell

Jonson, *Bartholomew Fair*

1987	Regents Park	Peter Barnes
1998	RSC Swan	Laurence Boswell

Jonson, *The Alchemist*

1991–92	RSC	Sam Mendes

Jonson, *The Devil Is an Ass*

1995	RSC Swan	Matthew Warchus

Jonson, *Every Man In His Humour*

1986	RSC Swan	John Caird

Jonson, *Volpone*

1983	RSC TOP–Pit	Bill Alexander
1995	RNT	Matthew Warchus
1996	DC	Michael Kahn
1999	RSC Swan	Lindsay Posner

Kyd, *The Spanish Tragedy*

1997	RSC Swan	Michael Boyd

Marlowe, *Doctor Faustus*

1979	OSF	Jerry Turner
1989	RSC Swan	Barry Kyle

Marlowe, *Edward II*

1990	RSC Swan	Gerard Murphy

Marlowe, *The Jew of Malta*

1987	RSC Swan	Barry Kyle

Marston, *The Fawn*

1983   RNT Cottlesloe   Giles Block

Middleton, *A Chaste Maid in Cheapside*

1997   Globe   Malcolm McKay

Middleton, *A Mad World My Masters*

1998   Globe   Sue Lefton

Middleton (?), *The Revenger's Tragedy*

1984   OSF   Jerry Turner
1987–88   RSC Swan–Pit   Di Trevis

Middleton and Rowley, *The Changeling*

1988   RNT   Richard Eyre

Webster, *The Duchess of Malfi*

1985–86   RNT   Philip Prowse
1995   Greenwich Theatre   Philip Franks
1996   Cheek by Jowl   Declan Donnelan

Webster, *The White Devil*

1991   RNT   Philip Prowse
1996   RSC Swan   Gale Edwards

Notes

I "LET IT BE HID": PRICE TAGS, TRADE-OFFS, AND ECONOMIES

1 Citations from Shakespeare are from the revised Riverside edition, ed. G. Blakemore Evans (Boston and New York, 1997). Citations from the First Folio are from *The Norton Facsimile: The First Folio of Shakespeare*, ed. Charlton Hinman (New York and London, 1968) and are accompanied by Through Line Numbers (TLN).

2 For an explanation of my abbreviations see page xi.

3 For overviews on such performance criticism see the essays collected in *Shakespeare and the Sense of Performance: Essays in the Tradition of Performance Criticism in Honor of Bernard Beckerman*, ed. Marvin and Ruth Thompson (Newark, Delaware, 1989) and *Shakespeare, Theory, and Performance*, ed. James C. Bulman (London, 1996). The wealth of material available includes volumes devoted to individual plays in Manchester University Press's *Shakespeare in Performance* series, Macmillan's *Text and Performance* series, and Cambridge University Press's *Shakespeare in Production* series as well as essays by individual actors in Cambridge University Press's *Players of Shakespeare* series. See also the revealing "case studies" provided by Martin White in his *Renaissance Drama in Action* (London and New York, 1998) – for example, an interview with Matthew Warchus that includes a discussion of cuts in his *Henry V* (RSC 1994) on pp. 50–51. I am especially indebted to the pioneering work of J. L. Styan and Homer Swander (and to the latter I owe the term *rewrighting*), but I have profited greatly from a wide range of practitioners (including many revealing post-performance comments from actors) and from interactions at a series of seminars at the annual Shakespeare Association of America meeting.

4 See Ralph Berry, *On Directing Shakespeare* (London, 1989), pp. 99–100.

5 *Peter Hall's Diaries*, ed. John Goodwin (New York, 1985), pp. 176–77. In a 1973 interview Trevor Nunn noted: "When you approach the text of *Hamlet*, the cutting virtually is the production. What you decide to leave in is your version of the play" (Berry, *On Directing Shakespeare*, p. 79). Comparable to Hall's restraint are the comments of Terry Hands on his approach to the *Henry VI* trilogy (RSC 1977–78). Although aware of the many negative judgments about these plays he decided "not to do even our own usual reshaping of a few corners and reorganizing the occasional speech" but chose rather "just to

put it all very crudely, very naively down on the stage – everything that was there, warts and all, in the hope that one or two of them would turn out to be beauty spots. There was something to learn" (quoted in Homer D. Swander, "The Rediscovery of *Henry VI*," *Shakespeare Quarterly* 29 [1978]: 149). From this naive, crude approach without reshaping or reorganizing (albeit with some lines cut) emerged a stunning production that was both a great success at the box office and a revelation to students of the history plays.

6　"Preparing the Text: *The History of Henry the Fourth, Part II*," *On-Stage Studies*, the Colorado Shakespeare Festival, Number 4 (1980), pp. 58, 62. A more moderate approach to "the nature of cutting" (from an academic as opposed to a theatrical perspective) is provided by Ralph Berry (*On Directing Shakespeare*, p. 12) who argues: "Essentially it is an affair of cutting the crystal, of presenting an object so as to reflect light at the desired angles." Building upon an example from *The Merchant of Venice* (see the end of this chapter) he concludes: "Cutting, then, should emphasise a certain quality, a certain source of vitality, in the full original. This is not to deny that cutting can be brutal, capricious, insensitive. Its function is nonetheless to illuminate, and not lay waste, the original text."

7　Director Lindsay Posner (RSC Swan 1999) provided another option for handling difficult terms by including in the program for *Volpone* a series of glosses (e.g., for strappado, *commendatori*, Aretine, *The Courtier*, Whitefriars' nation, Hospital of the *Incurabili*). Such a solution, however, presupposes an especially alert and retentive audience, for (as one actor in the company asked me) how is an auditor confronting a hard word in a darkened auditorium to retrieve such program copy? For some shrewd comments about the obstacles for actor or auditor posed by early modern English see Martin White, *Drama in Action*, especially pp. 5–8. For example, after wrestling with a Bosola speech from *The Duchess of Malfi* White notes wryly: "Perhaps unsurprisingly, the line is generally cut" (p. 6). White also (p. 2) reports actor David Troughton's comparison of "speaking Jonson's words to 'chewing beef stock cubes'."

8　Similarly, Michael P. Jensen tells me that the 1989 San Francisco Shakespeare Festival's *A Midsummer Night's Dream* featured an Asian–American actor as Snout/Wall, so that various references to the *chink* in the wall (e.g., "Show me thy chink" – 5.1.177) were changed to *hole* to avoid any semblance of a racial slur.

9　In his account of the RNT 1964 production Kenneth Tynan notes that "Othello's brief and dramatically pointless appearance is cut, in accordance with sound theatrical custom" (*'Othello': The National Theatre Production*, 1966, p. 11). In his SFC 1994 *Othello* Brian Bedford made a series of standard cuts in this script; omitted (in addition to Othello's appearance in 5.1) were his eavesdropping lines in 4.1, Desdemona's references to Othello's rolling his eyes and gnawing his lips (5.2.37–38, 43), and the interjections from Lodovico and Gratiano that come between Othello's last two speeches (5.2.357).

10　David Bell, *Backwards and Forwards: A Technical Manual for Reading Plays* (Carbondale and Edwardsville, 1983), pp. 83–84.

11 To be fair to Rylance's Globe choices, a striking moment was generated the afternoon I saw the show, for the tribunes' caustic comments to the crowd in 1.1 (e.g., "You blocks, you stones, you worse than senseless things!" – 1.1.35) not only silenced the actors planted in the yard but also the volatile and potentially raucous 1999 groundlings who initially seemed prepared to "cull out a holiday" (49). As a theatre historian I came away with the question: is this scene designed to shame not one but two sets of auditors into attentiveness?

12 As noted by Michael Shapiro, *playboy* is the term actually used in the period. See his *Gender in Play on the Shakespearean Stage: Boy Heroines and Female Pages* (Ann Arbor, 1994).

13 Jonson, unlike an in-house playwright like Shakespeare or Heywood, may not have set up his play with the available casting clearly in mind, so that such conjectures are even more suspect than those made about Shakespeare's plays (and those hypotheses are already very iffy). In casting *Volpone* boy actors are needed for (1) Celia, (2) Lady Would-be, (3) a female servant (a very small part), and possibly (4) the dwarf and/or the hermaphrodite. If three to five boys were indeed available for significant parts, conceivably one of them could have been available to play Peregrine.

14 Berry, *On Directing Shakespeare*, p. 12.

2 RESCRIPTING SHAKESPEARE'S CONTEMPORARIES

1 Citations in this chapter are from the following editions: *The Maid's Tragedy*, ed. T. W. Craik, Revels Plays (Manchester, 1988); *1 The Honest Whore* in *The Dramatic Works of Thomas Dekker*, ed. Fredson Bowers, 4 vols. (Cambridge, 1964), 2: 1–131; *The Shoemakers' Holiday*, ed. R. B. Smallwood and Stanley Wells, Revels Plays (Manchester 1979); *The Broken Heart*, ed. T. J. B. Spencer, Revels Plays (Manchester, 1980); *'Tis Pity She's a Whore*, ed. Derek Roper, Revels Plays (Manchester, 1975); *The Alchemist*, ed. F. H. Mares, Revels Plays (London, 1967); *Bartholomew Fair*, ed. E. A. Horsman, Revels Plays (London, 1960); *Every Man In His Humour: A Parallel-Text Edition of the 1601 Quarto and the 1616 Folio*, ed. J. W. Lever, Regents Renaissance Drama (Lincoln, Neb., 1971); *Volpone*, revised edition, ed. Brian Parker, Revels Plays (Manchester, 1999); *The Spanish Tragedy*, ed. Philip Edwards, Revels Plays (London, 1959); *Edward II*, ed. Charles R. Forker, Revels Plays (Manchester, 1994); *The Jew of Malta*, ed. N. W. Bawcutt, Revels Plays (Manchester, 1978); *Marlowe's "Doctor Faustus" 1604–1616*, ed. W. W. Greg (Oxford, 1950); *The Fawn*, ed. David A. Blostein, Revels Plays (Manchester, 1978); *The Revenger's Tragedy*, ed. R. A. Foakes, Revels Plays (London, 1966); *The Duchess of Malfi*, ed. John Russell Brown, Revels Plays (London, 1964); *The White Devil*, ed. John Russell Brown, Revels Plays (London, 1960). Throughout this book I have modernized the spelling of passages quoted from old spelling editions.

2 For an excellent discussion of these issues see Michael Warren, "*Doctor Faustus*: The Old Man and the Text," *English Literary Renaissance* 11 (1981): 111–47.

3 The re-run effect *was* included in Lucy Bailey's production at the Globe (admittedly a very different venue from The Other Place) and, for me, was one of the high points of the show.

4 Paul Taylor, *The Independent*, May 10, 1997.

3 ADJUSTMENTS AND IMPROVEMENTS

1 See *Measure for Measure*, ed. Mark Eccles, New Variorum (New York: Modern Language Association, 1980), p. 190 from which I have taken the Lever and Rossiter quotes. As noted later in this chapter, similar questions have been raised about the 3.1 positioning of the "To be, or not to be" soliloquy in the Second Quarto and the Folio.

2 In a long note in his Arden 2 edition (London, 1955) T. S. Dorsch accepts the traditional view "that the copy from which the Folio was printed contained two versions of the account of Portia's death, of which one was a revision, and that both were printed by mistake," so that the second account provided by Messala is the original and the first provided by Brutus himself is the revision (pp. 106–07). Michael Kevin (OSF 1991) and Edward Hall (RSC 2001) omitted Messala's version; Hall, moreover, did further streamlining of this scene (e.g., gone also were Varrus, Claudio, and Brutus's declaration that "I can raise no money by vile means" – 4.3.71–82) and considerably pared back Act 5 as well, most notably the presentation of the deaths of Cassius and Brutus (e.g., Dardanius, Clitus, Volumnius, and Strato disappeared, so that Brutus addressed all his requests for assistance in his suicide to one figure, Lucilius). In recent years, however, directors, who no longer hold an idealized vision of Brutus, usually keep both accounts of Portia's death and leave intact the deaths of Cassius and Brutus.

3 Streamlining of *Richard II* often eliminates elements that can reinforce such patterning but are deemed dispensable by a director. For example, the coda to the deposition scene in which the Abbot of Westminster, Carlisle, and Aumerle remain on stage to hatch a plot against the newly kinged Henry IV that "shall show us all a merry day" (4.1.334) is regularly cut (OSF 1980, OSF 1987, ESC 1988). However, this configuration of three plotters against a king who has just appropriated Richard II's crown parallels the coda to 2.1 where Northumberland, Willoughby, and Ross hatch their plot against another king, Richard II, who has just confiscated Gaunt's Lancastrian estate that rightfully belongs to Bolingbroke.

4 Robert Smallwood, " 'Beginners, Please'; or, First Start Your Play," *Jahrbuch 1993*, p. 73.

5 Richard Proudfoot, "The 1998 Globe Season," *Shakespeare Survey* 52 (1999): 216.

6 Cited in the Variorum edition, ed. Horace Howard Furness (Philadelphia, 1886), p. 237.

7 The adjusted version of 4.5 was:

Thus in the sty of the most deadly boar
My son George Stanley is frank'd up in hold
If I revolt, off goes young George's head;
The fear of that holds off my present aid
Yet will I hie to Richmond
And resolve him of my mind herein
Withal to tell him the Queen has heartily consented
He should espouse Elizabeth her daughter.

8 Michael Billington, *The Guardian*, May 2, 1998; Charles Spencer, *The Daily Telegraph*, May 4, 1998; John Peter, *The Sunday Times*, May 10, 1998; Alistair Macaulay, *The Financial Times*, May 4, 1998.

4 INSERTING AN INTERMISSION / INTERVAL

1 See Gary Taylor, "The Structure of Performance: Act-Intervals in the London Theatres, 1576–1642" in Taylor and John Jowett, *Shakespeare Reshaped, 1606–1623* (Oxford and New York, 1993), pp. 3–50.
2 Peter Holland cites this term, found in a Tom Stoppard letter, "which refers to the alleged need of a Broadway audience to urinate every 75 minutes." See his *English Shakespeares: Shakespeare on the English Stage in the 1990s* (Cambridge, 1997), p. 3.

5 WHAT'S IN AN ENDING? RESCRIPTING FINAL SCENES

1 Citations from the Quartos are taken from *Shakespeare's Plays in Quarto*, ed. Michael J. B. Allen and Kenneth Muir (Berkeley, 1981).
2 For a full discussion of this scene in the context of other contemporary tomb scenes see my *Recovering Shakespeare's Theatrical Vocabulary* (Cambridge, 1995), chapter 9.
3 Stephen Booth, "Speculations on Doubling in Shakespeare's Plays," *Shakespeare: The Theatrical Dimension*, ed. Philip C. McGuire and David A. Samuelson (New York, 1979), pp. 119–20; John C. Meagher, "Economy and Recognition: Thirteen Shakespearean Puzzles," *Shakespeare Quarterly* 34 (1984): 18–19.
4 See G. K. Hunter's Arden 2 edition (London, 1959), p. 124.

6 RESCRIPTING STAGE DIRECTIONS AND ACTIONS

1 Edmund Malone, "Preface," *The Plays and Poems of William Shakespeare*, 10 vols. (London, 1790), vol. 1, p. lviii.
2 E. A. J. Honigmann, *Myriad-minded Shakespeare*, Second Edition (London and New York, 1998), p. 187. To establish Shakespeare's carelessness with stage directions Honigmann notes: "He often omitted them, or left them incomplete, or inserted them in approximately but not precisely

the correct place. Secondly, some stage directions in the good Quartos, and many more in the Folio, were added or misplaced by scriveners, prompters, Folio editors or compositors. Thirdly, a very large number of the stage directions printed in modern editions which were added by eighteenth-century editors or their successors have only the authority of good sense (or not, as the case may be)" (187). For an alternative view see my *Recovering Shakespeare's Theatrical Vocabulary* (Cambridge, 1995), especially chapter 1.

3 For example, see S. P. Zitner, "Anon, Anon: or, a Mirror for a Magistrate," *Shakespeare Quarterly* 19 (1968): 63–70. In his *Shakespearean Negotiations* (Berkeley and Los Angeles, 1988, p. 43), Stephen Greenblatt treats the moment as one of "the play's acts of *recording*, that is, the moments in which we hear voices that seem to dwell outside the realms ruled by the potentates of the land." For my own reading see *Shakespeare and the Late Moral Plays* (Lincoln, Neb., 1986), pp. 69–70.

4 See chapter 7 of my *Elizabethan Stage Conventions and Modern Interpreters* (Cambridge, 1984).

5 For a wealth of detail on the performance history of these two scenes see *The Tempest*, ed. Christine Dymkowski, *Shakespeare in Production* (Cambridge, 2000), pp. 256–67, 274–86.

6 See John Jowett, "New Created Creatures: Ralph Crane and the Stage Directions in *The Tempest*," *Shakespeare Survey 36* (1983), pp. 107–20.

7 *The Shakespearean Stage 1574–1642*, Second Edition (Cambridge, 1980), p. 176. In the denouement of *The Wasp* (ed. J. W. Lever, Malone Society [London, 1976]), a manuscript play from the 1630s, a sumptuous banquet of "Viands" is suddenly transformed into something horrible to look at ("snakes toads and newts" – 2220–21) and then, later in the scene, reverts to its original condition ("these comfortable viands" – 2325). The stage direction for the first moment reads: *"the table turns and such things appear"* (2220–21); and for the second: *"Table turns"* (2324).

8 For this rescripted address to Richmond, Anne spoke two of her three lines ("Thou quiet soul, sleep thou a quiet sleep, / Dream of success and happy victory!" – 164–65); Prince Edward one of four ("Live and beget a happy race of kings!" – 152); Clarence one of three ("Good angels guard thy battle! Live and flourish!" – 138); Hastings one of two ("Arm, fight, and conquer for fair England's sake" – 158); Buckingham two of four ("God and good angels fight on Richmond's side, / And Richard falls in height of all his pride!" – 175–76); and the group spoke "Awake and win the day!" (145).

9 Citations are from Richard Brome, *The Queen's Exchange* in *The Dramatic Works of Richard Brome*, 3 vols. (London, 1873), 3: 453–550; Nathaniel Richards, *Messalina*, ed. A. R. Skemp, Materialien zur Kunde des älteren Englischen Dramas (Louvain and London, 1910); Thomas Goffe, *The Raging Turk*, ed. David Carnegie, Malone Society (London, 1974); George Chapman, *The Revenge of Bussy D'Ambois*, ed. Robert J. Lordi in *The Plays of George Chapman: The Tragedies with Sir Gyles Goosecappe*, gen. ed. Allan Holaday (Cambridge, 1987), 423–527. Dates attached to plays are taken from *Annals of English*

Drama, 975–1700, Third Edition, ed. Alfred Harbage, rev. S. Schoenbaum, rev. Sylvia Stoler Wagonheim (London, 1989).

10 Citations are from Thomas Heywood, *The Golden Age* in *The Dramatic Works of Thomas Heywood*, ed. R. H. Shepherd, 6 vols. (London, 1874), 3: 1–79; Thomas Middleton, *No Wit, No Help Like a Woman's*, ed. Lowell E. Johnson, Regents Renaissance Drama (Lincoln, Neb., 1976).

7 COMPRESSING *HENRY VI*

1 See Leah Marcus, *Puzzling Shakespeare* (Berkeley and Los Angeles, 1988), pp. 51–96; Gabriele Bernhard Jackson, "Topical Ideology: Witches, Amazons, and Shakespeare's Joan of Arc," *English Literary Renaissance* 18 (1988): 40–65; Nancy A. Gutierrez, "Gender and Value in *1 Henry VI*: The Role of Joan de Pucelle," *Theatre Journal* 42 (1990): 183–93; and chapter 4 of Phyllis Rackin, *Stages of History* (Ithaca, 1990). For a provocative interpretation of one episode in Part II, see Craig A. Bernthal, "Treason in the Family: The Trial of Thumpe v. Horner," *Shakespeare Quarterly* 42 (1991): 44–54.

2 See in particular J. P. Brockbank, "The Frame of Disorder: *Henry VI*," in *Early Shakespeare*, ed. J. R. Brown and Bernard Harris, Stratford-upon-Avon Studies 3 (1961), 72–99; David Riggs, *Shakespeare's Heroical Histories: "Henry VI" and its Literary Tradition* (Cambridge, Mass., 1971); and Edward Berry, *Patterns of Decay: Shakespeare's Early Histories* (Charlottesville, 1975).

3 Hereward T. Price, "Construction in Shakespeare," *University of Michigan Contributions in Modern Philology* 17 (1951): 24–37.

4 For accounts of this production see Homer D. Swander, "The Rediscovery of *Henry VI*," *Shakespeare Quarterly* 29 (1978): 146–63; David Daniell, "Opening up the text: Shakespeare's *Henry VI* plays in performance," *Themes in Drama* 1 (1979): 247–77; and G. K. Hunter, "The Royal Shakespeare Company Plays *Henry VI*," *Renaissance Drama* 9 (1978): 91–108.

5 *The Plantagenets* (London and Boston, 1989), pp. viii, xiv.

6 For example, owing to the transposition of elements young Clifford presented his angry speeches from the beginning of Part III (e.g., 1.1.161–62) *before* the death of his father at the end of Part II, the event that occasioned his pronouncement that "My heart is turn'd to stone" (5.2.50). Some of the elements from Part II's 5.1 were retained, but moving and reshaping them eliminated the climactic position of this first confrontation between the parties of York and Lancaster (and one potentially telling element, the choice by Salisbury not to kneel to Henry VI, was gone). To the degree that the sequence of elements is an integral part of theatrical meaning and effect, the treatment of the end of Part II and the beginning of Part III by all three directors constituted rewrighting.

7 Daniell, "Opening up the text," p. 257.

8 Bogdanov did some radical surgery here by transposing the beginning of 5.3 to 5.4 so that one sustained sequence involving Joan followed the Suffolk–Margaret part of 5.3. The juxtaposition of the two French women

remained, but the value of that link was changed (e.g., Joan's capture by York was not immediately followed by Suffolk's capture of Margaret). Bogdanov also cut Joan's shepherd father. His Joan, moreover, had her own distinctive music, but without the Folio fiends as a final comment this production offered no clear signal as to whether that music (and the auspices for her final moments) was holy or witchly. Here as elsewhere, Bogdanov provided an engaging story, but the original punch line as set up in the Folio had been drastically changed.

9 For treatments of 2.3, see especially Daniel C. Gerould, "Principles of Dramatic Structure in *Henry VI*," *Educational Theatre Journal* 20 (1968): 379–80; Berry, *Patterns of Decay*, pp. 1–28; James A. Riddell, "Talbot and the Countess of Auvergne," *Shakespeare Quarterly* 28 (1977): 51–57; and Alexander Leggatt, *Shakespeare's Political Drama* (London and New York, 1988), pp. 1–8.

10 Thomas Dekker, *Westward Ho*, 5.1.196–201 in *The Dramatic Works*, ed. Fredson Bowers, 4 vols. (Cambridge, 1953–61), 2:379. For a long list of examples see the *chair* entry in Alan C. Dessen and Leslie Thomson, *A Dictionary of Stage Directions in English Drama, 1580–1642* (Cambridge, 1999), p. 46.

8 THE TAMINGS OF THE SHREWS: RESCRIPTING THE FIRST FOLIO

1 Citations from 1594 are from *The Taming of a Shrew*, ed. Stephen Roy Miller (Cambridge, 1998). I know of no evidence that anyone in the 1590s or early 1600s distinguished between *A Shrew* and *The Shrew*.

2 Although now in disrepute, the term *bad quarto* has been used widely to denote a relatively small group of texts (e.g., the first printed editions of *Romeo and Juliet*, *The Merry Wives of Windsor*, *Henry V*, and *Hamlet*) that often differ considerably from subsequent longer versions. For a critique of this term see in particular Paul Werstine, "Narratives About Printed Shakespeare Texts: 'Foul Papers' and 'Bad' Quartos," *Shakespeare Quarterly* 41 (1990): 65–86.

3 For lucid summaries of the debate (along with arguments in favor of the "bad quarto" thesis), see Brian Morris's introduction to his Arden 2 edition (London and New York, 1981), pp. 12–50; H. J. Oliver's introduction to his Oxford edition (Oxford, 1982), pp. 13–34; and Ann Thompson's "textual analysis" appendix to her New Cambridge edition (Cambridge, 1984), pp. 164–74. In his useful 1998 Cambridge edition of *A Shrew* Stephen Roy Miller provides not only a thorough account of this debate (1–12) but also detailed comparisons of the sources and plots of the two versions (12–31), an account of the influence of *A Shrew* on the staging of *The Shrew* (40–55), and a scene-by-scene comparison of the two plays (127–43). For more extensive accounts of the performance history of *The Shrew* see Tori Haring-Smith, *From Farce to Metadrama: A Stage History of "The Taming of the Shrew" 1594–1983* (Westport, Conn. and London, 1985) and Graham Holderness, *The Taming of the Shrew* (Manchester, 1989).

4 Admittedly, some changes could be attributed to theatrical exigencies. For example, a playing area "above" is not needed in 1594 (where, in the second

scene, "*Enter two with a table and a banquet on it and two other with Sly asleep in a chair, richly apparelled, and the music playing*" – 2.0) but *is* needed at least twice in 1623. Several of the explanations for the two versions, moreover, are linked to the number of actors available, so that, in one formulation, the disappearance of Sly and his entourage after 1.2 in 1623 is necessary so that those actors could take on other parts, an exigency not faced, it is argued, in 1594. See, in particular, Karl P. Wentersdorf, "The Original Ending of *The Taming of the Shrew*: A Reconsideration," *Studies in English Literature* 18 (1978): 201–15.

5 For a summary and critique of such arguments, see Margie Burns, "The Ending of *The Shrew*," *Shakespeare Studies* 18 (1986): 41–64. Burns argues that "Sly's loss can be discussed as the play's gain, because the discontinuation of Sly's story actually helps develop the Kate–Petruchio story" (p. 41). She concludes (p. 61): "In the absence of textual or historical evidence, the idea of a missing ending must be regarded as myth with the usual function of myth, to explain puzzling sensations or puzzling phenomena, such as the impression created at the end of *The Taming of the Shrew* that much does indeed hang in the balance."

6 Peter Holland, *English Shakespeares: Shakespeare on the English Stage in the 1990s* (Cambridge, 1997), p. 129.

7 Like most recent editors (e.g., see Morris, Arden 2, pp. 37–39), I find such arguments unconvincing.

8 A comparable argument can be made against the co-presence in a modern conflated text of both Hamlet's last soliloquy ("How all occasions do inform against me" – 4.4.32–66) omitted in the Folio and the Folio-only material that follows Hamlet's allusion to "perfect conscience" (5.2.68–80) and includes "the interim's mine." The two passages cover comparable ground on *conscience* but do not co-exist in either Q2 or F.

9 I am building here upon Richard Hosley's distinction between *theatrical* and *fictional* stage directions. See "The Gallery Over the Stage in the Public Playhouse of Shakespeare's Time," *Shakespeare Quarterly* 8 (1957): 16–17. In Hosley's formulation, "theatrical" directions refer to "theatrical structure or equipment" (e.g., *within, at another door, a scaffold thrust out*) as opposed to "fictional" signals that refer "to dramatic fiction" (e.g., *on shipboard, enter the town*). Compare *enter above* and *enter on the walls* [of a city] as signals for the same action. Editors sometimes link "fictional" stage directions to authorial drafts as opposed to playhouse manuscripts or memorially reconstructed "bad quartos," but such distinctions are not supported by the extant evidence. The presence of "makes them come unto their husbands' call" is therefore not inconsistent with the putative "bad quarto" status of *A Shrew*.

9 THE EDITOR AS RESCRIPTER

1 E. A. J. Honigmann, *Myriad-minded Shakespeare*, Second Edition (London and New York, 1998), p. 187.

2 See in particular Cambridge University Press's Shakespeare in Production series, as with Christine Dymkowski's 2000 edition of *The Tempest* cited in

chapter 6 and Trevor R. Griffiths's 1996 edition of *A Midsummer Night's Dream.*

3 For a full discussion of *Much Ado* as a representative "foul papers" plays see Stanley Wells, "Editorial Treatment of Foul-Paper Texts: *Much Ado About Nothing* as Test Case," *Review of English Studies* 31 (1980): 1–16.

4 See Edward Berry, *Shakespeare's Comic Rites* (Cambridge, 1984), p. 185 and also Michael Friedman, " 'Hush'd on Purpose to Grace Harmony': Wives and Silence in *Much Ado About Nothing,*" *Theatre Journal* 42 (1990): 358 to whom I am indebted for the Berry passage. Friedman argues against Berry's conclusion that the mouth to be stopped is Benedick's. Rather, for him "the fact that Beatrice has completed a sentence does not exclude the possibility that she is about to begin a new one when her uncle interrupts her and gestures for Benedick to silence her with a kiss," an intervention that "endows Benedick with the patriarchal power to manage his wife's tongue." For me, either option is valid, with both keyed theatrically to the silencing and the kiss orchestrated by Leonato rather than Benedick.

5 Stanley Wells, "The Editor and the Theatre: Editorial Treatment of Stage Directions," *Re-editing Shakespeare for the Modern Reader* (Oxford, 1984), pp. 76, 68.

6 Margaret Jane Kidnie, "Text, Performance, and the Editors: Staging Shakespeare's Drama," *Shakespeare Quarterly* 51 (2000): 464. In my discussion of the Oxford edition I am indebted to this essay and to Leslie Thomson, "Broken Brackets and 'Mended Texts: Stage Directions in the Oxford Shakespeare," *Renaissance Drama* 19 (1988): 175–93.

7 For two arguments in behalf of such stagings in which bodies remain onstage see (on young Siward's body in *Macbeth*) Homer Swander, "No Exit for a Dead Body: What to do with a Scripted Corpse?" *Journal of Dramatic Theory and Criticism* (Spring, 1991): 139–52 and (on Sir Walter Blunt's body in *1 Henry IV*) Alan C. Dessen, *Recovering Shakespeare's Theatrical Vocabulary* (Cambridge 1995), pp. 83–84.

8 For a summary of the evidence see the *aside* entry in Alan C. Dessen and Leslie Thomson, *A Dictionary of Stage Directions in English Drama, 1580–1642* (Cambridge, 1999), pp. 15–16.

9 For a fuller discussion of early entrances and delayed exits see chapter 4 of my *Recovering Shakespeare's Theatrical Vocabulary.*

10 Why three of the Crane comedies in the Folio provide massed entries and two (*The Tempest* and *Measure for Measure*) do not remains a puzzle. For a full discussion of this anomaly and of Crane's characteristic procedures, see T. H. Howard-Hill, *Ralph Crane and Some Shakespeare First Folio Comedies* (Charlottesville, 1972). For a fuller account of this play see my "Massed Entries and Theatrical Options in *The Winter's Tale,*" *Medieval and Renaissance Drama in England* 8 (1996): 119–27.

11 For Pafford's discussion, see his 1963 Arden 2 edition, p. xx and also his essay in *Notes & Queries* 206 (May 1961): 176–77.

12 See the *nightgown* entry in *A Dictionary of Stage Directions*, p. 150.

13 In the elaborate stage direction that begins 2.4, "*The King takes place under the cloth of state; the two Cardinals sit under him as judges. The Queen takes place some distance from the King. The Bishops place themselves on each side the court, in manner of a consistory; below them, the Scribes. The Lords sit next the Bishops. The rest of the Attendants stand in convenient order about the stage.*" A marginal note in Holinshed (Arden 2, p. 195) refers to the queen's "lamentable and pithy speech in presence of the court." That speech is prefaced by: "And because she could not come to the king directly, for the distance severed between them, she went about by the court, and came to the king." Note also that in Holinshed "the judges commanded silence while their commission was read," but then Katherine "made no answer, but rose out of her chair," so that this account would support either interpretation of *Silence*.

14 A similar argument in behalf of *Silence* versus "Silence" is provided by Honigmann, pp. 185–86.

CONCLUSION: WHAT'S NOT HERE

1 As noted in chapter 1, my own contribution is a book on *Titus Andronicus* for the Manchester University Press "Shakespeare in Performance" series (1989).

2 As a caveat to would-be performance historians I should note that in the 1970s and early 1980s I had what now seems to me a naive faith in my memory and therefore disdained writing down the details of what I had seen. As might have been predicted, I then drew a blank when I later sought to invoke examples from such productions.

3 *Studies in Classic American Literature*, reprint (New York, 1955), p. 13.

4 *The Sunday Times*, April 30, 1995. With reference to the last question, I have been told that the practice at the Glasgow Citizens' Theatre is to leave one empty chair at the table for Shakespeare or any other playwright so that the author has the equivalent of one vote rather than a controlling presence.

5 "Shakespeare's Text on the Modern Stage," *Shakespeare-Jahrbuch 1967* (West), p. 189.

6 In a 1973 interview Nunn stated: "I must start with combing the text for its imagery, for its central ideas, for its visual ideas, and therefore I disdain the quick reading of the play which produces the superficial thought." He adds: "In that sense my loyalty to the text is total, because it is my starting point and my finishing point. But I am not a fundamentalist about the text, because my prime concern *must* be to make the plays work in a theatre to an audience living now. Therefore if I have to make cuts, if I have to make elisions, if I have to telescope, even – dare I say it – in certain limited circumstances, expand, I will do so." He also notes: "Not only do I think cutting necessary, but (unfortunately) it can become extremely enjoyable: the study exercise of making a slightly different scene from the one that exists on the page by linking certain speeches together or leaving a section out is most seductive." See Ralph Berry, *On Directing Shakespeare* (London, 1989), pp. 79–80.

Index

Lightning Source UK Ltd.
Milton Keynes UK
UKOW06f0430240815

257396UK00002B/80/P